terra australis 49

Terra Australis reports the results of archaeological and related research within the south and east of Asia, though mainly Australia, New Guinea and Island Melanesia — lands that remained terra australis incognita to generations of prehistorians. Its subject is the settlement of the diverse environments in this isolated quarter of the globe by peoples who have maintained their discrete and traditional ways of life into the recent recorded or remembered past and at times into the observable present.

List of volumes in Terra Australis

terra australis 49

Drawing in the Land

Rock Art in the Upper Nepean, Sydney Basin,
New South Wales

Julie Dibden

Australian
National
University

PRESS

ANU PRESS

Published by ANU Press
The Australian National University
Acton ACT 2601, Australia
Email: anupress@anu.edu.au

Available to download for free at press.anu.edu.au

A catalogue record for this book is available from the National Library of Australia

ISBN (print): 9781760462581
ISBN (online): 9781760462598

WorldCat (print): 1085244823
WorldCat (online): 1085245633

DOI: 10.22459/TA49.2018

Terra Australis Editorial Board: Sue O'Connor, Sally Brockwell, Ursula Frederick, Tristen Jones, Ceri Shipton and Mathieu Leclerc
Series Editor: Sue O'Connor

Cover design and layout by ANU Press. Cover photograph by Julie Dibden.

Contents

Acknowledgements

This research is an analysis of the rock markings on the Woronora Plateau, west of Wollongong. The land is within the Illawarra Local Aboriginal Land Council (ILALC) area. The ancestors of the local Aboriginal community inscribed their being in this land. I acknowledge my debt and gratitude to the ILALC and, in particular, to the late Mr Jim Davis, for allowing me to undertake this research.

The Sydney Catchment Authority (SCA) granted me access to the study area (the Metropolitan Special Area). My thanks to Kelvin Lambkin and Tony Kondek for this, and the field staff of the SCA who assisted in my fieldwork safety plans and other matters.

I conducted the 20 weeks of fieldwork with the assistance of a large number of people and gratefully acknowledge their help. Students from The Australian National University (ANU): Tasha Brown, Jillian Huntley (née Ford), Simon Lewis, Sophie Chessell, Russ Bradbury and Adrian Henham; students from the University of Sydney, who were supervised by Sarah Colley (thanks to Sarah also): Meg Cromie, Mathew Ling, Daniel Corke, Evan Raper, David Kooris, Mikael Pedlow and Nic Harrop; the University of New England: Lorien Watson-Keast; the University of St Petersburg: Mariana Koslova; school students doing work experience: Shay Zimmerlie and Sarah Manning; and, last but not least, family and friends: Oscar Rayner, Andy Pearce, Jenny Pink and Noel Ferguson.

Numerous people have helped with various aspects of my work for which I am grateful. June Ross was supportive and our discussions valuable. Melanie Thomson (Biosis Research) generously provided me with site data obtained during her fieldwork for the Dendrobium Coal Project. Meg Travers showed me how to use an ArcGIS function and Phil Boot assisted with support and provision of his PhD thesis. Norma Richardson assisted with support and editing. I am grateful to Jillian Huntley, not only for field assistance, but also clarification of certain matters, and patience. I extend my gratitude to Rebecca Parkes, for support, good advice and drawing my beautiful Figures 1.1 and 2.1. And, finally, to my friend Deirdre Russack for editing.

This project commenced some time ago as doctoral research at ANU, at which time my supervision was provided by Mary-Jane Mountain, Andree Rosenfeld and Howard Morphy. My more recent supervision was provided by Sally K. May, Jo McDonald and Peter Hiscock. I am tremendously grateful for what each have contributed to my project. Frankly, without Mary-Jane it would not have reached a conclusion; her assistance, encouragement and support has been tireless. I extend my gratitude to Mary-Jane and Barry Shaw, for their hospitality when I stayed with them on many occasions while working in Canberra. The influence of Andree's scholarship will be apparent in this work. I am so sorry she did not see an end product. Howard's enthusiasm for the rock art in my study area has been inspirational and validating. Ian Farrington has also been very supportive and his guidance towards landscape has been influential. I extend my deep gratitude to Sally, Jo and Peter, for assistance, editing and support during the last leg.

This project is based on the original field recordings made by the Illawarra Prehistory Group (IPG) on the Woronora Plateau. My work could not have been achieved without the extensive and comprehensive database they have compiled over the past 40 years. My analysis includes two separate databases, one being based on sites that I have not visited, and is, accordingly, compiled from the IPG site records. The other is based on my own fieldwork at 110 sites and, hence, is compiled from my own recordings. I am indebted to Caryll Sefton, in particular, for her support, information and allowing me access to her site files. Additionally, I thank Des Towne, John

Wyatt, Ken Kort and Bruce Scurr for introducing me to the Woronora Plateau and teaching me how to see its rock art and, in particular, that which is the most ubiquitous, ephemeral and faded—charcoal drawings. I acknowledge the valuable contribution of the IPG to Australian rock art recording.

Thank you to my husband Andy, and my son Oscar—for everything. Whoever would have thought that the word indeterminate could be uttered so many times and, in doing so, could be so hilarious!

Finally, thanks so much to the Terra Australis editorial team: Sue O'Connor, Sally Brockwell, Ursula Frederick and Katie Hayne.

Due to limited space, the appendices from the original thesis document have not been reproduced here. These are available in digitised form, along with the original thesis, in the ANU Open Repository (hdl.handle.net/1885/155274).

List of Figures

List of Plates

List of Tables

1

Introduction

The earth can be seen as a living record of the past; she bears on her 'body' the evidence of what has happened. (Lewis & Rose 1988:46)

We might profitably explore the contours of our material lifeworld and its recursive shaping of human experience. (Meskell 2005a:2)

The Nepean River is a significant drainage system in the Sydney Basin. It rises in a spring on a hillslope in the Southern Highlands where it commences a long, northerly traverse through the sandstone of the southern parts of the Woronora Plateau, becoming the Hawkesbury River along the western edge of the Cumberland Plain, and finally joining the Pacific Ocean at Broken Bay, north of Sydney. Before leaving the plateau, the Nepean captures the water from the Avon, Cordeaux and Cataract rivers. It is this sandstone country in the Upper Nepean catchment that is my study area. It has an extensive range of rock shelters and open sandstone platforms, which contain rock art and a suite of other types of rock marks. The land and stone through which these waters flow, and the human markings on the land, are the material objects of this research.

This monograph explores the materiality of these rock markings, and the manner in which they are embedded in the land, so as to explore change and transformation in social geography. In a seminal study, which integrates landscape and rock art, Bradley (1991:80) proposes that rock art is unique in respect of its link with the landscape: 'quite simply it had been applied to natural surfaces, and its study necessarily involve[s] *an archaeology of place*'. Similarly, Rosenfeld (1992:10) argues:

> The integration of motifs within the natural morphology of … sites clearly marks location as a cultural construct in which meanings of graphic units cannot be divorced from their spatial patterning. The rock is more than a blank canvas on which artists work – it is an integral component of the artistic system of meanings. The appropriation of the natural into the cultural may also operate at the level of graphic construction itself.

In Australia and its broader region, the analysis of location and rock art variability at both a broad landscape (e.g. Taçon 1989:112; Frederick 1997; Ross 1997; David 2002; Lee 2002) and micro-topographic scale (e.g. Rosenfeld 1991:137; David et al. 1999:20; Taçon 1999:47; Wilson 1999:95; Taçon & Ouzman 2004) has proved to be particularly rewarding for identifying spatial and chronological patterning and providing a firm basis for nuanced archaeological interpretations and narratives. The research conducted here is similarly framed within a landscape analysis and explores the nexus between imagery, other marks and location.

For conceptual and interpretive guidance, the research is situated within a theoretical framework that emphasises materiality, embodied practice and lived experience; it is this focus that has provided a basis for constructing an informing context. In particular, it has allowed a means of overcoming dualist concepts, which otherwise may limit understanding. Recently, practitioners from a wide range of disciplines endeavouring to understand either land and ecosystems (Head 2008), landscape (Thomas 2008), material culture generally (Boast 1997), *or* broader themes that reside at the heart of archaeology, such as time, culture and identity (Thomas 1996), have begun to respond to philosophical concerns with the post-Enlightenment conceptual separation between notions such as culture/nature, subject/object, mind/body, and so on. These conceptual separations are situated within a modern mode of thought, and a concern is now expressed regarding the assumption that an essential distinction exists between the natural world and the material things in it on the one hand, and human beings on the other (Thomas 1996:x; Boast 1997:181). These dichotomies may limit our appreciation of archaeological objects as they impose a modern or western understanding of the past; the people whose past we study may not 'have constructed their worlds using the same concepts or habits of mind as ourselves' (Thomas 1996:x, 11).

Modernist thinking separates humans from the earth. However, recent ethnographic studies emphasise the relational character of existence: that social life is lived out through the material world and that it is in the context of everyday life that humans become aware of themselves and their surroundings (Thomas 1996:12, 55, 234). It is via human lived experience that time, culture and identity emerge (Thomas 1996:235). Thomas (2008:304–305) argues:

> that if we wish to eschew the mind-body dichotomy … [within a landscape study] … we need to recognize that the 'objective' topography is quite different from the landscape that makes up the context of human dwelling … [and which] … is presumably the latter that an archaeology that concerns itself with experience, occupation, and bodily practice seeks to investigate.

Rather than being concerned with the exploration of the symbolic meaning of material objects in the landscape, Thomas (2008:305) argues:

> that a central concern would be with how a landscape was occupied and understood, and how it provided the context for the formulation and enactment of human projects. 'How did people relate to it?' in different contexts of engagement may be a more appropriate question.

These are some of the questions that this research seeks to address.

In order to explore aspects relating to social geography via an analysis of rock art, other markings on stone, and the stone and land itself, these concerns both structure the questions posed and concomitantly, the observations of materiality made. However, as Thomas (2008:305) cautions, in an archaeological analysis of such matters, the way we may make our observations is brokered by our modern 'contemporary skills, understandings, and practices of which we may be only partially aware'. Yet, nevertheless, *our* experience of a place or artefact in its landscape context is of value because the material object represents more than the product or outcome of an extinct pattern of social life; 'it represents an integral and still extant element of that pattern' (Thomas 2008:305). These elements potentially allow us to grasp the habitual mode of human conduct (cf. Thomas 1996:235); the charting of variability in these patterns over time has the potential to be informative of the historical dimension of change and transformation between humans and their world.

A notion underpinning this research is that humans live within a number of types of space. One is that of our lived and embodied experience in our environment, the 'space in which we habitually move and which is not external to us but a concomitant of our activities' (Dobrez 2009:5). Another space, which is directly relevant to rock art, is that of representations. This imagined space is no less real than a lived space, but is one that we inhabit as our lived space recedes and we experience space imaginatively when prompted by a visual narrative (Dobrez 2009:5–6). An example of the type of visual prompt, which may provoke such an imaginative space, can be seen in Plate 1.1, where the two marsupial gliders are drawn without their snouts, but with their partial heads against a natural bedding plane, suggesting that they are entering a crack in the rock. Rosenfeld (2002:74) describes the narrative quality of track alignments, which visually render movement and sometimes rise out of, or disappear into, natural fissures or hollows. Taçon and Ouzman (2004:60) also refer to similar relationships between imagery and stone. Still another space, which may be invoked by representation, is that which is experienced by viewing non-narrative rock art (e.g. see Plate 1.2 below), where the image is *read* as entering our actual lived space (Dobrez 2009:6–7).

In previous research conducted in the Sydney Basin, rock art located in shelters has been considered, at least implicitly, to be functionally equivalent across both space and time. The research here, by comparison, explores both synchronic and diachronic variability and gives consideration to the occupational and contextual diversity this represents. While the research is conducted without the support of any direct dating or archaeological context, it nevertheless seeks to discriminate temporal diversity in spatial patterns, and, concomitantly, reveals a part of the narrative of Aboriginal social life and history.

Plate 1.1 Images of marsupial gliders drawn in a way that visually suggests their movement into the rock (rock shelter A12).

Source: Photograph by Julie Dibden, 2011.

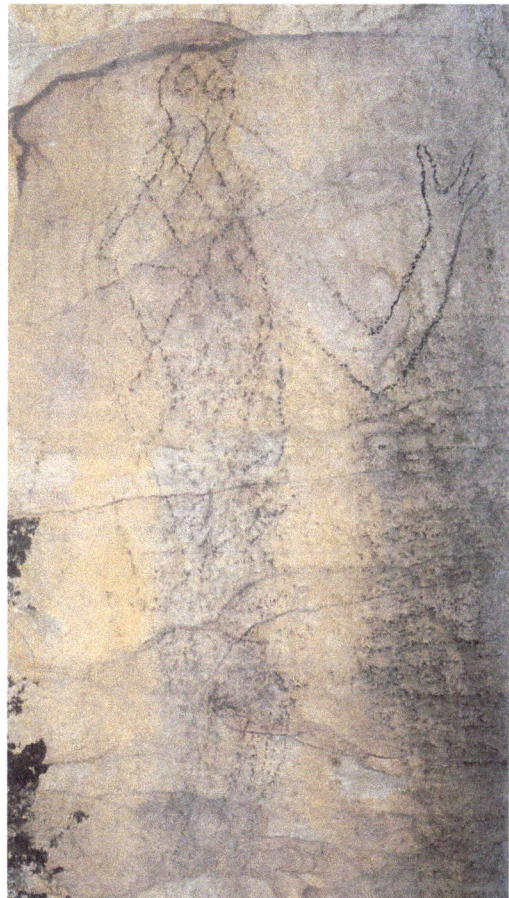

Plate 1.2 An unusually large anthropomorphic motif (160 cm high) drawn in a way that visually inhabits the viewer's 'lived' space (rock shelter UA36).

Source: Photograph by Julie Dibden, 2011.

1.1 Research Focus: Social Geography, Change and Transformation

In the quotation at the beginning of this chapter, Lewis and Rose (1988:46) refer to the marks on the earth left by the travels and activities of Dreaming Beings in the Victoria River district of the Northern Territory. Given the longer history of violence and dispossession, which occurred during the colonial and post-colonial period in south-east Australia, we are unfortunate not to have a similar living knowledge of Indigenous understandings of the features of the earth and how they were shaped. However, we do know that cosmogonic stories across Australia share a common trait in that they describe the journeys of Ancestral Beings as they traversed the land, transforming their bodies into landscape features and other natural phenomena (Tamisari & Wallace 2006:216). In so doing, the existence of all life forms (including people), and the correct and moral practices of life were established. This ancestral law in Aboriginal society simultaneously embraces religious, social and geographic realms (Swain 1993:117). Aboriginal geographies of country are grounded in explanatory frameworks, which refer to the creative actions of Ancestral Beings (Rosenfeld 2002:62).

A cultural landscape or social geography can be conceptualised as an enculturation of natural space. One mechanism by which this is achieved includes the identification and naming of nodes, or culturally ascribed significant places, in a spatial continuum (Rosenfeld 2002:62; see also Tilley 1994:34). However, Rosenfeld (2002:62) emphasises the importance of individual places that act to 'structure a sociopolitical framework of space … [country] … and in this way serve to define and to articulate a shared identity by its legitimate users'. It is in this manner that rock art has the capacity to be used in explanatory frameworks, which provide a 'cohesive ontology of country' (Rosenfeld 2002:62). In Aboriginal Australia, both spatial and temporal referents, which may serve in this process, are generally legitimised by the ancestral past. Rosenfeld (2002:63) remarks that '[t]he way rock art is located within the cultural praxis of such metaphysics is of interest to archaeology, because it is one of its more enduring expressions'.

One of the significant features of rock art, as social praxis, is its durability (cf. Rosenfeld 2002:61). The stone on which rock art is created 'has the potential for permanence, and that is almost certainly a factor in the choice of a rock surface in the first place' (Forge 1991:44). While the significance of rock art as practice and the nature of the relationship between the artist and locality in Australia is diverse, Rosenfeld (1997:291) notes several generalised points. First, 'most if not all Aboriginal rock art has in some sense a meaningful relationship to the locale in which it is executed'. She amplifies this point by noting that cultural constraints exist, which determine *who* may paint and *what* is appropriate to paint at any locality. In addition, the majority of rock art, other than mechanically imposed marks such as stencils, is concerned with the Dreaming, 'either explicitly or evocatively, or by negation via "trickster" spirits that stand in opposition to the ordering principles of the Dreaming' (Rosenfeld 1997:291; see, for a different emphasis, Taçon 1989). These general principles of rock art praxis underpin the conceptual framework in this research.

For locally appropriate conceptual and methodological guidance, the research draws upon anthropological understandings of rock art practice in Aboriginal Australia, and certain matters of relevance to an archaeological study are clear. In the absence of an ethnographically informed context and knowledge of the discourse in which rock art is, or was, situated, its cultural meaning is, and is likely to remain, largely unknown. This necessarily imposes epistemological limitations upon an archaeological study of rock art, and a recognition of this has significantly influenced the nature of enquiry in Australia, much of which has, until recently, been directed towards functional interpretations conducted under the umbrella of information exchange theory (Rosenfeld 1992).

Morphy (1999:21–22) suggests, however, that the possibility of some access to the meaning of art in archaeological contexts remains, and he emphasises that, given the relationship that can exist between form and meaning, this may be explored by first investigating the formal properties of art objects. That is, the archaeological question may be posed initially as to 'how something means', prior to questioning what it means (Morphy 1999:21).

Social science has conceptually privileged society in explanatory frameworks, and regards objects largely as representations of society; objects represent people—for example, the Bell Beaker culture. Archaeological studies of rock art in Australia, in which style theory, or an analysis of formal variation, has been employed, have considered stylistic and formal attributes as those that possess the social or meaningful aspect of rock art. Style in any one of its permutations, as Boast (1997:173) expresses:

> is that bit that we find most socially meaningful, the bit that is most human, added on beyond natural necessity. It is the bit that is most to do with the mind, with human intentions, with human communication. Style is seen as the key to the social.

It has been style itself, rather than the artistic tradition, or rock art as praxis, with which the archaeological study of rock art has been concerned because it is style that has been assumed to encode social information (cf. Wilson & David 2002:4). Style is something that is seen to be supplementary, and this view is arguably attributable to the modern separation of form and meaning from materiality (Thomas 2004:213). In stylistic or formal approaches, a dichotomy between form (style) and matter is conceptually fundamental, the former being afforded the greater consideration and analytical relevance, and it is this view that is now the subject of serious evaluation (cf. Boast 1997:174; Wilson & David 2002:4; Thomas 2004:212).

In this research, the theoretical focus is drawn from materiality studies, which attend very closely to the particular properties of material objects, and even recognise what is described as the false dichotomy between symbolic and materialist readings of the world (Meskell 2005a:2). Miller (2005a:212) expresses this in the following way: '[m]ateriality as a term always speaks to a paradox, which is the assumed greater reality of that which we do not apprehend over that which is merely evident'. By way of explication, Miller (2005a:212) refers to religions, for example, and the assumption that what we see materially as its expression is superficial, 'mere tokens and signs', and that the 'real' lies outside of the object and in the cosmological world. The paradox is that immateriality can only be expressed through materiality, and Miller (2005b) argues that a general rule is that the more humanity reaches toward a conceptualisation of the immaterial, the more important the specific form of its materialisation. In the field of religion, the more we feel the deity is beyond our comprehension, the more valuable the medium of our objectification. What makes materiality important is the systematic cultivation of immateriality (Miller 2005b:12).

Conkey (2001:272), who has paid much attention to the question of the use of the term 'art' in archaeological contexts, has welcomed the recent trend in material culture studies—she believes this allows for a more value-neutral analytical framework. She suggests that, if what we call 'art' were instead to be termed 'material culture', our attention might turn more appropriately to questions of how art works. The exploration of materiality resides at the core of contemporary material culture studies (Meskell 2005a:1).

A shift towards explorations of the materiality of rock art is exemplified by researchers such as Ouzman (2001) and Rainbird (2002), who, for example, in questioning the visual primacy of rock art and its analysis wherein the sense of vision is privileged, have instead explored non-visual aspects of rock art (see also Wilson & David 2002:4; Taçon & Ouzman 2004:61). Ouzman and Rainbird have both examined the role of sound in the production of rock art. Studies such as these exemplify a trend in which the deeper materiality of rock art is explored, and which seek to attend to 'uses of the imagery, the rock, the rock art site and the landscape that do not obviously fall within the *eye's compass*' (Ouzman 2001:238, my emphasis). Rainbird (2002:93) suggests that an adequate understanding of rock art may need to go beyond the motifs themselves in order to deeply consider rock art and the production of meaning. He argues that, rather than being an end product, the significance of rock art may have been in its productive context. While these types of studies are valued for their move away from what some have described as the tyranny of vision and sight, 'towards an understanding of place through perception and bodily experience' (Tamisari & Wallace 2006:221), they may be of limited use in contexts where there is an absence of supporting evidence with which to build linking arguments relating to the relevance of sound phenomena, and so on. Nevertheless, the importance of these studies is that they draw attention to the possibility of a deeper exploration of rock art as praxis.

Thus, if the 'eye's compass' is refocused in rock art sites, it is possible to explore more than meets the eye in rock art, the rock shelter and its location, and this may enable a deeper exploration of how rock art means. Taçon and Ouzman (2004:63) suggest 'the world is not always what it seems. Our everyday experience is literally at the surface of reality; a much larger universe lies beneath if we are willing and able to enter it'.

The view taken in this research is that rock art has particular (and potentially variable) properties, and that the investigation of these, conducted in respect of their materiality, may allow for a nuanced study of the object world and 'how something means' (cf. Meskell 2005a:2). This investigation is conducted with reference to the notion that the physicality of rock art is 'enmeshed in the work of praxis: cultural construction is achieved though action rather than simply conceptualisation' (Meskell 2005a:2). Thomas (2004:219) expresses a similar sentiment: '[w]hen a material is crafted poetically, it appears on the scene not as a dead object, with a series of attributes or qualities attached to it, but as a happening … [and its construction provides] … the context for a realisation of the potential for a relationship between people and their world'.

Rock art has many attributes that are limited, at least in part, only by the lens through which they are perceived. Not all of these are necessarily located within the formal or visual properties of the motif itself, but may include, for example, the nature of the pigment and the myriad of cultural and symbolic productive and narrative complexities it may possess. Rock art may also reside in a relationship of isomorphic congruence (where the shape of a motif mirrors that of, or incorporates within its materiality by some means, natural rock features [e.g. see again Plate 1.1]); the materiality of rock art may be very complex indeed, and, quite fundamentally, include the rock and land itself. All the attributes rock art may possess, its formal properties and material, micro-topographic situation within a rock shelter, geographic location and so on, are the result of choices made by the people responsible for its execution and, accordingly, provide an informing context in regard to the making and objectification of the thought world, and how the transcendent was made manifest and real. It is via material objects that the conviction of the transcendent is expressed or objectified (Miller 2005b:1).

As noted above, rock art in the Australian ethnographic 'present', other than mechanically imposed marks such as stencils, refers in some way to Ancestral Beings (Rosenfeld 1997:291, but see Taçon 1989). However, we cannot assume that this has always been the case (cf. David 2002), nor that rock art itself as a practice has always been an expression of Aboriginal life in all places, even where suitable stone is present. At different times in the past, people may 'have enjoyed different kinds of engagement with the material world' (Thomas 2004:219). This research examines how the practice of rock art and other marking of the land changes, and how human beings have related and engaged with the land differently over time. As with many forms of material culture, rock art has a complex temporality as it has the potential to remain extant long after its original production. In this context, observations may be made of both the instantiation of its creation, and the trajectory of its subsequent lifeworld. In Aboriginal Australia, rock art may become unrecognisable as having been created by human agency. It is in this sense that rock art may become something that has not been made by people, but is an Ancestral Being itself (Lewis & Rose 1988). In any case, in regard to rock art, in its 'grounded materiality of the object world', and with a consideration of its potential longevity, its 'residual force of matter has the ability to shape and influence the living' (cf. Meskell 2005a:3; see also Hiscock 2008:259). This notion that 'things make people, and people who are made by those things go on to make other things' (Pinney 2005:256) resides at the heart of materiality theory.

In this monograph, the historical dimension, in which people inhabited, occupied and experienced the landscape of the Upper Nepean catchment, will be examined by charting how rock markings, and the locations and places marked, changed over time; patterns of similarity, or contrast, in these variables will be examined within a temporal framework. It is known from the archaeological record that Aboriginal people have occupied the region since the late Pleistocene (Lampert 1971; Boot 1996:275; Attenbrow 2002:153; McDonald 2008a:36). That record has revealed temporal variability and chronological change in technology, occupation and land use, which is also synchronically spatially patterned and variable, perhaps reflecting contextual function (Boot 2002; Attenbrow 2004; Robertson et al. 2009:305). Something is also known, although with very little detail, of Aboriginal responses to the impact of European occupation.

The cultural change, which is both observed archaeologically and known to have occurred via historical sources, is likely to have been accompanied by 'developments in Aboriginal cosmologies and their mythic expression' (Rosenfeld 1992:1, see also Rosenfeld 2002:61). Layton (1992:245, 2000b:175) argues that Australian clan totemism developed around 5,000 years ago, and its emergence was expressed in new distribution patterns in the production of rock art. More recently, other researchers have explored, via rock art, the emergence of recent cosmologies, and consider those that correspond with ethnographically known systems to have developed within the last 1,000 or so years (David 2002; Rosenfeld 2002; Taçon 2008a:171). Also, Frederick's (1997) research, for example, has shown that within contexts of cross-cultural exchange, which ensued during the colonial encounter, rock art may express the forms of the Indigenous response.

There is no oral or textual (ethnographic, historical or anthropological) informing context with which to understand the practice of marking the land with rock art in the Upper Nepean catchment. A specifically archaeological approach to the measurement and explanation of variability in rock art in the absence of informing contexts has developed in Australia (cf. Clegg 1986:55), and there is now a long and established tradition of the use of rock art in defining temporal change and spatial variability in regional studies. A general pattern to have emerged is that of the definition of geographically widespread and uniform older (often inferred or known to be of Pleistocene or early Holocene antiquity) rock art styles, which give way to apparently more tightly bounded regional styles during the mid to late Holocene (e.g. Morwood 1980, 1984; Lewis 1988; David & Cole 1990; Taçon 1993). In several recent studies, enquiry has shifted towards examining changes, particularly in the recent past (both pre-European and after contact), in sociopolitical structures and ideational systems, and how these may be explored in rock art (e.g. Frederick 1997; Rosenfeld 2002:61; David 2002). A significant development has been to go beyond defining regional variation, to explore variability within regional rock art provinces (e.g. Officer 1984; McDonald 1994, 2008a; Ross 1997; Rosenfeld 2002:75). Officer (1984) and McDonald (1994) have examined sociocultural functional variability in the rock art of the Sydney Basin and identified a contrast between open context engraved and sheltered pigment rock art. While these studies have compared rock art in open and sheltered contexts, diversity within the latter will be explored in this research.

For archaeological research contexts, where rock art is no longer produced, and there is an absence of an ethnographic or anthropological context, Layton (1992:244–245, 2000a, 2000b) and Rosenfeld (1997:291) have developed models for the archaeological analysis of rock art. This research is guided by their concepts and methods. These models are premised on the notion that rock art may be produced synchronically within different functional and sociocultural contexts. Both authors emphasise a methodology that attends to the 'deployment of art in different ways' (Layton 2000a:170; see also Rosenfeld 1997:291, 1999, 2002), and the choice of sites and their location within the landscape, to provide clues to the social context of rock art, which does not depend on an understanding of its meaning and the cultural discourse of which it was a part. Rosenfeld (1997, 2002) also considers the relevance of attending to the nature of any associated archaeological evidence, such as domestic occupational debris, to further provide an informing archaeological context of the role of rock art in cultural praxis.

McDonald (1994:336, 2008b:343) has constructed a chronological framework for the rock art of the Sydney Basin. This chronology extends the production of rock art in this region from at least the mid-Holocene through to the period of the colonial encounter. In this monograph, synchronic variability of rock marking within defined temporal phases in the Upper Nepean catchment will be examined. In this sense it is assumed that, potentially, rock art functioned in different spheres of social life, and that, accordingly, diversity may reflect different social contexts—and also in light of the discussion above, differences in the modes of objectifying the immaterial. The Australian ethnography suggests that all rock art within a sociocultural context is unlikely to be equivalent in meaning and function. Rock art may express religious, secular and even subversive themes (Ucko & Rosenfeld 1967:160; Layton 1992:85, 2000b:176), and anthropological enquiry has revealed the 'multivalency of artistic expression' (Rosenfeld & Bahn 1991:vi).

The idea that different styles and functions of rock art may be contemporaneous within a region has been recognised for some considerable time (Ucko & Rosenfeld 1967:71; cf. Chippindale & Nash 2004:7). Layton (2000a:176) argues that in Australia totemic rock art frequently coexists with rock art produced in accordance with other themes such as sorcery and the everyday practices relating to hunting and gathering. From an emic perspective, people are able to differentiate between these different themes to deduce an authorised reading by attending to stylistic or iconographic traits, or the location of rock art within the landscape (Morphy 1999:14; Layton 2000a:176). A correspondence between synchronic rock art variability and different social contexts has been identified elsewhere in Australia (e.g. Morwood 1981:15; Officer 1984; Lewis 1988; 91; Rosenfeld 1997; David et al. 1999; McDonald 2008a). This topic of research is significant given that rock art variability that relates to social context has implications for the methods used to identify and analyse both spatial and temporal distribution patterns. As Macdonald (1990:60) remarks, 'if we fail to distinguish and disentangle complex levels of social process, we will fail in our analysis of style or anything else'. In this research, the conceptual basis for investigating variability in the material record specifically addresses the notion of social context. Human behaviour is recognised as being culturally and socially mediated, and accordingly:

> An immediate emphasis is placed on the social circumstances that tend to produce observable variation in that behaviour. That is, social context defines the limits and modal constraints on the appropriateness of social behaviours; human social behaviour is situational and context dependent (Macdonald 1990:52).

Specifically, in regard to rock art, Layton's (2000b:50) concern is with the referential context of social action, and he argues that this can be conceptualised on two levels. One is the broader cultural discourse in which rock art is practised, and the other is that of the world of perceived objects (Layton 2000b:50). In this sense, rock art motifs, while they may be read slightly differently between different members of a community are, nevertheless, produced within a framework of shared experience and meanings—that is, they are mutually intelligible within the 'intersubjective community of knowers' (Layton 2000b:50). On the other hand, the representational qualities of rock art, and whether or not these are ostensive or denotative, 'provide referential toeholds' into the world in which rock art was situated (Layton 2000b:52). David (2002:200) argues that the animals depicted in the late Holocene rock art on Cape York are evidence for the emergence of 'newly regionalized referential systems'. He argues that people did not merely and suddenly begin to produce rock art in new styles; '[w]hat took place involved also the referential signs through which peoples marked, understood, experienced and deferred to their worlds' (David 2002:199). David (2002:199–200) emphasises the importance of the concept of reference, this being the way in which the world is ordered in a 'chain of inter-connected signifiers', a process that involves the construction and relation of categories in a system of meaning. The analysis of the rock art in this research will seek to define the referential system and the 'universe of discourse' within which it was produced and employed, to construct and mediate the relationship between people and their world.

This research explores the manner in which people engaged in place, and how they experienced, modified and constituted their world, identity and history. Similar to David (2002), this research is concerned with the historical dimension of place marking. Given the physicality of landscape in which meanings and readings of landscape are situated, van Dommelen (1999:278) suggests landscape is where *history* most solidly resides; landscape and society are intertwined, for landscape itself is integral to the reproduction of social life. This research is an analysis of the material and object world and seeks to explore the social geography of the people of the Upper Nepean catchment.

1.2 Location: The Upper Nepean Catchment

The Upper Nepean River catchment occupies the southern end of the Woronora Plateau and is located immediately west of Wollongong and the Illawarra coastal plain (Figure 1.1). The plateau is deeply dissected by rivers and tributary creeks. The crests of ridges and catchment watersheds are gently undulating landforms (Plate 1.3). However, valley slopes are generally narrow, steep and frequently cliff-lined. All of the archaeological evidence examined in this research is comprised of marks on sandstone rock located within this highly variable yet generally rugged terrain.

Within its broader geographic context, the Upper Nepean catchment is geologically and topographically very different from the adjacent coastal plain and muted landscape of the Southern Highlands (Plate 1.4). It is separated from the coast by '[t]he Illawarra escarpment … [which] … is one of the most striking features of the NSW coast, for it runs like a great unbreached wall for some 120 kilometres, and dominates the narrow plains below' (Young 1980). The study area is a place in which the concept of human movement is particularly salient. Access from the coast is possible through isolated passes on the escarpment. Elsewhere, the steep-sided gorges of the rivers form barriers from the west. Once in the area, given its heavily dissected character, human movement and occupation is constrained and channelled along clearly defined natural routes (cf. Bradley 1991:80), which are the relatively level crests located between the rivers and their tributary streams. The manner in which the topography of the study area influences human movement and occupation forms a set of independent environmental variables with which to explore the archaeological signatures of occupation and land use, and the functional and sociocultural context of rock art as social praxis.

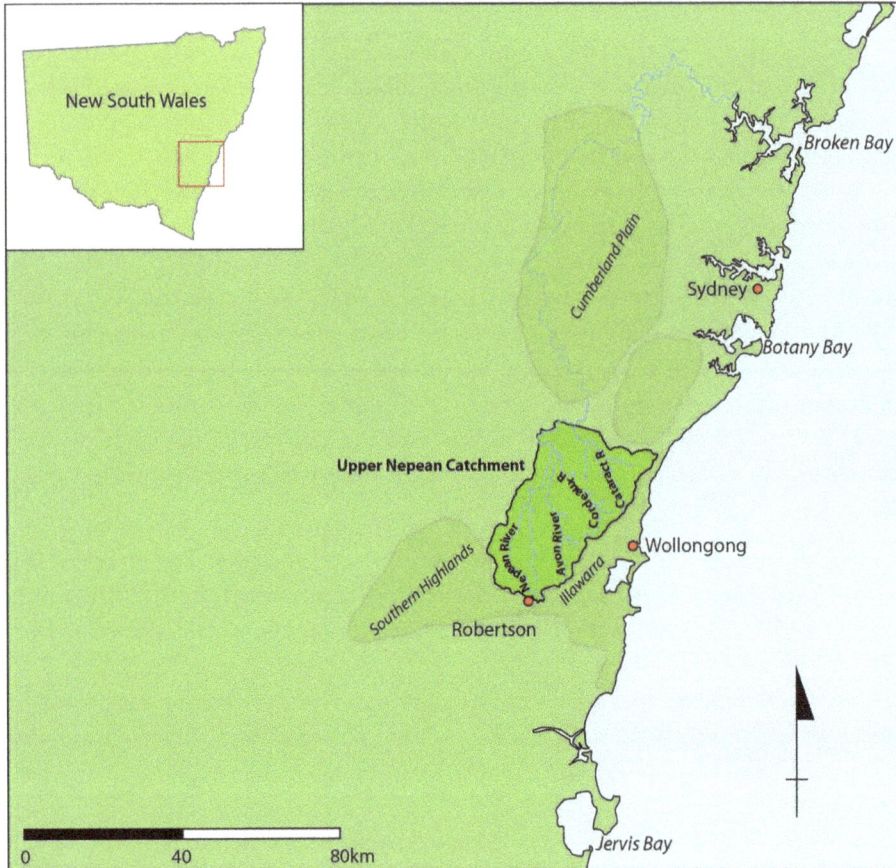

Figure 1.1 Location of the Upper Nepean catchment in a regional context.
Source: Map reproduced from Dibden (2011).

Plate 1.3 Lizard Creek flowing northward along the ridge crest situated to the west of the Cataract River. The abundance of water available on the plateau, rather than only in valleys, is an unusual and significant natural phenomenon of the study area.
Source: Photograph by Julie Dibden, 2011.

Plate 1.4 The Illawarra Escarpment looking west towards the Woronora Plateau from the coastal plain.
Source: Photograph by Julie Dibden, 2011.

1.3 Method

European occupation of south-east Australia in the late eighteenth century had an immediate and profound effect on Aboriginal individuals and society. Within a year after occupation there was significant loss of life due to introduced disease, and immense disruption to social, cultural, religious and economic life. While people were able to continue to dwell within, or at least visit, the Woronora Plateau area for some time, by the mid to late nineteenth century there was a virtual abandonment of country as people forged a life within the new settler society and economy. In the late nineteenth century, the country was further alienated when it was gazetted as a water reserve for Sydney and its suburbs, and subsequently dammed (Plate 1.5). The area is now controlled and managed by the Sydney Catchment Authority (SCA) and the New South Wales Office of Environment and Heritage (NSW OEH). Access is restricted, and Aboriginal people now visit only within the context of resource management conducted within the framework of environmental impact assessment. Given the passage of time since the abandonment of the plateau, there is now no social context of land use from which to obtain insight into the meaning and function of the rock marks in the study area.

The ethnohistoric records for the broader Sydney and Illawarra region are substantially incomplete (cf. Stanner 1969:32) and are virtually non-existent for the study area (cf. Attenbrow 2002:15). The records that do exist generally refer to chance encounters with Aboriginal people, with little or no mention made to social and economic life. Mathews and Everitt (1900) do refer to ceremonial activity, but these records were made approximately 100 years after contact and, accordingly, are limited.

Plate 1.5 The stored water of the Avon Dam, looking north-west from the rock art shelter site UA49.
Source: Photograph by Julie Dibden, 2011.

Contact imagery (drawings of sailing ships, stencils of steel axes and so on) is present in the wider Sydney Basin area, attesting to the production of rock art during the colonial period until the 1850s (Layton 1992:27; McDonald 2008a:248). However, the early European commentators in the Sydney region did not record either the purpose of rock art production or the meaning of imagery (Chippindale & Nash 2004:17; McDonald 2008a:3). McDonald (2008a:3) remarks that 'this has resulted in a regional body of art without anthropological or social context; one for which the meaning cannot be interpreted except by archaeological means'.

Given the absence of either relevant ethnohistoric records or a direct means of acquiring informed insight for interpreting the archaeology of the study area, this research has been conducted within the parameters of formal archaeological methods and analysis. All previous rock art research conducted in the Sydney Basin has, likewise, been undertaken by way of a formal archaeological methodology. Chippindale and Nash (2004:20) have succinctly described formal methods as 'any method of study that does not depend on inside knowledge, but works by the features that can be observed in the rock art itself, *or in its physical and landscape context …*' (my emphasis).

The development of archaeological methods of analysis is a defining signature of Australian rock art studies. When rock art analysis was being developed in the 1970s, researchers such as Maynard (1977) and Clegg (1983) stridently eschewed a search for meaning, considered such a goal as intractable and focused on developing methods for analysing visual form. Officer (1984, 1991:113, 1994) has subsequently further developed the analysis of the formal properties of rock art. However, with the strength of focus on the visual form, there has been, until recently, a tendency to isolate rock art from its archaeological context. Rock art has been treated as an archaeological artefact, but frequently has been analysed independently of other associated, contextual data. In early studies, motifs were the units subject to analysis, while the place (the stone, the rock shelter) in which these artefacts were situated was not incorporated in analyses. A recent development now places an emphasis on landscape and its relationship with art, the artist and the audience (Chippindale & Nash 2004:3). Greater attention is now afforded to the physical location of rock art—that is, the micro-landscape and macro-landscape context (cf. Chippindale & Nash 2004:21). The importance of this approach is exemplified by Frederick (1997), for example, who successfully explored change in social contexts of rock art production that occurred within the early period of Aboriginal and European interaction in Central Australia by closely analysing changes over time in graphic variability and changes in the geographic and environmental distribution of rock art. Similarly, Ross (1997), for her north-west Central Queensland study, utilised very fine-grained considerations of both environmental and micro-topographic attributes of motif location in her analysis and revealed very strong distribution patterns. This allowed her to demonstrate within-regional variability, and to argue that different categories of rock art were produced to fulfil different social strategies.

In Australian archaeology, the influence of the environment on change in the Aboriginal past has held a paramount explanatory position, both generally and particularly in relation to rock art analyses (Rosenfeld 1992). People have been viewed as having adapted to the environment, both responding to change and shaping the landscape itself (Head 2008:373). However, as Denham and Mooney (2008:365) argue, there has been a failure to explore the mutually transformative and temporal dimension of human-environment interactions. Previous rock art studies, which were conducted within a structural-functional perspective, viewed change to be precipitated by external factors (the environment). The processual paradigm was not up to the task of considering the role of endogenous social and cultural causes of rock art production, nor, for that matter, for explaining diachronic change (cf. Tamisari & Wallace 2006:205). Furthermore, human activities have frequently been 'read off' the archaeological record, and little attempt has been made to understand the historical, spatial and social contexts of changing human practices in response to environmental change (Denham & Mooney 2008:366). This has resulted in an archaeological account that, while being 'overtly' chronological, is profoundly ahistorical—that is, the 'socio-environmental inheritance' that contextualises and structures people's response is not taken into account (Denham & Mooney 2008:366).

Landscape is more than a set of 'objective' topographic features. Landscapes are constructed out of cultural and social engagement; they are 'topographies of the social and cultural as much as they are physical contours' (David & Thomas 2008:35). The conceptual approach to landscape in this research is based on a concern with experience, occupation and bodily practice (cf. Thomas 2008:305). Ingold (1993:153), in his argument relating to the temporality of landscape, advocates a dwelling perspective. He considers landscape as narrative and says 'the landscape tells—or rather *is*—a story' (Ingold 1993:153). The methodological approach adopted in this research attends particularly to location and relationality as a means of contextualising rock art as cultural practice. Given the nature of the physiography, different places within the Upper Nepean catchment are likely to have been utilised for different purposes and by different categories of people. As previously addressed, the Upper Nepean is not only difficult to enter, particularly from the coast, but, once there, human occupation and movement is constrained by the presence of steep, rocky slopes and cliff-lined gorges. The variable 'spaces' as embodied and experienced present a diverse suite of locales, and the location of rock art and other marks in different environmental and topographic contexts in the study area have the potential to be informative of different social contexts of production and perception. Landform and environmental elements, as measurable empirical space, will be employed methodologically to explore rock art as cultural praxis. Such an objective methodology may seem at odds with the research emphasis. However, for various reasons, not the least of which is the vast space encompassed by the study area, it allows for the identification, at a fine level of spatial resolution, of elements representative of the patterns of social life and how these may vary over space and time.

The morphology of the rock shelters in which rock art is present will also be investigated in the analysis. The size, shape and type of floors in shelters is influential in regard to the nature of their occupation and use. While it is sometimes expressed that rock art was made and meant for the place in which it is found (cf. Domingo Sanz et al. 2008:21), the relationship between rock art and its locale may be the result of choices made relating rather more pragmatically to the manner in which a rock shelter itself allows for the practical fulfilment of certain social practices in specific contexts. The micro-topographic context of rock art placement in rock shelters will also be examined. These independent variables have the potential to be particularly informative of experience and bodily action relating to rock art production and perception and, ultimately, variability in synchronic sociocultural context and temporal change and transformation.

Based on 'the proposition that not all features at rock art sites are the same order of cultural manifestation' (Rosenfeld 1997:291), the rock marks located in shelters will be initially categorised in accordance with their behavioural signatures. Two primary types are identified, graphic and non-graphic gestural marks. The first of these are conceptualised as being 'coherent sets of images the meanings of which are conveyed by virtue of their visual qualities as constrained by conventions of graphic construction' (Rosenfeld 1997:291). The graphic rock art will be subject to a detailed analysis in order to finely discriminate variability. Each image will be classified in accordance with its formal properties of graphic and material construction, figurative referent, as well as its imagined space. The other category of rock markings, which are described as gestural marks, are those that include mechanically imposed forms such as stencils (cf. Rosenfeld 1997:291) and others that result from gestural actions, such as pitted or rubbed surfaces, and non-graphic applications of pigment, which include, for example, applications of pigment to natural features on rock art panels (cf. Smith & Rosenfeld 1992:12).

The discrimination of rock marks in accordance with these two categories will be undertaken so as to explore the sociocultural context of rock art production and use from a behavioural perspective. The patterning that may exist between the site specific (shelter morphology, etc.) and the geographic and environmental location of these different categories of rock art is expected, in accordance with the models proposed by Layton (1992, 2000a, 2000b) and Rosenfeld (1997, 2002), to illuminate the social role of rock art in the Upper Nepean catchment. In accordance with an objective of this research to explore change and transformation patterns in the interplay of the variables will be examined within a framework of temporal change.

Analyses will include quantitative and qualitative approaches. Quantitative approaches to rock art have an established place in Australian archaeological research (Rosenfeld 2000:4), whereas a qualitative approach is less developed. Rosenfeld (2000:4) remarks that 'there has been a tendency to overemphasise the requirements of numeracy at the expense of qualitative evaluations'. She (2000:4) argues:

> there is now a need to place greater emphasis on the qualitative and contextual criteria of the art, and to focus on the rare or unique manifestations at rock art sites that tend to be masked in statistical analyses, including also individual site histories where this can be assessed. I believe only this finer scale of analysis will lead to a closer focus on the changing cultural contexts of rock art production and of rock art perception.

Ingold (1993:153) considers that '[t]elling a story is not like weaving a tapestry to *cover up* the world, it is rather a way of guiding the attention of listeners or readers *into it*'. This research employs a qualitative and descriptive analysis of the rock marking, its variability and its locational characteristics, so as to enable dealing with the nuances of the material, which is unlikely to be achieved solely by a quantitative analysis. Individual site histories presented in Dibden (2011:Appendix 1) are foundational to the analysis.

1.4 The Archaeological Material

The Upper Nepean catchment has approximately 810 known archaeological sites. The majority have been located and recorded by the Illawarra Prehistory Group (IPG). Over 500 are sandstone shelters with rock art. They have not been subject to previous comprehensive archaeological analysis, nor has the rock art been described systematically. The presence of such a large and yet unexamined body of rock art was the main impetus for undertaking the research in this area.

A number of studies have examined rock art in areas further to the north in the Sydney Basin (e.g. McMah 1965; Officer 1984; Sefton 1988; McDonald 1994, 2008a). The rock art of the study area falls within the geographic extent of the distinctive regional style of the Sydney Basin, which has been previously defined as a Simple Figurative style (Maynard 1979; cf. McDonald 1994). The work of Officer (1984), Sefton (1988) and McDonald (1994, 2008a:321) has expanded our understanding of the nature of this rock art and its variability. Nevertheless, the Sydney Basin rock art has the potential to be described in further detail, with the concomitant expectation that the use of fine levels of analytical resolution may enable deeper levels of understanding and interpretation. A wide range of rock mark types, which were produced by various actions and techniques, is present in the study area, and many of these have not been explored deeply before.

Rock markings are geographically widespread and occur in all landforms (Dibden 2011:Appendix 2). They are located on open exposures and in rock shelters. They mark the land in many ways—from boldly and colourfully, to secretly and subtly. The small eel motif shown in Plate 1.6 is located on a very low ceiling and is situated approximately 60 centimetres above a stone floor. To make or view this image, a person must crawl into the space and lie down. By comparison, the large eels in Plate 1.7 are located on a large rear wall in a commodious and tall shelter. The example of these two contrasting locations, in which images can be present, exemplifies

variability in experienced space, and suggests that different contexts of production and perception operated throughout the study area. These examples also show differences in their inscription and subsequent lifeworld. The lightly scratched eel has been produced expediently, while the others have been drawn with coloured pigment, which must have been brought to the site. Furthermore, the coloured eels have been redrawn at some time after their original creation.

Plate 1.6 Very small, lightly scratched eel motif. The head and fins are at the bottom of photo, slightly truncated by the camera frame (rock shelter BR12).
Source: Photograph by Julie Dibden, 2011.

The archaeological material is in open contexts, which primarily contain hatchet-grinding grooves (Plate 1.8), and sheltered contexts (Plate 1.9), which mostly contain rock art. The 20 weeks of fieldwork for this research focused on recording rock markings in sheltered contexts.

Archaeological excavation in the study area was beyond the scope of this research, which has been conducted independently of a local archaeological context. In the Upper Nepean catchment, there has been no excavation-based archaeological research. Accordingly, the analysis and interpretation rely solely on observations relating to the rock marks and the material contexts in which they are situated.

Plate 1.7 Large colourful eel motifs (rock shelter BR29).

Note the eel heads are at the top of the picture and these are three different coloured pigments: red, black and white.

Source: Photograph by Julie Dibden, 2011.

Plate 1.8 Grinding groove site in the sandstone bed of an upland dell (swamp) (open site UA3).

Note the small pothole with water at bottom right with a single groove at the front, and numerous grooves arrayed behind the hole to the top right. Note also a long, engraved groove channel extending across the rock surface in the centre of the photo.

Source: Photograph by Julie Dibden, 2011.

Plate 1.9 A small rock shelter in a boulder that has a relatively large number of graphic and non-graphic rock marks (rock shelter SCR4).

Source: Photograph by Julie Dibden, 2011.

1.5 Structure of Book

In Chapter 2, the environmental context of the study area is described, including its structure, geology, hydrological regime, vegetation and climate, and its variability over time. Consideration is given to constraints and opportunities afforded by the terrain in regard to human movement and occupation. Weathering and site formation processes in rock shelters are discussed as they have considerable relevance to contexts of human occupation and the preservation of rock art.

The wider geographic and environmental context, in which the study area is located is described in Chapter 2 to provide a broader context for the use and occupation of the Upper Nepean catchment in the pre-colonial and colonial periods. From the time of earliest occupation, presumably in the late Pleistocene, until the mid to late nineteenth century, Aboriginal people moved in and out of the Upper Nepean as they fulfilled their various economic, social, religious and familial activities and responsibilities. It is suggested in Chapter 2 that, during Aboriginal use of the region, the study area presented a geographic and environmental context that, differing as significantly as it does from its neighbouring terrain, provided a unique suite of constraints (as discussed previously) and opportunities regarding its occupation. The study area contains an abundance of sandstone surfaces, which allow for the possibility of the manufacture and sharpening of ground-edge implements and the recording of visual imagery in the form of rock art, which held some potential for permanence.

In Chapter 3, a framework of Aboriginal occupation of the broader Sydney Basin is outlined. It includes a summary of the archaeological understanding of the temporal framework of human occupation and change over time, the ethnographic context and a consideration of Aboriginal responses in the colonial period. This chapter sets out the chronological framework for Aboriginal people's occupation of the region from their earliest presence, as understood via archaeological observations and analysis, and how this changed through time. As far as possible, an ethnographic and historical review of Aboriginal life in the Sydney region will be outlined. However, our ethnographic understanding of Aboriginal people in this area, and the historical dimension of the colonial encounter, has been reconstructed from scant historical records produced during a context of death and dispossession (Swain 1993:115) and is sketchy and severely limited. Stanner (1977) has described the colonial and post-colonial past as a 'history of indifference', and this portrays both the substantive situation that prevailed and the general lack of regard for this history. However, historical scholarship has, in the recent past, become attentive to colonial processes, 'and in particular the dramatic and often violent events of the colonial frontier' (McNiven & Russell 2002:27).

Two recent religious histories are also discussed in Chapter 3, which address the intellectual and cultural milieu of the Indigenous people of south-east Australia in the colonial period, and which chart the startlingly swift and dynamic ritual response at this time (Swain 1993; Carey & Roberts 2002). By its nature, a historical narrative is derived from textual sources and is one that does not well breach and traverse the 'far side of the frontier', given the absence of an Indigenous voice in relevant texts (cf. McNiven & Russell 2002:27). Similar to the accounts set out in Chapter 3, McNiven and Russell (2002:28–31) describe numerous instances of ritual responses to colonial situations in Australia, and pose the question of whether or not these 'historical snippets of ritual activities [are] mere glimpses of an otherwise invisible domain of Aboriginal responses to European invasion?'. They suggest that, via archaeology and specifically the analysis of rock art, the 'complicated relationship between coloniser and colonised' may be understood.

The conceptual framework is outlined in Chapter 4. The archaeological context of rock art research in Australia is discussed to provide a paradigmatic framework. The research question and the conceptual focus of this research has been outlined in this introduction and, in Chapter 4, the theoretical underpinnings of this research will be developed further.

In Chapter 5 the database upon which this research is based is defined, and its biases and limitations are addressed. The methodology and nature of the data collection employed in the fieldwork and the post-fieldwork data treatment are described.

A general descriptive and quantitative profile of the database is presented in Chapter 6. Descriptive statistics are employed to explore the nature, diversity and distribution of open context and rock shelter sites, and the rock markings that each contain. Patterned relationships between different site types (and their identified variability) and geographic and environmental locations are defined and mapped. Hatchet-grinding groove sites are examined to provide a general context of people's habitual use of place. The rock markings and their diversity, contained within shelters, are quantified. Rock shelters are examined in regard to morphology, size and shape, as well as a number of other physical parameters, in order to consider their variability and potential in regard to human occupation and experience.

Earlier work dealing with the chronology of the Sydney Basin rock art is examined in Chapter 7, and the analysis of the relative temporal sequence of the rock art is documented. The temporal sequence in the current study area is explored by an analysis of superimpositioning of rock art.

Based on this analysis, an outline of temporal change, in both the rock art and the shelter and micro-topographic locational signatures of each phase of this sequence, is set out in Chapter 8. The rock art is analysed in detail in this chapter. Morphy (1999) argues that in order to define a body of rock art as a visual communicative system of meanings, it is essential to identify the manner in which it is constructed to convey meaning. A fundamental aim of this research is to explore the nature of the assemblage of rock marking in each temporal phase in order to define how rock art, as a visual communicative system of meanings, changes over time (cf. Morphy 1999). This will be undertaken by analysing each different mode of graphic and gestural expression and its intrinsic nature and variability. It is proposed that an examination of the different ways in which rock art is produced may provide clues as to its role in culture (Rosenfeld 2002), which, as Layton (2000a:170) emphasises, does not depend on reconstructions of meaning. In this sense, it is acknowledged that it is possible that rock art may express more than one core theme in a synchronic social context (Layton 2000a:172).

The analysis will be conducted using both quantitative and qualitative methods. In addition to rock art, shelters in the study area also contain evidence of other forms of gestural rock marking. These types of marks are not usually included in analyses of rock art, despite often being a real presence in shelter sites (Rosenfeld 1999). These marks are, however, the result of human behaviour, and can be described and quantified. They are, therefore, considered in this research to be a potentially significant data set of rock marks.

Various analyses will explore the manner in which rock marks articulate with the stone in which they are situated. A strong relationship of isomorphic congruence between images and natural rock features occurs in numerous instances in the Upper Nepean catchment, and this phenomenon will be described and quantified. In addition, images are present on a range of macro rock faces in shelters including walls, ceilings and concavities. In this regard, images can be located in either highly visible or hidden locales. The location of imagery and its variability in these different contexts is examined.

In Chapter 8 it will be demonstrated that, over time, marking the land became increasingly abundant and diverse. The temporal trends and patterns in rock marking, as defined in Chapter 8, will be explored further in Chapter 9 in a geographic and environmental framework. The spatial and landscape distributional signature of each temporal phase will be identified. The geographic location of specific categories of motifs will also be explored to determine if spatial patterning exists, which may indicate the emergence and existence of a totemic geography (cf. Layton 2000a). The spatial and locational patterning in the distribution of the most recent rock art will also be examined to explore whether or not rock art, as praxis, was a mechanism by which Aboriginal people sought to mediate their encounter with the British.

In Chapter 10, the results and implications of the analyses will be discussed. It will be argued that the practice of marking the land in the Upper Nepean catchment was a dynamic dialectic, both constitutive and transformative, of being and place. Over time, people drew the land into an object world that became, with ever-increasing inscription and embellishment, a marked and painted landscape, both productive of and reflecting a complex history.

2

Environmental Context

This chapter outlines the physical context of the Upper Nepean. The location and boundaries are delineated, and the topography, geology and vegetation are defined. The broader geographic and environmental context, in which the study area is situated, is also described. The four catchments are discussed individually. They each have different overall characteristics, which would have presented a different suite of opportunities and constraints to human occupation. It is assumed that the area is likely to have been used by Aboriginal people since the late Pleistocene through to the historic era. Accordingly, consideration is given to climatic variation and corresponding changes to the physical environment over that time. The weathering and site formation processes, which created and continue to form rock shelters, are described. These processes have considerable relevance to the nature of human occupation of shelters and to their potential to preserve the rock art they host.

2.1 Introduction

The study area is located on the Woronora Plateau, situated between the Illawarra Escarpment and the watershed divide between the Nepean and Bargo rivers. The plateau is deeply dissected, and is drained by six major rivers: the Georges, Woronora, Cataract, Cordeaux, Avon and Nepean (Figure 2.1). The study area is defined on a catchment (the Upper Nepean) and land use basis (it is confined to the Metropolitan Special Area), and it occupies the southern extent of the Woronora Plateau. The Metropolitan Special Area measures c. 78,000 hectares and is managed jointly by the SCA and the NSW OEH. Public access has been restricted for a considerable time, and it is now a significant naturally vegetated and largely undeveloped area (Mills et al. 1985:5). A considerable part of the Nepean's upper catchment is outside the Metropolitan Special Area. This extraneous area is predominantly private property and is situated largely on Wianamatta group soils or the overlying Robertson Basalt. It has been extensively cleared (Mills et al. 1985:2).

The Upper Nepean catchment includes four main rivers: the Cataract, Cordeaux, Avon and the headwaters of the Nepean. The Cataract, Cordeaux and Avon join the Nepean at the north-west boundary of the study area. The Nepean River thereafter drains to the north where it becomes the Hawkesbury (near Windsor, north-west of Sydney), and finally flows eastward to meet with the sea at Broken Bay, north of Sydney. The drainage of the Upper Nepean system is unusual given its proximity to the eastern seaboard, in that the rivers flow in a north-westerly direction rather than flowing eastward to the sea.

The Woronora Plateau is located on the southern margins of the geological feature known as the Sydney Basin (cf. Branagan et al. 1979), and is comprised of Triassic and Permian strata (Sherwin et al. 1986). The surface geology of the plateau coincides with the surface of the Triassic formation, comprised of Hawkesbury Sandstone, which is dominant, and intermittent exposures of the underlying shales, claystones and sandstones of the Narrabeen Group (Sherwin et al. 1986). The sedimentary sequence of the Sydney Basin was deposited in a relatively stable tectonic period, and is, therefore, generally conformable and remains essentially horizontal (Young 1985). All the archaeological material examined in this research is located within or on the weathered features of the Hawkesbury Sandstone strata of this sequence.

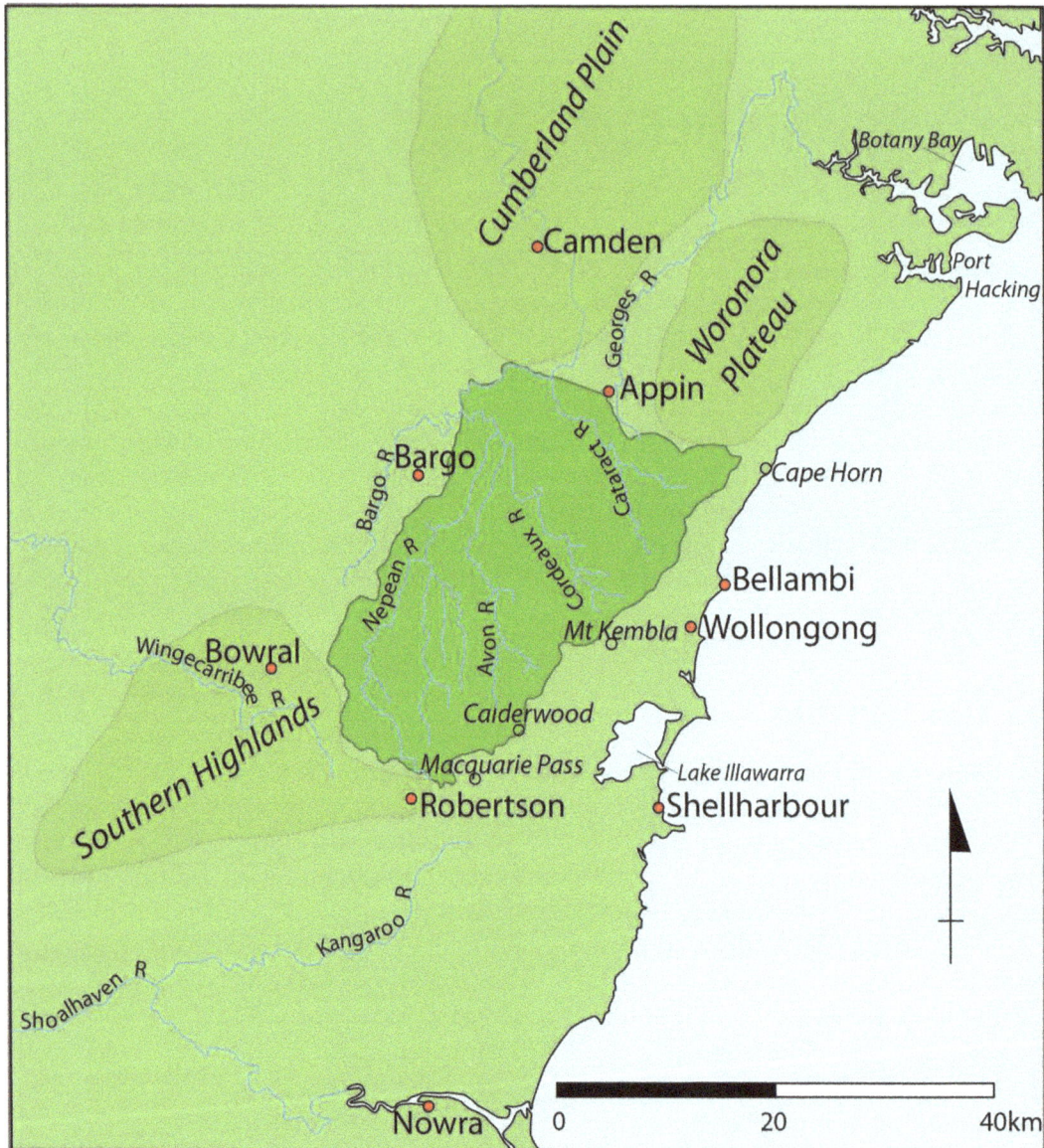

Figure 2.1 The Upper Nepean catchment in a regional context.
Source: Map reproduced from Dibden (2011).

Altitude in the study area ranges from 730 metres (Australian Height Datum [AHD]), at its southern boundary, to 449 metres (AHD) in the north. The major rivers follow this fall in land surface, which coincides with the surface and dip of the Hawkesbury Sandstone formation, and which falls to the north-west at an average slope of less than 1° over 15–20 kilometres (Young & Johnson 1977). The Woronora Plateau is dominated topographically by the river systems and the ridge/divides of the plateau from which they initiate. First- and second-order streams rapidly become narrower with increased gradient, eventually flowing through canyon-like gorges much of their length. These are narrow and deep, and their valley sides are nearly vertical (Young 1985). The crest landforms at plateau level vary between being either narrow or broad. At plateau level, dells (upland swamps) are located within the first- and second-order valleys of the Cataract, Cordeaux and Avon (Young 1982).

2.2 Climate

The context of climate change in Australia underpins much interpretation of observed changes in the archaeological record. Climate change, specifically relating to temperature and effective rainfall, is outlined in this section. The Illawarra region currently experiences a temperate climate. The average annual rainfall is 1,200 millimetres. The orographic effect of the Illawarra Escarpment is pronounced, with annual rainfall on the plateau in the vicinity of the escarpment being 1,700 millimetres on average. On the western boundary, average rainfall is about 900 millimetres per year (Mills et al. 1985:5).

During the time Aboriginal people have occupied south-east Australia, average temperatures and effective precipitation have been variable. During the Last Glacial Maximum between 24,000 and 17,000 years BP, the climate was much drier and colder than present, with periods of extreme coldness and aridity (Kershaw et al. 1991; Attenbrow 2004:204). Sea levels at this time were c. 135 metres lower, and the continent was approximately one-third larger than now (Black et al. 2008:438). While glacial or periglacial conditions prevailed at this time in regions with elevations above 1,000 metres, the east coast and foothills of the Great Dividing Range are likely to have experienced less extreme conditions due to oceanic influences (Attenbrow 2004:207). The late Pleistocene recovery from the glacial period, from c. 15,000 years BP onwards, saw a gradual increase in precipitation and vegetation growth rather than an abrupt change (Attenbrow 2004:207).

While generally warmer and wetter than the late Pleistocene, the Holocene has also witnessed climatic variability, particularly during its middle period (Dodson & Mooney 2002:456). In south-east Australia during the early Holocene, climate was relatively stable and this is perhaps related to reduced seasonality (Black et al. 2008:438). The significant environmental change during the early Holocene was the reduction in landmass resulting from rising sea levels. Based on the expansion in woody taxa, Kershaw et al. (1991) argue that recovery from glacial conditions is evident between 11,500 and 8,500 years BP. Maximum effective precipitation, and perhaps also warmth, occurred between 7,000 BP and 5,000 years BP (Black et al. 2008:438), and this is believed to have peaked between 6,000 and 4,000 years BP, when maximum warming was 1°C, and effective precipitation was about 30 per cent higher than the present (Dodson & Mooney 2002:456). At this time, an expansion of wet sclerophyll and rainforest species occurred in south-east Australia (Black et al. 2008:438). After this time, there was a return to a cooler and drier climate. A more variable climate has been experienced in south-east Australia in the last 5,000 years (Shulmeister 1999:83). At about 5,000 years BP, a sharp decline in effective precipitation occurred, resulting in falling lake levels, a reactivation of continental dunes and a decline in rainforest elements.

Additionally, the modern Eucalypt grasslands in the woodlands of south-east Australia replaced the Casuarina/Asteraceae associations (Kershaw et al. 1991). Between 4,000 BP and 2,000 years BP, effective precipitation was lower, and it was also possibly cooler (Black et al. 2008:438). This period saw an intensification of the El Niño–Southern Oscillation (ENSO) climatic pattern, which was causal of these changes, and productive of increased variability in seasonality and precipitation (Attenbrow 2004:207). During the last 1,500–1,000 years, temperature and precipitation increased until reaching the climate currently experienced today (Attenbrow 2004:206).

Attenbrow (2004:203) argues that environmental changes resulting from global climatic change were of sufficient magnitude to affect both the land and subsistence resources (relative abundance and/or spatial distribution of resources) in the Sydney region, and that this would have led people to modify land use and extractive methods, with ensuing changes in habitation patterns, tool kits and so on. Attenbrow (2004:203) is careful to stress that these responses to environmental change, which may be visible in the archaeological record, are indirect changes mediated by people's decisions and choices. In summary, over the course of Aboriginal occupation in south-eastern Australia, major climatic oscillations occurred resulting in changes to sea levels, landforms, temperature and precipitation, and vegetation structures. In Chapter 3, archaeological models relating to Aboriginal responses to these changes will be discussed further.

2.3 Geology

The Hawkesbury Sandstone is highly quartzose, being composed of medium-coarse, poorly sorted quartz grains with an argillaceous matrix of secondary quartz siderite (iron carbonate) cement (Standard 1964; Packham 1969). The average composition of Hawkesbury Sandstone includes 68 per cent quartz in a 20 per cent carbonate and clay rich matrix, which includes 2 per cent siderite (Packham 1969:408–412). The carbonate and clay-rich cement component makes the sandstone very susceptible to weathering processes. Both the chemical and physical weathering processes, which have created and continue to shape the rock shelters in the study area, represent complex formation processes and histories (Huntley et al. 2011).

Both the lithology and bed dimensions of the Hawkesbury Sandstone are variable (Conaghan & Jones 1975). The sandstone facies are up to 10 metres thick, while the mudstone facies are typically 0.3–5 metres thick. Coupled with the characteristics of the sandstone, as comprised of relatively discontinuous layers, its cross-bedded nature results in rock shelter formation, which is often highly irregular in morphology. Walls are commonly comprised of short, bedded sections located between bedding planes. Bedding planes, from which blocks of sandstone have previously fallen (roof-fall), often form shelter ceilings. Ceilings in shelters can be numerous and they are often low. Shelter floors, likewise, are frequently comprised of rock, either broad expanses, or as roof-fall boulders. As indicated in Chapter 1, considerable variability in shelter characteristics and morphology exists in the study area. For this research, the physical characteristics of shelters (shape, size and floor characteristics) are quantified, in order to explore whether or not they exercised any control in regard to their use as potential occupation sites and in the production of rock art (Plate 2.1).

During the weathering of exposed sandstone, the siderite is hydrated to iron oxide plus water, and mobilised to the surface of the outcrop where it is oxidised and may hydrate to form a crust on the surface. These surfaces are rich in iron minerals such as goethite, hematite and/or limonite, and the predominance of one or the other depends on local, site specific weathering conditions (Watchman, pers. comm., in Sefton 1988). The iron oxide deposits intermix with the quartz and clay, at or near the surface. Chemical weathering of the sandstone occurs behind crusts whereby the siderite and silica are mobilised by water action to the surface of the stone. As these surfaces form from within the stone, they produce an impermeable crust. Behind the crust the sandstone continues to weather, disintegrating and changing chemically. Siderite cement can oxidise to form goethite or hematite beneath the silica skin. The skin then begins to detach, which results in the disintegrating sandstone spilling to the floor. The chemical processes both create case-hardened surfaces upon which rock art was produced, and, at the same time, act to facilitate their eventual disintegration and the removal of imagery. It has also been determined that some of the coloured pigment, which is likely to have been utilised for rock art production on the Woronora Plateau, may have been sourced locally from within shelters, as minerals are released during these weathering events (Huntley et al. 2011).

Plate 2.1 Typical rock shelter floor comprised of roof-fall boulders (rock shelter EC36).
Source: Photograph by Julie Dibden, 2011.

The formation processes in shelters are likely to have contributed significantly to the preservation or otherwise of rock art (cf. Hughes 1976). The majority of the sheltered rock art in the study area is highly weathered, and is now indeterminate in regard to its original form. This phenomenon is not new or recent. In the late nineteenth century, Mathews (1895:272) commented that rock art located in a shelter in the northern Woronora Plateau was highly weathered owing to the 'natural decay of the rock'. Weathering processes, in which imagery is removed and/or covered with silica skins, can be highly active (Plate 2.2). For example, graffiti (names and dates) has been observed to be almost entirely obscured by mineralisation (pers. observ.). In another example, a comparison of pigments and rock surfaces photographed at an interval of two years, between 2001 and 2003, reveals significant loss of both pigment and the crust on which it rests (pers. observ. of photographic records of J. Dibden & J. Huntley). The hostile nature of the physical and chemical processes that occur in the Hawkesbury Sandstone has significant impact upon the art surfaces and the imagery itself, and this is recognised generally for the Sydney Basin, with the implication that much of the extant rock art is unlikely to be old.

Hughes (1976) conducted a study of three sandstone shelters located to the south of the Woronora Plateau, to measure the rates of rock weathering and roof-fall. His study has established a strong relationship between rates of weathering and site usage—specifically, that the more a site was occupied, the greater the rate of roof-fall. The implication of this finding is that rock art present at the time shelters were occupied is likely to have been removed due to accelerated weathering and roof-fall (Hughes 1976:52). Hughes (1976:53) argues that where rock art has survived in shelters known to have been used as habitation sites, it is likely to have been produced late in their occupational histories. He suggests also that the reduced weathering occurring in the absence of human (Aboriginal or European) usage is a likely contributor to the preservation of rock art.

Plate 2.2 Example of weathering processes on rock art.

Note the mineral skin and exfoliation of rock surface. Each process is, respectively, covering and removing parts of the image (rock shelter DCC30).

Source: Photograph by Julie Dibden, 2011.

In regard to rock art located on open sandstone platforms, weathering rates are significant to the point that engraved images of sailing ships (which can only be c. 200 years old) in the Sydney Basin have been reported to be virtually invisible (Edwards 1971:361). However, it is noted that, according to Jo McDonald (pers. comm., Feb. 2011), contact engravings are apparently thinly incised into rock, and this may have a causal relationship with their swift deterioration. Maynard (1979:93) refers generally to the outline engravings 'on the soft Sydney sandstone in the Sydney–Hawkesbury area, which suffer erosion to the point of obliteration'. Edwards (1971:361) suggests that a combination of soft sandstone, salt-laden air and exposure to high levels of rainfall combine to accelerate weathering of engravings in open sites. Hughes (1976:52) also indicates that rock art located on open rock exposures is likely to undergo ongoing deterioration from exposure to rain and running water. These aspects of site formation processes, which operate in the Sydney Basin, have obvious implications in regard to the antiquity of extant rock art.

2.4 Soils and Geomorphology

Two major soil landscapes have been defined for the Upper Nepean catchment: the Hawkesbury Sandstone Soil Landscape, which is a colluvial landscape; and the Lucas Heights Soil Landscape, which is residual. The Hawkesbury Sandstone Soil Landscape is confined to the major rivers and larger tributaries. It is characterised by rugged sandstone escarpment and ridges, with moderate to steep slopes and narrow, deeply incised valleys. Sandstone outcrops are common, occurring as boulders, benches and large blocks. They often form scarps of up to 10 metres in height. The soils in this landscape are subject to mass movement as the principal geomorphological process; they are shallow, discontinuous and generally sandy (Hazelton & Tille 1990). The Lucas Heights Soil Landscape is confined to ridge tops and gentle slopes. It is comprised of gently undulating crests, ridges and plateau surfaces, with low local relief and slopes of less than 10 per cent. Soils in this landscape are generally yellowed to lateritic podzolic, and are generally shallow (Hazelton & Tille 1990). Soils in the study area are infertile; one reason why the sandstone country was avoided by early settlers (Mills et al. 1985:5).

The rivers and streams have dissected the Woronora Plateau to varying degrees. Creeks flow from major ridges and divides in narrow, steep-sided gullies joining the major rivers in wider valleys. As the rivers proceed northwards, these valleys narrow and become sheer, cliff-lined gorges. Dells are present in the Cataract, Cordeaux and Avon catchments. Dells are swampy sediment traps containing sedge-heath vegetation communities, located in headwater valleys at plateau level. Most dells are located in first- and second-order valleys, generally on valley floors, but sometimes on benches or steep valley sides (Young 1982:16). They occur on the east side of the plateau where elevation is greatest, and precipitation substantially exceeds evaporation. Dells consist of deep deposits of sediment provided by downslope movement from adjacent higher slopes. Their initiation is largely a factor of geomorphic processes (Young 1982:49). Deep, permanent pools are present in the larger dells, thus providing an important source of water, particularly in droughts (Young 1985). Elsewhere in dells, water is stored in long furrows running parallel to land contours (Young 1985). The sediments in dells have been dated to c. 17,000 BP. Dells are relatively stable, their boundaries do not change over time, and they do not encroach on neighbouring forested areas.

The Cataract catchment has gentle slopes, generally with 88 per cent having less than a 10º gradient, whereas the Cordeaux and the Avon have fewer gentle slopes. Local relief is far greater in the latter two catchments, which are deeply dissected and average local relief exceeds 100 metres, while in the Cataract local relief is 65 metres (Young 1982:13). The Hawkesbury Sandstone has been considerably breached in the Cordeaux, and the correspondingly low dell numbers, in part, reflect this feature (Young 1982:12). The largest dells are located in the Cataract catchment; the largest is located at Sublime Point and Maddens Plains. It measures 2.5 kilometres in width (at its widest) with several arms measuring 2–3 kilometres long by 300–500 metres wide (Young 1982:11). The dells on Lizard Creek in the Cataract, are 5 kilometres long. However, most dells measure less than 1 kilometre in length and approximately 200 metres in width [<13 hectares] (Young 1982:11). Dells contain acidic, swampy soils, and accordingly support almost treeless vegetation dominated by sedges, restiads and water-tolerant shrubs (Young 1985). While potable water is also available at plateau level away from dells, they are important occupational determinants in that they are likely to have provided Aboriginal people with a reliable, if not abundant, source of fresh water on the ridge crests. Given the late Pleistocene age of dells, this scenario is likely to have some considerable antiquity.

The Woronora Plateau contains patches of Ferricrete (laterite) preserved (and believed to be still forming) on undissected, relatively flat ridge crests. This Ferricrete is hard, orange-brown nodular material believed to form via iron migration through the Hawkesbury Sandstone (Young 1985). It is possibly a raw material that was used for the production of red pigment for use in rock art and other decorative purposes. To date, this notion has not yet been confirmed.

2.5 Regional Context

The Upper Nepean catchment area is bounded in the east by the Illawarra Escarpment. This natural physiographic boundary is the easterly divide between the rivers of the study area and the shorter streams of the coastal plain. The escarpment is a visual and physical barrier to human movement between the coast and the plateau, although not one that is insurmountable. The northern boundary of the study area is the east–west-oriented divide that separates the Cataract

River catchment from the rivers and streams that flow in a northerly direction, emptying into either Botany Bay (Georges River, Woronora River) or Port Hacking (Hacking River). The land to the north of the study area is the north section of the Woronora Plateau and is of the same geology and comparable topography with that of the study area. The southern boundary of the study area coincides with the headwaters of the Nepean's tributaries and the Avon River. This area is also marked by a localised topographic and geological boundary, comprised of Wianamatta Shale, and is associated with a marked and subdued topographic physiography. The area is also comprised of pockets of remnant volcanic geology (Mills et al. 1985).

For the purposes of providing a wider geographic and environmental context to the study area, each of these areas adjacent to the study area is described in more detail below. As Officer (1984:7) remarks, the landscape of the Hawkesbury Sandstone provides a dramatic contrast between open and fertile plains and the 'rugged, poorer and inaccessible highland'. Officer (1984:7) also draws attention to the possibility that this division in the landscape may have determined human access and communication. In this regard, Officer identifies various routes between the plateau and the coast. The one relevant to the current study is the divide between the Georges and Woronora rivers and the Cataract River on the northern boundary of the study area.

2.5.1 The Illawarra

This narrow band of undulating land is located between the base of the Illawarra Escarpment and the littoral zone of the Pacific Ocean. The northern part of the coastal land is situated at a point located 1 kilometre to the east of the north-east boundary of the study area. This area is coincident with Cape Horn, and is where the cliffs of the Illawarra Escarpment meet with the sea cliffs that line the coast along the north-eastern margin of the Woronora Plateau. Southwards from Cape Horn, the coastal margin increases gradually in width to measure approximately 16 kilometres (as measured from the base of the escarpment at Macquarie Pass to Shellharbour on the coast) adjacent to the south-east boundary of the study area.

The Illawarra Escarpment rises dramatically from the coastal plain. It comprises an upper near-vertical cliff line measuring up to 50 metres high, below which very steep slopes fall to the coastal plain. The escarpment in many areas is a barrier to human movement and, accordingly, access from the coast to the plateau is possible only in few places so that movement into the study area is highly constrained and channelled. The western part of the coastal margin comprises the foothills of the escarpment, drained to the east by short first- to third-order streams. The moderate to steep slopes of the foothills extend variously to within a few hundred metres or less of the littoral zone in the north, to 2 kilometres at Bellambi, and approximately 3 kilometres at Wollongong and the western margins of Lake Illawarra. The streams drain into beaches located between bedrock headlands. Beaches vary from a few hundred metres to several kilometres in length. Lake Illawarra dominates the topography in the southern part of the coastal plain. Early commentators described the vegetation of the Illawarra as luxuriant tree-cover, including rainforest and wet sclerophyll forest communities (R. L. Jones 1990:37–38). During the late Holocene, the Illawarra was covered continuously with Eucalypt forest (which may have been wet sclerophyll) and probably patches of rainforest (R. L. Jones 1990:43).

Along the coastal plain and behind estuaries, extensive wetland development occurred during the past 5,000 or so years, after the post-glacial sea level rise and stabilisation (R. L. Jones 1990). The marine influence in these wetlands has changed during the late Holocene. At Terragong Swamp in the Minnamurra Valley, for example, sediments dated to between 4,300 and 2,500 BP were deposited in an inter-tidal environment. Pollen and spore data indicate that wetland species at this time were saline plant vegetation. After c. 2,500 BP, however, a significant change in wetland plants occurred, with freshwater aquatic species appearing, reflecting a change to a freshwater wetland environment. Significantly, the plant species that became abundant in the swamp at this time were those that are known to have been important Aboriginal plant foods, such as Typha and Blechnum (R. L. Jones 1990:45; cf. Gott 1999). The coastal zone, including the ocean and its rock platforms and estuaries, would have provided Aboriginal land users with an abundance and diversity of plant and faunal resources likely to have exceeded that which exists in the study area today.

2.5.2 The Southern Highlands

The area to the west of the study area is a north–south-oriented divide between the Nepean catchment and the Bargo River. This divide is a major north–south passage between the Cumberland Plain of the Central Sydney Basin and the Southern Highlands. The underlying geology is Hawkesbury Sandstone, and the landforms are dissected similar to the Woronora Plateau. The landscape of the Southern Highlands proper, which is situated to the south and south-west of the study area, is of subdued relief. The geology is comprised of Wianamatta Shales and Narrabeen Sediments with pockets of volcanics (Herbert 1980). The land drains westward to the Wingecarribee River, and it too eventually joins the Nepean River much further to the north after skirting west of the Bargo and other rivers. Immediately to the south-east of the study area, the Kangaroo River begins its south-westerly passage to eventually join the Shoalhaven. The latter proceeds easterly to its confluence with the sea at Nowra.

The contrast between the Southern Highlands and the Upper Nepean area of the Woronora Plateau is dramatic. The former is gently undulating and of subdued relief; the country between Berrima and Moss Vale was described by Wilson in 1798 as 'a most beautiful country, being nothing but fine meadows with ponds of water in them; fine green hills, but very thin timber' (cited in Andrews 1998:12). While it is considered possible that these contrasting environments provided some influence over Aboriginal land use, it is unequivocal that European settlement has been strongly defined by these background conditions (Mills et al. 1985:5).

2.6 European Land Use

Until the 1880s, the majority of the Upper Nepean catchment was unalienated crown land. Given the nature of the topography, and its poor soils and forest cover, it was largely unsuited to agriculture (Mills et al. 1985:5). Accordingly, and unlike the Cumberland Plain, Illawarra and Southern Highlands, the Upper Nepean was not taken up by European settlers except for small areas of land at the headwaters of the Cataract and Cordeaux rivers where local relief is more subdued and soils deeper (these lands were resumed by the crown in the 1910s).

The Upper Nepean water catchment was gazetted in 1880 as a water reserve for Sydney and its suburbs. The area measured 924 square kilometres and encompassed the Cataract, Cordeaux, Avon rivers and the headwaters of the Nepean River (i.e. the study area). This was followed in 1888 by the commencement of works on the Upper Nepean Water Scheme. A program of dam construction on all four rivers occurred between 1907 and 1935 (Mills et al. 1985). Impacts relating to these works, while including denudation of the main valleys, all otherwise occurred within the immediate vicinity of the dam wall construction sites. Other European impacts in the area are generally confined to linear features including two public east–west-orientated roads (the Appin and Picton roads), numerous fire trails, an unfinished railway and several power transmission lines. Minor surface impacts occur in the vicinity of above ground facilities associated with underground longwall coal-mining operations. Public access to this country has been restricted for many years (Mills et al. 1985:5), but there is an ongoing incidence of unlawful entry. Recreational fishermen have for years camped, and in some instances continue to camp, in rock shelters situated along some of the lake edges, and this activity has resulted in significant impact on archaeological deposit and rock art.

Table 2.1 shows the area covered by dam water in each of the four catchments. The land of the study area totals 866.6 square kilometres, 30.05 square kilometres of which is flooded by dam water. This figure represents 3.5 per cent of the study area in total, and presents a bias in the study in terms of any analysis relating to site location and distribution. Generally, it is the sections of the valleys of each catchment that are wide and shallow that are dammed. Any archaeological sites in the valley bottoms of these locations are now destroyed.

Table 2.1 Summary of catchment areas, dam areas and percentage of each catchment denuded by flooding.

Statistics	Cataract	Cordeaux	Avon	Nepean	Total
Area dammed (ha)	850	780	1,015	360	3005
Total catchment (ha)	20,557	16,656	17,447	32,000	86,660
% of catchment dammed	4.1	4.7	5.8	1.1	3.5 (av.)

Source: After Mills et al. (1985).

2.7 Vegetation

In January 2001, during the period of fieldwork undertaken for this research, a wildfire swept through much of the Cataract, Cordeaux and Avon catchments. The consequence of this on the vegetation was, as would be expected, dramatic, and particularly so in its effect as to make movement across the area considerably easier. Prior to the fire, the thick understorey often acted to impede movement significantly. The modern vegetation structure and composition of the study area may now be different from what it was when the land was occupied by Aboriginal people. Information regarding Aboriginal fire regimes in south-east Australia is scant, although it is known that elsewhere fire was used to clear vegetation and to propagate new plant growth (Gott 1999) and encourage animal activity. Certainly, it is likely that Aboriginal people used fire for land management within the study area, and this is likely to have kept the woodland relatively open. Studies of Holocene changes in vegetation and fire are discussed below in order to give consideration to the pre-European environment.

Studies of sediments conducted in the Sydney Basin reveal the presence of charcoal in deposits that occur in variable densities throughout the late Pleistocene and Holocene. However, distinguishing between natural and cultural agencies, which may account for this variability, is problematic (cf. R. L. Jones 1990:43; Dodson & Thom 1991; Black et al. 2008). In the Illawarra, R. L. Jones (1990:43) found that burning of vegetation occurred throughout the late Holocene, but not on a large scale. He observed a sharp peak in charcoal in sediment from the Terragong Swamp at c. 2,500 BP. In the Mill Creek catchment, situated 70 kilometres north-west of Sydney, Dodson and Thom (1991) found that, during the entire Holocene, frequent fire, which may have been influenced by human activity, had acted to restrict the abundance of rainforest, and that Eucalyptus-Casuarinaceae forest and heath had dominated the landscape for the past 9,000 years. More recently, Black et al. (2008:445) argue that a climatic solution explains all periods of change in the fire history of the landscape at Goochs Swamp in the Blue Mountains, but that peaks in charcoal that coincide with ENSO-like climatic variability may reflect anthropogenic fires, which may have been a response to climate variability. This interpretation is somewhat at odds with previous ideas that Aboriginal people in Australia strongly controlled prehistoric fire activity (Black et al. 2008:437).

Johnson (2000) has carried out a fine-grained palaeoecological study of sediments from the Mill Creek Valley. The study sought to examine land system responses to Aboriginal and European land management over the past 820 years. The results can be extrapolated with caution to the study area given its proximity and the comparability of land system, geology and vegetation structure. Johnson reached a number of conclusions, and those that may be salient to an understanding of the pre-European environment of the study area are listed below:

- Prior to European settlement, the environment is likely to have been well vegetated. The vegetation community comprised a stable sclerophyll association on valley sides and a significant wetland community on the valley floor. While the vegetation structures are currently undergoing successionary processes that are returning to those that occurred earlier, the current terrestrial vegetation types compare well with those that were present prior to European occupation.

- Prior to European settlement, charcoal input was relatively low (R. L. Jones [1990] obtained a similar result in the Illawarra) and is not linked to vegetation abundance. Johnson (2000) suggests that this result may distance Aboriginal burning practices from vegetation dynamics.

- A notable change in fire regime corresponds with the lower limit of pollen from introduced species. The present charcoal supply pattern appears to be similar to that which existed prior to European settlement.

- Prior to European settlement, sedimentation rates were significantly lower (Johnson 2000:221, 223, 229).

Providing that these results are, as suggested, relevant to the study area, they support a view that the current vegetation is both structurally and compositionally comparable with that during Aboriginal occupation, at least during the late Holocene. However, a recent study has found that long-term changes in understorey vegetation occur in the absence of fire in dry sclerophyll forests of south-east Australia, and that species richness declines significantly in the absence of frequent fire. This decline was also found to be associated with significant changes in species composition (Penman et al. 2009:535). In this study it was found that of 51 species, predominantly shrubs and herbs, declined over time in the absence of fire. This is relevant because those species that decline in the absence of regular burning all occur in the study area and are known to have been Aboriginal food plants (cf. Penman et al. 2009:537). The biodiversity values of vegetation communities in the study area, which existed at the time of Aboriginal occupation, therefore, should be considered to be somewhat uncertain.

The vegetation of the Woronora Plateau is now comprised mostly of sandstone plant communities—woodlands or open woodlands (Mills et al. 1985:6). These communities are dominated by Eucalypt species and possess a species-rich understorey of heath or shrubland. They are relatively homogenous across the study area. The understoreys present on the Narrabeen Group, however, are generally dominated by grasses and are less species rich. In the larger gullies, open forests occur, and some support simple rainforest communities. In the east, the sedgeland/heathland communities of the dells are extensive (see below). Where isolated pockets of other geologies are present, such as to the south where small areas of Robertson Basalt occur, tall Eucalypt forests grow. A small area in the Upper Cordeaux catchment is covered with a subtropical rainforest, which has developed on the Cordeaux Crinanite.

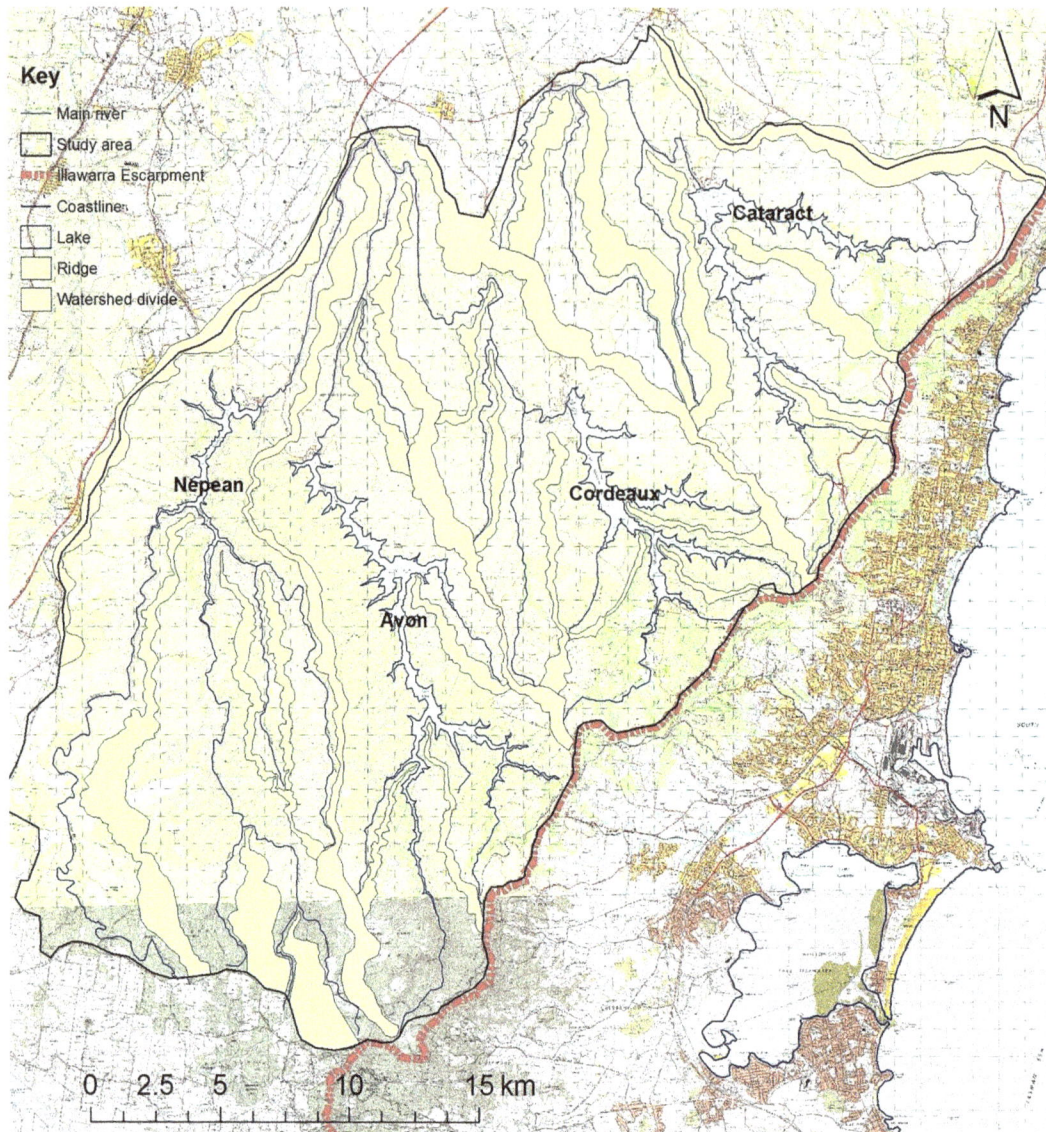

Figure 2.2 The Upper Nepean catchment in a local context.
Source: Map reproduced from Dibden (2011).

On ridge tops, woodland and open forest communities grow to a maximum height of 15 metres. These communities are comprised of a range of Eucalypt species (Silvertop Ash and Scribbly Gum) and Red Bloodwood, with a small tree layer of Old Man Banksia and Paperbark Ti-tree. Numerous species occupy the shrub and ground layers of which *Gahnia sieberi* and *Persoonia levis*, respectively, provided seeds for flour and the other fruit. Gully forest occupies slopes and gullies. This dry forest community is dominated by Red Bloodwood and Sydney Peppermint, growing to a height of 25 metres. A species-rich understorey contains numerous Acacia species. The tubers of orchids (*Acianthus* spp. and *Dendrobium speciosum*) and fruits of *Persoonia* spp. and *Dianella caerulea* in these communities are potential foods.

Warm temperate rainforest is present in restricted areas of the catchment and is mostly confined to the east where it occurs in gullies on south- and east-facing slopes. A closed canopy of Coachwood and Sassafras grows to a height of up to 30 metres, shading a range of small trees including Blackwood, of which the seeds were processed for flour, and Lillypilly, the fruit of which was eaten. Cabbage Tree Palms, of which the tip of the palm is edible, also grow in this community. Seeds and rhizomes from commonly occurring plants such as *Gahnia sieberi*, *Acacia rubida*, *Lomandra longifolia* and *Pteridium esculentum* were processed for food. Plants across the plateau also provided a range of other resources including medicines, bark, fibres and wood.

The vegetation communities in dells are low heaths and sedgelands, ranging in height from 0.5 to 3 metres. They are dominated by coarse sedges (Cyperaceae family) and rushes (Restionaceae family), usually growing into tussocks up to 1.5 metres high. Additionally, low shrubs (Proteaceae and Myrtaeae families) grow along drainage lines and some hillslopes, but are mostly scattered. The occasional, generally isolated Eucalyptus (usually *E. heamtastosa*) is present (Young 1982:74– 75). A variety of aquatic and terrestrial faunal species, many of which are represented in the rock art, were available for food, and also for tool-making. Given the high diversity of habitats, most native species occurring in the region are present (Mills et al. 1985:19). It is concluded that the study area is likely to have presented Aboriginal land users with a relatively abundant and spatially continuous distribution of natural resources.

2.8 The Individual Catchments

Each of the four catchments is described separately in this section. The intention is to summarise the main structural features of each area, and to describe their general character. These physical variables will then be considered as boundary conditions relating to Aboriginal land usage and human movement in each catchment (Figure 2.2).

2.8.1 Cataract River

The Cataract catchment extends from the escarpment in a north-westerly alignment between its northerly watershed with the Georges/Woronora rivers, and its southerly watershed/divide with the Cordeaux. The landforms of both watersheds are relatively broad and gently undulating. Today, the Appin and Picton roads traverse them, and are major local thoroughfares between the coast and interior. These routes are likely to have been utilised similarly by Aboriginal people. The divide between the Cataract and the Georges/Woronora rivers is recognised to have been an Aboriginal travel route between the Cumberland Plain and the coast. The explorer Throsby was shown this particular thoroughfare by two Aboriginal men in the early 1800s (McDonald 1966:27).

The Cataract River is comprised of two main arms, the Loddon and Cataract, both of which commence their drainage at the Illawarra Escarpment. The Loddon drains from Maddens Plains in the north-east of the study area, at c. 1.5 kilometres from the coast, and flows westward for 9 kilometres. The Cataract rises on the escarpment at c. 5 kilometres from the coast and flows north-west for a distance of c. 11 kilometres to the confluence of the two arms. This point is near to where the Cataract becomes a gorge (now coincident with the Cataract Dam wall). The Loddon and Cataract flowed through relatively wide valleys prior to the construction of the dam. Given the nature of these valleys, before they reach the gorge, they are likely to have been utilised for travel from the coast into the interior of the catchment. Likewise, the large ridge separating these two arms, being wide and gently undulating, is also likely to have been a thoroughfare into the catchment. To the west, three major creeks (Lizard, Wallandoola and Cascade) flow northward from the Cordeaux/Cataract divide, to where they each join the Cataract at various points along the gorge. In terms of human movement, the northerly extent of the landforms between these creeks, given that they join the Cataract where it is cliff-lined, are effectively dead ends. However, the Cataract catchment generally presents relatively little constraint to human activity and movement. Local relief and slope gradients are low. Ridge crests and valley bottoms (at least in the mid and upper reaches) are likely to have been used for access and as thoroughfares.

2.8.2 Cordeaux River

The Cordeaux catchment extends from the escarpment in a north-westerly alignment between its northerly watershed/divide with the Cataract and its southerly watershed with the Avon. The slopes falling to the Cordeaux River from the Cordeaux/Cataract divide are generally of moderate gradient only, and this contrasts with the remainder of the Cordeaux catchment, which is commonly steep. Similar to the Cataract/Cordeaux divide, the ridge between the Cordeaux and Avon is relatively broad and gently undulating, and is likely to have been a major thoroughfare between the coast and the interior of the Upper Nepean. At their confluence, the Cordeaux and Avon become unpassable cliff-lined gorges. However, from midway along the Cordeaux/Avon divide, human movement is possible to the north across the Cordeaux, and to the west across the Avon and Nepean rivers.

The Cordeaux River rises at a point on the Illawarra Escarpment immediately to the north of the Avon drainage system. Access between the escarpment and the coast is possible at this southern section of the catchment via the hillslopes of Mt Kembla. The Cordeaux drains to the north-west, and its upper reaches flow through a relatively wide valley that is likely to have been used as a thoroughfare into the catchment. However, from near to where the Cordeaux dam wall is now, and further to the north-west, the river is narrow, and it is highly unlikely that people would have used that section of the river as a thoroughfare. At c. 6 kilometres short of its confluence with the Avon, the river valley becomes very steep and cliff-lined. Several tributary creeks flow northward from the Cordeaux/Avon divide including Sandy, Wongawilli and Donald Castle creeks. All three flow through steep slopes and are often flanked by cliffs and rocky scarps. The creeks themselves were unlikely to have been habitually used for travel, but the minor divides between these were. The Cordeaux catchment contrasts with the Cataract primarily in terms of its greater local relief, steeper slope gradients and frequent occurrence of high, long cliff lines extending along valley slopes. The terrain in the Cordeaux is such that it is likely to have exerted constraints to human movement. It is considered most probable that people would have utilised the ridges of watershed divides and crests of minor divides between creeks to travel through the catchment.

2.8.3 Avon River

At its southern margin, the Avon catchment is bounded to the east by the Illawarra Escarpment and to the west by the divide between the Avon and the Nepean rivers. The southernmost area drains from a point where the escarpment at Calderwood changes its orientation from north–south to east–west. Calderwood is also the most southerly access point between the coastal plain and plateau. The Avon catchment extends from the escarpment in a predominantly northerly alignment between the Cordeaux and Nepean rivers. The watershed between the Avon and Nepean is relatively broad and gently undulating, and is likely to have been a major thoroughfare between the coast and the interior of the catchment. At their confluence, both rivers are impassable cliff-lined gorges.

For a distance of approximately six kilometres from the escarpment, the Avon River is located within a narrow steep gully and is fed by short tributary streams. It is bounded to the east by the escarpment. Two third-order creeks (Gallahers and Native Dog) flow from the escarpment, forming short ridges jutting into the catchment. As the Avon proceeds northwards, the catchment width is restricted to about 6 kilometres. Generally, only first- and second-order tributary creeks flow into the Avon. The majority of the Avon catchment is steep and deeply dissected. Cliffs line the river valley and tributary creeks along the majority of the length of their course. The terrain of the Avon catchment is likely to have strongly influenced the manner in which it was occupied. It is most probable that people would have utilised the crests of watershed and minor divides to travel through the catchment.

2.8.4 Nepean River

The Nepean River rises in a spring near Robertson, immediately to the south of the study area. The southernmost area of the catchment is at a point located c. 4 kilometres west of the Illawarra Escarpment. Macquarie Pass on the escarpment is an access point between the coastal plain and the plateau, and is situated some 3.5 kilometres to the south-west of the Calderwood access point. A number of tributaries flow from the Southern Highlands and join the Nepean.

The upper reaches of the Nepean traverse relatively large expanses of flat and swampy country before the tributaries and the Nepean itself begin to incise the sandstone. Three major tributaries—Little Burke River, Explorers Creek and Burke River, which are each oriented north–south—are situated to the east of the Nepean. The creeks and rivers form steep-sided and narrow gullies that are generally impassable south of the dam. These gorges have high continuous cliffs at the valley bottom and ridge-top levels (Sefton 2000; Sefton 2003a). The ridge crests would have presented the only viable thoroughfare passages in the catchment. All four rivers join within 2 kilometres of each other at the southern margin of the dam water. While the valley sides are narrow in the area of the dammed water, passage along the valley of the Nepean from this point northwards is probably possible. At the dam wall the catchment area is c. 4.5 kilometres wide. From the dam wall the river proceeds northwards through a steep-sided gorge located c. 2 kilometres to the west of the similarly formed Lower Avon gorge. The Nepean is relatively easily crossed at the point where it meets with the waters of the Cordeaux and the Avon.

2.9 Summary

The environmental context of the study area is significant in regard to a number of factors relevant to this research. The country of the Upper Nepean catchment is physically very different to its surrounds in the east (the coastal plain) and to the south (the Southern Highlands). The Upper Nepean has deeply dissected and rugged terrain, which contrasts with the more gentle and muted topography of the coast and Southern Highlands. Human movement between the coast and Upper Nepean entails breaching the cliffs of the escarpment, which can only be achieved in a few places. Except for the Cataract catchment, where the main river valleys are generally trafficable, human movement in the Upper Nepean is significantly constrained by the presence of steep, rocky valley slopes or narrow, cliff-lined gorges that occupy the majority of the valleys.

It is proposed that, given the nature of the topography, the landforms that people are most likely to have used, for access into and movement within the Upper Nepean catchment, are the watershed divides and ridge crests, which are gently undulating and relatively easy to move along, in comparison with the valley slopes and gorges. The watershed divides and ridge crests possess reliable and, in some places, abundant fresh water (Plate 1.3), which is available year round and in all years, including during periods of drought. Therefore, it is proposed that these divide and ridge landforms in the Upper Nepean are likely to have been the focus of domestic habitation and hence the location of base camps (discussed further in Chapters 3 and 5). The exception to this is the Cataract catchment where the valleys are also likely to have been utilised for habitation, given their accessibility due to the low local relief, generally low valley slope gradients, and their favourable amenity. The variability between different landforms, particularly crests versus valley slopes, is likely to have presented different constraints and opportunities in regard to human movement and occupation. Accordingly, landform categories are utilised in this research as independent variables in analyses of site distribution relating to sociocultural contexts of occupation and land use.

The study area can be considered to have possessed a wide variety of faunal, floral and other resources, and these are generally spatially continuous in distribution. Similarly, potable water is available across all landforms, including watershed and ridge crests (Plate 1.3). It is, however, possible that the Upper Nepean catchment may have been peripheral to the coastal margin where resource abundance is arguably higher, given the presence of marine and estuarine environments, in addition to that provided by the terrestrial context (cf. Attenbrow 2004:111). However, in contrast to both the coast and the majority of the Southern Highlands, the Upper Nepean possesses something locally distinguishing—that is, sandstone rock surfaces. While these may have presented people with constraints and challenges in regard to access and movement through country, significantly, they provided a number of locally unique opportunities such as shelter, abrasive surfaces for the manufacture and sharpening of tools, and sheltered surfaces, which have the potential to be marked with rock art.

The rock shelters in the Upper Nepean catchment are, however, not all equivalent in size, morphology and floor characteristics. Accordingly, their ability to satisfy people's needs as shelter, or for the fulfilment of other goals, is considered to be variable. The physical properties of rock shelters are used in this research as independent variables, against which to assess the social context of rock art production and use.

Climatic variability and corresponding environmental change, from the late Pleistocene and through the Holocene, has been described in this chapter. The country of the Upper Nepean catchment is unlikely to have experienced significant structural and landform change during this time, compared with the coastal region. Certainly, geomorphological processes are likely to have been generally unchanged within the time frame of Aboriginal occupation. However, climatic variability and its impacts relating to effective precipitation and temperature are likely to have been significant in the region, requiring a human response and the development of accommodating strategies in economic, technological and social spheres (cf. Attenbrow 2004:203).

Early European settlers did not occupy the Upper Nepean sandstone country as it was comprised of rugged terrain, forest cover and poor soils. This contrasts with all surrounding areas (the Cumberland Plain, Illawarra and Southern Highlands), which were occupied by the 1820s, thus significantly marginalising Aboriginal access and use of country in the local region. It is proposed that the Upper Nepean may well have remained in use by Aboriginal people during the period of the colonial encounter. Furthermore, it is considered possible that rock art was produced during that period for the pursuit of social strategies relating to the mediation between Aboriginal people and Europeans at that time.

3

Aboriginal Occupation

It seems to follow that one cannot make full sense of the development of European life in Australia without reference to the structure of racial relations and the persistent indifference to the fate of the Aborigines; in short, without an analysis of the Australian conscience. Part of such a study would be the apologetic element in the writing of Australian history, an element that sticks out like a foot from a shallow grave. (Stanner 1977:22)

This chapter outlines a broad archaeological, anthropological and historical framework of Aboriginal occupation of the region. A review of archaeological research conducted in the Sydney Basin, and the adjoining south coast, is presented. General temporal and archaeological trends are identified, which are relevant because they are comparable with those that were likely to have occurred in the Upper Nepean catchment. Models developed to explore the nature of Aboriginal occupation, land use and subsistence strategies in south-east Australia, and the manner in which people occupied and exploited the resources of the coast and its hinterland, are considered. In the absence of detailed archaeological research, and in particular the lack of excavation in the Upper Nepean, this review aims to establish, as much as is reasonable, a model of temporal change and Aboriginal occupation in the study area.

The occupation and settlement of New South Wales by the British in 1788, and during the colonial period, was predicated on 'two quite opposite and irreconcilable requirements … one the need to assure settlers their legal rights to possess land (and dispossess the Aborigines); and the other the moral requirement that the Aborigines should be treated well and their rights as human beings protected' (Plomley 1990–1991:1).

The broad demographic and social context in which Aboriginal people encountered Europeans in the region is discussed in this chapter. It is well established that rock art was produced in the Sydney region in the early period of European occupation (McDonald 2008b). Given that the Upper Nepean catchment was largely unoccupied by European settlers, it can be considered to have been located actually beyond, or on the *far side* of the frontier (cf. McNiven and Russell 2002). Historical records are scanty in regard to Aboriginal use of this land during the colonial period; however, there is evidence that indicates people did retreat to the Woronora Plateau to recover from introduced disease. It is possible, if not probable, that some rock art present in the Upper Nepean was produced at this time. The review of the colonial period takes into consideration contemporary conceptual issues relevant to the exploration of Aboriginal intellectual and cultural responses to the frontier.

Knowledge and understanding of Aboriginal social life and organisation in south-eastern New South Wales at the time of European occupation is minimal. Fundamental details relating to kinship, clan, territorial and religious organisation are, by and large, unknown (cf. Attenbrow 2002). The main sources of information relating to Aboriginal social life in the south-east derive from the work of Howitt (1904) and Mathews (1898), which was compiled during the late nineteenth century, well after Aboriginal people had adjusted to the new settler economy. Their work was framed by assumptions and ethnographic models 'which laid emphasis on a rather limited view of social and cultural life' (Rose 1990:8). The work of Mathews is considered 'slight and unreliable' by some (Flood 1982:29), and by others as sober and thorough (Rose et al. 2003:17). Howitt is often found to be contradictory and must be approached with caution (Swain 1993:118; Rose et al. 2003:16). A consideration of Aboriginal social life and organisation is set out in this chapter with reference to contemporary anthropological concerns and understandings.

3.1 The Archaeological Context

South-eastern New South Wales has been occupied since the late Pleistocene (Attenbrow 2004:72; Boot 1996:288; Lampert 1971:9). The dated occupational sequence in the Sydney region extends back 30,000 years (JMcD CHM 2005:3; and see Stockton & Holland 1974). Further to the south, Lampert (1971:9) and Boot (1996:288) report Pleistocene dates for occupation of the south coast and its hinterland, which extend back to c. 20,000 years BP. Several occupation dates have been obtained from the northern Woronora Plateau (cf. Attenbrow 2002:18,19) and, at this time, the oldest date of occupation is 7,450±180 BP, obtained from Curracurrang 1 rock shelter (Megaw 1974:35). While no dates of cultural deposits have yet been obtained in the Upper Nepean catchment, it is probable that the study area would have been utilised by Aboriginal people in a similar time frame as in the broader south-eastern region.

A basic chronological sequence of human occupation in south-east Australia is the Eastern Regional Sequence, proposed by McCarthy (1964) and more recently refined by Lampert (1971:68), Stockton and Holland (1974:53), Attenbrow (2004:72) and McDonald (1994; 2008a). McCarthy's (1964) three-phased sequence extends from the Pleistocene through to the late Holocene, and is based on observed changes over time in stone artefact assemblages. The phases identified by McCarthy were the Capertian, the Bondaian and Eloueran (the latter being the most recent). Later researchers, such as Lampert (1971:64) at Burrill Lake, found a general agreement with McCarthy's sequence. However, the sequence has undergone revision (Lampert 1971:68). At Upper Mangrove Creek Catchment (UMCC), Attenbrow (2004:72) identified four cultural phases based on changes in artefact typology and raw material in the stone artefact assemblages from four radiocarbon-dated sites. These changes were considered with reference to other studies conducted in the south-east in defining the phases and assigning dates to them.

Attenbrow (2004:72–75) identified the following broad sequence of change in the UMCC catchment:

- Phase 1 (Capertian): c. 11,200 – c. 5,000 years BP: Assemblages consist primarily of flakes, cores and flaked pieces. Implements include amorphous flakes with retouch/usewear, dentated saws and small numbers of backed artefacts. Fine grained siliceous stone and quartz dominate assemblages.
- Phase 2 (Early Bondaian): c. 5,000 – c. 2,800 years BP: Backed artefacts become more archaeologically visible and ground-edge implements appear at c. 4,000 years BP. Fine-grained siliceous stone and quartz dominate assemblages.
- Phase 3 (Middle Bondaian): c. 2,800 – c. 1,600 years BP: Backed artefacts reach a peak in abundance. During this time quartz dominates assemblages.
- Phase 4 (Late Bondaian): c. 1,600 years BP through to just after European occupation: Backed artefacts are rare, bipolar artefacts and ground-edge implements continue to increase in abundance; quartz continues to dominate raw material categories.

Regional, and sometimes local, variations in the assemblages of each phase of the sequence have been identified and, furthermore, each phase has been found to begin at slightly different times in different regions (Attenbrow 2004:219). Attenbrow argues that these differences are possibly due to local environmental conditions and local responses to climatic change, as well as to regional variations in social organisation, territoriality and subsistence patterns. As discussed below, considerable regional variation exists in the archaeological record. In consideration of the absence of detailed archaeological investigation of the study area, extrapolating the evidence from elsewhere for use in this research necessarily requires caution.

While supporting the general sequence of change, archaeological enquiry undertaken since McCarthy proposed his regional sequence now considers the behavioural and demographic implications of observed change. Much attention has also been given to explaining phenomena such as the timing of initial site occupation and other indicators, such as changes in artefact numbers in sites. A picture of apparent intensity of site occupation during the mid to late Holocene has been explained in terms of a corresponding population increase (Hughes & Lampert 1982), and this notion has gained currency in the literature (see, however, Hiscock 1981, 1986; Attenbrow 1987, 2004; Boot 1996, 2002). Attenbrow (2002:21; 2004) devotes considerable attention to this issue, and concludes that distinguishing between behavioural (such as changes in technology or mobility patterns), geomorphological and demographic change to account for observed changes in the archaeological record is not straightforward. She argues that answers to these questions are still unresolved, and that at this time it is not known how populations may have grown or changed from the time of initial occupation.

This problem of unresolved issues relating to population change is an important consideration in any study dealing with rock art because notions of population increase reside at the explanatory heart of many previous studies (e.g. Morwood 1980; David & Cole 1990; David 1991; McDonald 1994, 2008a). McDonald (1994:67, 80) argues that the archaeological evidence indicates that the region was most intensively occupied during the last 3,000 years, and that occupation patterns became more complex during that time. McDonald (1994:348) considers that a dramatic increase in population density occurred at c. 3,000 years BP, and that this and associated social pressures provided the impetus for the development of 'social mechanisms to control interaction and to make such interaction less stressful'. However, others note that population growth at this time is not easily demonstrated using quantitative evidence (e.g. Attenbrow 2002:17, 2004; Hiscock 2008:158).

The nature of Pleistocene occupation in south-east Australia is generally thought to have been sporadic and of low intensity, reflecting low population levels (McDonald 1994:67). For sites located immediately to the south and south-east of the Upper Nepean catchment, such as Sassafras, Burrill Lake, Bass Point and Currarong, it has been argued that they possess evidence of increasing intensity of site occupation and population during the mid to late Holocene (Hughes & Lampert 1982). Based on observed increases in sedimentation rates and implement discard in rock shelters in the southern part of the Sydney Basin, Hughes (1977; Hughes & Lampert 1982:26) proposes that a region-wide intensification in site use and population increase occurred between 5,000 and 2,000 years BP. This argument has been critiqued by a number of researchers. As Boot (2002:19) summarises:

> The archaeological evidence is still not understood well enough to support definitive statements about Aboriginal occupation in the different ecological zones of the hinterland, let alone any alleged changes in subsistence strategies and population levels in the region.

As more work has been undertaken in more sites, and in sites with long periods of occupation, both the substantive and theoretical foundations of this model have required review.

Boot's (2002:220) research identified that the south coastal hinterland and adjacent coast were first occupied before 19,000 years BP, and that early occupation of the hinterland 'appears not to have been intensive'. Throughout the Holocene, occupation levels fluctuated with sites being temporarily or permanently abandoned at different times, and the intensity of occupation varied between sites (Boot 2002:220). Boot (2002:225, 244) argues, that since the late Pleistocene, the archaeological evidence indicates that a generalised subsistence economy was practised in the south coast region, and that there is no evidence of a region-wide increase in artefact discard rates and intensity of site use during the mid to late Holocene. Instead, it was found that not only was there evidence of considerable inter- and intra-site variability in rates of artefact discard and intensity of site use, the notable pattern was one of a series of peaks and troughs indicating significant variations in the intensity of site use, both from the late Pleistocene through to the early Holocene, and during the mid to late Holocene (Boot 2002). Boot (2002:245) argues that the evidence reveals numerous fluctuations in intensity of site occupation over time and, furthermore, he argues that these variations could not be correlated directly with long-term variation in environmental changes.

As already noted above, Attenbrow's (2004) research has been specifically directed towards an examination of the causes of quantitative changes over time in the region's archaeological record. The UMCC data displays a lack of correlation in the 'timing and direction of dramatic late Holocene changes in number of sites and artefacts', and Attenbrow (2004:1) suggests that this seriously questions notions that chronological changes in numbers of sites and artefacts correspond to population changes. The UMCC data indicates that there is also a lack of correspondence in timing of changes in sites and artefact numbers, and changes in stone artefact assemblages, and that dramatic changes in different indicators occur at different times (Attenbrow 2004:1, 217). This result questions the epistemological premise that broad suites of archaeological materials may be precisely contemporaneous, and that changes in all indices occur at the same time (cf. Pinney 2005).

While Attenbrow (2004:217) does not discount the fact that broad-scale demographic change may be invoked for explaining quantitative change in habitation and artefact indices, she focuses on addressing behavioural explanations and processes, which may have contributed to observable patterns. Attenbrow's (2004) investigation was, therefore, geared towards examining habitation indices in terms of habitation patterns and subsistence organisation, and artefact accumulation rates in relation to subsistence methods and equipment. In investigating habitation patterns and subsistence organisation, Attenbrow (2004:219) assumes the possibility that habitation sites are not all equivalent in function. That is, they may not all have been used for the same types of activities and, furthermore, she recognises that a single site's function may have shifted over time. This is important because, as discussed later in this chapter, one of the characteristics relating to Aboriginal settlement and mobility is that they conform to a 'collector' model (after Binford 1980), whereby people form home bases and make logistical forays from these home bases (Keen 2004:104). Employing the Binford (1980) model, Attenbrow (2004:220, 223) distinguishes between *base camps* and *activity locations*, and she identifies a number of salient points. These are listed below because the potential for shelter function to vary across space and time is considered to be potentially relevant in this research:

- Of seven long-term habitations, only one appears to have been used as a base camp throughout its history (first established in the fourth millennium BP). The function of the remainder changed over time from activity location to base camp. The majority of these sites became base camps at, or after, 3,000 years BP.

- Twenty-two habitations were used solely as activity locations, and most of these were first used in the last 2,000 years.

In the UMCC, the commencement of use of base camps was limited in the early Holocene, and it was not until after 4,000 years BP that base camp occupations became established. This coincides with the appearance of ground-edge technology (Attenbrow 2004:243). Attenbrow

(2004:223) argues that in the third millennium BP there was significant change, including a substantial increase in base camps, and this timing was earlier than the dramatic increase in habitation indices, which subsequently occurred during the second millennium BP. In the second and first millennium BP, activity locations increased, corresponding also to a more diverse use of the landscape, including topographic zones previously not used (Attenbrow 2004:223). It is also notable that Attenbrow (2004:223) argues for a correspondence during the last 4,000 years, and 'perhaps more commonly in the last 2,000 years', between the activities that occur within 'habitations' and the addition of ground-edge implements, which were manufactured and maintained on sandstone where water was available such as in creek beds (represented by open context grinding groove sites). Attenbrow (2004:243) argues that changing habitation and land use patterns involving shifts in subsistence and mobility patterns may explain the dramatic late Holocene increases in habitation indices. Attenbrow (2004:223) summarises these patterns as '[v]ariations in the number of base camps and activity locations in different millennia … support the proposition that habitation patterns and subsistence organisation in the catchment changed over the last 11,000 years, and that change of an unprecedented scale and nature began in the third millennium BP'.

Detailed use-wear analysis and residue studies on backed artefacts from three UMCC shelters shed further light on functional variability in shelters located within a single catchment (Robertson et al. 2009:296). While the primary focus of the Robertson et al. (2009:302, 305) study was to emphasise the general purpose and multiple use of backed artefacts, it was also found that various characteristics of use of these artefacts differed between shelters. It was concluded that '[t]he pattern is one of a distinctive combination and emphasis of backed artefact tasks at each location in the landscape, perhaps reflecting dissimilar resources in the immediate neighbourhood of each site and/or different activities habitually undertaken at each site' (Robertson et al. 2009:303). This latter point is of particular interest in this study, because it indicates that shelters in the region do possess evidence of functional variability and that, hence, in the Upper Nepean catchment, there is the potential that inter-site variability may occur, which is due to differences in site use and social context.

A new adaptive model, based on analyses of backed artefacts, has also been proposed, which has implications for behavioural change during the late Holocene. Backed artefacts have been made and deposited in south-east Australia since 9,500 years ago (Hiscock & Attenbrow 1998). They dramatically peaked in abundance c. 3,500 years ago, and sustained until 2,000 years ago when their number began to decline. Hiscock (2008:156, 158) hypothesises that the backed artefact proliferation was a response to economic risk associated with the onset of drier and more variable climatic conditions in southern Australia related to the intensification of the El Niño system. Additional factors that may have triggered higher foraging risk have been posited, including landscape colonisation, redefinition of social space, landscape change, reduction of resources and greater foraging mobility (Hiscock 2008:158). It is noted also that ground-edge hatchets were adopted as a new technology in south-east Australia at c. 3,500 years ago at the same time as the backed artefact proliferation. This technology is also likely to have helped deal with foraging risk.

While the above discussion has focused on chronological change in the archaeological record, researchers have also examined the subsistence strategies employed in coastal areas, and how people organised themselves in respect to coastal and hinterland resources. For the south coast, several models of Aboriginal occupation have been proposed (cf. Boot 2002:7). Bowdler (1970:5, 111) argues that, during summer, Aboriginal occupation of the coastal zone was intensive and dense, and that some inland exploitation occurred during seasons when coastal resources were limited. Lampert (1971:63) proposes a model based on a mixed coastal economy involving the exploitation of littoral, estuarine and terrestrial resources. Similar to Bowdler, however, Lampert argues that littoral resources contributed a much higher component to the Aboriginal diet than that which may have been obtained from the forest. Lampert's model includes a differentiation of coastal sites based on different forms of resource exploitation, including main sites (base camps), specialised sites and a third category of overnight camps (Lampert 1971:62–64). Poiner (1976) proposes a model of seasonal differentiation in which semi-nomadic occupation of the coast occurred during summer, with nomadic winter occupation of both hinterland and coastal areas. This model assumes that hinterland sites are small, widespread and few in number (Boot 2002:7).

These early models have been subject to various reviews. Attenbrow's (1976:66, 121–3) model of resource exploitation and movement posits that the hinterland and coastline were occupied on a year-round basis, and that movement occurred only at the family or small group level, rather than as seasonal movement of entire populations. While arguing that coastal occupation was greater during summer when the resources of the sea were more abundant, Attenbrow suggests that people living on the coast would also have harvested terrestrial resources. Attenbrow also considers in greater detail the nature of hinterland occupation and argues that, in summer, large groups would have occupied valleys, while small family groups exploited resources in the mountains. Conversely, family groups would have been more widely dispersed throughout the hinterland and along the coast during winter. Each of these groups, and particularly those on the coast, had a higher proportion of animal foods in their diet during the colder months. Vallance (1983:27–8) also moves beyond a strictly seasonal model and argues the economy was likely to have been based on a range of subsistence strategies that varied within and between seasons, and from year to year. Vallance (1983:62–64) argues that short-term climatic variation would have affected subsistence strategies rather than longer term seasonal variation. Hiscock (1982:43) argues that considerable movement between the south coast and its hinterland occurred. He found associations of stone from hinterland sources with stone derived from the coast, and argues that this indicates that occupants of hinterland sites had an intimate knowledge of resources in both areas and that they were therefore not just 'short-term refugees' escaping winter coastal food scarcity.

3.2 The European Encounter

The British settlement and occupation of New South Wales commenced in 1788 with the arrival of the First Fleet and was premised upon an assumption that Australia was *terra nullius* or unowned land (Troy 1990:13). Governor Arthur Phillip was under instruction to open friendly intercourse with the Aboriginal inhabitants and to protect them from convicts and settlers. It was effectively a policy of protection and segregation (Bell 1959:345). It was not until 1825 that an official policy was introduced, which aimed to 'civilise and convert them to Christianity', although this policy was largely ignored (Bell 1959:345). By 1838, spurred by humanitarian concerns in England, Aboriginal Protectors were appointed. Once again, the civilising policies that were their charter were never, or were ineffectually, implemented (Bell 1959:345; Shaw 1992:265, 269).

The injustices of the colonial period were the result of failed government policies and the antipathy of settlers and pastoralists, the latter having considerable bearing on the inability of contemporary governments to enforce any policy of which the settlers or squatters did not approve (Shaw 1992:265). The colonial encounter resulted in Aboriginal people systematically and inexorably losing their land. As Shaw (1992:266) expresses, '[t]he tragedy which ensued was the almost inevitable result of a conflict between the settlers and the Aborigines', and this conflict was one fought over land with both parties wanting the same land.

The Aborigines, for their part, wanted to continue to occupy their land. They literally lived off it. They used its flora and fauna for food, clothing and shelter. … [T]hey had strong emotional and spiritual ties with the land which they had lived on for so long. Here were their sacred sites – the homes of their Dreamtime ancestors, whose spirits still dwelt among their rocks and rivers and caves and where natural features had been settings for the great deeds of those ancestral heroes who had given life and shape to the various clans (Shaw 1992:267).

That Aborigines believed that particular tracts of country belonged to each group was recognised by some, in particular Archdeacon Broughton, who presented such evidence to the 1834 Select Committee Inquiry into the state of Indigenous people in British settlements (Shaw 1992:269). This fact, and its corollary, that settlement was effectively shutting Aboriginal people out from what they regarded as their property, was recognised by others also, but there remained the position that the government of the late 1830s would not protect the Aborigines' land, denied that they owned any, and, in fact, encouraged encroachment of it by the introduction of the Squatting Acts of 1836 and 1839 (Shaw 1992:275).

While the obvious impacts of the colonial encounter include the loss of life from disease and massacre, loss of land and access to resources and special places and so on, it has only recently been recognised that an understanding of Indigenous responses entail considerations of agency and resistance, and that the forms by which responses can be expressed are sometimes startling (Comaroff & Comaroff 1989, 1991; Lattas 1993:103; McNiven & Russell 2002:27). In the wider Sydney region, it is clear that death, dispossession and 'titanic population declines' followed colonisation (Swain 1993:115). The Aboriginal response was to regroup, fight, in some instances to attempt to accommodate the invaders within pre-existing social structures, and, significantly, instigate a new sky hero into their cosmology to mediate the encounter and wrest back control of life and land (Swain 1993). It is very clear that, during the colonial period, Aboriginal people had very little interest generally in adopting the culture and practices of the British (Shaw 1992:276). This is important because, while there is no fundamental reason for rock art produced during the colonial encounter to refer exclusively to introduced objects (cf. Taçon 2008b:220), there is a significant reason why it may not.

The most obvious and immediate impact following the arrival of the First Fleet was the introduction of disease, the most lethal of which was smallpox (Butlin 1983). Three major smallpox epidemics were recorded in Australia: in 1789, one year after European settlement, in 1829 and in 1866 (Curson 1985). The 1789 epidemic had a devastating effect on the local Aboriginal people living close to the British settlement at Port Jackson, and it was reported that the region was evacuated until the disease had disappeared (Bell 1959:345). At the end of the 1789 epidemic, when Aboriginal people began returning to the shores of Port Jackson, it was estimated by Governor Phillip that smallpox had claimed at least 50 per cent of the population (Butlin 1983). In the years immediately after the epidemic, its effects were observed in locations well outside the 1789 European frontier. The second smallpox epidemic, beginning in 1829, coincided with the commencement of the dramatic expansion of the pastoral frontier across the south-eastern interior of New South Wales (Carey & Roberts 2002:822).

Flow-on effects of disease included difficulties for people to obtain food and carry out socio-religious obligations. It affected demography and the social structures of Aboriginal populations. After the 1789 epidemic, individual groups were so reduced in number that individuals were required to forge new groups (Collins 1798:496; Attenbrow 2002:60). It has been estimated that by the 1830s, approximately only 500 people remained within a 200 kilometre radius of Sydney (Swain 1993:115). In short, smallpox 'initiated cultural disorientation for the … people of NSW during which the direct impact of the disease was compounded by the effects of European colonization, military action, and losses from other introduced diseases' (Carey & Roberts 2002:822). It has been argued by Carey and Roberts (2002:822) that, in addition to the demographic impact of smallpox and other introduced diseases, 'the deeper intellectual and cultural responses of Aboriginal people' precipitated the development of a new cult, 'that reflected deep hostility to both the presence of Europeans and the diseases associated with them'. This will be discussed further below.

Until c. 1813, European settlement of the Sydney region was confined, at least officially, to Sydney Harbour and that area of the Cumberland Plain, situated east of the Nepean River (Troy 1990:1). As settlement expanded, conflict between the British and Aborigines escalated, and two methods of segregating the Aborigines were adopted. One was by punitive expeditions, and the other by the issue of Government Proclamations and General Orders to control their contact with whites (Bell 1959:345).

A permit system began in 1821, which allowed for the movement of cattle beyond the Cumberland Plain. Many exploratory journeys proceeding south from Sydney took place prior to this time, some of which traversed the study area, while others skirted around it. In addition to official or 'respectable' journeys of exploration, Europeans made their way out of the arena of European settlement to live with Aboriginal people (Andrews 1998). This phenomenon would have added to the already dynamic social and economic changes taking place within Aboriginal society at this time. Cattle had already penetrated the interior, west of the Nepean, growing to immense herds, and significantly impacting local environments. Caley visited an area, which later became Appin, in July 1807, when he travelled to the Appin Falls on the Cataract River (c. 1 kilometre west of the now Cataract Dam wall). Caley recorded the Aboriginal name of the falls as Carrung-gurrung. In 1811, a series of land grants were made and from this time settlers began to occupy, clear and farm the Appin district. This occupation resulted in a period of conflict during 1814 after Aboriginal people apparently raided crops. A report from 1814 indicates that Aboriginal people from Jervis Bay had banded with mountain people from the west for the purpose of 'kill(ing) all the whites before them' (Sydney Gazette 1814:Jun 4, cited in Officer 1984:12). This was not an isolated event. At this time the early white settlers were required to defend themselves and their property. In a number of recorded events, both Europeans and Aboriginals were killed (Whittaker 2005). Other attacks occurred within the broader area, including Bringelly and Camden, which provoked Governor Macquarie to order the military to round up all Aborigines in the Hawkesbury and Southern Districts. A regiment, accompanied by two Aboriginal guides, spent one month in the area around Glenfield and Appin in a largely unsuccessful campaign, which was thwarted by the settlers of Appin who were sheltering the Aboriginal people. It is also possible that Aboriginal people were themselves finding refuge within the gorges of the plateau further to the south (in the study area). However, 14 Aboriginal people were killed in a single event at the Cataract River when they were shot or driven over the cliffs on 17 April 1816 (Whittaker 2005).

An article in the 1820 *Sydney Gazette* (1820:Dec 16, in Officer 1984), which is of specific interest, refers to Aboriginal people who, after sustaining significant loss from influenza in the winter of that year, went to the coast and into the 'bushy and broken country, where there were quantities of honey', and where it was expected that they would remain until the summer. The area referred to is almost certainly the Woronora Plateau. At Wollongong a decade or so later, a deputy surveyor reported to Tyerman and Bennett (1840:193) that Aboriginal people were numerous, and that they had come from the interior (likely to be the Woronora Plateau) to 'obtain fish, oysters, water fowl, grubs'. While references regarding people continuing to use the Upper Nepean catchment after the beginning of colonial period are scanty, there is every reason to consider that they did so, although the intensity and nature of that use is less certain.

3.3 Social Geography and Worldview

Historical records relating to Aboriginal social geography and worldview in the early years of European occupation are very few; they are significantly incomplete and superficial (Swain 1993:115). Stanner (1969:32) reviewed the early record of Aboriginal and European relations in Sydney and concludes that the enquiry relating to Aboriginal people has resulted in a picture that is 'sketchy, ill-proportioned and often malevolently drawn'. Everything we know of Aboriginal social life in the region comes from records made after the huge population decline resulting from the death and dispossession that ensued following the arrival of the First Fleet in 1788 (Swain 1993:115). The social geography and an understanding of the relationship between land and the people who inhabited the study area is, therefore, limited and difficult to overview. It was not until the 1880s that Europeans began to look intently at aspects of Aboriginal social organisation and worldview, by which time (i.e. after 100 years of European occupation) Aboriginal people had forged a new life within the settler economy.

3.3.1 Social Geography

Close scrutiny of the early records offer some observations of relevance in consideration of Aboriginal social geography and relations to land in the Sydney region. In the eighteenth century, David Collins noted that in Port Jackson, Bennelong considered Goat Island to belong to him and he advised that, similarly, other people 'possessed this kind of hereditary property' (cited and quoted in Williams 1986:143). Threlkeld, later in 1828, was able to define the boundaries of the country of the Awabakal people, near Lake Macquarie, and understood that this group considered it to be their own land (Gunson 1974:30). Threlkeld understood that '… every tribe has its district the boundary of which must not be passed without permission from the tribe to which it belongs' (Gunson 1974:186). Williams (1986:144) notes that early nineteenth-century explorers also recorded that Aboriginal people knew with great accuracy, the boundaries and limits of their own land.

The early records also reveal that the land was named and ordered at an extremely fine level of resolution. Lang, in 1847 (cited in Williams 1986:147), remarked that Aborigines named all features and areas of land, 'every rock, river, creek, mountain, hill, or plain' so exactly, that meeting places could be specified with great accuracy. Many early commentators indicate that natural land features clearly defined the boundaries of tracts of country to which people identified and occupied. It is also notable that places clearly also possessed specific significances, given that during particular parts of initiation ceremonies, which took place in the region, 'the men shout the names of *remarkable* places in the novice's country' (Mathews & Everitt 1900:279, my emphasis).

In the late nineteenth century, Mathews identified three broad cultural areas in south-eastern New South Wales, extending from Port Macquarie to the New South Wales–Victorian border, across which people had similar cultural practices and beliefs (Mathew 1898; cf. Attenbrow 2002:126–127). The central cultural area, which includes the area in which Sydney is located, extended from the Hunter River–Newcastle area south to the Georges River–Botany Bay area. The southern cultural area, which includes the study area, extended from the Georges River south to the New South Wales–Victorian border (Mathews 1898).

By the early twentieth century, it was becoming clearer to commentators that Aborigines' division of groups, which were associated with particular tracts of land, was an important aspect of their social organisation, and Baldwin Spencer, for example, reported at length about land-owning groups, which he called 'tribes' (cf. Williams 1986:150). It was also recognised that while a 'tribe' could be regarded as owning definitive tracts of country, the boundaries of these areas were known to that group, and also were *recognised* by others (Williams 1986:150). In this sense, knowing the location of boundaries probably did not require the aid of non-verbal communication such as style and so on (cf. Wobst 1977).

Tindale (1974) formalised the notion of tribal boundaries and identified those in the study area. Tindale (1974:191, 195) identified the Tharawal as having occupied land that included the coast from the southern shores of Botany Bay to Bulli, and westward to include that part of the Woronora Plateau drained by the Georges and Port Hacking rivers, and the area to Camden and Picton. The Wodi Wodi land was identified as that which extended along the coast from Bulli south to the north shore of Jervis Bay, with a westerly margin that extended from the headwaters of the Nepean River and its tributaries, south to the northern drainage system of the Shoalhaven River. On the basis of Eades's (1976) linguistic work, it is understood that a common language, Dharawal, was spoken across both the Tharawal and Wodi Wodi tribal boundaries. Early researchers equate language group areas with tribal boundaries (e.g. Capell 1970:22). According to Tindale's analysis, the study area can be considered to be located within the boundaries of the Wodi Wodi country.

The notion of the boundedness of social groupings, and concept that tribes functioned as politically cohesive, corporate groups, does not retain its anthropological currency (Rumsey 1989:76). Tindale's tribal groups were conceptualised in accordance with a model of social organisation, in which the tribal group equates to a linguistic group, which is seen as a defining structural feature in Aboriginal social organisation, with the implication that tribes or language groups were territorial groups. These concepts are no longer regarded as valid. It is now recognised that conceptualising language groups as bounded social groupings is not appropriate because Aboriginal people were multilingual, that linguistic groups were not necessarily spatially contiguous, and that social affiliations are/were at any time, highly fluid (Sutton & Rigsby 1979). Furthermore, language groups and social networks are not necessarily spatially isomorphic (Sutton & Rigsby 1979:717).

Aboriginal cultures in Australia share comparable underlying features. In the secular sphere, these hunter-gatherer communities foraged in highly flexible bands, in which membership was fluid and ephemeral (Layton 1992:31). Social groups, therefore, are likely to have been multidimensional and fluid (spatially and generationally), and at any one time comprised of people with different clan, gender and age identities. Individuals are likely to have resided in different places, at different times, as they fulfilled various familial, social and individual responsibilities. The flexibility in band composition is, however, 'counterpoised against a relatively stable structure in the spiritual sphere' (Layton 1992:31). Across Australia, Aboriginal men and women belong/ ed to small descent groups, each of which possesses 'a distinct body of religious property', which includes a suite of sites, waterholes, caves, rocks and other environmental features imbued with the spiritual power of Ancestral Beings who created the landscape during the heroic period. These sites form clusters that correspond to what is known as a clan's estate (Layton 1992:31). Clans are not, however, autonomous and, instead, are linked by shared religious traditions, the exchange of marriage partners and overlapping foraging rights (Layton 1992:31). Clan membership is attained by descent, usually through the father and, in the Sydney region, it is generally believed that clan groupings were based on patrilineal descent, and that local clan membership appears to have been the significant manner by which social organisation was structured (Attenbrow 2002:58).

A person's identity in Aboriginal society is multifaceted. Layton (1989:5) argues that in order to assess artistic systems—for example, in the archaeological record it is useful to distinguish between the egocentric and sociocentric status of individuals. The former is exemplified by kinship. This status is fluid and varies in accordance with those with whom a person interacts. Sociocentric status, on the other hand, is exemplified by clan, age and gender groupings, and this is less fluid. A person's sociocentric status, as defined according to membership of one of these groupings, means that s/he has that status towards everyone, at all times (Layton 1989:5). These groupings, however, are not mutually exclusive, nor are they always in existence everywhere and at the same time. Social groupings, as groupings, are contextually relative and do not endure in all social contexts (Rumsey 1989:76). That is, social grouping is context specific and is mobilised according to specific contexts, at specific times and for specific purposes (Smith 1994:5). Smith (1994:5) argues that cultural constructions of groups are activated according to contexts of interpretation, which are informed by the broader social and historical context in which an individual lives.

The general underlying features of Aboriginal social organisation and identity, as set out above, are invoked in this research in the absence of an ethnographic context for the Upper Nepean catchment.

3.3.2 Worldview

Religion is a dominant feature of Australian Aboriginal society. Every aspect of life can be considered to be intertwined with religion (e.g. cf. Berndt 1969; Myers 1986; Swain 1993). Aboriginal beliefs and practices are, however, complex and varied. The motives behind them, their purposes and significance are heterogeneous (Keen 1986:46). Beliefs are the products of complex histories. Keen (1986:46) states that although beliefs may vary in detail, the forms taken by Aboriginal religions in general 'have a lot to do with governance and politics'. He argues that religious beliefs and practices are key aspects of governance and provide the basis of authority. Social practices are thus arbitrated via religious law and the rules and categories that were 'established by ancestral Spirit Beings' (Keen 1986:46). In south-east Australia, aspects of social organisation such as marriage were regulated, at least in part, by totemic affiliations. Totemic affiliation to an animal, plant or other object was inherited by sons and daughters patrilineally and formed one basis for the choice of marriage partners. Marriage between individuals of the same totem was forbidden (Mathews & Everitt 1900). It is probable that similar to elsewhere, land tenure in the south-east may also have been governed by the politics of religion.

From the late nineteenth-century accounts, the dominant belief at that time in the south-east was in an All-Father being known by various names, including Baiame and Daramulan (Attenbrow 2002:128). These two beings are in some places the one, but with different names, while in others, Daramulan is the son or half-brother of Baiame (Knight 2001:59; Attenbrow 2002:128). In the late nineteenth century, Howitt emphasises the heaven-dominated cosmology that is central to the Baiame/Daramulan belief, and which is described by Swain (1993:203) as a utopian tradition, whereby humans and ancestral spirits are removed to a sky realm. Swain (1993) contrasts the cosmological orientation emphasised in south-east Australia with what he calls the locative tradition found elsewhere in Australia, which 'emphasises the association between creative powers and sites, and the affiliation of human spiritual essences with these places …[and] stresses ubiety and earth-based powers'.

Given this significant contrast between a heaven-dominated cosmology of south-east Australia with an earth-based religious cosmogony, anthropologists have for some time suggested that the belief in the All-Father arose following contact with missionary teaching (cf. Swain 1993:117; Carey & Roberts 2002:823). Swain (1993:117) provides the most controversial account of the emergence of the All-Father belief, which is based strongly on the notion that Aboriginal conceptions of existence within the colonial frontier could have adapted to accommodate the devastating effects of European occupation upon social and territorial organisation. Swain (1993) offers well-documented and compelling evidence (Rose et al. 2003:21–22) that charts the historical trajectory of the emergence of the utopian tradition in south-east Australia. Swain describes major changes that occurred in the relationship between people and place as a result of depopulation and dislocation, describing this as a revolution in the Aboriginal understanding of space. Aboriginal people sought to accommodate the invaders in their 'pre-existing structures of space', yet this failed and, based on their understanding via experience, they began to subsume key elements of Western ontology, notably 'that the earth was impoverished and that power now resided in the sky'. Swain also contends that people's predicament became one regarding time, specifically a concern with the end of the world.

Swain (1993) focuses his attention on the Aboriginal response, and the dynamic restructuring of Aboriginal world views, which occurred during the period of early European occupation. He argues that the coexistence of dual cosmologies in post-colonial Australia is well documented and widespread, and that there is ample evidence that this was also the case in south-east Australia. Recognising that significant limitations apply in any attempt to reconstruct pre-colonial religious life in the south-east, Swain (1993:119) nevertheless strongly claims that a locative tradition did exist prior to and in the very early years of the colonial encounter. He refers to the existence in south-east Australia of increase ceremonies and abundant references in the literature to Ancestral Beings transforming into identifiable places in the landscape. Swain (1993:121) thus argues that the association between creative powers and sites, and the affiliation of human spiritual essences with these places, existed prior to the emergence of Baiame. Swain (1993:121–122) maintains that, within the early colonial period, a twofold cosmological orientation therefore existed. He argues that, while the dual cosmological orientation is unremarkable in colonial Australia, what is peculiar to the south-east is that the belief in the sky realm view became dominant. However, Swain (1993:204) indicates that in the south-east the utopian vision achieved a dominant position in Aboriginal cosmology; he attributes this to the specific context of the colonial period here where, for Aboriginal people, 'invasion was for them a reality so devastating as to render impossible the maintenance of a locative religious life'.

Swain's (1993:122) argument is essentially that the Aboriginal response to invasion was an intellectual one, which was to locate conquest in a moral order. As described earlier in this chapter, the settlement of south-east Australia resulted in widespread death, which devastated traditional social networks and resulted in dispossession and the alienation of people from their lands—in this context the ability to maintain 'the cosmos through a locative tradition' became impossible. The challenge for Aboriginal people, in response to this, was to establish a means of accommodating those who were seen as a fundamentally immoral and brutal people (Swain 1993:124). Swain (1993:124, 229) argues that this entailed subsuming some of the ontological principles of the invaders' own cosmology, not in the manner of a synchretic or mythic borrowing, but rather via a major reformulation of their understanding of the nature of existence, and that '[i]n a single move the All-Father created a new, potentially pan-Aboriginal, social base and removed the cosmological centre of gravity beyond known places to an unspecified realm in the sky'.

There is no mention of the All-Father Baiame in the accounts of the earliest commentators in the Sydney region. Swain (1993:145) argues that the earliest mention of Baiame dates to the 1830s, in the Wellington Valley mission, in central western New South Wales, and that Baiame was introduced to that area from closer to the Sydney frontier. Carey and Roberts (2002:822–823) examine in detail the records (many of which have previously been overlooked) from the Wellington Valley mission, and argue that Baiame, and an associated dance ritual, *waganna*, was a phenomenon linked to the aftermath of smallpox. Their research is also concerned with exploring the intellectual and cultural response to the impacts of disease and death. At Wellington, Baiame was associated with an adversary, Tharrawiirgal, who was believed responsible for the bringing of smallpox because of his wrath due to his loss of a tomahawk (Carey & Roberts 2002:830–831).

Smallpox reached the Wellington Valley in 1830, and was particularly severe. It has been estimated that a third of the population died (Carey & Roberts 2002:827, 829). The Wiradjuri, via a range of Indigenous and/or borrowed natural and/or magical explanatory frameworks, began to search for an explanation and possibly control of 'so virulent a misfortune' (Carey & Roberts 2002:831). They argue that, from 1830, there is evidence that suggests that one cultural response was the creation of new dance rituals and mourning ceremonies, and that, by c. 1833, these responses had been elaborated into a *waganna*, or dance ritual.

Missionaries recorded that some dance rituals were held at this time specifically in regard to smallpox (Carey & Roberts 2002:832). Over a period of time they were performed on a regular basis and with increasing intensity and ritual elaboration. By 1835, there was also a shift in focus from smallpox to the issue of sexual access by white men to Aboriginal women and children, and an insistence on the traditional practice of nose piercing (Carey & Roberts 2002:833, 837–838). Between 1833 and 1935 it was also strongly believed, as Swain (1993) similarly documents, that the end of the world was a possibility, and specifically that the world was to be destroyed by flood.

The Baiame *waganna* cult at Wellington lasted for two years only, and during this time missionaries recorded what Carey and Roberts (2002:843) describe as the formation and transformation of the Baiame travelling cult. They observed major changes in the prophecies. The concern with smallpox shifted to the issue of the sexual abuse of women and children by white men and a focus on the instigation of traditional practices. The cosmology saw a decline in the acknowledgement of Tharrawiirgal, who was regularly replaced by Daramulan, and to a 'magnification of the authority of Baiame' (Carey & Roberts 2002:843). The evidence from Wellington is testament of dramatic and swift change in Aboriginal people's beliefs and concerns, which could take place in a very brief period to time.

It is inconceivable that the Aboriginal people from the Upper Nepean catchment and environs did not also adapt their world view and conceptions of existence to meet the demands of life within the colonial milieu.

3.4 Summary

Given that the broader region was occupied from the Pleistocene, it is probable that the Upper Nepean catchment has been used by Aboriginal people since that time. Certainly, it is likely that Aboriginal occupation of the study area occurred throughout the Holocene and until the 1840s (at least), as documented in written texts. Whether or not imagery of Pleistocene or even early Holocene antiquity (and, indeed, occupation deposit) is present in the study area is unknown given the lack of research into this question in the Upper Nepean.

The archaeological evidence described in this chapter charts a mosaic of change in a variety of indices relating to technology, subsistence and occupation in the south-east, although explanations that account for the impetus of change are contested. Nevertheless, on a fundamental level, changes in technology, subsistence strategies and land use, which are evident in the archaeological record, are likely to have been accompanied by reformulations in legitimating ideologies and world views (cf. Rosenfeld 2002:61; Hiscock 2008:159). The discussion above forms the basis for conceptualising in very general terms, change and transformation in the Upper Nepean catchment that may have been expressed and indeed brokered, at least in part via the production of rock art.

A general model of temporal variability in the regional archaeological record is evident. In respect of technological innovations during the late Holocene, Hiscock (2008:159) argues that 'it is likely that these technological reconfigurations were accompanied by ideological reconfiguration, as the new life ways involved in using altered toolkits found expression in socially defined views of the ancient world'. He suggests that new ideologies were likely to be a component of, rather a reason for, technological shifts. An ideological reconfiguration in the late Holocene may well leave an archaeological signature in the rock art sequence of the Upper Nepean catchment. This proposition will be discussed further in subsequent chapters. Here, however, it is noted that while referring to Central Australia, the archaeological record indicates that in the recent past Aboriginal culture underwent significant transformations in technology, subsistence strategies and the demographics of mobility and territoriality. Rosenfeld (2002: 61) remarked as follows: 'It is improbable that such transformations did not also require reformulations of the legitimating ideologies that underly [*sic*] social praxis'.

In contrast to many other places in Australia, a deeply informed knowledge and understanding of the social geography and worldviews of Aboriginal people of the south-east that prevailed at the time of European occupation are not available, and this has been acknowledged in this chapter. In the south-east, throughout the early colonial period and beyond, commentators did report on Aboriginal people's deep attachment to land, and this is in keeping with what is known more broadly in Australia. With British occupation, and the pastoral expansion in the south-east, Aboriginal people lost not only sovereignty over their land but possibly also their ability to maintain conceptions of existence, which may have been founded in an ontology of place (cf. Swain 1993).

That such an ontology of being existed has generally been denied to the Aboriginal people of south-east Australia and, instead, the sky-based All-Father being has been widely considered to have been the basis of religious life. In this chapter, a review has been conducted of two religious histories that, contrary to this view, argue that the All-Father being arose during the colonial period as a ritual response within the context of cross-cultural exchange. Swain (1993:121) refers to many examples hidden in the literature, which strongly suggest the existence of a totemic geography in the south-east that is comparable with cosmologies found elsewhere, and which emphasises the association between creative powers and places, and the affiliation of people with these places.

David (2002:205) argues that the ethnographically known Dreaming has a history, and his work has sought to reveal that social history via archaeological analysis. The Dreaming of south-east Australia is clearly not well understood, and it is almost misleading to consider that there is an ethnography relating to it. However, the signatures of a totemic geography are potentially recognisable in rock art (Layton 2000a:179). This research seeks to explore the social geography of the Aboriginal people of the south-east, and questions whether or not there is evidence of a totemic ontology, which Swain (1993) argues prevailed at the time of European occupation, prior to the ascendance of Baiame.

The European occupation of the region was an agricultural enterprise. Accordingly, shale and volcanic landforms, which previously existed as open woodlands, were the focus of this endeavour. The forested sandstone country, especially that which is dissected with gorge and escarpment systems such as the Upper Nepean catchment, was not occupied by European settlers (see Chapter 2). While it is recognised that there is variation in responses to colonialism at local levels, in this study it is assumed that within the colonial and post-colonial period, a ritual response to accommodate change, as is documented elsewhere in the country, may also have occurred in the Sydney Basin. McNiven and Russell (2002:27) argue that Aboriginal people's activities and responses to the colonial encounter were often conducted on the far side of the frontier, and that, therefore, historical sources alone are inadequate for the task of exploring this phenomenon. In this chapter, various references to Aboriginal people's continued use of the Woronora Plateau during the colonial period have been discussed, and in Chapter 2 it was noted that this country was largely unoccupied by colonists. It can, therefore, seriously be considered that the plateau may have continued to have been used by Aboriginal people during the period of the colonial encounter.

However, it cannot be assumed that an Aboriginal response to European occupation necessarily entailed marking the land with imagery. At any time people may enjoy 'different kinds of engagement with the material world' (Thomas 2004:219). While people may have used the plateau country during the colonial period, this may not have been accompanied by the production of rock art. Indeed, McDonald (2008b:109) expresses the view that, given the paucity of contact motifs in the Sydney Basin rock art, the arrival of Europeans resulted in the 'termination of the Sydney region's symbolical and artistic culture'. She argues that there is no evidence that rock art production continued after European occupation. The question of whether or not rock art was produced within the context of cross-cultural exchange in the south-east has not yet been the focus of a systematic analysis, so the view in this research is that it cannot be discounted that some rock art in the Upper Nepean catchment may have been produced at this time.

Frederick's (1997, 1999) research has in many ways legitimised the study of contact rock art in Australia. Prior to her work in Central Australia, discussions regarding contact rock art were largely descriptive and incidental to the concerns of 'prehistoric art' (and see also, Smith & Rosenfeld 1992). Contact rock art was defined solely by introduced subject matter and this 'implicitly asserts a model of acculturation' (Frederick 1999:133). One reason for seriously entertaining the notion that some rock art in the Upper Nepean catchment may have been produced within the context of the colonial encounter is that the historical records, as discussed above, clearly chart the emergence of and change in novel ritual practices that, in their motivation, were also startlingly dynamic and contingent upon the immediate and changing concerns of people (i.e. at Wellington mission, the Baiame *waganna* was originally concerned with smallpox, but within two years its focus had shifted to a concern about the sexual appropriation of women and children by white men). Cultural construction is achieved through action, not merely through conceptualisation (Meskell 2005a), and it is potentially via rock art as praxis that Aboriginal people may also have sought to mediate the colonial landscape and their place within it.

4

Research Focus and Conceptual Guidance

> What has been so revealing about this turn to 'material culture' is that material culture is often now taken to be inseparable from the immaterial, and, quite powerfully, so much of this 'material culture' is intimately bound up with all sorts of social and cultural phenomena, such as … gender, power relations, exchange, colonialism, tourism, and more. (Conkey 2001:272)

In this introduction, it is acknowledged that the persistence of the use of the word 'art' and the modern inheritance embedded within the term is problematic. Conkey (1997:413, 2001:270), amongst others, draws attention to the fundamental differences in regard to the role of art in Indigenous and western societies. The deeply entrenched view of art, and by extension rock art, as being an artefact quite distinct from its more mundane archaeological counterparts, such as stones and bones, requires consideration. In this regard, Tomásková (1997:268) remarks:

> The nineteenth century understanding of creativity as a special separate practice that only few endowed individuals engaged in, separate from profane unimaginative skilled work, remains with us to this day, and has deeply affected our investigation of prehistoric symbolic activities that we label art.

Soffer and Conkey (1997:2–3) refer to two problems with the use of the term: on the one hand, it implies an aesthetic function which should not be assumed; and, on the other, art is 'transcendent and therefore provides us with transcendent values', which limit the nature of our enquiry.

Conkey (2001:272) points out that in recent material culture studies, the inclusion of items of form and media that do not readily conform to notions of art has led to the recognition that material culture is often inseparable from the immaterial (e.g. see also Miller 2005a, 2005b). Conkey (2001:285) remarks in this regard:

> the material and visual culture of some hunter-gatherers is just as much about the core cultural and social concepts of everything from daily life and gender relations to overarching understandings of how the world came to be, as they are about object shape, form aesthetics, colour, or utilitarian function. These latter are the usual categories that we think of, perhaps, when faced with trying to study what we call 'art', but it is both more complex and richer than this.

Conkey (2001:272) therefore argues that if we were to consider art as material culture, then questions relating to the ways in which art works would become more central to our line of enquiry.

In Australia, we have abundant ethnographic evidence that indicates that rock art is produced in a variety of social contexts, and we know that the motives behind its production can be extremely varied (Taçon 2002:124). Layton (2000a:172) emphasises that art can express more than one core theme in a local culture, and that this possibility deserves consideration in the interpretation of rock art. Some ethnography indicates rock art was produced within a ritual context. Although this evidence is rare (cf. Ross & Davidson 2006:307), Layton (1992) refers to abundant examples from the ethnographic literature of ritual, particularly associated with increase ceremonies, occurring in rock art sites and with reference to specific imagery. The ethnography also reveals many examples of the production of art for religious purposes (Morphy 1999) and in secular contexts for a variety of motivations, many of which are individually inspired, such as those that are commemorative of personal events, hunting and gathering, and the practice of sorcery (Lewis & Rose 1988:47; Layton 1992; Taçon 1994:123; Rosenfeld 1997:296). Rosenfeld (1997:296) remarks that 'rock art can be variously an ancestral creation, a human creation about the dreaming or a human creation about human concerns'. Furthermore, not all rock art is equivalent in its behavioural expression (Rosenfeld 1997:291, 297, 1999).

A fundamental premise underpinning this research is the recognition that a regional body of rock art may possess such diversity of themes and behavioural signatures. It also raises serious questions in regard to the epistemological appropriateness of inclusive interpretative umbrellas (cf. Conkey 1997:419). Tomásková (1997:268) argues that the preconceptions that come with the term 'art' leave 'only a narrow corridor for interpretation'. The notion of context in this regard is also problematic for it is here that the modern inheritance presents its gravest limitations for rock art analysis. Tomásková refers to the 'investigation of context in art history which involves two clear poles of production and consumption (the artist and the audience) *that remain uncertain in prehistoric settings*' (1997:269, my emphasis). It is now clear that it is not possible to generalise about the purpose of imagery production in hunter-gather societies. Conkey (2001:277) remarks:

> We cannot say, for example, that hunter-gatherers made art primarily for ritual purposes related to the food quest, or that they engaged in making art in order to negotiate identity. Both these 'reasons' for art might have been at work in some places, at some times, and according to some people's perspectives, but we have to enquire into each differing context to approach the 'whys'.

In regard to rock art as a category in analyses, a shift has occurred away from attending to its visual and/or formal properties alone, and as the basic analytical unit, towards a greater consideration of its deeper materiality and what this may imply (e.g. Ouzman 2001; Rainbird 2002; Wilson & David 2002). Closely tied in with these considerations of the materiality of rock art is a growing concern with its physical, locational and archaeological context (Rosenfeld 2002; Taçon 2002). In order to expand the interpretive potential of rock art, enquiry is moving well 'beyond art' (cf. Conkey 1997:361). However, what ties all these recent threads together is a conceptual emphasis on image-making as cultural practice—a regard for human agency as well as the agential properties of material culture itself—in attempts to infer how rock art functioned meaningfully.

The theoretical and conceptual approach used to guide this research has been discussed in Chapter 1. In this chapter, the first section considers briefly the historical background of rock art research in Australia and specifically the approaches and results of work conducted in the Sydney Basin. The rock art of the Upper Nepean catchment has not been subject to any prior detailed or systematic analysis. However, two previous studies have included a selection of sites from the area. These studies provide information in regard to general archaeological patterns (Sefton 1988; McDonald 1994, 2008a). Thirty-one art sites from the Upper Nepean were included in McDonald's (1994) regional rock art analysis, and a substantial number from areas further north on the Woronora Plateau. Sefton's (1988) work included the sites in the Cataract River catchment, which forms the northern area of the Upper Nepean. Officer's (1984) analysis of rock art in the Georges River catchment is also described.

Next, a review is presented of the anthropological understanding of the role of art in Aboriginal Australia, with reference in particular to the work of Layton (1992; 2000a) and Morphy (1999). Layton's comprehensive overview of rock art in Australia, from both an ethnographic and archaeological perspective, provides particular insight into the pitfalls of transposing generalisations and analogies from one region to the next, and both scholars clearly explain the many limitations faced by archaeologists who seek to interpret rock art in the absence of an informing context. Cautiously, Layton and Morphy offer avenues of enquiry for the development of hypotheses about how art encodes meaning, and its functional purpose, which may not exceed what is empirically viable. Both Layton and Morphy consider the analysis of context to be central to a valid archaeological approach to rock art, and, in this regard, Layton (2000a) specifically addresses the relevance of attending to how and where rock art is distributed in the landscape arguing that, from an Indigenous perspective, location also provides interpretive clues in regard to meaning.

While geographic distribution and environmental location, and also the micro-topographic situation (where it is placed within rock shelters), of rock art (including different types) can be defined at a high level of spatial resolution, and on the face of it may appear to be objective data (which is not necessarily perceived to be a good thing, e.g. see Bradley 1991:77; Ingold 1993:153; Thomas 2008), its interpretation from a landscape perspective can be highly subjective to the point of being arbitrary (cf. Brück 2005). As noted above, reconstructing context in rock art research, which is traditionally the bread and butter of archaeology (Meskell 2005a:2), is neither straightforward nor without its pitfalls and limitations. Original conceptions of landscape, as proposed and applied archaeologically by Tilley (1994:7–11) and others, reject the concept that landscape is neutral space onto which human activities can be mapped and instead view landscape 'as something we travel through and in; it is a participation that articulates the experience of life' (David 1999:295). 'These insights have inspired novel ways of engaging with the material remains of the past' that attend to notions of the embodied experience of landscape (and monuments and artefacts) and which, methodologically, are often based on the archaeologist's own embodied experience and interpretation of place (Brück 2005:47, 54, 56). Notwithstanding the many critiques relating to the philosophy and substantive issues that have been raised (many of which are summarised in Brück 2005), it is concepts relating to experience and embodiment that are drawn upon in this research for the purposes of examining the distribution, location and context of rock art in the Upper Nepean catchment.

4.1 Archaeological Approaches to Rock Art in Australia

One of the most important and influential papers in early Australian rock art research is Macintosh's (1977) reappraisal of Beswick Creek cave. In this paper, he shows that the meaning of Aboriginal rock art could not successfully be determined in the absence of appropriate and knowledgeable informants (Macintosh 1977:197). Macintosh reports that, even at the fundamental level of species identification, figurative motifs, which he had identifies with confidence, were actually incorrect according to his Aboriginal informants. Australian archaeologists have since eschewed a search for meaning in rock art per se, considering such a goal as intractable, and have instead concentrated on the analysis of visual form, distribution and context (cf. Layton 1992:2; Rosenfeld 1992:1).

Prior to the publication of Macintosh's papers, several quantitative analyses, which sought patterns in motif distribution, had been undertaken (cf. Maynard 1977:387). This approach was recognised as methodologically important and Maynard (1977:387) proposes a comprehensive and standardised classification scheme to facilitate quantitative analysis. The issue of classification was a research theme subsequently developed further by Officer (1984, 1991, 1994), as discussed below.

McMah's (1965) analysis of engraved art in the Sydney Basin set the stage for a purely archaeological approach to rock art analysis in Australia. McMah (1965:7) looked at 285 open context engraved rock art sites with the aim to produce a typology and examine spatial variability and distribution. The quantitative study indicates significant differences in subject representation and form between the northern (around the Upper Hawkesbury) and southern extremes (south of Botany Bay) of the region, and between the inland and coastal areas. The area situated south of Botany Bay was also differentiated by lower site density. McMah (1965:75) argues that these differences may be ascribed to cultural causes, except for those which relate obviously to the stimulus of different environments.

Since McMah's seminal study, archaeological approaches to rock art in Australia have been rigorously objective in the manner in which the material has been handled, and a strong tradition of formal analysis, quantification and analysis of spatial distribution has become central to the discipline. Since the 1970s, the use of archaeological approaches (Morwood & Smith 1994:20) has been vibrant, resulting in a large and rich corpus of theoretical and substantive work. Studies have generally been closely allied to mainstream archaeological objectives, and this in part is reflected in the research questions that have been addressed and approaches adopted. In seminal projects, Rosenfeld (1975) and Morwood (1980) explicitly explored the relationship between rock art and changes in excavated archaeological materials. Others have since adopted this integrated approach (e.g. David 1991; McDonald 1994, 2008a). Excavations conducted as a component of rock art investigations have provided some researchers a direct means of dating rock art when panels are found buried by habitation deposit (Rosenfeld 1975:37; McDonald 1994), and an archaeological context in which to situate and infer temporal and spatial ordering in rock art (e.g. Morwood 1980; McDonald 1994, 2008a).

Arguably, the dominant theoretical and explanatory approach used in rock art studies during the 1980s and early 1990s—information exchange theory—likewise has been adopted in accordance with the 'central paradigm of Australian prehistory which focused on adaptive strategies of hunter-gatherer populations in a range of highly contrastive environments' (Rosenfeld 1992:3). Within this interpretive framework, rock art styles have been identified and their inherent spatial variability set out within a chronological framework whereby different styles are equated with different periods of time. Style has been viewed as functioning within a process of information exchange, which is conceived as a cultural mechanism for establishing social links and boundaries that confer an adaptive advantage in determining access to resources within synchronic contexts (Rosenfeld 1992:3). For example, a widespread geographic distribution of a rock art style is viewed as reflecting open networks of communication, which function socially to facilitate access to resources, while restricted distributions of rock art styles are seen to reflect boundedness, and closures of communication networks, usually in response to ameliorated climatic and environmental conditions, and often conceptualised as reflecting population increase (cf. Rosenfeld 1992:3; and see e.g. Morwood 1984; Lewis 1988; David & Cole 1990; McDonald 1994). In these studies, the concept of meaning was reinstated as a central issue, not as a search for explicit meaning, but 'rather by integrating the concept of systems of communication into models of Australian prehistory' (Rosenfeld 1992:2).

As indicated above, a dominant strand of research in Australia has been the integration of rock art studies into mainstream archaeological research and, in particular, the establishment of regional prehistories (cf. Rosenfeld 1992:2). A seminal and influential project in this regard was Morwood's (1980) doctoral research in which he explored diachronic and synchronic variability in two primary artefact categories—rock art and lithics—as well as other types of evidence, in the Central Queensland Highlands. The processual approach was the first in Australia to fully integrate rock art within an archaeological analysis. Morwood (1980:iv) describes his approach:

As two strands in the web of evidence documenting the workings of a cultural system, a combined study of art and stone offers potential for yielding a more detailed account of the processes by which archaeological observations relate to their cultural context, and the manner in which this reflected environmental and external ideational influences.

Morwood's (1980) approach was a particularly significant methodological development given the manner in which he explored the structural patterning and relationships between rock art and a number of other lines of contextual evidence, not only lithics but also shelter morphology, environmental categories and intra-site positioning of art. This approach, utilising comprehensive and multiple strands of evidence, has also been adopted by Ross (1997) and will be discussed further below.

Morwood (1980:408) identifies a pattern of relatively homogeneous, widely distributed and older rock art and lithics which, in the mid-Holocene, gave way to restricted distributions of both mediums that exhibited regionalised character. Morwood (1980:410) suggests that these trends may reflect fundamental changes in the social organisation of Aboriginal groups and inter-group communication. This general trend in the temporal and spatial patterning of rock art was to be subsequently identified in structural analyses conducted elsewhere in Australia, and was accompanied in some studies by the integration of concepts of information exchange theory (e.g. Morwood 1984; Lewis 1988; McDonald 1994, 2008a).

Lewis (1988) analysed changes in the Arnhem Land corpus of rock art with reference to postulated social strategies developed in response to changing environmental conditions. His theoretical position (Lewis 1988:79) is grounded in information exchange theory, which was at this time developing internationally (cf. Wobst 1977; Conkey 1978; Gamble 1982), whereby art is conceived as being a part of an 'integrated information system'. An information system, in this model, is seen to be both determined by, and constitutive of, social strategies of adaptation to particular ecological systems. Art style is 'interpreted as a marker of social identity' (Lewis 1988:79). Lewis developed a chronology based on a methodology that was focused on variability in human figures and their associated items of material culture. Material culture items that possessed at least one temporal boundary were considered as key for the purposes of defining relative art style periods. By identifying the material culture and its associated motifs, Lewis (1988) was able to then define the stylistic features of the imagery. The earliest period identified (Boomerang Period) is widely distributed across the Arnhem Land plateau. This characteristic of the style provided Lewis (1988:80–81) with the circumstantial evidence to suggest its age. The linking argument behind his hypothesis, that the style is dated to a time prior to the full physical effects of the post-glacial sea level rise, is that its widespread distribution is indicative of a large information exchange network. At this time, the country was semi-arid and, accordingly, it was argued that a large ecological territory would have been required by a sociolinguistic group. In addition, in such an ecological environment, communication between small local groups needed to be open. Similarity is emphasised over difference so that local groups have access to economic resources that are widely distributed. The widespread stylistic similarity of the Boomerang Period is seen as a reflection of people emphasising regional integration. The subsequent period defined by Lewis (1988) is the 'Hooked Stick'/Boomerang Period. This period is comprised of two distinct yet interrelated stylistic units, including regionally distinct styles and the widespread and relatively homogeneous Rainbow Snake complex. The regionalism inherent in this period is seen by Lewis (1988:86) to reflect an increased social concern with local territories. The regionalism is explained by reference to environmental conditions that ameliorated at the end of the post-glacial maximum and allowed social groups to occupy smaller territorial areas and, via rock art, emphasise group difference.

A similar pattern of an earlier geographically widespread homogeneous rock art corpus, which gives way in the late Holocene to regionalised rock art styles, has been identified in north-eastern Australia (David & Cole 1990; David 1991). The argument presented by these authors to explain late Holocene regionalism was tied in with a contemporary archaeological debate in regard to a perceived major structural change (intensification) of socioeconomic systems in Australia at that time (David & Cole 1990:788). The earlier widespread rock art style was seen to have operated in an extensive open sociocultural network, which acted to minimise the risk of resource shortages during the period of Pleistocene aridity. By contrast, the late Holocene regionalism in north-eastern Cape York rock art was explained as reflecting increases in population, a fragmentation of groups and regionalism of inter-group activity (David & Cole 1990:803).

The premise underlying studies of rock art as functioning systems of non-verbal communication and information exchange is that 'art functions (in part) as an expression of social identities, but for inter-group identity markers to operate meaningfully, stylistic differences must remain within the bounds of mutual intelligibility' (Rosenfeld 1992:3). The contrastive models of open versus closed communication systems has been described by Rosenfeld (1992:6) as an oversimplification of both environmental constraints on human adaptations, and of the range of social networks that operate within Aboriginal societies. In the European context where, in similarly conceived projects, researchers have inferred boundaries within society based on bounded visual styles of artefacts, this has been described as 'an imaginative leap', whereby in the direct move from metaphor to reconstruction, the reading of the evidence 'becomes increasingly capricious' (Bradley 1991:78).

These studies often deny or at least fail to explore the possibility of functional variability within single periods of time. That is, art is ascribed one function only, which is to express social identity (Rosenfeld 1992:3). Also, these approaches have been pursued within the structural/functional theoretical paradigm of processual archaeology and, accordingly, have been largely ahistorical. While concerned with cultural process rather than culture history (Morwood & Smith 1994:21), these types of studies do not address the transformation of social change, but merely correlate different periods of rock art styles with different environmental/ecological periods. In these types of studies, distribution patterns in rock art are used as circumstantial evidence to assign a recognised style to a particular period, and rock art is seen to reflect change in social organisation, interaction and patterns of settlement. They do not deeply explore the actual practice of rock art as functioning as a messaging mechanism in systems of information exchange (Rosenfeld 1997:290), but, rather, the function is assumed.

Officer (1984) examined the pigment art of the middle and upper reaches of the Georges River, located immediately to the north of the Upper Nepean catchment, with the aim of examining formal variation within a 'discrete regional sample', in order to explore the function of medium and style. Officer (1984:76) found that the rock art is similar in terms of broad conventions with the wider region but that regional variations were evident. Officer (1984:76) found the assemblage to be 'fundamentally diverse', and that dominant forms were lacking. He raises the issue that his fine-grained classification scheme may have contributed to the diversity but rejects this explanation by comparing the Georges River rock art with both the pigment and engraved art situated further to the east. Officer (1984:65, 77) found that, in terms of major figure shapes, the amorphous character in outline and infill, and the range from naturalistic to formalised, the pigment art is similar to sites in the east. Officer (1984:68) also concludes that the engraved component was similar to that located to the east of his study area. Accordingly, he discounts a style boundary existing between the Georges River and the coastal margin (Officer 1994:70), and, like McMah (1965, see above), finds a style boundary at the Georges River demarcating the north from the south.

Officer (1984:71) argues that the open context engraved motifs were more strictly bound by formal conventions compared with the sheltered pigment rock art in the region. While he argues for stylistic unity between the two media, he suggests that the differences may reflect functional variability. Officer (1994) looked directly at the formal qualities of the art itself to provide the key to understanding this variability. Invoking the proposition that art has more potential to possess multiple and abstract meanings if it is more formalised and less constrained by figurative detail, Officer (1984:83) argues that the 'casual use of form …[in the pigment art]… could reflect a loosely defined or secular operational context. Carved figures on the other hand, appear to have required a more consistent representation, perhaps in order to communicate the established and more conventional'. This research was based on an assumption of contemporaneity of all the sheltered pigment rock art; the notion of sequential change was not considered. While this assumption may not be valid, Officer's fine-grained analysis of formal variability was a significant methodological advance in rock art studies in Australia.

Sefton's (1988:20) study of the central Woronora Plateau was more broadly focused, and not specifically aimed at analysing rock art. Her primary aim was to explore archaeological patterning in relation to historically documented territorial boundaries, specifically a territorial boundary between the Tharawal and Wodi Wodi. Sefton also sought to define whether or not differences between coastal and inland areas were evident. In regard to shelter sites, Sefton (1988) conducted a series of multivariate analyses, which revealed strong patterns of inter-site variability. The most significant separation occurrs between shelter size and various site associations; large shelters are located in close proximity to other archaeological site types, while small shelters are located at distance from other archaeological sites. Chi square analyses were carried out on the results of the correspondence analysis in order to test for significance in relation to the archaeological question of variability in settlement patterns between catchments and the inland and coastal areas. The results indicate a significant difference between the two catchments and, to a lesser degree, in relation to the inland/coastal sectors; large shelters in the Georges River and coastal sector are close to another archaeological site, in contrast to the Cataract and inland areas, where they are not. While of less importance, shelters in the Georges River and coastal sector contain imported stone artefactual materials and higher counts for charcoal drawings. Sefton (1988:108) interprets this evidence as being informative of differing settlement patterns between the two catchments and coastal/inland areas.

Sefton concludes that the results of her analysis confirm the presence of the Tharawal and Wodi Wodi boundary and, to a lesser extent, a coastal/inland separation of settlement patterns. While it may be questioned whether these results are indicative of a tribal boundary, they do show strong patterning in regard to factors including site density, location and associated inter-site variables. On their own, these factors are equally suggestive of patterned variability in terms of site function, settlement and land usage rather than as indicators of territorial differences. However, the spatial patterning evident from Sefton's analysis of site and artefact distribution on the central Woronora Plateau suggests that a search for spatial patterning in the Upper Nepean catchment could be similarly rewarding and, if this was tied in with a detailed examination of the art itself, it may provide greater explanatory potential.

As researchers have sought to examine regional rock art assemblages at higher theoretical levels, it has become evident that the degree of analytical resolution of classificatory schemes used may not adequately serve these goals (Officer 1991:113, 1994; Rosenfeld 1992:235; Davidson 1997:218). Rosenfeld (1992:235) describes this problem as '[t]he classificatory systems and comparative analyses used have not been geared to an examination of the dynamics of image production and perception in information exchange'. This issue is especially relevant in regard to figurative bodies of art, which are inherently difficult to break down into constitutive components or elements and which, furthermore, by their very nature, encourage a figurative classification.

In a significant departure from conventional methodologies, Officer (1984) classifies imagery in terms of its formal construction rather than figurative motif type categories. Officer (1984:15) recognises that the categorisation of rock art into figurative types led to the clumping of motifs that possessed a diversity of form and that, furthermore, much of the art remained unclassifiable as it was indeterminate in terms of figurative models. Officer (1991:113) poses questions such as when is an anthropomorphic image actually a lizard, for example, which emphasises the subjective and problematic nature inherent in figurative motif type classifications. He describes the problem as '[f]igurative categories tend to be used as appropriate units within supposedly formal and stylistic analyses. That the category may be hiding rather than revealing the graphic vocabulary is often overlooked' (Officer 1991:113).

While inherently problematic, in terms of subjectivity and substantive relevance, broad figurative motif classification systems are unable to handle variability and diversity in graphic form. This is a critical problem in the exploration of regional assemblages where the identification of patterns of heterogeneity and/or homogeneity in rock art underpins the basis of explanatory and interpretive analysis. Many researchers now seek to classify their material in a manner that affords greater analytical control over the form and graphic construction of imagery (cf. Taçon et al. 1996; Frederick 1997; Ross 1997; McDonald 1999; Gunn 2005). While this approach is relevant in enabling greater analytical rigour and control on variability, and hence on the exploration of chronological and spatial patterning, it is considered in this research as intrinsic to approaches that seek to explore the nature of imagery as a system of meanings (cf. Morphy 1999). However, while appropriate in a strictly structural analysis, a purely formal analysis as proposed by Officer (1994) potentially divorces the object of investigation (usually the social or cultural in one form or another) from the material evidence itself (this is discussed further below).

Demographic issues underpin McDonald's (2008a) explanatory framework in her 1994 doctoral research, in which she examined the Sydney Basin rock art in a broad regional study. McDonald's (2008a:1, 350) research was aimed at exploring stylistic variability in engraved and sheltered rock art in terms of synchronic and diachronic variation, medium and reconstructed site context (the latter being a crucial basis for her interpretations). The theoretical approach was informed by information exchange theory, with style defined as a particular way of doing things or producing material culture that signals similarly constituted but different groups of people (McDonald 2008a:1). Anchored to an interpretation of changes in social organisation throughout the Holocene, McDonald (2008a:349) argues that art practice intensified between 4,000–1,000 BP, and was related to a period of increased population. Rock art, she argues, acted during this period as a social mechanism to mediate 'uncontrolled and possible conflict-marked interactions'. From 1,000 BP, a posited shift away from the occupation of shelter sites to open habitation contexts was argued to imply a shift in the social system, which McDonald (2008a:350) suggests increased further the need for social mechanisms to facilitate large-scale group cohesion. She suggests that many engraved open context sites may have been produced in this period.

McDonald (2008a) found that clinal-style patterning correlated with ethnohistorically defined Aboriginal language group areas. Further patterning was evident based on drainage basins located within language areas that, she argues, may be indicative of the operation of smaller local group territoriality. Patterning between engraved and sheltered art was also identified. The engraved rock art located in open contexts displays relative homogeneity across the region; McDonald (2008a:350) argues this demonstrates that this art system functioned as a broad-scale cohesive mechanism. Conversely, McDonald found that the shelter rock art is of greater heterogeneity, demonstrating localised group-identifying behaviour. The Guringai language area in the central Sydney Basin appears to be its central source of cohesion. However, this influence seems to be non-existent in the south of her study area, including, at least partially, the Upper Nepean catchment. A previously identified style boundary at the Georges River was confirmed by McDonald's analysis (cf. also McMah 1965; Officer 1984). This defined style boundary is based on the presence and proportions of different motifs and overall schematic differences (McDonald 1994:333). McDonald argues that this is indicative of either a reduction in the level of broad-scale group cohesion between groups to the north and south of the Georges River, or alternative social strategies operating south of the Georges River. Given that McDonald's study did not deal with the entirety of the Upper Nepean, a detailed analysis of the rock art and its associated inter-site patterning will provide a greater understanding of this area.

Ross (1997:32) emphasises the necessity for establishing, independently of style theory, the behavioural context in which art is produced, and has developed a strong contextual approach to satisfy this endeavour. Ross's (1997:1) research was focused specifically on the analysis of one rock art motif type in north-west central Queensland: a distinctive anthropomorph that occurs in a discrete regional area and dominates the local art assemblage. In order to explore the 'operation' of the art system, specifically in processes of the negotiation of social strategies, Ross (1997:18, 21) examined the formal attributes of the motif, its inter-site and intra-site distribution, its relationship with other motifs, and details of the geographic, environmental and archaeological context of the sites in which it occurs. Ross's (1997:25) approach was to explore the interrelationships between these various variables, which she considered to be attributable to 'the choices the artists made when producing art', and the 'organising principles which provide the patterns which characterise the art system'. Coupled with a behavioural theory of style as a social strategy, Ross (1997:32) argues that recourse to independent evidence that addresses the 'ways in which the artist has utilised, manipulated or modified the art in order to mediate a particular social outcome', is necessary to provide explanations for patterns. Her analysis revealed that the anthropomorphic motif was a spatially and temporally discrete art style, and that it separated into two types, Basic Motifs and Detailed Motifs, and that each occurred in different environmental contexts. Ross (1997:131) argues that this spatial discreteness suggests that the motif may have been related to a purposeful process of boundary maintenance, and that this may have arisen within the context of widespread trade networks, which operated in the region during the late Holocene. This research is particularly interesting in regard to the high level of patterning revealed by Ross's analysis of the interrelationships between a wide range of associated variables. She argues that these patterns are informative about why they may have been produced and under what circumstances the patterns may have appeared (Ross 1997:155).

Frederick (1997:209) has also explored patterns in various aspects of the graphic structure of rock art, and how these relate spatially to the use of the physical environment, in an analysis of the rock art at Watarrka National Park in Central Australia. Frederick identifies a chronological sequence, which includes two distinct phases of rock art production, identified as a shift in the technical mode of art production, corresponding to changes in the structuring of graphic designs and in the frequency of production (Frederick 1997:271). In order to examine inter-site variability for the purposes of correlating site distribution patterns with changes in land use or differences in site function, the physical environment was ordered into three spatial units based on topographic and geomorphological criteria (Frederick 1997:97). By distinguishing between the different environments within the broader landscape, Frederick (1997:210) was able to look at spatial variations in rock art density and site associations. For example, site complexes containing larger sites surrounded by a 'constellation of smaller sites' were identified in some units. Frederick (1997:209) sought to distinguish the fundamental characteristics of the assemblage in a detailed classification of the art. This included an assessment of diversity in media and technique, the frequency and spatial distribution of graphic categories (stencils, figurative, non-figurative, track and indeterminate graphics), graphic classes and basic graphic elements. The analysis of these variables was contextualised within the spatial configuration of the three environmental units of the study area. The earlier phase of art is characterised by the use of a wide variety of pigment colours, little evidence of re-marking, a small range of graphic vocabulary and little variability. The few elaborate graphics were found to be site specific, which Frederick argues is suggestive that they were definitively associated with particular places. Art representative of the earlier phase is present in 92 per cent of rock art sites, and is evenly distributed across the landscape. The art of the recent phase, however, differs significantly to the earlier patterns in that there is a restriction in the range of pigment used, an increase in the diversity of graphic designs, an efflorescence of re-marking, and changes in landscape use. The identification of both continuities and discontinuities in the production of rock art was hypothesised by Frederick (1997:271, 335) to reflect and express changes in the social context within which it was produced during the transformation of the social geography and land use that occurred at the time of Aboriginal and European contact.

Numerous archaeological studies in Australia have referred to the symbolic meanings embodied in stone artefacts, and of stone itself (McBryde 1986; R. Jones 1990; Taçon 1991; Paton 1994). Similar approaches, which consider deeply the role of rock art as a system of symbolic expression and meaning, and how it may encode the Dreaming or totemic geographies, are now also beginning to emerge (e.g. Taçon et al. 1996; Layton 2000a; David 2002; Taçon 2008a:164). In the Laura region of north-east Australia, Rosenfeld (1982:216) found that certain motifs tend to occur in association with one another, and that the pattern of site clustering, each with an identifiable suite of motifs, may reflect different cultural connotations. She argues that the different imagery may relate to the depiction of variable topics such as ancestral figures, sorcery or secular themes. Taçon et al. (1996) hypothesise that elements of the ethnographically known Rainbow Serpent mythology in northern Australia may have emerged in the early Holocene, when Rainbow Serpent imagery appears in the rock art in Western Arnhem Land. More recently, David (2002:200) has argued that the recent regionalism in Cape York rock art indicates not only a changed geographic structure, but also 'newly regionalised referential systems'. David (2002:204), in moving beyond a formal analysis, explicitly addresses the referential properties of the animal motifs in recent Cape York rock art. These motifs, David (2002:204) argues, 'emerged as meaningful … as components in regionalised networks of reference that served to order social space and meaning in the world'.

In summary, earlier rock art research in Australia was predominantly focused on the visual form, which methodologically and conceptually is highly abstracted from its materiality and physical associations with other imagery, its material support and location within the landscape. With a strong focus on the formal properties of imagery in Australian research, there has been a tendency to abstract rock art from its archaeological context. Studies that have focused on a broader suite of contextual data, and, in particular, the incorporation of detailed geographic and environmental locational variables, have enabled deeper explorations of patterns in rock art diversity. Another significant development, informed by the recognition that rock art predominantly relates in some way to ideology and religion, is the recent enquiry into the emergence and transformation of beliefs via an analysis of rock art.

4.2 Anthropological Exegesis

Rosenfeld's (1997:289–290) important critical review of the social context of rock art production in Australia sought to examine how it expresses group identity and territoriality, which she argues remained an implicit but poorly explored concept in archaeological investigations. The examination of the social contexts of rock art production in varied environment and art style regions allowed Rosenfeld (1997:297) to recognise the inherent complexity in regard to the relationship between rock art and the manner in which it expresses a social landscape, which goes well beyond the 'model of reciprocity of access to resources between members of territorial groups'. In regard to regions that archaeologically are defined via rock art as being geographically bounded with an internally coherent stylistic expression, Rosenfeld (1997:292) argues that not only is their internal homogeneity variable, but that rock art articulates with a 'very different expression of sociality and territoriality'; differences obtained between regions in the nature of rock art, social significance of rock art localities (including the artist's affiliation to that locality) and of the social contexts of rock art production (Rosenfeld 1997:292).

For example, Rosenfeld compares the rock art produced in the Central Queensland Highlands with that of the West Kimberly. In the Central Queensland Highlands, rock art is comprised predominantly of stencils, and it occurs mainly at or near camping sites. Rosenfeld (1997:292) argues, therefore, that this art is marking patrilineally determined territory, which is the habitual foraging range and resource of related men and their families. In addition, in this area, rock art is also associated with burials, and this art, which consists of formal motifs, marks the affiliation between the deceased and a locality. Rosenfeld suggests that the rock art in this region is an individualised expression of habitual residence and affiliation. By comparison, in the West Kimberly, Wandjina motifs mark focal localities in a patrilineal clan's estate, which define a totemic locus for clan members' ritual obligations and the expression of their socially constituted identity. These localities are totemic increase sites, and less dominant motifs (plant, animal and other), which occur in association with Wandjina motifs, are highly site specific. Given that, in this area via affinal relationships, a group's foraging composition and range (and rights) extend far beyond a patriclan's estate, Wandjina rock art expresses men's socially constituted identity and ritual (clan-based affiliation to territory), but it does not articulate habitual interpersonal relations, and hence does not determine access to resources (Rosenfeld 1997:293). Despite the rock art from these two different regions functioning in two different structures of sociality and land affiliation, and expressing two very different aspects of identity, Rosenfeld (1997:293) notes that from an archaeological perspective both bodies of rock art possess stylistic unity (they are regionally distinct and possess a uniformity of style and dominant motifs), which is predicted by their closely bounded social networks. However, the two bodies of rock art do not reflect the different social contexts and identity that they each express.

Rosenfeld (1997:293–296) also compares the production of rock art in Western Arnhem Land with that of the Central Ranges, Central Australia. These are two highly contrastive environments, where in both places rock art is produced in at least two separate social contexts. Western Arnhem Land rock art is comprised of a widespread, distinctive rock art province (with clinal rather than exclusive stylistic patterning), and is produced in a ritual context comprised of art of the Dreaming (a secular context of art about the Dreaming) and anecdotal art. Rock art is not a central feature of a sacred locality, but where rock art of the Dreaming is produced, it marks patriclan-owned localities, and marking is constrained according to totemically sanctioned relationships (Rosenfeld 1997:294). In Western Arnhem Land, residence and foraging groups are loosely patterned, and there is a high degree of fluidity relating to access to territory and resources, which is mirrored in the fluidity of rights to produce non-sacred paintings (Rosenfeld 1997:294). While rock art in this region may visually encode territorial affiliation as constituted via social identity, or merely through rights of residence, it is not unambiguously evident from an archaeological perspective (Rosenfeld 1997:294). Rosenfeld (1997:294) concludes that in this region the 'essentially secular use of formal imagery has blurred the archaeologist's ability to distinguish between expressions of individual and supra-individual identities'.

In the Central Ranges, rock art, at least superficially, is also comprised of a widespread and uniform style, and Rosenfeld (1997:295; see also 2002) identifies two main site classes, each of which contain different types of rock art: camp site shelters, which contain secular art (individualised stencils and loosely structured graphic imagery), and restricted sites, some of which are totemic increase sites that contain highly formalised and often unique imagery. Rosenfeld (1997:296) argues that these two categories of rock art sites seem to reflect very different aspects of territorial affiliation. The former relates to people's habitual foraging ranges, while the latter expresses formal relationships. In this area, a patrilineal totemic affiliation prevails; however, other totemic affiliations can also be emphasised by people to negotiate social relations and access to territory and resources (Rosenfeld 1997:295). Rosenfeld (1997:296) argues that the parallelism between Western Arnhem Land and the Central Ranges in dual contextual traits of rock art, which occurs in two highly contrasted environments, 'suggests that our models of style in relation to environmental adaptation are inadequate to deal with the full complexity of the realities of rock art production'.

In a summary of her analysis, Rosenfeld (1997:296) argues that rock art practice is an expression and mediation of social relations instead of an explicit expression of territorial affiliation. Rosenfeld explores this issue by distinguishing between two categories of rock marking, each of which is an archaeological indicator of particular expressions of social identity. One of these is graphic images, which are produced according to conventions of graphic construction, while the other is marks that result from purely mechanical processes, such as hand stencils. Rosenfeld argues that the former relates to supra-individual identity and is concerned with religion operating '… primarily to visually express and mediate supernaturally sanctioned power relationships', while the latter is concerned with individual identity (Rosenfeld 1997:291). As a result of this research, Rosenfeld (1997:296, 297) comes to a number of conclusions:

> The creation or maintenance of ancestral images is restricted to individuals according to their structurally determined identities and that art created in such contexts is narrowly constrained in terms of style and motif, and that subject matter and style emphasise the nature of the artist's contextualised relationship to a locale. In its reference to appropriately expressed concepts of the dreaming it expresses his/her structurally determined interests in the locale as defined via the legitimacy of the ideational system of social relations.

This predicts a correspondence between rock art, which is expressive of religious themes, and its formal properties. However, it also sets out an avenue of enquiry into the expression of identity that resulted in the production of rock art: 'The creation or renovation of such paintings is an act of expressing … classificatory and contextual identity, and of relationship to place via the spiritual power of the "law"' (Rosenfeld 1997:296). Rosenfeld (1997:296) therefore states that religious rock art functions to express and mediate social relations rather than explicitly territorial affiliation, and that this is 'an affirmation of territorial affiliation via social relations as constructed through cosmological principles'. On the other hand, the execution of rock markings and non-sacred designs is generally concurrent with rights of residence that are much more inclusive. This rock art does not evoke rights of control over place, nor of ritual affiliation to it, and it refers to a person's individual identity but does not define socially constructed identity (Rosenfeld 1997:297).

In Aboriginal geographies of country, the explanatory framework, which provides a cohesive ontology and legitimating basis, is encoded in the mythology of the creative actions of Ancestral Beings (Rosenfeld 2002:62). As David (2002:205) reminds us, the genesis and sociopolitical inheritance of the Dreaming, as it is known ethnographically, has a history, and, as he and others (Taçon et al. 1996; Rosenfeld 2002; Taçon 2008a) argue, this may be explored archaeologically. All of these studies have used rock art to illuminate such research. Rosenfeld (2002:62) specifically argues that the role of rock art in such archaeological analysis is appropriate, as it is one of the more enduring expressions of the cultural praxis associated with a social geography, which is underwritten by such metaphysics. However, the ethnographic material in Australia makes clear that rock art is produced in a diversity of cultural contexts (Layton 1992:17). Layton (1992:17) notes that rock art may be the object of increase ceremonies, such as in the Western Kimberley or in Central Australia, and in other contexts it is illustrative of Ancestral Figures, but, without being the object of ritual focus, it may simply record secular events.

Nevertheless, it is emphasised by anthropologists that in Aboriginal Australia, art, including all its various manifestations (rock art, body painting, sand drawings, etc.), is a form of spiritual power: 'it is an intervention of the world of the mythical past in the present', and for this reason art exists in people's heads until such time as it is created to fulfil a specific purpose (Morphy 1999:13). Art is information, and the means by which knowledge is transmitted regarding the 'creative forces that shaped the world and will enable it to continue into the future'; it is for this reason that Aboriginal art is referential (Morphy 1999:13). Aboriginal art encodes meaning in two primary representational modes: iconic (figurative) that is based on 'look-alike criterion'; and non-iconic (geometric) that bears no formal resemblance with that which it represents (Morphy 1999:13). The question of meaning is not only an outsider's problem, but, as Morphy (1999:13) notes, an insider's question as well. According to Layton (1992:86; see also Morphy 1999:21), like any system of communication, contextual information is necessary in order to understand Aboriginal rock art:

> The successful functioning of the art in its cultural context depends on the ability of other members of the community to decode its meaning at one or more levels. Visual clues are therefore deliberately encoded in both style and iconography to convey messages according to local convention.

Both Morphy (1999:15) and Layton (2000a:179) consider the different systems and manner by which Aboriginal peoples produce and interpret art, and offer to an archaeological audience a consideration of these principles, so that the conduct of analyses can reasonably proceed within contexts where the original discourse and meanings are unknown.

Layton (1992:29), recognising that Aboriginal Australia is not culturally uniform, questions whether or not any regular patterns in the content or distribution of rock art, revealed by anthropological understanding, could be used reliably in an archaeological research context. He argues positively in this regard, and indicates that the spatial organisation of rock art, both within and between sites, can provide a key to interpreting its various functions. According to Layton (1992:77), secular rock art is patterned differently from that which is totemic art. The sites containing secular rock art are not spaced in such a way as to 'map the focal points of a clan estate'. In addition, secular rock art is represented by a greater range of subjects (Layton 1992:77). Likewise, sorcery rock art can be distinguished from art by its style and distribution (Layton 1992:86).

However, Layton (1992:87) provides many cautionary examples of cross-cultural differences in Australia in regard to the significance of various features of art. For example, while in some areas the elaboration of a motif's infill will distinguish it as religious as opposed to secular, elsewhere this principle does not apply. In another example, Layton (1992:88) suggests that where secular rock art is produced with no restrictions on whom may paint, it may be expected that a site will contain art over all surfaces, and that there will be random selections of subjects depicted. However, the production of sacred rock art can result in the same pattern, and, therefore, the difference between sacred and secular contexts may be archaeologically invisible.

According to Morphy (1999:20), Aboriginal religious art is mostly non-iconic, because it conceals meanings and is, therefore, suited to a system of restricted knowledge. Iconic or figurative art, on the other hand, is predominantly secular, and Morphy (1999:20) explains that this is because the schema of a figurative system does not easily represent the metaphysical concepts underpinning the complexity of an Aboriginal worldview. While non-iconic art is surficially obscure, upon adequate instruction, an initiate is enabled to see the different levels in which relationships between people, Ancestral Beings and land are encoded via art, in order to understand the shape of the landscape and become aware of its transformational history (Morphy 1999:20). By contrast, a figurative system is less able to illustrate or represent metaphysical concepts relating, for example, to the shape-changing properties of Ancestral Beings, and the blurred boundaries between the animate and inanimate (Morphy 1999:20).

Davidson's (1995:891) argument, that in representational systems the relationship between form and meaning is *arbitrary* and hence requires people to interpret meaning, implies that over time those meanings become unrecoverable. His concern in this regard is that, from an archaeological perspective, this means that we may not, therefore, go beyond purely utilitarian interpretations towards an understanding of symbolic systems. While in general agreement, Morphy (1999:21) nevertheless suggests that an archaeological interpretation of meaning is possible, insofar as it is the structured relationship between form and meaning that allows an analysis to proceed, and from which it is possible to hypothesise about how the art in question encodes meaning.

Layton (2000b:51) argues that visual representations point in two directions: one outward via ostensive reference to a world of experience, which can be perceived by an audience; and the other inward, which is the world of possible meanings. He is particularly concerned that the representational (iconic) qualities of figurative rock art should be recognised analytically for how they function within an intersubjective sphere of interaction: 'iconic forms point to a tradition of usage through which ambiguities are reduced, and are symptomatic of an inter-subjective world defined by the artist's cultural tradition' (Layton 2000b:51). This means that attention needs to be paid to the manner in which rock art, as communication, is employed as a social strategy, and meanings should not be considered as entirely open ended because:

> during social strategies through which elements of an artistic system are utilised, reference is made either to objects or agents (through denotation or ostension), or to a broader cultural discourse, which exists outside the message itself (Layton 2000b:49).

There are two types of referential contexts of social action in which rock art is situated: the broader cultural discourse; and the world of perceived objects (Layton 2000b:50). In Australia, the cultural discourse of rock art as praxis is about landscape and the creation period. The reference to objects, which may be meaningful on a number of levels to different individuals within that cultural discourse, is nevertheless meaningful within a framework of shared experience and meanings (the intersubjective community of knowers) (Layton 2000a:49). In this sense, Layton (2000b:49, 52) argues that if the pattern of references is sufficiently habitual as to leave an archaeological trace, referential contexts may be explored by analysis of the representational qualities of rock art and their distribution in the landscape.

Like Layton, Morphy (1999:21) emphasises the role of the formal properties of the art system in communicating messages. As a first step in any analysis of art, the form of art objects should be investigated in order to question how something means, for 'it is this that reveals the nature of the system of interpretation, and enables art to be connected to its interpretive context' (Morphy 1999:21). Thus, Morphy (1999:21) emphasises that in archaeology it is both the reconstruction of context, which enquires about 'to whom it means, and in what contexts', and an investigation of the formal properties, which enable it to be 'interpreted in the ways it is', that provide the empirical foundation for research. Layton (1992:88; 2000a:176) emphasises the value of considering the location of rock art in the landscape in analysis, and indeed suggests that Indigenous people also read art in this way, in order to deduce meaning (see also Merlan 1989). Layton (1992:88) and Morphy (1999:22) consider that archaeological investigations of the interpretive context of rock art, while possible, will necessarily be incomplete.

4.3 Summary: Breaking Down Dualist Concepts

An epistemological respect for the multivalency of rock art expression has been a foundation of research in Australia, if not an impetus for its paradigmatic trajectory. While the complexity of the social function of rock art has also been recognised for some time (cf. Rosenfeld & Bahn 1991:vi), this notion has not been fully integrated in formal methodological and theoretical approaches to the same degree. The use of Wobst's (1977) overarching theory of style, as non-verbal social communication and information exchange, and the notion that rock art expresses group identity and territoriality, has been a significant trend in Australian rock art research. Rosenfeld (1997:290), however, notes that the manner in which rock art operated in networks of communication is little understood. Her review of the social contexts of rock art production, as outlined above—which shows that comparable structural patterns in rock art may exist between different regions and in highly contrastive environments and, furthermore, do not reveal differences regarding social context and identity—indicates that models of style in relation to environmental adaptation are inadequate for dealing with the full complexity of rock art production (Rosenfeld 1997:296). The use of overarching interpretive frameworks often denies that rock art is complex in its social function, and potentially diverse in terms of the motivations that lead to its production and use. Such frameworks tend towards a conceptualisation of rock art production that is synchronically uniform in its purpose and social function and, in Australia, the ethnography reveals that this may not necessarily be so.

The emphasis on the use of style in archaeology is based in an ideology of modernism, which prioritises the way in which we know things in visual terms (Conkey 1990:7; Thomas 2004:212). The identification and interpretation of similarities, differences, homogeneity and heterogeneity in artefacts and cultural products of the human past has always been a concern of archaeology, and in these endeavours the concept of style has dominated material culture studies (Conkey 1990:5; Boast 1997:173). Formal variation and style came to be seen as equivalent (Conkey 1990:10). The privileged position that style has attained is arguably because it has been seen as that aspect of material culture providing a key to the social (Boast 1997:174):

> Style has been seen as pervasive and universal to all forms of human production. Style is seen as that which distinguishes us not only from nature but from each other, both as cultures and individuals. It is that which situates the object in society as a social object—it is that which represents identity.

Style came to be used in the service of accessing social groupings or units, boundaries and interactions (Conkey 1990:10). Conkey (1990:10) notes that with the employment of style in this manner 'an extremely optimistic and productive period of archaeological research' ensued in America; arguably, the same could be said for rock art research in Australia. Whether conceptualised as passive or accidental—such as isochrestic style (Sackett 1986) active and deliberately employed in the negotiation of identity (Wiessner 1983), or symbolic and meaningfully constituted with the dynamic capacity to actively represent and act back on society (Hodder 1982)—style maintains an analytical separation between form and matter (Thomas 2004:213). The focus on style, and that it may be informative of the social, may have been something of a red herring; the nature of rock art itself as a behavioural manifestation has been largely unexamined in archaeological research contexts (Rosenfeld 1997:290).

Boast (1997:184) argues that style is not a meaningful category with which to define the social. The foundation to Boast's critique is based on a recognition that style, rather than being a universal cross-cultural phenomenon, is a contemporary concept based on a modern subject/object dualism (Boast 1997:174). However style is defined, whether as the material product of cultural systems or as a language to be read by social actors, 'an a priori distinction between the human actor and the material world' is implied. In this view, the material and natural world, to which the social is added by human activities, is based on a premise that 'there exists a basic essence or purpose to things prior to them becoming social'.

The recent concern with materiality in archaeology is related fundamentally to the conceptual distinction between form and matter that is, as Thomas (2004:202–209) describes, also a largely modern way of thinking.

Thomas (2004:202) argues that the conceptual separation of form and matter occurred within medieval scholasticism when the complementary distinction between them—but together making up a substance (as conceived earlier by Aristotle)—changed into a concern about the essential qualities of things being the key to an understanding of their behaviour. To illustrate this view, the form of a living creature is considered to be intrinsic to it, while the form of an artefact is considered to be imposed. It was this view of the opposition between matter and form that provided the possibility of viewing material things as the passive recipients of labour, and '[w]hen this version of form as a source of coherence that was exterior to material things eventually collided with the Cartesian opposition between mind and body, a closed conceptual framework resulted which emphasised the role of the dynamic human subject acting upon the dead matter of the object' (Thomas 2004:202, 203). Once thought was separated from materiality, substance became 'just there … a bearer of qualities and attributes'. This, coupled with the idea that humans give form to matter, constitutes our understanding of archaeological evidence (Thomas 2004:204, 210).

The Cartesian philosophy of matter has been described by Thomas (2004:204–205) as 'the most austere of all', and conceives of matter as inert and only distinguished by its occupation of space, and from this view is derived the proposition that our knowledge of things must rest upon as abstract and mathematical a foundation as possible, because our experience of things is not up to the task. The modern theory of representation distinguishes thoughts or words from things (Thomas 2004:203). The notion that rock art motifs are symbols or signs associated by convention with that which they signify holds a powerful sway (Ross & Davidson 2006:325). Hodder's (1982) contextual and symbolic approach advocates that material culture is potentially transformative of human behaviour because the efficacy of artefacts resides in their meaning—that is, material culture is considered to be meaningfully constituted and this is via the agency of humans (cf. Thomas 2004:214). In this sense, humans invest meaning in things, but things themselves do not inhabit a world of meaning (Thomas 2004:214).

However, the meaningfulness of rock art may not reside solely within its symbolic properties. Rock art may not be just a symbol, nor only a social strategy employed in the service of achieving particular goals. It is feasible that instead rock art is no more or less than what is already present in the land. Isomorphic congruence is a term that describes the formal relationship between a rock art mark and a natural feature of the rock (cf. Rosenfeld 1991:137), when the graphic form has been produced to mirror the shape, or to be in a situated relationship with a specific feature of the rock. A drawn circular-shaped motif located in a circular concavity may be considered to be an instance of isomorphic congruence. This practice has been recognised as a characteristic of European parietal rock art (Ucko & Rosenfeld 1967:48; Thomas 2004:220–221), and is occasionally reported in Australian contexts (e.g. David & David 1988:153; Rosenfeld 1991:137; Taçon 2008b). Taçon et al. (2006:232) describe an example in the Wollemi National Park of an engraved bird head 'attached' to a natural depression, the shape of which resembles a bird's body, and they argue that the depression is likely to have inspired the bird head to be engraved where it is. Isomorphic congruence also features in the Americas (cf. Taçon & Ouzman 2004:41), South Africa (Lewis-Williams & Dowson 1990; Ouzman 2001) and presumably in other places as well. The practice of integrating rock art with the natural morphology of rock, therefore, appears to be common. However, the incorporation of isomorphic congruence within archaeological analysis in Australia is not. The only work that explicitly analyses isomorphic congruence in Australia is that of Taçon and Ouzman (2004:46), who explore the phenomenon with reference to the notion of inner and outer worlds. They refer to animal figures depicted in a manner suggesting that their heads appear to disappear into cracks and crevices, for example, and argue that this reflects a concern with inner rock worlds (Taçon & Ouzman 2004:46). Taçon and Ouzman (2004:39) suggest that rock art sites are places where both inner worlds of extraordinary experience and the outer world of everyday existence are connected.

According to Ucko and Rosenfeld (1967:48–49), in Europe this relationship is explained in terms of the natural rock feature having suggested to the Palaeolithic artist the shape of an animal or part of an animal. Rosenfeld (1992:10–11) suggests that this may also be the case in Australia, whereby the 'appropriation of the natural ... may operate at the level of graphic construction itself', and that the integration of motifs within the natural morphology of the rock suggests that it 'is an integral component of the artistic system of meanings'. In respect of rock art and its material situation on rock, specifically where it is placed in a formal relationship with natural morphology, Thomas (2004:221) suggests that rock art practice, rather than being representational of animals 'distant from the cave', may instead be elaborating something considered to be already in the rock. Lewis-Williams and Dowson (1990:14) argue that painting is a ritual act employing two principal elements, rock and paint, each of which have their own significance that cannot be separated from meaning. It is clear that an archaeological analysis of rock art may profit from a much deeper examination of its materiality than that commonly undertaken.

The charting of change in rock art abundance and stylistic uniformity or otherwise, within a temporal framework, resides at the methodological heart of research in Australia. The general model to emerge from analyses that consider the longue durée reveals a pattern of low-density and widespread distributions of rock art in the late Pleistocene to mid-Holocene that give way to regionalised and abundant distributions in the late Holocene. These patterns, generally, are interpreted to reflect the trajectory, over time, of increasing population levels and, correspondingly, increasing needs to mediate social complexity, access to resources, and so on. However, the notion of the one-to-one correspondence between rock art and population density has not received the scrutiny that, for example, stone artefact densities vis-à-vis population have (Hiscock 1981). Notwithstanding a consideration of site formation processes that may contribute to some archaeologically observable patterns, a deeper historical investigation, which considers the impetus for change within an endogenous framework, might approach the question differently.

5

Research Methodology

> Rather than the properties of materials, technological processes and functional performance being seen as boring sidelines to the goal of social meanings, they need to be seen as crucial pathways towards this goal. Properties should be studied as essential information to be investigated with our senses and technologies in order to provide ideas about social contexts. Such knowledge and sensory experience can then inform an understanding of objects as individualised pieces as the material evidence of past concepts of materiality. (Hurcombe 2007:538)

The methodological approaches adopted for conducting this research are outlined in this chapter. Two separate sets of data are used in the analysis. The Research Database (R/DB) includes data gathered from 110 rock shelters recorded during 20 weeks of fieldwork undertaken for this research. The Illawarra Prehistory Group Database (IPG/DB) includes the remaining 700 open context and rock shelter sites in the Upper Nepean catchment. Throughout this monograph, it will always be made clear which of the databases is being referred to; although, it is noted that in some instances analyses are conducted on single data sets compiled from both sources. In this chapter, the selection of material for the databases is described and the basis on which this was made is outlined. The field-recording techniques and processes and post-fieldwork analytical techniques are described. The limitations and problems associated with the data and any identified biases are also discussed.

5.1 Illawarra Prehistory Group Database

Since 1970, the Illawarra Prehistory Group (IPG), a local interest group, led by archaeologist Caryll Sefton, has conducted a systematic and comprehensive survey of the Woronora Plateau, aimed at locating and recording the Aboriginal archaeological resource (Sefton 1988:2, 1989, 1990, 1991, 1994, 1995, 1996, 1997, 2000, 2003a, 2003b). More than 2,000 sites have been recorded. As indicated in Chapter 1, the sites in this database, and present in the Upper Nepean catchment, have not been subject to a detailed and comprehensive analysis.

The analyses conducted in this research, which are focused in part on distributional patterns in the landscape, are therefore contingent upon the nature of sample, which the IPG recordings comprise. The field survey methodology employed by the IPG is described in Sefton (1988:14) and can be considered to be systematic, as their aim and strategy has been to inspect *all* areas of land for archaeological evidence. Sefton (1988:16) documents a check of IPG survey coverage undertaken in the Georges River basin, the results of which generally confirmed the completeness of the earlier surveys. Accordingly, the IPG recording can be considered to be reasonably comprehensive and, on a practical level, fundamentally representative of site variability and distribution. More recent surveys undertaken in areas previously surveyed by the IPG have, nevertheless, resulted in the recording of a few additional sites (see below). This result is not unexpected given the terrain and the nature of the often impenetrable vegetation.

The level of detail in the recordings made by the IPG is commensurate with their goal, which is primarily to locate sites rather than to undertake a detailed site recording. The information recorded encompasses basic locational and environmental information, shelter morphology variables (including drawn plans and cross-sections) and a brief description of art including motif categories and numbers, technique, colour, superimpositioning and weathering information. The recordings also include sketch drawings of the rock art.

The previous recordings of the IPG comprise a significant archaeological resource and have provided the means to conduct the present research. The existing information has enabled the selection of sites for re-recording and, more importantly, provided positional information so that they could be relocated.

5.2 Sampling Strategy

A total of 810 archaeological sites are known to be present within the boundaries of the study area. Given time and resource constraints, a selection of a sample of sites to be recorded during fieldwork was made. Detailed re-recording has been based on a variety of determining factors as described below.

5.2.1 The Inherent Characteristics and Nature of the Site

An aim of the fieldwork has been to record graphic imagery and evidence of temporal change. Generally, but not exclusively, sites were selected for re-recording that were known to contain: a) reasonably intact (unweathered) images; b) a reasonable number of intact images; and c) superimposition of motifs. This naturally introduces a bias into the sample, so sites with single or few images or weathered imagery have been re-recorded also, especially if they have been situated on or near to the walking route to other sites or located in close proximity. With the focus of the monograph on graphics, sites with stencils only have generally not been re-recorded. In regard to stencil sites, it is considered that the information in the relevant site cards is adequate for handling stencil data. Open context grinding groove sites have generally not been re-recorded because the information available from previous recordings provides a sufficient level of information for use in this study. Six open context engraved rock art sites are present in the study area, none of which have been re-recorded. Attempts to record several of these failed as they could not be relocated.

5.2.2 The Inherent Characteristics and Nature of Site Distribution

Sites distributed in clusters (higher relative density) in some locations have, as much as possible, been re-recorded. Given a focus of the research question, which is to consider inter-site variability, site clusters provide some potential to examine this issue at a high level of resolution. Accordingly, in these cases, recordings have been made of a fuller range of site types, including sites that possess incomplete imagery only, which otherwise might have been rejected in the selection process. Additionally, sites were chosen on the basis of their distribution along drainage systems. The goal was to sample sites in a reasonably comprehensive and even spatial distribution along the entire length of each catchment, and in a range of environmental contexts. It is noted, however, that this objective was not achieved in regard to the Upper Nepean catchment where, for logistical reasons and time constraints, a very small and uneven sample of shelters has been recorded.

5.2.3 Logistics

Given the nature of the topography and terrain, the majority of sites are accessible by foot only, and overnight camping was not allowed in the study area (accordingly, limited time was available at sites, some of which required six or more hours walking to get to and from). As a result, the issue of accessibility was to a certain extent a determining factor of site selection. A larger number of sites have been re-recorded that are located within reasonable proximity to fire trails (<4 hours walking). While it is recognised that this method of sampling is at best described as ad hoc, it, nevertheless, was the practical option. The use of data from the remainder of the IPG records lessens the biases and limitations posed by the sampling strategy.

5.3 Recorded Variables

In regard to the rock art itself, it was recognised prior to fieldwork that, as it is highly weathered, its capacity for use in analyses relating to graphic form and so on was going to be somewhat limited for the majority of rock marks. Given the high degree of weathering, the majority of graphic marks are indeterminate in regard to form and, in many instances, marks are so weathered it is uncertain if they are graphic or gestural marks. Therefore, in order to utilise the rock art data to its maximum potential in these circumstances, a number of strategies have been devised to allow the recording of as much behavioural information related to the practice of rock art as possible, which does not solely reside in the mark form. These strategies are discussed below and they tie in with the objectives of this research, which is to explore the embodied and experiential use of the study area, and rock art as cultural practice.

Data collection has entailed attending to a wide range of different contextual and situational variables including environmental, topographic (and micro-topographic), locational, site morphology and other archaeological data sets, such as the presence or otherwise of grinding grooves, stone artefacts, etc. For sites included in the database that have not been re-recorded, this information has been extracted from site forms compiled by the IPG (and others), and reports produced by Caryll Sefton, which document the IPG surveys.

All field data were recorded on forms constructed specifically for the fieldwork. Certain aspects relating to rock art had not been previously recorded by the IPG—for example, rock pitting or rubbing, and the phenomenon of isomorphic congruence. These variables had nevertheless been listed on the recording form in the anticipation that these little recognised or otherwise ignored features of rock art may well be present. As fieldwork progressed, the recording form was modified to capture more efficiently and consistently the level of recording that was made at each site. A cue card prompt was used for the detailed visual inspection (and drawing) and recording of rock surfaces, so that each rock surface and each image could be analysed and recorded comparably and efficiently.

The variables recorded in rock shelters are set out below in three broad categories: geographic, locational and environmental; shelter; and rock mark.

5.3.1 Geographic, Locational and Environmental Variables

All sites documented are identified by their site name, which is usually abbreviated (e.g. Caddie 44 = C44). The maps used for fieldwork were the 1:25,000 topographic series produced by the Central Mapping Authority of New South Wales and included the following: Picton 9029-4-S (2nd ed.); Appin 9029-1-S (2nd ed.); Bargo 9029-3-N, (2nd ed.); Bulli 9029-2-N (2nd ed.); Avon River 9029-2-S (2nd ed.); Robertson 9028-4-N (2nd ed.) and Wollongong 9029-2-S (2nd ed.). This series of maps uses the Australian Geodetic Datum AGD66 coordinate system. The grid references for sites re-recorded during fieldwork have been obtained using a Hand Global Positioning System set to WGS84. These have subsequently been transformed to Geocentric Datum of Australia (GDA) coordinates for post-fieldwork Geographic Information System (GIS) mapping and analysis.

In this research, environmental and geographic contexts, both broadly conceived and at the site specific level, are viewed as being potentially informative of a range of constraints and/or opportunities and behaviours associated with Aboriginal occupation and experience. At the level of individual locales, natural features such as rock shelters are also both enabling and constraining of human experience given their individual size and morphological characteristics.

The reality of the physical world is such that human occupation, and certain cultural practices and behaviours, cannot be equivalent and always possible everywhere: 'environments constitute arenas of human action and being, they yield resources to be exploited, and they impose constraints and provide enabling conditions for practices' (Keen 2004:3). In Chapter 3, reference has been made to what is, in Australia, a general model of subsistence organisation—a collector model, whereby people in groups formed home bases, from which they made foraging forays and returned, for the sharing and distribution of food (Keen 2004:104). In this model, people make few residential moves, and those made are often to locales valued as much for the presence of water or firewood as they are for food (Keen 2004:104). Geographic and environmental data is used in this research for anticipating where in the landscape people may have habitually resided in base camp scenarios, and how the patterns in rock art location, and other places such as grinding groove sites, relate to those landforms.

Unlike, for example, Morwood (1980) and Rosenfeld (1982:215; 2002), who were able to identify social contexts relating to habitation and/or more restricted ritual contexts based on the presence or absence of informing archaeological materials (food grinding slabs and so on, which suggest a domestic context), in the study area there is very little additional archaeological material present in shelters that can be potentially informative of social context. Stone artefacts (flaked stone debris) and hatchet-grinding grooves are frequently found to be present in rock art shelters, and in those that contain sediment, as opposed to rock floors, it is almost certain that archaeological deposit would be present. However, inferring social context on the basis of the presence or absence of these is not straightforward. The presence of stone artefacts (in the absence of analysis that has been beyond the scope of this project) does not necessarily imply a domestic occupational context, nor for that matter does the presence of grinding grooves. Numerous shelters that do contain grinding grooves have either highly irregular rock floors or otherwise very limited optimal living space (see below), and, therefore, could simply not have functioned as an occupation site.

Given the limitations here for inferring social context archaeologically, it is the land and earth itself that is used to provide an informing context for the interpretation of different spheres of sociality. In this research, various analyses will explore whether or not there are correlations between the archaeological evidence and geographic and topographic location, and specific features of rock shelters. It is, however, recognised that inferences drawn about social context from any patterns that may emerge may not all be equally secure (Layton 1992:229). Nevertheless, the ethnography in Australia shows certain distribution patterns to be characteristic of certain cultural functions; given this, Layton (1992:229) argues that 'on the balance of probabilities, then, if different distributions occurred in the past, the cultural context was also different'. Geographic and environmental variables in this research therefore constitute a line of independent evidence for use in analyses to discriminate patterning. Specific aspects and attributes of these variables will also be evoked in some instances to infer experience and being, and, hence, to explain variability across space and time.

The following geographic and environmental variables were recorded for each site:

River catchment: The coarsest geographic level of site location has been classified according the major catchment in which it is situated—that is, the Avon, Cordeaux, Cataract or Upper Nepean rivers.

Stream order: Site locations are defined according to the stream order classification of the creek valleys in which they are situated. In the study area, first- and second-order streams form on either gentle crests or steep slopes. First- through to third-order streams are called headwater streams and constitute any waterways in the upper reaches of a watershed. As streams increase in size and strength, those that are classified as fourth- through to sixth-order are medium streams. Given that no streams are larger than fourth- or fifth-order, the *rivers* in the study area are actually medium-sized streams.

Landform: Variables utilised are based on standard terminology taken from the Australian Soil and Land Survey Field Handbook (R. McDonald et al. 1998), and are used in the analysis for the characterisation of fine-grained site locational attributes and other behavioural correlations. The following landform variables were recorded:

Morphological type:

- Crest: element that stands above all or almost all points in the adjacent terrain—smoothly convex upwards in downslope profile. The margin is at the limit of observed curvature.
- Simple slope: element adjacent below crest or flat and adjacent above a flat or depression.
- Open depression: element that stands below all or almost all points in the adjacent terrain.

The majority of slopes in the study area are simple slopes and do not strictly conform to the definition of Upper, Mid or Lower Slopes (cf. R. McDonald et al. 1998). However, for heuristic purposes, sites have been assigned an Upper, Mid or Lower Slope position, so as to allow explorations of fine-grained locational variability from an embodied perspective.

Thoroughfare: This variable is based on broad landform categories and includes Major Divide (watershed, e.g. between Avon and Nepean), Spur off Major Divide, Minor Divide (between major tributary streams in individual catchments and defined as being at least 5 kilometres long) and Spur off Minor Divide. These four attributes are used for exploring site location with reference to the notion of thoroughfare or human movement. Their categorisation is based on an assumption that people would have moved through the study area primarily via the crests of major landforms.

Slope class and value:

- Level – 0°20' average
- Very Gentle – 1° average
- Gentle – 3° average
- Moderate – 10° average
- Steep – 23° average

For the purposes of the analysis, the slope class attributes Level, Very Gentle and Gentle have been conflated into Low gradient, on the basis that from a human-embodied point of view, there is very little difference between the three categories. The Moderate and Steep categories, however, are considered to be potentially relevant, and are kept as separate attributes. Slope has been recorded for gradient located above and below a site. The study area is variable in terms of ease of human access and movement. Combined with other landform variables, such as slope position (i.e. Upper, Mid or Lower), and a consideration of the presence or absence of cliffs, or other obstacles, slope class provides an objective measurement of accessibility.

Accessibility: The variable of accessibility is a descriptive category relating to the physical ease, or otherwise, of approaching a site. It is very much a qualitative variable taking into consideration factors such as physical barriers (cliffs and gorges) and the general nature of the terrain. It is primarily based on rockiness and slope. For example, a site located on an upper slope of low or moderate gradient, without significant physical constraints, such a formidable rock outcrops, would be assessed as highly accessible. By comparison, a site located high in a cliff face, in a lower slope position, with access via steep, rocky slopes, is assessed as difficult level of accessibility.

Aspect: The cardinal point to which the site faces.

View: Closed = <100 m; Limited = <1000 m; Moderate = between 1000 and 5000 m; Broad >5000 m.

Distance to water: Two measurements of distance to water have been calculated: the first being distance to the closest water source irrespective of its stream order; and second, distance to a fourth-order water body. These variables have been recorded primarily for the purposes of considering site location within the broader landscape context, rather than for considering the availability of water for Aboriginal land users. While not everywhere the same, water is usually available at plateau level—that is, within lower order stream contexts. This means that in the study area water is generally readily available in those landforms, such as crests on divides and watersheds where human movement is most accessible.

Type of sandstone exposure: Shelters occur in Boulders or Clifflines, while open grinding groove sites occur in creek beds on horizontal exposures. Engraved rock art occurs both in open horizontal exposures and rock shelters.

5.3.2 Shelter Variables

A scale plan of each shelter has been drawn for two primary purposes: first, to enable an analysis of behavioural constraints and opportunities at sites such as the availability and size of living areas; and second, to enable analysis of the spatial placement of imagery within sites.

The following variables relating to shelter size and morphology were recorded:

Shelter space: The shelter dimensions recorded include measurements of length, height and depth.

Internal shape (geometry): The internal geometry of rock shelter sites in the study area is highly variable; however, it conforms to a set of generalised shape categories, as defined below. This variable, in conjunction with size measurements (height of ceiling and so on), is informative of the type of physical human activity that can take place at a site.

- Wedge: generally at least as deep as high, and with a horizontal or gently sloping floor and ceiling.
- Square: an internal space that is square in profile.
- Dome: a cavernous internal space with a dome-shaped ceiling.

Dome-, square- and wedge-shaped internal spaces provide actual shelter, although it may not be possible for an adult to stand, while the two categories listed below are shallow, vertical exposures with little or no actual shelter.

- Scallop: generally higher than the width, these sites are formed usually by cavernous weathering processes that expose a shallow cavity in a vertical rock surface.
- Open: generally higher than the width, these shelters are often simply high vertical rock surfaces that slope slightly outward with increased height.

Both shelter size and shape are likely to have governed a number of human behavioural responses, such as the numbers of people present at any one time, and whether or not the site could be utilised for shelter and/or camping.

Floor: Shelter floor variables are important for defining the nature of human use of shelters (see further below in regard to living space and optimal living space). The following type of shelter floors have been recorded:

- Primarily rock.
- Primarily sediment.
- Half-rock and half-sediment (approximate).

Living space area (measured in square metres): Living space area is the floor surface within a shelter that is assessed to be a 'living or working space'. This is the area of the shelter floor that is located behind the drip line. It is relatively dry and level, contains no significant rock and has a vertical space above the ground exceeding 1 metre (cf. Officer 1994:105).

Optimal living space area: Optimal living space area is defined as that part of the living space area containing predominantly sediment floor (cf. Officer 1994:105). In this sense, it is that area within a shelter in which people could comfortably sleep. This variable is considered to be informative of the different types of social activity and behaviour that may have occurred in rock shelters.

Level area adjacent to shelter: If an area of level ground is associated with the shelter, this is identified.

Location of shelter in respect of the ground level: Some shelters are located within cliffs and have a steep drop of c. 3 metres or more to the ground below. Sites such as these may well be indicative of a specific social context of use, and may also have both temporal and synchronic significance.

Rock surfaces: In order to analyse the spatial organisation of rock art within a shelter, individual art panels have been recorded. Panels have been defined as generally broad yet coherent spaces on walls, within concavities, ceilings or under ledges that have relatively clear boundaries. They have each been assigned a coded name. Basic measurements relating to area and height above ground have been recorded, as well as a description of the rock surface and weathering processes.

In addition, an attempt has been made to quantify the amount of art present on panels, as follows (cf. Officer 1994:105–106):

- Potential Art Surface Area (PASA) is that area of panels that is assessed to be suitable for art production.
- Surviving Art Surface Area (SASA) is that area of panels that contains art.
- Unassessable Surface Area (USA) is that area of a panel for which an assessment of whether or not art is present cannot be made, due to weathering.
- Available Surface with Existing Art (ASEA) is a percentage calculation taking into consideration PASA, SASA and USA. The calculation is: SASA divided by the product of the PASA minus the USA multiplied by 100.

This assessment provides an indication of the amount of art production undertaken at a shelter, and can be considered to be an important behavioural variable. However, it is acknowledged that the area estimates which form the basis of the ASEA calculation are problematic. For example, while measurements made in regard to PASA and SASA are relatively straightforward to quantify, estimating the USA, given the highly dynamic site formation processes of the Hawkesbury Sandstone, is difficult and inexact. The ASEA can be considered as indicative only.

Different resource zones in the study area have not been defined. As documented in Chapter 3, in general terms, floral and faunal resources are considered to be uniformly distributed across space. From the point of view of Aboriginal subsistence organisation, which is based on a collector model, it is also arguable that fine-grained explorations of discrete resource areas are not necessarily relevant, as people foraged widely from base camps. Furthermore, the value of base camp locales, as Keen (2004) argues, relates to the presence of water and firewood, both of which are present everywhere in the study area.

5.3.3 Archaeological Traits

In this research, 'rock marking' refers to all marks present on shelter surfaces, and includes graphics, non-graphic marks such as stencils, other non-graphic pigment marks, and non-graphic extractive marks such as pitted or rubbed areas. These different mark types each reflect different behavioural expressions, and so are recorded and analysed as separate categories of rock marking. The different rock mark categories are described below:

Graphic marks: Graphic marks are defined as those that are assessed to have been produced according 'to culturally regulated conventions of form' (Rosenfeld 1999).

Gestural marks: Gestural marks are defined as those that 'derive from a gestural system of expression' (Rosenfeld 1999) rather than from a structured and corporately mediated referential visual system. Two categories of gestural marks have been defined for this research: additive (non-graphic additions of pigment); and subtractive (non-graphic removal of the rock surface). These categories and sub-categories are defined below:

Gestural Marks—Additive

Stencils and prints: In her classificatory scheme for Australian rock art, Maynard (1977) classified stencilling as a mechanical technique, to distinguish it from that which is 'delineated' as created by drawing or painting. Later, Forge (1991) and Rosenfeld (1999) concluded that they are qualitatively different from a system of referential visual symbols that function in corporate processes of power negotiation. Forge argues that stencils are a different form of rock art, and separate to graphics, given that stencils are mechanically produced and not representational. This means that a stencil's form neither derives from, nor is mediated by, a cultural symbolic system. In this view, stencils are/were marks of individuals (Forge 1991:40).

While Forge (1991) was dismissive of the utility of stencils in rock art studies, considering their use to be a 'minor and common cultural fact', Rosenfeld (1999) makes the distinction between stencils and graphics for the purposes of providing greater analytical power in archaeological investigations of the ideational and societal context of rock art. She stresses the utility of treating gestural marks (inclusive of stencils) as separate analytical units, because they may relate to different facets of societal expression.

The following stencil and print variables have been defined:

- Colour: red, white, cream and black.
- Object: those classified in the study include human and animal, hand, feet and paws, and material objects.

Non-graphic pigment gestural marks are applications of pigment to a rock surface that do not conform to a visual system of structured and referential graphic marking. This category of mark has rarely been described in the Australian literature (however, see Smith & Rosenfeld 1992; Rosenfeld 1999). These marks possess traits indicating that they are simply applications, albeit deliberate, of pigment to a rock surface. In this study, marks that are classified as such include discrete blobs or smeared applications of wet pigment (Plate 5.1), and a variety of drawn, generally linear marks that often have been applied to natural features of the rock, such as concavities or slightly raised ridges (Plate 5.2).

Plate 5.1 Pigment blobs with stencils (rock shelter C39).

Source: Photograph by Julie Dibden, 2011.

Plate 5.2 Pigment marking: drawn non-graphic charcoal pigment marking (very faint) of the natural coloured lines in a hidden concavity (rock shelter SCR3).

Source: Photograph by Julie Dibden, 2011.

Plate 5.3 illustrates an example of what is defined as a drawn type of non-graphic pigment mark (circles). The example also highlights the problematic process of classifying the mark as being non-graphic given that within a highly heterogeneous and weathered body of art, such as that in the study area, the mark may well be representational. However, in this instance, this mark is considered to be of a different order to the representational rock art for a number of reasons, including that the drawing strongly reflects the geometry of the concavity and its internal features, rather than being an imposed formal arrangement of lines. Given that this mark is located in a 'hidden' location within a shelter, it suggests that the mark was an individualised expression, rather than one that is compliant and responsive to a corporate graphic system.

Plate 5.3 Drawn non-graphic charcoal pigment mark (rock shelter SCR3).
Source: Photograph by Julie Dibden, 2011.

In the study area, a number of different non-graphic pigment application forms have been identified. Given that they are each physically different forms of expressive behaviour, they have been categorised individually and include the following:

- Pigment circles: as implied, this category is expressed as circular applications of pigment that are always dry charcoal. They are frequently located in small concavities (Plate 5.3).
- Pigment marking: the application of pigment to specific natural features of the rock surfaces, such as raised ridges or edges.
- Pigment smear: thin smears of pigment.
- Pigment blobs: usually small and discrete, thick applications, which look occasionally as though they have been thrown onto the rock surface.
- Pigment strokes: usually repeated vertical, short lines of pigment.

Gestural Marks—Subtractive

Non-graphic subtractive gestural marks are the result of the removal of part of the rock surface and their appearance is governed entirely by mechanical processes (cf. Rosenfeld 1999; Taçon & Ouzman 2004:52). Rosenfeld (2002:73) refers to Central Australia, where rubbed patches bear witness to the practice of rubbing rock during ritual.

These marks have been classified in accordance with the method of rock removal into following categories:

> **Scratches:** Scratched rock surfaces are lightly scratched. It is noted that some graphics are also produced by light scratching. Given the shallow nature of both types of marks, distinguishing whether they are graphic or non-graphic is sometimes difficult; in such instances, marks are simply categorised as indeterminate.
>
> **Abraded (rubbed) patches** are smooth areas of the rock surface and are always present on vertical walls. Their broad area, extremely shallow nature and location are suggestive that they are produced for non-utilitarian purposes. They are generally associated with graphic imagery. Numerous instances of abraded and pitted rock surfaces, created within a ceremonial context, are reported in Mountford (1976) (see also Rosenfeld 1999).
>
> **Pitted rock surfaces** are always located on vertical surfaces and are generally associated with graphic imagery. These are lightly pitted features. This definition differs somewhat from that defined by Rosenfeld (1999), who described actual 'pits', which it is assumed are small, discrete depressions. Instead, in this study, the pitted surface category actually fits more readily with Rosenfeld's (1999) 'battered rock ridges' category.
>
> **Bashed edges:** Battered ridges entail the deliberate removal of the edges of generally thin rock, which is often the edge of a case-hardened surface. This category fits closely with Rosenfeld's 'flaked rock' category. However, given the implication of the appearance of negative flake scars (which are not present), this is not appropriate as a classification in this study.

5.3.4 Locational Variables

The location of imagery and marks within a shelter is behaviourally determined, i.e. it is considered that the location was chosen, presumably accordingly to a limited number of conditions, some of which may have been socially sanctioned, and others of which may have been materially determined. A number of variables relating to the physical situation of a mark within a shelter have been recorded as defined below:

General location: The following attributes in this category are possible: Wall, Ceiling and Concavity.

Visibility: Open = i.e. clearly visible; Moderate = for the image to be seen one is required to kneel down or perform some similar bodily contortion; Hidden = images that are located in concealed locations, such as below very low ledges or ceilings, or behind vertical projections.

Height above the floor: Height of the bottom of an image as measured from the floor. Given that the majority of rock art in the study area is located on surfaces adjacent to rock floors, this measurement has some relative relationship to the artist. However, in those instances where the art is adjacent to a sediment floor that may have increased in height over time, this relationship cannot be directly inferred to have been relevant at all times of shelter use.

Isomorphic congruence: This variable refers to whether or not a pigment mark, graphic or non-graphic is formally congruent with natural features of the rock surface. For example, the relationship between the mark shown in Plate 5.3 and the natural morphology of the rock is identified as being one of isomorphic congruence.

Spatial association: This variable describes the spatial physical relationship of an image with other images across a rock surface face. It attempts to address whether an image is a part of a composition. If an image has no justifiable spatial relationship with another, it is simply assigned a 'No attribute'. However, if a relationship is inferred, this is defined according to the basis on which the inference is made, including if the image is adjacent to one or more other images that are of the same schema, or are otherwise in a composition that appears related by proximity and/ or surface geometry.

Superimposition association: This variable describes the superimposition relationship of an image with other images on a rock surface. While this variable is important for temporal ordering of imagery, it is also an indicator of other behavioural actions that may or may not have a time-based significance. The possible attributes in this category are: Above, Below, Indeterminate or No.

Gesturally marked: This variable refers to whether or not an image has been marked with either a pigment (this is frequently by a stencil) or by non-pigment gesture such as, for example, pitting. The mode of gestural marking is recorded.

Re-marked: This variable refers to older images that have been subsequently redrawn.

Imagery was recorded in the field by drawing (and annotation) and photography. Given that a goal of this research is to discriminate graphic variability at a high level of analytical resolution, the imagery was recorded in such a way as to enable further detailed graphic analysis to be undertaken off-site. Accordingly, fieldwork aimed to record in detail all graphic marks, and any other relevant material expressions of behaviour such as gestural marks, rather than simply recording numbers of motif types, etc. The primary recording technique involved detailed scrutiny of the rock surfaces, and then the sketching onto art paper all observable marks. Additionally, a note was made of relevant graphic, taphonomic and locational information. The aim of the photography was to have a more accurate visual recording of the imagery, and spatial relationships with other imagery and the rock surfaces, so as to assist in the later analysis. Photographs included both the shelter itself, rock art panels and details of the imagery.

5.3.5 Post-Fieldwork Data Treatment

A Microsoft Access database has been built for data storage and management. The database is comprised of linked nested forms. Four forms have been constructed as defined below.

Site data includes summary locational, environmental and basic contents data for all sites used in the analysis. Site data includes data retrieved from both the IPG site forms (for sites not re-recorded) and data from 110 rock shelters recorded during fieldwork (total n = 810 sites). The variables and associated attribute options in the Site Database are listed below in Table 5.1.

Shelter data includes all observations recorded in regard to shelter morphology. The shelter data entered in this form is based only on those sites recorded (n = 110) for this research, given that a number of the variables have not been included in previous site recordings. The variables and associated attribute options in the Shelter Database are listed below in Table 5.2.

Table 5.1 Site data variables and attributes.

Variable	Attribute
Site name	As per IPG naming system, or that of another recorder
Re-recorded	Yes or No
Easting (AGD)	As per GPS
Northing (AGD)	As per GPS
Catchment	Avon, Cordeaux, Cataract or Nepean
Catchment area	Upper, Mid, Lower, and East or West of river
Creek	As per named creeks or code assigned
Stream order	1, 2, 3 or 4
Broad landform	Divide, Ridge or Spur
Small-scale landform	Crest, Simple Slope or Drainage Depression
Slope element	Upper, Mid or Lower
Distance to third-order stream	In metres
Aspect	N, NE, E, SE, S, SW, W, NW or open
Gradient above site	Low, Moderate or Steep
Gradient below site	Low, Moderate or Steep
Distance of view (approximate)	Metres
Travel route	Major Watershed Divide (between catchments), Minor Divide (within individual catchments), Spur off Major Divide, Spur off Minor Divide
AHD	Australian Height Datum
Context	Shelter or Open
Graphics	Present: Yes or Absent: No
Black graphics	Present: Yes or Absent: No
Red painted graphics	Present: Yes or Absent: No
Red drawn graphics (according to Ford [2006], these may actually be painted; they appear different from those above)	Present: Yes or Absent: No
Red-and-black graphics	Present: Yes or Absent: No
White graphics	Present: Yes or Absent: No
Other coloured graphics (includes scratched)	Present: Yes or Absent: No
Engraved graphics	Present: Yes or Absent: No
Red stencils	Present: Yes or Absent: No
White (includes cream) stencils	Present: Yes or Absent: No
Black stencils	Present: Yes or Absent: No
Handprints (red only)	Present: Yes or Absent: No
Non-graphic pigment rock marking (pigment blobs, etc.)	Present: Yes or Absent: No
Gestural rock marking: additive (i.e. added non-graphic pigment)	Present: Yes or Absent: No
Gestural rock marking: subtractive (i.e. pitted or ribbed rock surface)	Present: Yes or Absent: No
Total number of rock markings (not including grinding grooves)	Quantified i.e. counts
Grinding grooves	Quantified i.e. counts
Stone artefacts	Present: Yes or Absent: No
Cache (artefacts)	Present: Yes or Absent: No
Shell	Present: Yes or Absent: No
Engraved groove channels	Present: Yes or Absent: No
Quarry (flaked pebbles in bedrock)	Present: Yes or Absent: No
Temporal	1 = One Temporal Phase, 2 = Two Temporal Phases

Source: Table reproduced from Dibden (2011).

Table 5.2 Shelter data variables and attributes.

Variable	Attribute
Length	Metres
Height	Metres
Width	Metres
Volume	Cubic metres
Floor area	Square meters
Optimal living area	Square meters
Shelter shape	As defined previously
Level in front of shelter	Present: Yes or Absent: No
Floor composition	Primarily Sock, Primarily Sediment, Mixed Rock and Sediment (c. half and half)
Moisture regime	Dry, Wet, Mixed
SASA	Percentage
PASA	Square metres
Shelter above ground level > c. 3 metres above ground	Yes or No
Location of rock art vis-à-vis optimal living space	Adjacent Wall, Adjacent Ceiling, Adjacent Wall and Ceiling, Away, Not Applicable

Source: Table reproduced from Dibden (2011).

Mark location: All marks recorded in shelters have been given a unique location identifier. This identifier is numeric data simply 1–2,423. The purpose of giving each mark a locational identifier in a separate form in the database is to facilitate analysis of superimpositioning. For a mark not in a superimposed relationship with another, it will be the only mark in a specific mark location. Alternatively, mark locations, which contain superimposed marks, will contain two or more marks. The position of each mark within a layer or superimposed relationship is defined in the Mark Data form. Each mark location is also defined according to its location within the micro-topography of the rock shelter. The categories include wall, ceiling and concavity.

Mark data: Mark data includes all observations recorded in regard to the motifs and other marks in shelters recorded during fieldwork. The variables and associated attribute options in the Mark Database are listed below in Table 5.3.

Table 5.3 Mark data variables and attributes.

Variable	Attribute
Mark ID (unique identifier number in database)	Numbers are sequential and range from 1–2,565
Mark ID (unique identifier number in individual rock shelter)	Numbers are sequential and range from 1–206. The purpose of assigning a shelter mark ID is simply to allow reference back to original recordings (drawings, photos and notes)
Layer (numeric position in relation to its superimposed association or otherwise in a mark location [as defined above])	Layers are numeric and range from 1–4. A mark that is either a single mark in a mark location (i.e. NOT superimposed), or at the bottom in a superimposed relationship, is assigned the value 1; a value of 2 is ascribed to a mark that is above the mark that is layer 1, and so on.
Mark type	Indeterminate (i.e. cannot distinguish between graphic or gestural mark categories) Graphic Gestural Additive: stencil, print, pigment blob, pigment circles, pigment marking, pigment smear, pigments strokes, pigment random Gestural Subtractive: non-graphic scratching, rubbing, pitting, and ridge bashing

Variable	Attribute
Height above floor	Millimetres
Isomorphic congruence	Yes or No
Colour	Black, red, white, cream, yellow, crimson, brown, orange, scratch, black and white, black and yellow, black and red, black, red and white, and Not Applicable (i.e. for pitting)
Technique	Indeterminate, Dry Pigment Application, Wet Pigment Application, Scratched, and Not Applicable
Size (area)	Square millimetres
Notation (relevant to graphics only)	Indeterminate, Outline, Outline, and Infill, Solid and Line
Boundedness (relevant to graphics only)	Indeterminate, Bounded, Unbounded, Not Applicable (i.e. for stencils)
Completeness (relevant to graphics only)	Indeterminate, Complete, Incomplete, Part Complete, and Not Applicable
Symmetry (relevant to graphics only)	Indeterminate, Symmetrical, Asymmetrical, Part Symmetrical, and Not Applicable
Complexity (relevant to graphics only)	Counts of components to graphic
Association: spatial	No Obvious Association, or Indeterminate, Part of a Composition (i.e. cluster of stencils in discrete area), Same Schema, and Not applicable
Association: temporal	No Obvious Association, or Indeterminate, Below, and Above
Remarked	Indeterminate, Yes and No
Gesturally marked	No, or Pitted, Rubbed, Scratched, Stencil, Pigment blob, and Pigment Marked (non-graphic)
Infill	Indeterminate, Not Applicable, Complex, Cross-Hatch, Diamond, Diagonal Line, Lines Perpendicular, Lines Longitudinal, 'V' Lines, Solid, Zig Zag, Random
Model	Indeterminate, Unknown, Human, Imaginary Anthropomorph, Female Anthropomorph, Male Anthropomorph, Human (Life-like), Bird, ?Cow, ?Horse, Unknown Animal With Joey, Dog, Echidna, Fish, Glider, Wombat, Tortoise, Snake, Marsupial (Other), Macropod, Lizard, Koala, and Not Applicable
Motif code	A total of 265 possible—see Appendix 3 in Dibden (2011)
Orientation	Indeterminate, Horizontal, Diagonal, Vertical, Not Applicable
Stance	Indeterminate, Action, Formal, Not Applicable
Visibility	Open (i.e. visible when standing), Moderate, Hidden

Source: Table reproduced from Dibden (2011).

All rock art marks, irrespective of whether they are graphic or gestural, have been classified via a coded system (Dibden 2011:Appendix 3), in order to explore analytically their abundance, preferential location and diversity. The classification developed for coding the graphic rock art has sought to discriminate the formal variability that it possesses at a fine-grained level. In essence, each formally distinct graphic is coded by number. The formulation of the code has been focused on capturing like or very similar graphic forms, and the exercise has negotiated a path somewhere between distinguishing diversity yet avoiding undue splitting. Graphic coding, in this way, is expected to be useful in investigating issues such as diversity within and between different temporal phases, and whether individual graphic forms are located within one or more of these phases.

6

Database Profile

This chapter provides a broad overview of the locational distribution of rock markings within the study area and considers what these patterns may indicate in respect of occupation, land use and sociocultural context. A summary of the database is presented, and the different types of site contexts and rock markings are quantified. The overall structure of the database in terms of site context, distribution and density is outlined first. The context of each site and the nature and distribution of their rock markings are then examined to identify variability and trends in spatial distribution. These patterns will be used to inform the analyses of temporal and spatial variability in rock art, presented in later chapters.

6.1 The Database

A total of 810 sites are in the Site Database, which includes data from the Illawarra Prehistory Group Database (IPG/DB) and the Research Database (R/DB). A summary of the different site contexts, their catchment location and frequency are shown in Table 6.1. The major site context in the database is rock shelters (n = 627; 77.4%). Open contexts account for 183 (22.6%) of the total site count. The Cataract contains the highest site count; the Nepean, the lowest. The difference in the density of sites in each catchment is explored below. Site density differences may reflect varying levels of occupation and land use.

Table 6.1 Number and percentage of site contexts (open or shelter) by river catchment (compiled from IPG/DB and R/DB).

Catchment	Open	Shelter	Total per catchment	Percentage per catchment
Cataract _Area: 207 sq km_	90	194	284	35.1
Cordeaux _Area: 165 sq km_	37	127	164	20.3
Avon _Area: 173 sq km_	32	171	203	25.1
Nepean _Area: 246 sq km_	24	135	159	19.6
Total _Area: 791 sq km_	183	627	810	100
Total contexts (%)	22.6	77.4	100	

Source: Table reproduced from Dibden (2011).

The total study area covers c. 791 square kilometres and the average site density in the Upper Nepean catchment is 1.02 sites per square kilometre. The site density for each catchment is listed below:

- Cataract: 1.37 sites per square kilometre
- Cordeaux: 1 site per square kilometre
- Avon: 1.17 sites per square kilometre
- Nepean: 0.64 sites per square kilometre

The Cataract contains the highest site frequency and the highest overall site density. Likewise, the Nepean contains the lowest site frequency and the lowest overall site density. The Cordeaux and Avon each contain comparable sites densities, which are slightly lower than the Cataract but considerably higher than the Nepean. This pattern of decreasing site density from north to south is a continuation of the density patterns between the Georges/Woronora and Cataract rivers identified previously by Sefton (1988). Site density will be examined further in respect of specific site types and the abundance of their various traits.

6.2 Open Site Contexts

As indicated, open site contexts account for 22.6 per cent of the total site count in the database. All open sites except one (EC12) contain grinding grooves. Of the 182 sites with grinding grooves (see Plate 1.8), 11 contain engraved groove channels (described below) and five have engraved rock art. In the following sections, grinding groove sites will be examined first and then open sites with engraved groove channels and engraved rock art.

6.2.1 Grinding Groove Sites

Grinding groove sites form a significant component of the archaeological record within the Upper Nepean catchment. Here, as in Attenbrow's Upper Mangrove Creek study (2004:148), they are regarded as indicators of Aboriginal land use. The grinding groove data are used to examine, amongst other aspects of social life and subsistence, spatial variability with regard to the nature of Aboriginal occupation and land use. Patterns in the variable distribution of grinding groove sites in respect of topography have been observed elsewhere in the Sydney Basin. Attenbrow (2004) found that these sites were generally restricted to ridge landforms. Sefton (1988:54) also found that grinding groove sites on the northern Woronora Plateau were most frequently located at or near plateau level.

Grinding groove sites have a range of different groove counts. It is expected that by exploring count variability, correlated with environmental location, information might be gleaned regarding the foci of occupation and land use and this may be broadly informative of sociocultural context. Here the distribution of these sites and their variable groove counts is examined in respect of a number of geographic and environmental variables. First, the nature of these sites, their estimated antiquity and other matters relevant to this research are discussed.

Grinding groove sites contain grooves in rock surfaces that are produced through the shaping and/or sharpening of ground-edge stone hatchet heads (Attenbrow 2004). Groove size and morphology is known to be variable in the broader Sydney Basin, which suggests that they can result from the sharpening of a variety of different tools, and the preparation of food (Attenbrow 2004:43). In the study area, groove dimensions indicate that all are hatchet-grinding grooves.

A broad temporal framework for the age of grinding groove sites can be inferred on the basis of the age of ground-edge hatchet heads found within archaeological deposits. Across Australia, there is significant variation in the timing of the introduction of ground-edge hatchet technology and, in the south-east, the earliest hatchet heads date to the fourth millennium BP (Dibden 1996:35; Attenbrow 2004:241), and no earlier than 3,500 years ago (Hiscock 2008:155). The Pleistocene age of ground-edge hatchets elsewhere in Australia is well established (Morwood & Trezise 1989:78; Clarkson et al. 2015; Hiscock et al. 2016). Kamminga (1982:103) states that their later appearance into south-east Australia can be understood as the introduction of a pre-existing technology into new areas. At the southern margins of the Sydney Basin, hatchet heads found in excavated sites date to the last 3,000 years (Bowdler 1970; Lampert 1971; Flood 1980; Boot 1994:334). Using these dates and evidence from further north, it is suggested that grinding groove sites in the study area can be no older than 3,500 years. Given that hatchets were still used at the time of European occupation, the use of some grinding groove sites may have spanned this temporal range.

Morwood and Trezise (1989:85) suggest that the introduction of new technologies, such as ground-edge tools, in southern Australia acted to increase extractive efficiency and was adopted as a response to increased demands placed on regional production systems, due to population increase. According to Attenbrow (2004:241), the introduction of ground-edge technology in the Sydney Basin in the fourth millennium BP coincides with changes in climate that saw the advance of colder and drier conditions. She suggests that ground-edge implements may have been a part of risk minimisation strategies adopted for negotiating changes in vegetation and faunal communities associated with environmental fluctuation. In the Sydney Basin, there was a further change in the second and first millennia BP when a diversification in subsistence methods using ground-edge implements occurred (Attenbrow 2004:241; McDonald 2008a). Based on the presence of hatchet heads and fragments of ground edges in dated assemblages, Attenbrow (2004:223) argues that while grinding groove sites in the Upper Mangrove Creek catchment were used during the past 4,000 years, they were perhaps more commonly produced in the last 2,000 years. It is reasonable to assume that grinding groove sites in the study area may also have been used with greater frequency in the past 2,000 years.

It is well recognised that ground-edge stone hatchets played a significant role in Aboriginal subsistence activities (Sharp 1952:69; Binns & McBryde 1972:1; Dickson 1978:19, 35; Giopoulos 1986:2). Hatchets were used for a range of utilitarian purposes and functioned as a general multi-purpose tool (Dickson 1978:35).

While grinding grooves were formed as the result of specific technological activity and can be considered functional expressions of behaviour, they also have the potential to be informative of social aspects of life. Given the central importance of ground-edge implements in the economic life of Aboriginal people during the late Holocene, it is considered here that the location of grinding groove sites, particularly those with large groove counts, is potentially informative about areas in the Upper Nepean catchment that were habitually utilised within a specific social context. Whether or not that related to an exclusively gendered domain, general domestic space or some other mode is, however, unknown. It is also considered that grinding groove sites may have been imbued with cultural meaning and significance entirely independent of their functional context. This is plausible given that hatchets feature in the rock art of the Sydney Basin, as pigment and engraved graphics, and stencils, from which can be inferred the suggestion of their sociocultural meaningfulness.

It is well documented that in historic times, some stone hatchet heads were imbued with a high culturally constituted value and significance and that they featured as prestige items in formal contexts of gift exchange in the south-east (Sharp 1952; McBryde & Harrison 1981; McBryde 1984; Dibden 1996). An ethnographic study of the Yir Yoront in northern Queensland revealed that hatchet exchange was mediated by kinship structure and thus played a social role in generalising and standardising interpersonal relationships (Sharp 1952). Sharp also argues that hatchets in that area were imbued with masculine symbology.

Both men and women used hatchets, but the literature emphasises that they were most commonly men's tools. When not in use, hatchets were worn tucked in men's belts (Dickson 1978:19, 30). Hatchets can be considered to have been a form of material culture physically associated with the bodily appearance of men. It is feasible to consider that hatchets may have been gendered objects and that they could potentially have encoded information relating to, amongst other things, social identity, age, status and differing degrees of ritual knowledge. An analysis of hatchets from south-eastern New South Wales, including a number from the study area and adjacent coastal plain, established that they exhibit stylistic variability, which may indeed signify that they were used in strategies relating to the negotiation of social identity (Dibden 1996).

Grinding hatchet heads on stone can result in the formation of grinding grooves, which, similar to rock art, creates indelible marks on the rock surface and land. Grinding groove sites may have become significant and meaningful locales over time given their reference to an important item of material culture and their strong material presence in the landscape. Sites containing high groove counts are now visually significant marked locales. While the original motivation that led people to choose to grind hatchet heads at a specific place is now not understood, it is possible over time and, as places became increasingly embellished with grooves, that the meaning and significance of that locale was correspondingly changed. Grinding groove sites may have provided a physical and conceptual reference to the ancestral past and activities of previous generations. Because of the enduring physicality of grinding groove sites, they may have been meaningfully constituted expressions of place and mnemonic of past events and personal and group history (cf. Peterson 1972:16). This notion is explored further in later chapters.

A total of 182 grinding groove sites are distributed across the study area and 2,015 grooves occur in these (Dibden 2011:Appendix 4). A small number of grinding groove sites contain other rock markings in the form of engraved rock art and engraved groove channels. These additional traits will be discussed further below.

The Cataract has almost half of all open grinding groove sites (n = 90; 49.5%) and more than half of the grinding grooves (n = 1,086; 53.9%). The Avon and Cordeaux catchments contain similar numbers of sites; however, the Cordeaux contains markedly more grooves than the Avon. The Nepean contains relatively low site (13%) and groove counts (11%). The difference in the density of site numbers and groove counts between each catchment is explored further below.

The open context grinding groove site density in the entire study area is 0.2 sites per square kilometre and average grinding groove density is 2.5 grooves per square kilometre. The grinding groove site and groove density in each catchment is as follows:

- Cataract: 0.4 sites per square kilometre; grinding groove density is 5.2 per square kilometre.
- Cordeaux: 0.2 sites per square kilometre; grinding groove density is 2.6 per square kilometre.
- Avon: 0.18 sites per square kilometre; grinding groove density is 1.6 per square kilometre.
- Nepean: 0.1 sites per square kilometre; grinding groove density is 0.1 per square kilometre.

Grinding groove site and groove densities diminish from north to south. The Cataract contains the highest grinding groove density and the Nepean contains the lowest overall site and groove density. The Cordeaux and Avon contain similar site densities as each other, but the Cordeaux contains the highest groove density. There is a strong correspondence between the open grinding groove site numbers and densities in each of the catchments and the overall site frequencies and densities as outlined previously in Section 6.1.

In all catchments, the minimum groove count per site is one. The maximum number of grooves per site differs, with the Avon possessing the lowest maximum count of 41 grooves per site and the Cordeaux having the highest count of 92. The average groove count per site is 11.1. The majority of sites in all catchments possess low numbers of groove counts. The most frequently occurring groove count per site (mode) for all catchments is one and the overall median is five. Sixteen sites only possess groove counts of 31 or more. Approximately 70 per cent of open context grinding groove sites have 10 or less grooves.

The sites containing higher groove counts are predominantly located in the north-east sector of the study area (Figure 6.1). Large grinding groove sites occur on, or within very close proximity to, the main watershed divides and ridge crest landforms. As suggested in Chapter 2, these landforms are potentially areas habitually used for domestic occupation and movement through country.

A total of 129 sites have 10 or less grinding grooves. Most sites contain very low grinding groove counts, and the pattern of decreasing sites counts with higher numbers of grooves is a general trend. Almost 45 per cent of sites with 10 grooves or less possess one or two grooves only. This suggests that the majority of grinding groove activity is generally ad hoc, is expedient and not spatially focused. By comparison, those with large groove counts can be considered to reflect repeated and intensive use, albeit possibly over a long period of time, and this suggests that they have been produced as a result of a strong spatially focalised motivation.

The following analyses explore the distribution of these sites in accordance with a number of environmental variables. The majority of sites are located in upper valley slope contexts (n = 152; 84%). All sites with groove counts of 21 or more are located in upper valleys.

The majority of grinding groove sites are located in areas corresponding to the main thoroughfares in the study area (n = 146; 80%): the Major Divides, Spurs off Major Divides and Minor Divide landforms. Fewer sites are located on Spurs off Minor Divides, which are generally landforms located in the interior. The larger sites are located in upper valley slopes and on landforms corresponding to the main thoroughfares.

The majority of grinding groove sites (n = 171; 93%) are located in first- and second-order stream contexts. This is not surprising, given that most of these lower order streams are located on the upper valley slopes. Far fewer sites are in third- and fourth-order streams. The sites containing high grinding groove numbers (>10) are *all* located in first- and second-order stream contexts.

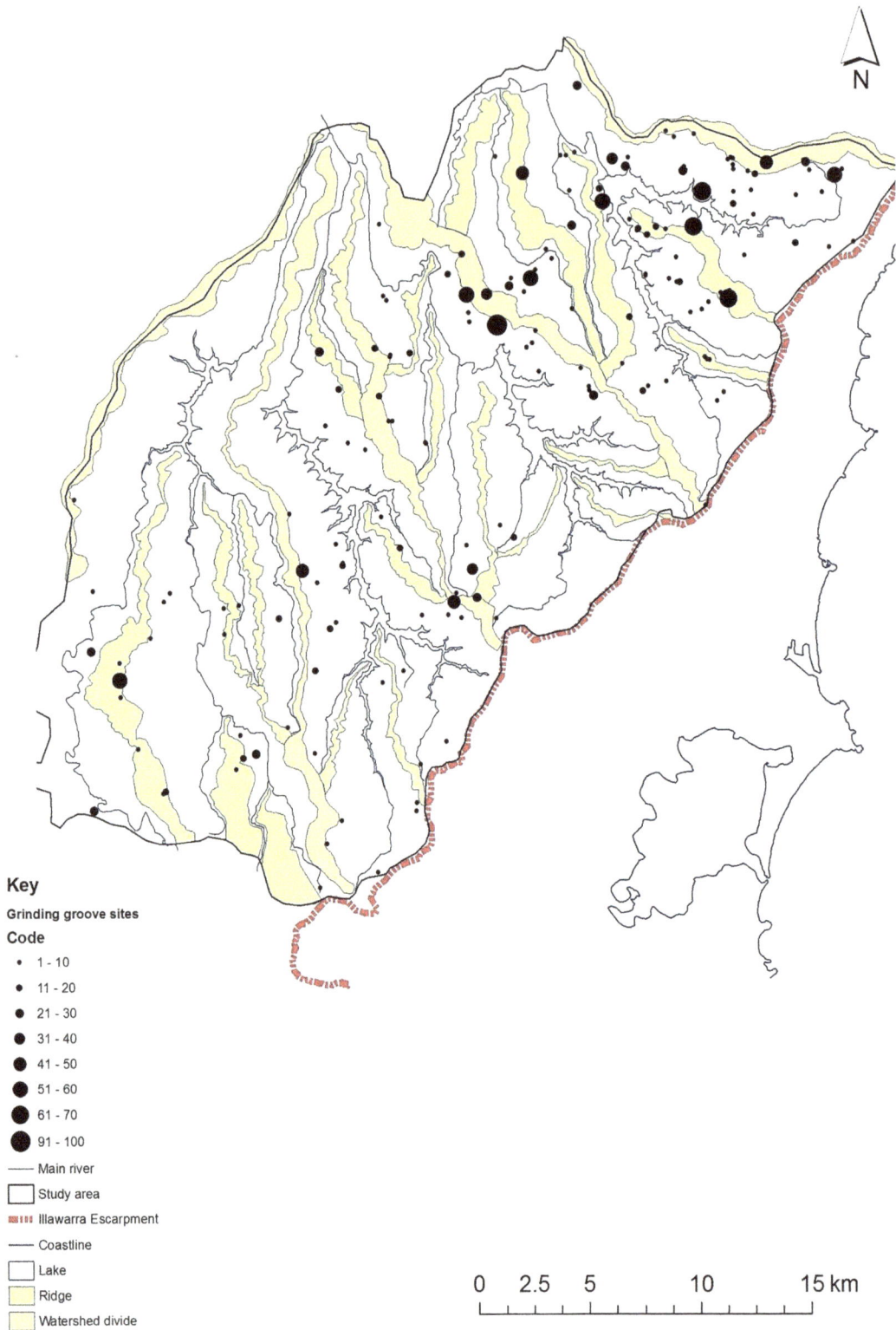

Key

Grinding groove sites
Code
- · 1 - 10
- · 11 - 20
- • 21 - 30
- ● 31 - 40
- ● 41 - 50
- ● 51 - 60
- ● 61 - 70
- ● 91 - 100
- —— Main river
- ☐ Study area
- ▰▰▰ Illawarra Escarpment
- —— Coastline
- ☐ Lake
- ☐ Ridge
- ☐ Watershed divide

0   2.5   5   10   15 km

Figure 6.1 Location of size coded (as per grinding groove counts) open context grinding groove sites.

Source: Map reproduced from Dibden (2011).

6.2.2 Engraved Groove Channels

Engraved groove channels form a very minor component of the archaeological record in the study area (Table 6.2). Their function is uncertain, and it is not known whether they served a utilitarian purpose or otherwise. Despite their rarity and uncertainty in regard to function, they are a significant material and visual component of open context sites (Plate 1.8). Engraved groove channels occur across the Sydney Basin (Sefton 1988:65). While their function is occasionally surmised, they have not been the subject of a specific study and analysis. Sefton (1988:65) suggests that they appear to be functional, acting to control water flow around potholes. However, more often than not (94 per cent of sites), grinding groove sites do not possess engraved groove channels, and so a purely utilitarian purpose is questionable. It is beyond the scope of this research to conduct a detailed analysis of engraved groove channels. However, their distribution will be examined in respect of their relationship with other rock marks, and a number of geographic and environmental variables.

Engraved groove channels are linear (usually longer than 1 metre), narrow (c. 3 centimetres wide), shallow (c. 2 centimetres deep), incised or pecked into open rock platforms. Engraved groove channels can be relatively straight or sinuously curved. Although most groove sites do not have channels, when they are found, channels are typically at groove sites rather than in isolation; they can also occur with engraved rock art. They are usually in sites that have large numbers of grinding grooves. The age of engraved groove channels in the Sydney Basin is unknown. Given their association with grinding grooves, they may be of a comparable age range and antiquity.

Table 6.2 Summary description of sites with engraved groove channels (description as per IPG Site Cards).

Site	Catchment	Stream order	Graphics	Grinding grooves (gg)	Engraved groove channels (egc)
BMS1	Cataract	1	Yes	68	1 egc
C29	Avon	1	No	17	1 'L' shaped egc, which diverts water to ggs & away from pothole
C41	Avon	2	No	1	1 egc from 1 pothole to another
DCC28	Cordeaux	1	No	1	1 egc around pothole; gg below pothole
EC2	Cordeaux	1	Yes	26	1 egc keeping seepage out of a pothole
Gill51	Cataract	1	No	54	1 egc extending from a small pothole diverting water past a large pothole
Lod31	Cataract	1	No	30	1 egc with pick marks visible; 1 egc extending from gg
Lod5	Cataract	1	No	45	1 egc at top of shallow pothole
T1	Cordeaux	1	No	59	1 egc diverting water from main water flow to side of the site
UA3	Avon	1	No	41	1 egc extends from a grinding groove in an alignment with water flow
Wall15	Cataract	1	No	52	2 egcs

Source: Table reproduced from Dibden (2011).

A total of 12 engraved groove channels are present in 11 open sites in the study area. Most sites contain one engraved groove channel only. The Cataract contains the highest count (n = 5). The Avon and Cordeaux contain three and there are none in the Nepean. The majority are associated with relatively large numbers of grinding grooves. All engraved groove channels are located in upper valley slope contexts, and all but one is located within first-order streams. The majority of sites (n = 9) are situated on main thoroughfares in the study area (Figure 6.2). It is evident that engraved groove channels are patterned preferentially in regard to topographic variables. This feature of their environmental context is shared with large grinding groove sites and engraved rock art.

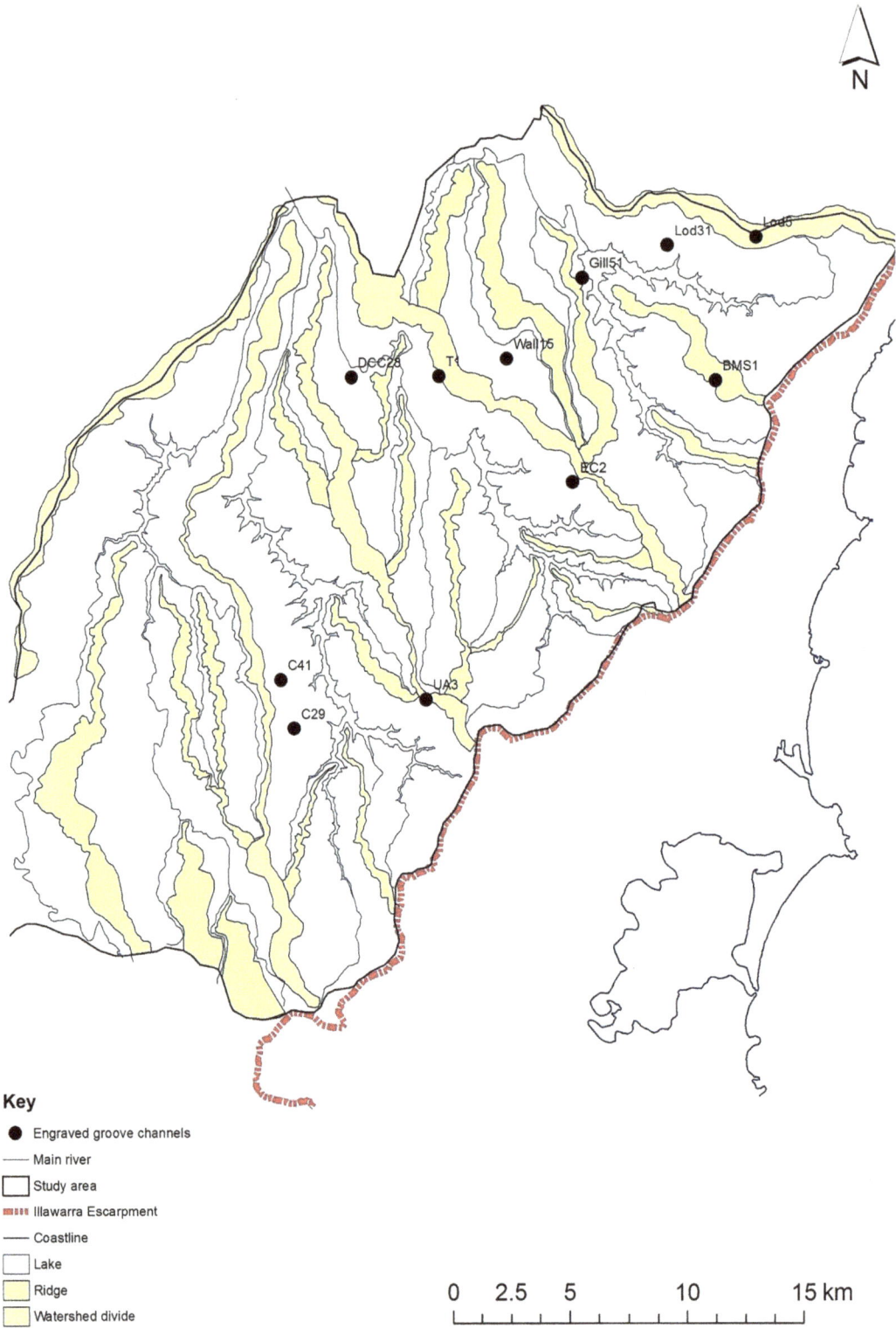

Key

- ● Engraved groove channels
- —— Main river
- ☐ Study area
- ▰▰▰ Illawarra Escarpment
- —— Coastline
- ☐ Lake
- ☐ Ridge
- ☐ Watershed divide

0   2.5   5   10   15 km

Figure 6.2 Location of sites with engraved groove channels.

Source: Map reproduced from Dibden (2011).

6.2.3 Engraved Rock Art

The open context engraved rock art on the Woronora Plateau consists of pecked and abraded motifs of tracks, symbols, human figures, fish and macropods (Sefton 2003a:9), and is formally consistent with the regional Sydney–Hawkesbury engraving style (cf. McMah 1965; Attenbrow 2002:146; Sefton 2003a:9; McDonald 2008a). Engraved imagery is believed to have been produced by 'conjoined-puncturing', whereby a series of pits (measuring up to 3 centimetres in diameter and up to 1 centimetre deep) have been punctured into the bedrock; pits can overlap to form a continuous groove or may remain unjoined (Clegg 1985). In some instances, pits have been subsequently abraded. The objects used to create engraved graphics are unknown but may have included stone, shell, bone, wood and hatchet heads (Attenbrow 2002:147).

Approximately 50 open engraved rock art sites are on the Woronora Plateau. Sefton (1988:63) describes 22 of these in her study, and notes their restricted distribution within 11 kilometres of the coast. McDonald (1994:331) analysed 717 open engraved sites possessing 7,904 motifs in the wider Sydney Basin. South of the Georges River, engraved rock art sites were found to decline in both number and assemblage size (McDonald 1994:333).

The antiquity of the Sydney–Hawkesbury engraved rock art is not known, although it is certain that some engraved imagery was produced during the early period of European occupation (Edwards 1971:361; Attenbrow 2002:150). McDonald (2008a) argues that they date from the early Bondaian because of their stylistic similarity with shelter pigment art, but that the majority may have been produced within the last 1,000 years. Sefton (2003a) also argues that on the basis of weathering processes, they cannot be very old.

Of the Upper Nepean's six open context sites containing engraved imagery: five contain one image and the other contains four (Dibden 2011:Appendix 5). These sites are located in the Cataract and Cordeaux and in the north-eastern corner of the study area, and none are located more than 11 kilometres from the coast (Table 6.3). This pattern conforms to the one Sefton (1988) identified. The decline in site numbers and density south of the Georges River, as identified by McDonald (2008a), continues southward across the Woronora Plateau. The most southerly occurrence of the Sydney Basin open context engraved rock art (EC2 and EC12) is at the mid/ eastern end of the Cordeaux/Cataract divide (Figure 6.3).

Table 6.3 Description of engraved rock art in open contexts (per IPG Site Cards).

Name	Location	Motif description and associations
EC2	Cordeaux	One engraving, described by the IPG as a female symbol: an engraved circle with a central pit. 26 grinding grooves and one engraved groove channel.
EC12	Cordeaux	One whale motif.
BC3	Cataract	One macropod motif; one grinding groove.
BC4	Cataract	One emu motif; 12 grinding grooves.
BMS1	Cataract	Four motifs described as male and female symbols; 68 grinding grooves and one engraved groove channel.
Lod47	Cataract	One female with an axe in her right hand, with headdress, a waistband, one left breast and 'clear female symbol at fork of legs'; 10 grinding grooves.

Source: Table reproduced from Dibden (2011).

As with large grinding groove sites and engraved groove channels, engraved rock art exhibits strong patterning in relation to environmental variables. All are located on thoroughfares on major watershed or minor divide landforms. All engraved rock art is found on upper slope and crest landforms, and in first-order stream contexts. Most of the engraved imagery is associated with substantial numbers of grinding grooves. Two engraving sites also contain engraved groove channels. The clustering of open engraving sites in the north-east sector of the study area is comparable with the general pattern of large grinding groove site distribution. Given the paucity of all these site traits (large grinding groove sites, engraved groove channels and engraved rock art) in the study area, their general spatial co-occurrence and similar environmental and topographical locational patterning are notable. The significance of this pattern in respect of a cultural landscape will be explored further in Chapter 9.

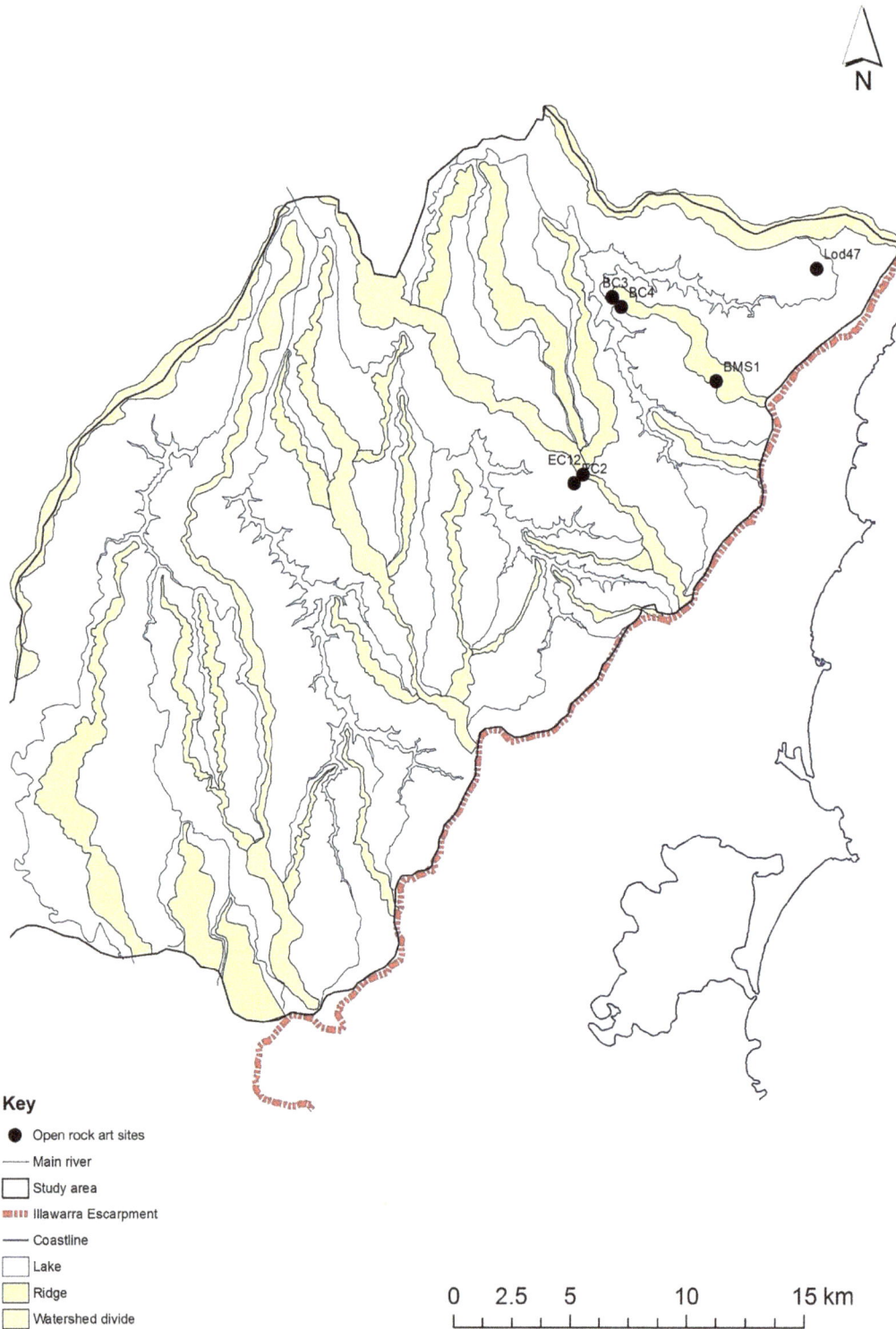

Figure 6.3 Location of open context engraved rock art sites.

Source: Map reproduced from Dibden (2011).

6.2.4 Open Context Sites—Summary

A number of notable features and geographic and environmental patterns are discernible in the open context site locational and distribution data. These are summarised as follows:

- The majority of open context sites contain grinding grooves only. A small percentage contain engraved grooves channels (n = 11; 6%) and/or engraved imagery (n = 5; 2.7%). One open site contains an engraved image only.

- The Cataract catchment contains almost half the grinding groove sites and more than half of the groove counts. The frequency and density of grinding groove sites and numbers of grooves per catchment diminishes from north to south.

- Engraved groove channels occur in highest frequency in the Cataract and do not occur in the Nepean catchment.

- Open context sites with engraved imagery occur in a restricted geographic area at the north-east of the study area and within 11 kilometres of the coastline. The two sites in the Cordeaux catchment represent the southern extent of engraved Sydney–Hawkesbury rock art.

- Grinding groove counts vary between 1–92, with a mode of one and median groove count of five. The majority of sites contain low grinding groove counts. The range in median groove count is comparably low in all catchments. This comparable structural patterning suggests that the different densities of these sites between catchments are a reflection of variable intensities of land use in the Upper Nepean.

- The majority of grinding groove sites contain single or otherwise very low groove counts suggesting that, generally, hatchet-grinding activity was not spatially focused. However, the pattern of a considerably fewer number of sites containing high groove counts does indicate that those sites are of a different order of significance. These locales were the focus of repeated activity.

- The majority of grinding groove sites are located in upper valley slope/first-order stream contexts and landforms that are likely to have been thoroughfares in the Upper Nepean catchment. In Chapter 2, it was proposed that these landforms are those that people were likely to occupy habitually. The presence of the larger grinding groove sites in these places cannot necessarily be seen to confirm this, although the relationship is suggestive that this may be the case. In addition, given that the maintenance of such an important tool is likely to take place in a domestic or base camp context prior to embarking on hunting, foraging or journeying, the presence of the majority of these sites in these landforms gives further weight to this argument.

- All grinding groove sites with large groove counts, all engraved groove channels and all engraved imagery are located in upper valley slope/first-order stream contexts. Large groove counts, engraved groove channels and engraved rock art frequently co-occur. Furthermore, the majority of sites that contain these traits are located on thoroughfare landforms and are clustered in the north-east sector of the Upper Nepean.

The following discussion compares these patterns with those identified by Sefton (1988) in her study area (Georges/Woronora and Cataract catchments). Sefton's (1988:54) area contained 3,912 grooves in 316 open sites, with an average count of 12.4 grooves per site. This mean calculation is slightly higher than in the Upper Nepean and the range of groove counts (1–209) is considerably greater. However, both study areas show remarkable agreement in structural patterning. Sefton (1988:55) also found that 70 per cent of sites contained 10 or fewer grooves.

Sefton (1988:62) examined the density of grinding grooves, and found that higher densities occurred in the Georges/Woronora River basin than the Cataract. She argues that this pattern indicates a greater Aboriginal population in the former area. The ratio between grinding grooves and rock art sites in each catchment is equivalent, and she argues that this supports her assumption that grinding grooves are indicators of settlement patterns and density of catchment usage. The patterns identified for the Upper Nepean provide further support of a trend on the Woronora Plateau, of diminishing grinding groove site and groove count density, from north to south. Sefton (1988:54) identifies that most grinding groove sites are located at or near plateau level, and in swamps or creek beds at the heads of creeks. They are rarely found in valley bottom locations. She argues that, while suitable sandstone is not distributed everywhere in the landscape, not all outcrops contain grooves where it does occur, and that sites did not appear to be overused. This is also the case in the Upper Nepean and, accordingly, grinding groove site distribution can be regarded as a factor of choice rather than as having been ultimately determined by environmental constraints. Attenbrow (2004:224) identified a similar pattern of grinding groove distribution relative to topography in the Upper Mangrove Creek catchment, where grinding grooves have a more restricted distribution than any other archaeological trait. She found that most sites with grinding grooves (74%) occur in upper elevations in periphery ridgetop zones (comparable with *major watershed divide* landforms as defined in this research).

The locational patterning of engraved groove channels in Sefton's study area is also comparable with the Upper Nepean catchment, in which all but two of 21 sites are located at plateau level. The remaining two are located in creek beds in upper valley slope contexts (Sefton 1988:67). All engraved groove channels, except one, occur in association with grinding grooves. All sites with engraved groove channels (except one, which is interpreted to be unfinished) contain high numbers of grooves. While the frequency of grinding groove sites and engraved groove channels is high in the northern catchment, the proportional frequency of engraved groove channels and grinding groove sites is the same in both (Sefton 1988:67). All 22 engraved rock art sites in Sefton's (1988:63) study are located in either ridge-top or near plateau-level locations. Sefton found that while the geographic distribution of engraved rock art (as confined to the eastern sector) and grinding groove sites do not coincide, the frequency of both diminishes from north to south, and the proportional frequency between the two is the same for both catchments.

The patterns in open context site contents and geographic and environmental location identified in this section, along with broader trends, as identified north of the Upper Nepean catchment by Sefton (1988), will be discussed again in conjunction with patterns in sheltered rock art in Chapters 8 and 9.

6.3 Shelter Site Contexts

Shelter site contexts account for 627 (77%) of the total site count in the database. Of these, 509 contain rock art, of which 110 have been subject to detailed recording for this research (Figure 6.4). As with open context sites, data relating to the remaining shelter sites have been obtained from the IPG site recordings, its various reports (Sefton 1989, 1990, 1991, 1992, 1994, 1995, 1996, 1997, 2000, 2003a) and others (Biosis 2007). The analyses of shelter contexts and their traits is undertaken on two levels. The first is based on general geographic, environmental and site contents data compiled from the IPG/DB and R/DB, and the second is based on detailed shelter morphology and rock art micro-topographical locational data from the R/DB. These latter data are based on a sample of the sites in the study area, and so the analyses of shelter morphology and micro-topographic location are conducted to indicate only the diversity and range of situational contexts that exist in relation to sheltered rock art. In subsequent chapters, analyses will be undertaken in respect of these variables to investigate their relationship with rock art in more depth, and whether or not there is a temporal signature to this diversity.

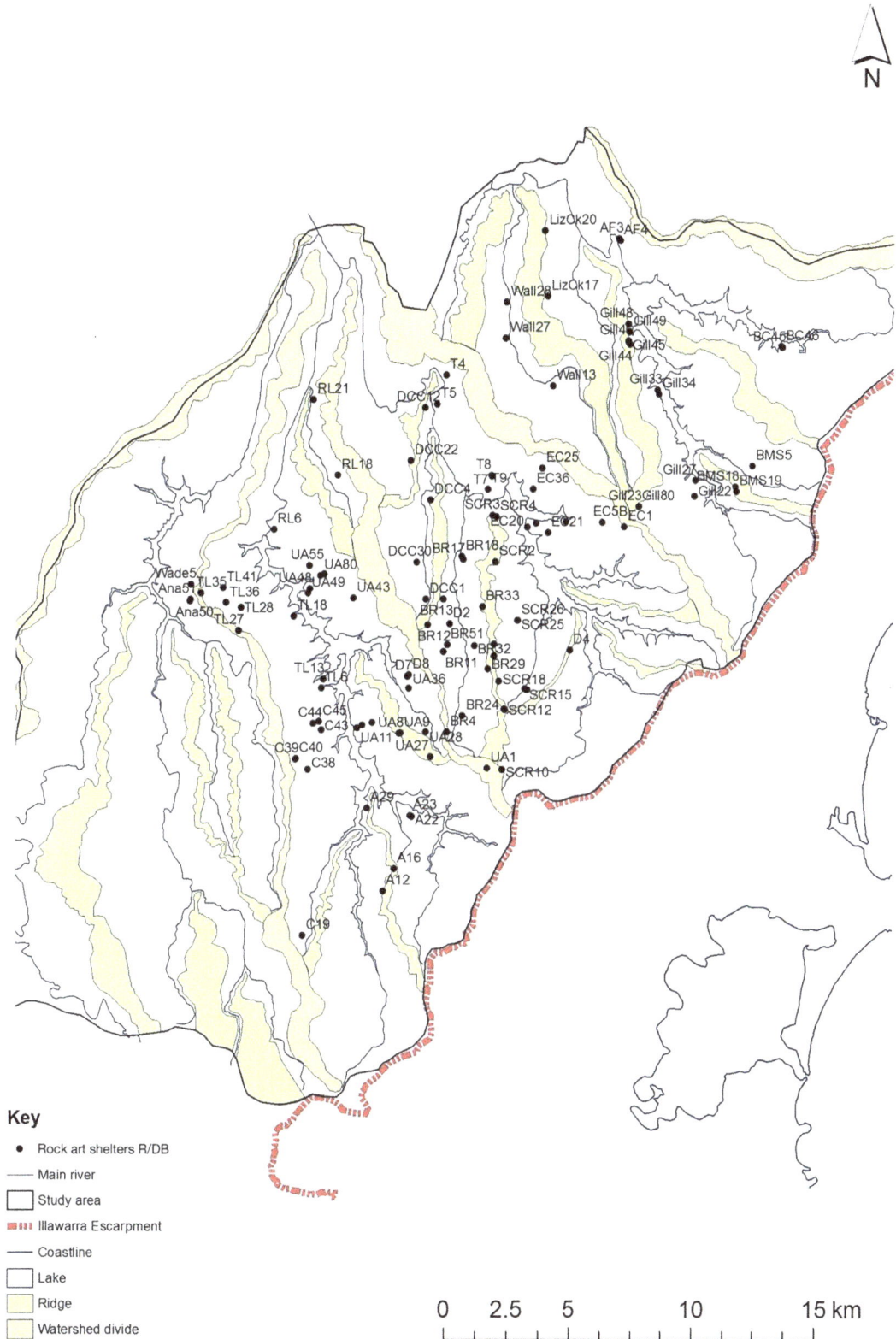

Figure 6.4 Location of rock art rock shelters in the Research Database.

Source: Map reproduced from Dibden (2011).

The IPG have not recorded rock shelters that do not contain observable 'direct' evidence of use, although many have been encountered during their surveys (Sefton 1988:70). Sefton (1988:71) refers to Attenbrow's (1987) work in the Upper Mangrove Creek catchment where, upon excavation, 60 per cent of such sites were found to contain deposit. The implication is that shelters with archaeological deposit are likely to be underrepresented in the IPG/DB. This underrepresentation is uniform across the entire Upper Nepean and, hence, is unlikely to influence site density calculations. This data limitation is of minor importance to the main thrust of this research.

6.3.1 Shelter Contents—General

The majority of shelters (81%) contain rock art in the form of graphic and gestural (stencils and prints) marks (Table 6.4; Dibden 2011:Appendix 6). Other archaeological traits may also be present. Grinding grooves are present in 21 shelters. Stone artefacts have been recorded in 278 shelters, 118 of which do not contain rock art. Small numbers of other features, such as the caching of stone tools and 'quarrying' of quartz pebbles, have been recorded.

Table 6.4 Summary of archaeological traits per shelter in the Upper Nepean catchment (IPG/DB and R/DB).

Catchment	Stone artefacts	Grinding grooves	% with ggs	Rock art	% with art	Art counts	% art count	Total shelters
Cataract	85	12	57.1	160	31.4	1,424	27.8	194
Cordeaux	46	1	4.8	114	22.4	1,494	29.2	127
Avon	72	4	19	140	27.5	1,562	30.5	171
Nepean	75	4	19	95	18.7	640	12.5	135
Total	278	21		509		5,120		627

Source: Table reproduced from Dibden (2011).

The density of shelters with rock art, across the entire study area, is 0.6 sites per square kilometre. A total of 5,120 graphic and gestural marks are distributed at an average density of 6.4 per square kilometre. The site and rock art mark density in each catchment is as follows:

- Cataract: Sheltered rock art site density is 0.8 sites per square kilometre; rock art mark density is 6.8 per square kilometre.

- Cordeaux: Sheltered rock art site density is 0.7 sites per square kilometre; rock art mark density is 9.1 per square kilometre.

- Avon: Sheltered rock art site density is 0.8 sites per square kilometre; rock art mark density is nine per square kilometre.

- Nepean: Sheltered rock art site density is 0.4 sites per square kilometre; rock art mark density is three per square kilometre.

Similarities and differences are evident in patterns of sheltered rock art site density compared with open context grinding groove data. The Nepean catchment contains the lowest overall site and rock art mark density. In contrast to open sites where the Cataract catchment contains significantly higher site and groove densities, the Cordeaux and Avon catchments contain sheltered rock art site densities that are comparable with that found in the Cataract. The Cataract contains a lower density of rock art marks compared with the Cordeaux and Avon. This pattern is unexpected given trends in various other lines of evidence (Section 6.1.1 and 6.2), which reveal a pattern of site and trait decline from north to south. It is also notable that the Cordeaux and Avon both possess higher frequencies of rock art motifs in fewer shelters, compared with the Cataract and Nepean. The question of what may have influenced this different geographic pattern in sheltered rock art distribution is analysed further in Chapter 9.

Over half (57%) of the rock shelters with grinding grooves are in the Cataract catchment. This distribution is comparable with open grinding groove sites in which 49.5 per cent are in the Cataract. Also, comparable with open contexts, the Cataract has the highest frequency (68.1%) of grooves in shelters. This correspondence of grinding groove frequency between open and shelter contexts in the Cataract suggests that the pattern relating to the geographic distribution of sheltered rock art density is different, and potentially informative of different behavioural expression relating to rock art.

The sheltered grinding groove site density in the entire study area is 0.02 sites per square kilometre; average grinding groove density is 0.09 grooves per square kilometre. The sheltered grinding groove site and groove density in each catchment is as follows:

- Cataract: 0.057 sites per square kilometre; grinding groove density is 0.236 per square kilometre.
- Cordeaux: 0.006 sites per square kilometre; grinding groove density is 0.006 per square kilometre.
- Avon: 0.023 sites per square kilometre; grinding groove density is 0.064 per square kilometre.
- Nepean: 0.016 sites per square kilometre; grinding groove density is 0.045 per square kilometre.

Sheltered grinding groove site and groove densities diminish significantly between the Cataract and the southern rivers. The Cordeaux, however, contains the lowest site and groove density, and this contrasts with the open site density pattern. The Avon contains higher sheltered grinding groove density than the Nepean, which is comparable with the open site pattern.

The descriptive statistics for shelter context rock art marks reveal a number of additional similarities and differences between the catchments (Table 6.5). The maximum number of rock art marks per site differs between catchments. The Nepean possesses the lowest maximum count of 41 rock art marks per site and the Cordeaux has the highest count of 206. The average rock art mark count per site is 10. The median count is four for each of the Cataract, Cordeaux and Avon catchments.

Table 6.5 Summary statistics relating to shelter contexts with rock art marks per catchment (IPG/DB and R/DB).

Catchment	Number of sites	Total image count	Range of counts	Average count	Median	Standard deviation
Cataract	160	1,424	1-146	8.8	4	15.7
Cordeaux	114	1,494	1-206	13.1	4	26.8
Avon	140	1,562	1-108	11.1	4	18.3
Nepean	95	640	1-41	6.7	3	8.4
Total	509	5,120	1-206	10	4	18.6

Source: Table reproduced from Dibden (2011).

Very few sites have large rock art mark counts. Nearly 80 per cent of shelter context rock art sites have 10 or less rock art marks. Less than 5 per cent of sites have rock art mark counts of 31 or more. This pattern of distribution is similar to that encountered in the exploration of grinding groove counts in open contexts. The production of rock art also appears to conform to a pattern of spatially focalised activity represented by sites with high rock art counts on the one hand and, on the other, a much more situationally diffuse activity characterised by limited and often *one-off* events.

The locations of size-coded sheltered rock art sites are shown in Figure 6.5. The most obvious spatial pattern is that the Nepean catchment does not contain shelters with large rock art counts. The remaining catchments all contain large sheltered art sites, but each has different locational patterns. The largest site in the Cataract is located in the valley near the dam wall and in the centre of the catchment. This contrasts with the Cordeaux and Avon, where large sites are located on or within close proximity to watershed divides or ridge crests of minor divides. There is some tendency for these large sites to be relatively close to the Illawarra Escarpment, rather than within the interior of the plateau.

As the majority of shelter contexts contain 10 or fewer rock art marks, the distribution in these sites is explored further. Rock art counts of one or two occur in 34.8 per cent of the total number of shelters in the study area. Shelters with one (n = 89) or two (n = 88) rock art marks account for 44.3 per cent of this group of shelters.

While shelters with low rock art counts are possibly representative of marking activity undertaken within discrete time frames or temporal phases, those with large rock art counts may represent accumulations of imagery over significantly longer periods of time and in successive temporal phases. An analysis of the spatial distribution of sheltered rock art sites will be undertaken in Chapter 9, which explores locational patterns further and examines variability between different temporal rock art phases.

The following discussion explores the distribution of sheltered rock art sites in accordance with the same suite of environmental variables used to examine grinding groove sites. Given that temporal variability may be a significant determinant in regard to rock art location, the purpose of these analyses is to reveal the range of environmental variability only. Approximately half of shelters with rock art (55.6%) are located in upper valley slope contexts. The remainder are distributed almost equally between mid and lower slope contexts. This distribution of rock art differs significantly from the pattern in open grinding groove sites, although there are slightly more sites with rock art counts of 60 or more in upper valley slope rather than mid or low contexts.

The Cataract catchment contains rock art shelters in comparable densities in all slope contexts. However, the remainder of the catchments, generally, contain more sites on upper slopes, particularly in the Nepean. The physical differences between each catchment were described in Chapter 2, and it was noted that occupation and travel within the Cataract valleys was likely to be less constrained than in other catchments. The pattern in different site locations between each catchment most likely reflects the differences in topography between them, and a general preference to occupy all valley locations in less treacherous terrain, or the converse.

The majority of rock art sites (71%) are located in areas that correspond to the main thoroughfares in the study area. This pattern of preferential location near major thoroughfares is comparable with that relating to open grinding groove sites, although to a lesser extent (see Dibden 2011:Table 6.20). The different terrain of the Cataract catchment is likely to be influencing this distribution to some degree.

The location of sheltered rock art sites in relation to stream order also diverges when compared with that identified for grinding grooves sites. While the majority are located in lower order stream contexts, they are also commonly located in higher order contexts, and this is commensurate with the greater numbers of sites located on mid and lower slopes. Significantly, sites with high rock art counts are preferentially located in lower stream order contexts.

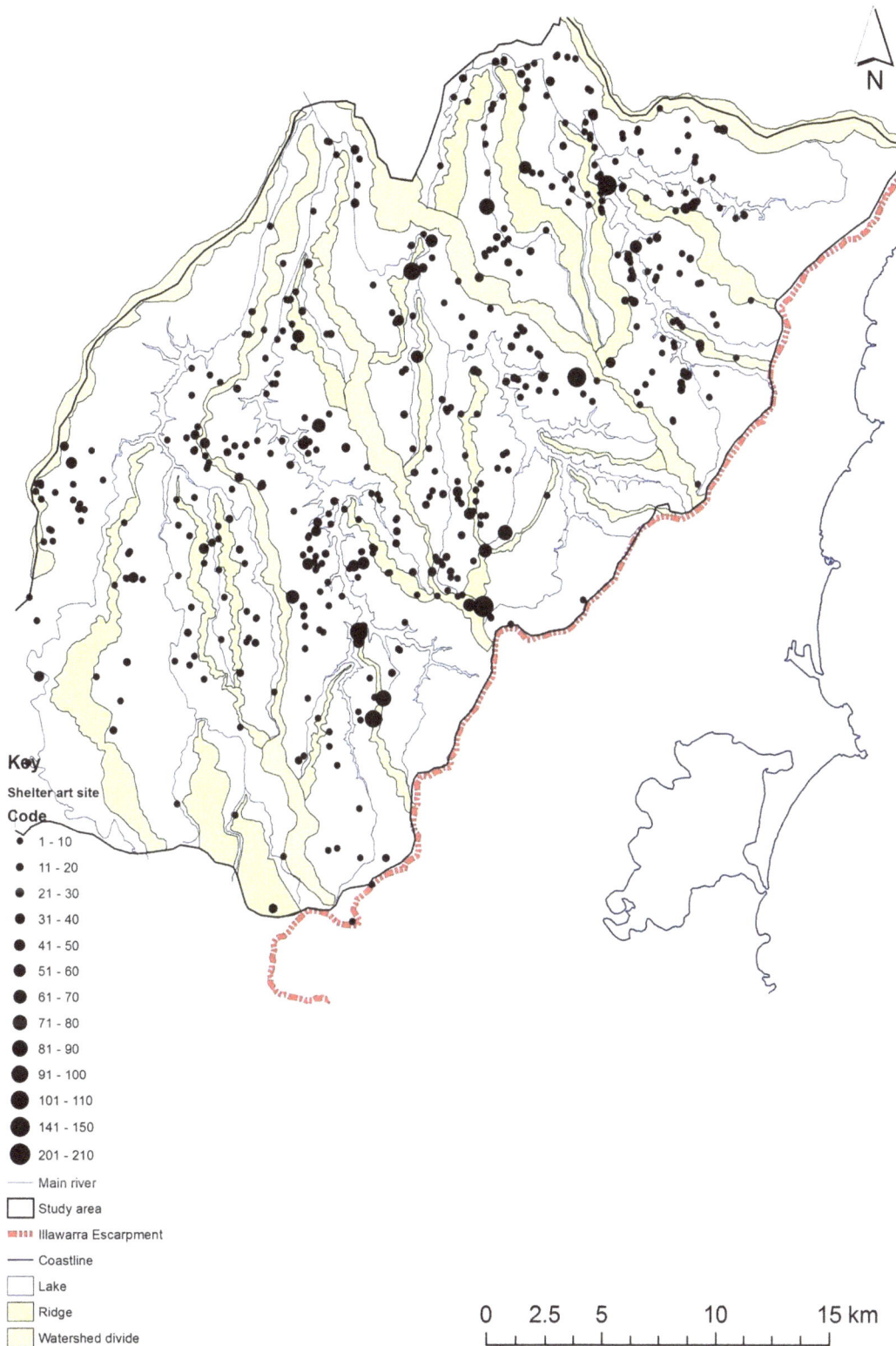

Key

Shelter art site

Code

- 1 – 10
- 11 – 20
- 21 – 30
- 31 – 40
- 41 – 50
- 51 – 60
- 61 – 70
- 71 – 80
- 81 – 90
- 91 – 100
- 101 – 110
- 141 – 150
- 201 – 210

— Main river
☐ Study area
▪▪▪▪ Illawarra Escarpment
— Coastline
☐ Lake
☐ Ridge
☐ Watershed divide

0   2.5   5   10   15 km

Figure 6.5 Location of size coded (as per rock art counts) sheltered rock art sites.

Source: Map reproduced from Dibden (2011).

6.3.2 Shelter Rock Art—Marks

In this section, shelters with rock art and their variability in respect of different categories and counts are examined briefly. Pigment graphics occur in 461 of the 509 rock art shelters. Stencil imagery occurs in 130 shelters. Prints are relatively uncommon (five sites). Gestural applications of pigment marks occur in 23 sites, and gestural subtractive marks such as pitting occur in 21. The latter categories are likely to be underrepresented because, except for large red pigment smears, these mark types have not been recorded by the IPG. Engraved graphics occur in two shelters.

Rock art occurs in shelters in three main groupings: pigment graphics only, stencils only and graphics and stencils (Table 6.6). The majority of shelters (74.5%) possess graphics only. Forty-seven sites (9.2%) contain stencils only, and 83 (16.3%) have both graphics and stencils.

Table 6.6 Data on number and percentage of the main rock art categories in each catchment (IPG/DB and R/DB).

Catchment	Graphics only	% only graphics	Stencils only	% only stencils	Graphics & stencils	% graphics & stencils
Cataract	104	65%	16	10%	40	25%
Cordeaux	90	79%	8	7%	16	14%
Avon	108	77.1%	15	10.8%	17	12.1%
Nepean	77	81.1%	8	8.4%	10	10.5%
Total	379	74.5%	47	9.2%	83	16.3%

Source: Table reproduced from Dibden (2011).

The relative percentage frequencies of these groupings vary between catchments. The Cataract catchment has more shelters with stencils and fewer with graphics only, compared with the southern catchments. This difference in the relative abundance of a specific trait between the Cataract and other catchments has been identified previously in regard to other data. The greater frequency of stencilling in the Cataract is explored at a deeper analytical level in Chapters 8 and 9.

6.3.3 Sheltered Rock Art—Shelters

Rock art occurs in a wide range of shelter morphological types and sizes. Shelter variability is explored here with data from the Research Database (see Dibden 2011:Appendix 7:Shelter Database). In all aspects relating to rock art shelter size, living space and art panels, shelters are highly variable. While the minimum length, height, width and volume calculations are very low, the largest shelters are of enormous dimensions. Given the mode of zero in respect of living space categories, it is common that shelters provide space that is neither suitable for use as a living/work area, nor as a sleeping space. The range in size of rock art surfaces is also significant and is between 1 and 103 square metres.

In Table 6.7, shelter variability is described further in respect of shape, the nature of floors and dampness, location of rock art in respect of optimal living space, and location within elevated rock faces. These shelter categories will be examined in later chapters in relation to the nature of the rock art and temporal ordering. Of note here is the predominance of highly uneven rock-floors in half of all rock art shelters, and this accounts for the low number of shelters with Living or Optimal Living Space. It is also notable that eight shelters are perched in elevated contexts within vertical rock faces.

Table 6.7 Numbers of morphological types and other shelter characteristics (n = 110: R/DB).

Category		Shelter counts
Shape	dome	15
	open	20
	scallop	14
	square	25
	wedge	36
Floor	Primarily rock	56
	Primarily sediment	38
	Half/half	16
Relationship to ground surfaces	Shelter perched in elevated rock faces	8
Location of art to relationship to Optimal Living Space	Not Applicable (i.e. no Living Space)	41
	Away	4
	Adjacent ceiling	2
	Adjacent wall	52
	Adjacent wall and ceiling	11
Dampness	Dry	95
	Mixed	9
	Wet	6

Source: Table reproduced from Dibden (2011).

The variability that the rock shelters possess suggests that marking the land with rock art is likely to have been motivated by a range of purposes and meanings. The different variables relating to shelters provide opportunities and constraints to human beings as embodied individuals.

6.3.4 Sheltered Rock Art—Micro-topography

Rock art occurs in a range of micro-topographic contexts within shelters (Table 6.8). Variability in rock art location is explored in this section with data from the Research Database (see Dibden 2011:Appendix 8:Mark Database). A total of 2,565 rock marks have been identified in the 110 rock shelters recorded for this research. The majority of rock marks have been produced on walls and in open visibility contexts. Eighty-three marks have been identified to be in a relationship of isomorphic congruence with natural features on the rock art panels. The lowest mark is 5 centimetres above a shelter floor, and the highest is c. 3 metres. The average height is 106 centimetres, and the median and mode are both 100 centimetres. Plates 6.1, 6.2 and 6.3 illustrate variable visibility contexts in which rock marks can occur.

Table 6.8 Numbers of locations and visibility characteristics of rock marks (R/DB).

Category		Rock mark counts
General location	Wall	2,034
	Ceiling	269
	Concavity	262
Visibility	Open	2,134
	Moderate	261
	Hidden	170
Isomorphic congruence	In a relationship of isomorphic congruence	83

Source: Table reproduced from Dibden (2011).

Plate 6.1 Location of a 'hidden' motif on the roof (50 centimetres above the rock floor) of a small concavity in the rear wall of a shelter (rock shelter SCR14; mark ID 2459).

What is particularly interesting about this shelter is that the rear wall contains abundant suitable rock art panels that are devoid of art, other than the small hidden motif that cannot be seen unless one kneels down and looks up into the roof of the concavity.

Source: Photograph by Julie Dibden, 2011.

Plate 6.2 Location of a highly visible motif situated c. 3 metres above the ground (as measured from base of image to the ground) on an outside face of a shelter (rock shelter DCC12; mark ID 1534).

Source: Photograph by Julie Dibden, 2011.

Plate 6.3 Close-up of mark ID 1534.

Source: Photograph by Julie Dibden, 2011.

6.3.5 Shelter Context Sites—Summary

The notable features and geographic and environmental patterns discernible in the shelter context site data are summarised as follows:

- Shelters with rock art are distributed in different densities between the catchments in a pattern that contrasts with open context grinding groove site distribution, except in the Nepean.

- The Avon and Cordeaux catchments contain comparable site densities with the Cataract, but higher densities of motifs.

- Grinding grooves in shelters have a comparable density distribution with that found in open grinding groove sites.

- The Avon and Cordeaux catchments contain more motifs in fewer shelters than the other catchments.

- Rock art counts per shelter vary between 1–206, with a mode of one and median count of four. The majority of shelters contain low rock art counts.

- Generally, rock art activity was neither intensive nor spatially focused. The fewer number of shelters that contain high rock art counts suggests that more intensively marked sites were utilised within a different sociocultural context to smaller sites.

- Rock art shelters are distributed relatively evenly between landforms, but larger sites are almost exclusively located on landforms in which domestic occupation and movement through country is inferred. In the Cataract catchment, large sites occur in valley bottoms. Elsewhere, they are located most frequently on watershed divides or the crests of ridges.

- Shelters contain predominantly graphic rock art with lesser frequencies of gestural marks. The Cataract catchment has a greater proportional frequency of stencils.

- Rock art shelters are extremely variable in their morphology and dimensions, and the majority have highly uneven rock floors. The majority of shelters do not possess attributes that would have allowed for their use as domestic habitation sites. The sociocultural context of rock art production and perception may not have been equivalent in all shelters.

- Rock art is predominantly on shelter walls in contexts of open visibility. However, rock art occurs in a range of micro-topographic contexts within shelters, suggesting that the sociocultural context of rock art production and perception was highly variable.

6.4 Summary

In this chapter, an overview of the database has been presented and the broad categories of archaeological material and the contexts in which these occur have been quantified. General trends in the variability of site and trait frequency, and their spatial density across the study area have been identified. The Cataract catchment contains the greatest numbers of sites and the highest overall site density. Site density in the Cordeaux and Avon catchments is comparable, but lower than the Cataract and higher than the Nepean. This pattern has been mirrored, if not amplified, by the grinding groove site data. The structural comparability between each catchment in the Upper Nepean, and with areas to the north (Sefton 1988), suggests that the pattern of variable site density is real and not a reflection of sampling bias. The spatial trend of site frequency and density decreasing from north to south is possibly an indicator of differential levels of Aboriginal land use across space in the period since c. 3,500 BP, when it is assumed that ground-edge stone hatchets began to be used in the region. This spatial pattern, in regard to site density, is only behaviourally meaningful if an equitable opportunity exists for rock platform and shelter use in all catchments of the study area. It has been beyond the limits and scope of this project, and possibly any research, to quantify the availability of suitable stone exposures across the study area in order to test for this. Based on personal observation and the IPG records and documents, it is the case that stone platforms and exposures are abundant across all catchments. The geology and geomorphology are relatively uniform. Accordingly, the site-density patterning in the Upper Nepean is believed to be a result of human choice, rather than being environmentally determined.

It has also been identified that open context rock art and engraved groove channels occur in greater numbers in the Cataract catchment than elsewhere, and not at all in the Nepean. The southerly limit of open context engraved rock art in the Cordeaux catchment, and engraved groove channels in the central area of the Avon, marks the cessation of practices that were clearly of decreasing and less importance in the area of the southern Woronora Plateau. In subsequent chapters, the question as to what these patterns in the Upper Nepean may indicate will be addressed.

An unexpected pattern, identified in this chapter, is that sheltered rock art abundance in the Cordeaux and Avon catchments does not mirror the decreasing density trends found in other site patterns. The Cataract catchment contains densities of sheltered rock art sites comparable with that found in the Cordeaux and Avon, but has lower densities of rock art marks. This suggests that the Avon and Cordeaux catchments were the focus of more intensive shelter context rock marking than when compared with the Cataract.

Open grinding groove and sheltered rock art sites possess a similar diversity in the number of marks they contain, and predominantly have low counts of grinding grooves or rock art. On the other hand, small numbers of both site types contain a contrastingly high number of marks. This variability may be inferred to reflect differences in respect of the use of land, which may be the result of their production within different sociocultural contexts.

The variability in rock art shelters, including their environmental and topographic location, morphology, the nature of the rock marks they contain, and the micro-topographic location of marks, has been defined in this chapter. The topographic location of rock art shelters has been found to be more variable than open context grinding groove sites. This cannot be accounted for by the availability of suitable sandstone shelters and exposures.

The examination of diversity in the physical location of rock marks, whether on a macro- or micro-topographic scale, focuses attention on questions of sociocultural context, occupation and meaning. Further analyses will be undertaken in following chapters to address the questions that have arisen in this chapter.

7

Relative Temporal Sequence

The Sydney Basin rock art has been previously identified as possessing temporal variability, and various relative and chronological sequences have been proposed (McCarthy 1988a; McDonald 1994:336, 2008a:343). However, the temporal ordering of the sheltered rock art of the Upper Nepean catchment has not yet been subject to detailed analysis. Officer (1984) and Sefton (1988) both analysed spatial variability in the northern Woronora rock art based on an assumption of general contemporaneity.

This research aims to investigate if temporal change can be identified in the study area and, if so, to characterise that change over time in terms of the nature and form of the rock art, and also in regard to the environmental and micro-topographic locations chosen for marking. In the first section of this chapter, previous research that focused on temporal change in the Sydney Basin rock art is reviewed. Next, the methodology employed in the analysis is defined. This is followed by an analysis of superimposed relationships identifiable in the Upper Nepean rock art. A temporal sequence is then presented, which sets out the nature of the rock art in terms of colour and technique in each of the identified 'phases'. This sequence will be used as a framework for charting change over time in the rock art for analysis and discussion in subsequent chapters.

7.1 Introduction

This introductory section presents a review of the temporal ordering of Sydney Basin pigment rock art, as defined by previous researchers. All previous work, other than two Accelerated Mass Spectrometry (AMS) radiocarbon dating projects, is based on superimpositioning analysis and, in the case of McDonald's research, a chronology has been proposed based on posited correlations between rock art and archaeological deposit (McDonald 1994; 2008a). The pigment characterisation project undertaken in the Upper Nepean catchment by Huntley (née Ford) (Ford 2006; Huntley et al. 2011) has implications for the likely recent age of white stencilled rock art. Hughes's (1976:52) analysis of the high rates of weathering of the Sydney Basin sandstone provides a framework for considering the potential longevity of the pigment rock art in the study area, and that it may be relatively recent in age. The age of the open context engraved rock art in the Sydney Basin has not been subject to a detailed analysis. However, Sefton (2003a) argues that it is likely to be recent due to high rates of weathering, and McDonald (2008a:350) suggests that many engravings may have been produced during the last millennium.

Officer (1984:3) considers the rock art of the upper and central Georges Basin to be no more than 2,000 years old based on a consideration of the high rates of weathering of the Hawkesbury Sandstone. McDonald (1994:336; 2008a:343) subsequently produced a relative chronology for the rock art sequence of the Sydney Basin based on her analysis of 65 sites in the Upper Mangrove Creek catchment. Her sequence suggests an antiquity for the pigment rock art in the region at c. 4,000 years BP, and she also defined a three-phased sequence of change. McDonald (2008a,

2008b) and others (e.g. Clegg 1986:60; McCarthy 1988a:16) recognise that rock art production continued to be practiced in sheltered and open contexts in the Sydney Basin into the contact period. Assuming a broadly comparable archaeological context for this part of the Sydney Basin, rock art in the Upper Nepean also was likely to have been produced from at least the mid-Holocene and into the colonial period.

Early studies of (usually) individual shelters identified superimpositioning in the Sydney Basin pigment art, although an exploration of the chronological implications of this was rarely undertaken (e.g. Mathews 1895:271). Mathews refers to black drawings over white hand stencils in two (north Sydney Basin) shelters. In a northern Woronora Plateau site, Clegg (1971:38) identifies 'two pieces of evidence that the drawings [in the shelter] were made during at least two periods'. The first is that red drawn 'lines' (being parts of motifs) were underneath black and white lines, and the second is that newer marks were on a fresh erosional surface that once would have contained the upper parts of motifs, which now only remain at the bottom of the panel. However, Clegg (1986:56) was generally not hopeful of establishing a relative sequence.

McCarthy (1979; 1988a:18) proposes the first relative sequence for the pigment rock art based on his recordings of superimpositioning at individual sites across the wider Sydney Basin, including Conjola in the south and Canoelands in the north (McCarthy 1959, 1961). McCarthy does not recognise an engraved component in the shelter art, nor does he attempt to correlate the art with the archaeological sequence of the region (McDonald 1994:162).

McCarthy's relative sequence was subject to critical review. Clegg (1977:262) argues that he found no evidence of different phases at Canoelands, and Officer (1984:3), likewise, argues that there was no evidence of this sequence in the Georges River area. In defence, McCarthy (1988a:18) refers to numerous other early studies, which he argues confirm the sequence (including Cox et al. 1968; Vinnicombe 1980; Smith 1983). McCarthy (1988b:40) later emphasised that at least two major phases exist, one being an early stencil phase and the other a later black drawing phase (i.e. his phases 1 and 3 respectively: Table 7.1). As stated by McDonald (1988) in a series of review papers, McCarthy's model does not 'stand up' to the increased data produced by subsequent research. McDonald (1988) questions the validity of McCarthy's single motif Polychrome phase, and the usefulness of a sequence that has several probable contemporaneous phases, and a lack of a chronological and cultural, or archaeological, alignment.

Table 7.1 McCarthy's Sydney–Hawkesbury shelter art sequence.

Phase	Description	Period
1 Stencil phase (wet paint)	Stencils of hands, feet and artefacts, in red and white, also yellow. Also imprints of hands and feet. An occasional outline figure.	Earliest
2 Red-and-white phase	Drawings in dry pigment in outline, solid and various infilled styles of culture heroes, humans, animals and artefacts.	Not specified
3 Black phase	Drawings in dry charcoal in a wider range of subjects than Phase 2, in outline, solid and various infilled styles, with an important series of black-and-red, black-and-white, black-and-yellow bichromes, red, white and black trichromes; *the richest phase*.	Recent
4 Polychrome phase	Known only in one figure: a culture hero in four colours.	Recent (probably contemporaneous with Phase 5)
5 White stencil phase	A very rich phase of stencils of hands, feet, animal paws, a wide variety of artefacts, parts of plants and other subjects.	Recent (probably contemporaneous with Phase 4)

Source: Table reproduced from Dibden (2011).

Officer (1984:3) does not consider 'sequential change over time' in his study of the Georges River sheltered rock art due to a lack of evidence of a clear chronological sequence, and also because of the high rates of rock art deterioration. Officer (1984:3) draws attention to problems associated with differential rates of weathering, which make cross-correlations as a relative dating technique 'impossible to verify'. He suggests that, given the rate of deterioration of the Hawkesbury Sandstone, the rock art of the Georges River is unlikely to exceed an age of 2,000 years. Officer considers all pigment rock art in his study to be roughly contemporaneous. Officer (1984:25–26) does not record any graphic rock art made with wet pigment applications, a technique identified by McDonald in one of her art phases (see below). However, while Officer (1984:37) identified systematic superimpositioning of drawn figures over stencils (this partially supporting McCarthy's model), he questions the extent to which this sequence was systematic across the broader region, and argues that its chronological significance was, at that time, impossible to determine.

Sefton (1988:154–157) does not explicitly explore chronological patterns (as this was outside the focus of her research), but identifies superimpositioning patterns relating to stencils in her study area. The following notable relationships were identified (Table 7.2):

- white drawings are always above any other colour/technique combination when in a superimposed relationship
- white stencils are always above any other colour/technique combination, including red stencils, when in a superimposed relationship
- charcoal drawings are mostly over any colour/technique combination in a superimposed relationship, although one instance of being under a red stencil, and two of being under a red painting are identified. However, the four instances of red paintings under charcoal drawings, and 11 of charcoal being over red stencils may indicate the dominant trend.

Table 7.2 Sefton's superimposition sequence in the Georges/Woronora and Cataract rivers area.

Over	White drawing	White stencil	Charcoal drawing	Red drawing	Red stencil	Red painting
Charcoal drawing	8	11	—	0	1	2
Red drawing	2	3	10	—	0	0
Red stencil	0	5	11	0	—	0
Red painting	0	2	4	0	0	1

Source: Table reproduced from Dibden (2011).

While it was acknowledged that differential rates of preservation between red and white stencils may be relevant, Sefton (1988:156) argues that, chronologically, red stencils are earlier than white stencils. Sefton (1988:56) also notes that there is greater object diversity in the more recent white stencils, than when compared with the earlier red stencils, which further emphasises temporal difference and its nature.

Sefton (1988) finds that black drawings generally occur over red drawings and, in a subsequent paper, she identified differences in motif types between red and black drawings (Sefton 1992:3). In particular, an absence of profile human motifs was identified in red drawings, and Sefton concludes that this reflected a chronological shift. This proposition was further tested using a correspondence analysis for 62 shelters from Heathcote National Park and 91 from the Cordeaux catchment. The correspondence analysis (CA) supports a chronological difference between red ochre and charcoal drawings (Sefton 1992:3, 4). Sefton (2003b:40) also argues that the high levels of weathering of red drawings, which are comparable with that of black drawings, are further confirmation of an age difference, given that red pigment adheres in a stronger bond with stone and would generally be expected to survive longer than charcoal.

McDonald et al. (1990) conducted an AMS dating program that sought to test the feasibility of the technique and to date rock art from the Sydney Basin. Pigment, presumed to contain charcoal, was extracted from motifs in three shelters, although five samples collected from Native Animals shelter on the McDonald River in the north Sydney Basin had insufficient carbon for dating (McDonald et al. 1990:86, 89). Two dates were obtained from two separate indeterminate painted motifs (with charcoal in the matrix) collected from Waterfall Cave in the south Sydney Basin, one being 635±50 BP and the other modern. These dates were considered to reflect a late relative position within the rock art sequence. In regard to the modern date, it was suggested that this probably indicated rock art production being undertaken during the contact period (McDonald et al. 1990:90). It is noted here, however, that the technique represented in the motifs at the Waterfall Cave site is rare, and localised to the area in question, so that extrapolating the results from this site broadly across the Sydney Basin is of limited utility. Two widely divergent dates (6,085±60 BP and 29,795±420 BP) were obtained from a single black-and-red non-figurative motif from Gnatalia Creek (another southern Sydney Basin site). The interpretation of these two dates is unresolved, but it clearly demonstrates the problems associated with dating organic materials in rock art pigments (see also Ridges 1995).

McDonald (2000:91, 2008a:181) reports further AMS dates for rock art in the Sydney Basin. Four samples, taken from two charcoal drawings in UDM shelter in the Central Sydney Basin, produced dates ranging from c. 280±90 BP to indistinguishable-from-modern (three of the latter). McDonald (2000:91) questions these dates, suggesting that the modern dates may indicate contamination, although she canvasses the possibility that the dates could indicate the art production during the contact period. Dates were eventually obtained from Native Animals shelter, three from a charcoal macropod, and one from a 'koala' motif. The age estimates produced from the macropod ranged from 760±205 to 1770±205 BP, and that for the koala was 1080±210 BP (McDonald 2000:91). The range in age-estimates for the macropod suggests the possibility of contamination; the very small size of the charcoal samples was also argued to be problematic (McDonald 2000:91). The range of different dates, from individual motifs, was suggested by McDonald (2000:4) to demonstrate more about sampling difficulties in the application of AMS analysis than they do about the age of charcoal drawings in the Sydney Basin sandstone shelters.

McDonald (2008a:342) sought to explicitly define the temporal significance of rock art variability and produced a broad relative sequence and chronology for the Sydney Basin, based on an examination of 65 shelter sites in the Upper Mangrove Creek catchment (Table 7.3). She assumes that the majority of the art coincides with the more recent archaeological evidence in the region—that is, the late Holocene Bondaian sequence with its three dated phases. At Yengo 1, McDonald explored the correlation of intaglio engraved rock art with excavated deposit, and she tested three other rock shelters to explore the contemporaneity of the art with the occupation deposit. McDonald (2008a:241, 249) defines the earliest art (Phase 1) as being the small assemblage of intaglio engravings, which occur in a very restricted range of motifs (and sites). She assigns Phase 1 a minimum age of 4,000 years BP, possibly extending back c. 6,000 years BP. These intaglio engravings are rarely found in a superimposed relationship, as they are mostly located at the base of shelter walls or sloping rock floors. However, when they are, McDonald (2008a:236) found that they were always under pigment motifs. Notably, the engravings at Mount Yengo were covered by deposit that was 4,000 years old, hence the minimum age designation given to them. More recently, an oxalate skin overlying a pecked emu track (a 'Panaramitee'-style intaglio engraving) sampled from a vertical wall in Emu Cave in the Blue Mountains returned an AMS date of 1,900±220 BP, thus establishing a minimum age for the engraving (Taçon et al. 2006:231). In comparing the pecked engravings from Emu Cave with similar forms in sheltered sites elsewhere in the region, Taçon et al. (2006:234) conclude that this art is the earliest in the Sydney region. McDonald (1994:179) argues that Phase 1 and Phase 2 are probably temporally discrete.

McDonald's Phase 2 rock art consists of red paintings in a relatively restricted range of motifs that includes 'other' (mostly dots), macropod tracks, circles and men, similar to that found in Phase 1. Additionally, anthropomorph, goanna, snake, quadruped and complex non-figurative motifs, and red and white stencils were found to occur in Phase 2 rock art. This phase was placed between 4,000 years and c. 1,600 BP (McDonald 1994, 2008a:249). The most recent art phase, which includes a proliferation of techniques, colours and motifs (with a greater focus on figurative motifs), was argued to extend from 1,600 years BP through until European occupation (McDonald 2008a:249).

The dating of these phases was inferred by assuming contemporaneity between the main phases of occupation deposit in the shelters and the rock phases. There are notable differences in the dating of the sequence as proposed initially, and then subsequently published (cf. McDonald (1994:336, 2008a:249, 343). McDonald now considers that Phase 2 is likely to be older than 4,000 years, while Phase 3 is designated to extend from 4,000 years to the contact period (McDonald 2008a:343, 349). This adjustment has been made to correlate the rock art sequence with a more recently defined chronology in the regional Bondaian sequence (McDonald 2008a).

Table 7.3 Relative chronology for the Mangrove Creek Art Sequence produced by McDonald (1994). Note text in italics denotes changes made by McDonald (2008a).

Art Phase	Correspondence with Bondaian Sequence	Description	Period
Art Phase 1	Pre- or Early Bondaian	Pecked engravings of tracks and circles.	>4,000 years BP ~ (*minimum*)
Art Phase 2	Early Bondaian	Red paintings and red and white hand stencils that do not co-occur.	<4,000–c. 1,600 years BP ~ *>4,000 years BP*
Art Phase 3	Middle to Late Bondaian	A proliferation of techniques and colour use, perhaps starting with plain dry black and dry red motifs and developing into a range of paints, dry bichromes, stencils of various colours, polychromes and incised motifs. Outline only motifs end the sequences of many shelters, with contact motifs in white stencils and drawn in red-and-white outlined and infilled forms.	c. 1,600 years BP – European contact ~ *4,000 years BP – European contact*

Source: Table based on McDonald (1994:191, 196, 2008a:343).

Huntley (Ford 2006; Huntley et al. 2011) conducted characterisation analyses of pigment harvested from nine sites in the Upper Nepean catchment. The pigment was recovered from graphics and gestural marks, the latter including white stencils and white 'amorphous smears', both of which have been applied to the rock by blowing from the mouth. The temporal implication, which arose from Huntley's (Ford 2006) findings, relates primarily to the white stencil pigments. Carbon was found to be present in the six samples taken from stencils, and largely absent from white graphics. Huntley (Ford 2006:92) argues that the presence of carbon in the stencil pigment is derived from saliva, as a result of both the preparation and process of blowing pigment from the mouth. On the basis that organic specimens in paint are fragile and do not survive long, Huntley (Ford 2006:94) argues that the presence of carbon implies a very recent age (not more than a few centuries) for the white stencils. It is also notable that red stencil pigment, which Huntley had sought to analyse, was unable to be collected because it remained as a stain in the rock only; the red stencils did not possess any residual surface pigment. Sefton (1988) previously described this feature of red stencils and argues that it suggests that they are of some antiquity.

To conclude, it is clear from previous research in the Sydney Basin, and within the Woronora Plateau, that there is some basis for anticipating that an analysis of superimposed rock art motifs in the study area will reveal the presence of a relative sequence. In the absence of direct dates for the rock art, or of any associated archaeological deposit, establishing the timing of this sequence for the Upper Nepean catchment with any certainty is not possible. However, as discussed above, for a variety of reasons that include consideration of the unstable nature of the Hawkesbury Sandstone, the composition and characteristics of much of the pigment used, and reference to other direct dates obtained (or inferred, see Ford 2006; McDonald 2008a; Huntley et al. 2011) from rock art in the Sydney Basin, the period encapsulated by the sequence, particularly relating to pigment rock art, is unlikely to be long.

7.2 Relative Sequence Analysis: Methods and Limitations

The superimpositioning analyses were conducted on the two separate databases: Illawarra Prehistory Group Database (IPG/DB) and the Research Database (R/DB). The results of these separate analyses will be synthesised.

In establishing the relative sequence of the Upper Nepean rock art, consideration was given to the material properties of various pigments used to infer the potential antiquity, or otherwise, of imagery. Generally, drawn charcoal imagery is believed to be of a relatively recent age because, as a dry application, it does not bond well with the rock (Rosenfeld, pers. comm., 2003). White pigment imagery that survives on rock surfaces is generally thought to be of a recent age (cf. Lewis 1988:46; Rosenfeld 1991:141; David 2002:195) because the pigment is fragile. It is noted that McDonald (1994:173) indicates that all stencilled European contact objects are white in the Sydney Basin. On the other hand, red pigment is more chemically durable and tends to penetrate and bond with rock surfaces. Red pigment has the potential to survive longer and, therefore, to be relatively older than black or white pigment (cf. Lewis 1988:46).

Superimpositioned relationships do not encompass the full suite of motifs in the study area, and this limits the potential to reveal more than very broad trends. Furthermore, given high rates of weathering of the rock art and relatively high levels of formal diversity, identifying detailed temporal trends for the full range of motif variability is also likely to be limited. Another substantive issue is that early rock art occurs in low frequency and distributional density. Panaramitee-style rock art occurs extremely infrequently in Sydney Basin rock shelters. Accordingly, the potential for superimposed relationships to occur, with respect to this type of rock art, is correspondingly low. Further, if at any time artistic production proliferated in a suite of shelters for the first time, such art is unlikely to be superimposed over older art, so determining where it falls within the sequence is difficult. Motifs from earlier sociocultural contexts may be deliberately curated by subsequent generations by either avoidance of those areas, image re-marking or even image 'repair'. Conversely, there may also be continuity of graphic or gestural expression between different sociocultural phases. These scenarios recognise some of the fundamental limitations inherent in temporal ordering via superimpositioning analyses. However, disentangling the archaeological signatures is likely to offer illumination in regard to not only temporal variability itself, but also to the nature of change and the meaningful use of rock art in processes of social change and transformation.

Plate 7.1 Superimposed imagery (rock shelter BR32). A black drawn graphic is over red handprints and stencils.

Note: white is mineral skin.

Source: Photograph by Julie Dibden, 2011.

Discernment of the exact superimpositioning relationships between motifs in the rock art of the study area is often difficult (see Plate 7.1). This is not unique and is often remarked upon as a problem elsewhere (e.g. Haskovec 1992:64). However, this is not always the case, and many instances of pigment from a particular motif clearly overlying another have been identified in the study area. In the Research Database, where a superimposed relationship has been established for this analysis, the stratigraphical relationship is believed to be unambiguous.

Another consideration is determining whether or not a superimposed relationship between images has a temporal significance of sufficient magnitude as to have a historical dimension. (cf. Maynard 1979:90). Superimpositioning was regarded by Leroi-Gourhan and Laming (cited in Ucko & Rosenfeld 1967) in regard to European Palaeolithic cave art as compositions and, accordingly, they deny its relevance for establishing relative chronologies (Ucko & Rosenfeld 1967:145). Ross and Davidson (2006:322), in reference to rock art panels that have a dense overlay of imagery, suggest that these may indicate that the locale may represent 'specified contexts' and, hence, may hold a particular significance within a broader complex. In such instances, the motivations that result in superimposed relationships can occur as the result of events separated in time by minutes or years, rather than centuries or millennia. An awareness of the various possible permutations of the temporal significance of superimposing is thus necessary for establishing chronological patterns on the one hand, and the variability of rock art practice in synchronic contexts on the other.

7.2.1 Analysis of IPG Database Superimpositioning

In this section, superimposed rock art relationships recorded by the IPG are analysed. The individual superimposed relationships upon which this analysis is based are listed and described in Dibden (2011:Appendix 9). The analysis describes the relative positions of motifs in accordance with pigment colour and technique variables. An additional analysis was carried out on the relative positions of the IPG motif categories. It is not included here, as it was not considered to be interpretively useful, particularly given that most are formally indeterminate, and because of the arbitrary nature of motif categorisation (see also Dibden 2011:Appendix 9).

The following patterns emerge from the IPG superimpositioning data (Table 7.4). The location of the rock art sites referred to are shown in Appendix 2 in Dibden (2011).

Stencils

Red stencils are in superimposed relationships in 13 cases. In all instances except one, they are located below other motifs, including four white stencils, one red drawn graphic, five charcoal graphics, one white graphic, and two scratched graphics. Red stencils and red wet graphics do not co-occur in superimposed relationships. In two additional cases in the one shelter (Gill1, these stencils are not listed in Table 7.4), red stencils occur in a three-part superimposed relationship as follows: charcoal eel over red drawn snake over red stencils; and charcoal macropod over red drawn snake over red stencil. These two examples hint at a three-part pigment sequence of red drawn graphics being younger than red stencils, but older than charcoal graphics.

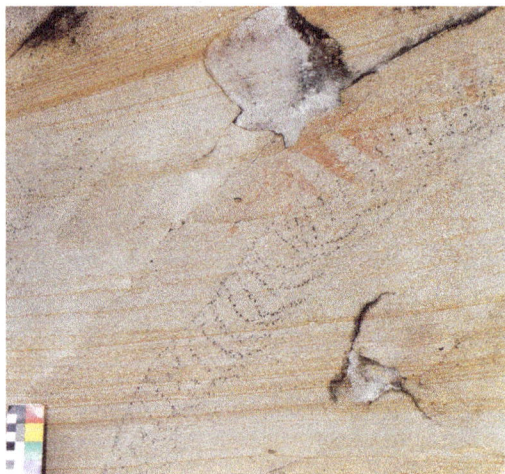

Plate 7.2 Superimposed imagery (rock shelter SCR3). A black drawn graphic over a red hand stencil.

Source: Photograph by Julie Dibden, 2011.

While red stencils are almost always under any other motif in superimposed relationships (Plate 7.2), this contrasts with white stencils, which in 11 relationships are over any other motif, including four red stencils, five charcoal graphics and two red drawn graphics. White stencils do not occur in superimposed relationships with red wet, white or scratched graphics.

Graphics

Red wet graphics occur in only two superimposed situations and, in each, are situated under charcoal drawings. One red drawn graphic is over a red stencil, and six red (including one red-and-black bichrome) graphics and one orange drawn graphic are located under charcoal drawings. As noted above, the examples in Gill1 also indicate that red drawn graphics (included in the count of six) overlie red stencils, but occur under black graphics.

Charcoal graphics occur over red stencils in five instances, and over red graphics in eight. The notable exception is one recording of a black graphic situated under a red stencil. There are no recordings of charcoal graphics over white stencils or white graphics, whereas they occur under white graphics twice.

Scratched graphics occur in three superimposed relationships twice over red stencils and once over a charcoal graphic.

Three additional superimposition relationships of pigment within individual bichrome motifs (all of which are eels) are noted by the IPG, and both entail charcoal outline and infill overlying the red component of the graphic. This example may have no temporal significance, and might simply represent the bichrome construction of the motif with charcoal being the last pigment application; alternatively, the charcoal may be a later redrawing of an earlier image and, hence, this may have a temporal dimension.

Table 7.4 Numbers of superimposed relationships per pigment colour and technique (IPG/DB).

Colour and technique combinations	Superimposition	Number of instances	Superimposition	Number of instances
Red and white stencils	White over red stencils	4	Red over white stencils	Nil
Charcoal graphics and red stencils	Charcoal graphics over red stencils	5	Red stencils over charcoal graphics	1
White graphics and red stencils	White graphics over red stencil	1	Red stencils of white graphics	Nil
Scratched graphics and red stencils	Scratched graphics over red stencils	2	Red stencils over scratched graphics	Nil
Red wet graphics and red stencils	Red wet graphics over red stencils	Nil	Red stencils over wet red graphics	Nil
Red drawn graphics and red stencils	Red drawn graphics over red stencils	1	Red stencils over red drawn graphics	Nil
Charcoal graphics and red wet graphics	Charcoal graphics over red wet graphics	2	Red wet graphics over charcoal graphics	Nil
Charcoal and red (and orange) and red-and-black bichrome drawn graphics	Charcoal graphics over red and red-and-black bichromes graphics	6	Red and red-and-black bichromes graphics over charcoal graphics	Nil
Charcoal graphics and white stencils	White stencils over charcoal graphics	5	Charcoal graphics over white stencil	Nil
Red drawn graphics and white stencils	White stencils over red drawn graphics	2	Red drawn graphics over white stencils	Nil
White graphics and white stencils	White stencils over white graphics	Nil	White graphics over white stencil	Nil
Charcoal and white graphics	White graphics over charcoal graphics	2	Charcoal graphics over white graphics	Nil
Scratched and charcoal graphics	Scratched graphics over charcoal graphics	1	Charcoal graphics over scratched graphics	Nil
Scratched and white graphics	Scratched graphics over white graphics	Nil	White graphics under scratched graphics	Nil
Scratched and wet red graphics	Scratched graphics over wet red graphics	Nil	Wet red graphics over scratched graphics	Nil
Scratched and red dry graphics	Scratched graphics over red drawn graphics	Nil	Drawn red graphics over scratched graphics	Nil
Scratched graphics and white stencils	Scratched graphics over white stencils	Nil	White stencils over scratched graphics	Nil

Source: Table reproduced from Dibden (2011).

Summary—IPG Database

This small IPG Database suggests the following basic temporal trends in regard to extant rock art based on the superimposition relationships of pigment and technique:

- Red stencils are likely to be a component of the earliest pigment rock art.
- Red drawn graphics may typically be more recent than red stencils, but older than many charcoal graphics.
- Charcoal graphics typically appear to occupy an intermediate position, as they occur over older red stencils, wet red graphics and red drawings, and under recent white stencils, and white and scratched graphics. They are, nevertheless, likely to be a component of the most recent art.
- White graphics and stencils are likely, normally, to be a component of the most recent rock art.
- Scratched graphics are likely to be a component of the most recent rock art.

7.2.2 Analysis of Research Database Superimpositioning

Of the 2,565 motifs in the Research Database, 524 (20.4%) have been identified to be in superimposed relationships. The majority of these are stratified associations involving two motifs, although a number of associations include three or more. These superimposed relationships occur in 42 of the 110 rock art shelters recorded for this research. The comparatively high number of shelters with superimposition in the Research Database reflects the intentional selection for more detailed recording, based on previous IPG observations, of shelters that contain these relationships. For heuristic purposes, not all motifs in superimposed relationships are included in the superimpositioning analysis documented below. For example, where one graphic is superimposed over several red stencils, one stencil only is counted.

The frequency in which pigment colour and mark type occurs, either over or under in superimpositions, including those that include two, three or four motifs, are shown in Table 7.5. For superimpositions including three or more motifs, *under* refers to the motif on the bottom and *over* is ascribed to any subsequent motifs. The following patterns are evident:

- Black charcoal pigment occurs most frequently in superimpositions (n = 192), and is typically (79.2%) situated over other coloured pigments. However, in 20.8 per cent of superimpositions, it is under other colours. All except one black motif occur as graphics or indeterminate (probably graphic) mark types. One instance of the gestural category, *black pigment marking*, is recorded as being over in a superimposed relationship (in EC5b: over a red indeterminate drawing).
- Red pigment is also common in superimpositions (n = 164) and is most frequently (95.1%) situated under other coloured pigments. Eight red motifs (all graphic or indeterminate marks) are over other colours. The majority of red pigment motifs are graphics or indeterminate (either graphic or gestural marks). Forty-six marks are gestural, including 42 handprints and/or hand stencils, and four are pigment blobs or smears. All red gestural marks are under other marks in superimpositions.
- Crimson is present in one superimposition and is under another colour. Orange is also infrequently superimposed and, in all instances, is under other colours.
- White pigment occurs in 39 superimpositions and is most frequently (89.7%) over other colours. The majority (n = 29) of white motifs in superimpositions are gestural marks, including stencils, pigments blobs and smears. There are four instances where white stencils are under in superimpositions.
- All cream-coloured pigment, all of which are gestural marks (stencils and pigment blobs), are over any other colour.

- Yellow (a graphic) is recorded once in a superimposition and is over another mark.
- Scratched marks, both graphics and gestural (in this tabulation defined as a colour), occur in 14 superimpositions, and are always over any other colour. Likewise, rubbed and pitting marks are always over other colours.

Table 7.5 Numbers of marks in superimposed relationships by mark type and pigment colour (R/DB).

Colour and mark type	Over #	Over %	Under #	Under %	Total
Black (total)	152	79.2	40	20.8	192
graphic	106	77.4	31	22.6	137
indeterminate	45	83.3	9	16.7	54
pigment marking	1	100			1
Black and white (total)	7	87.5	1	12.5	8
graphic	7	87.5	1	12.5	8
Black and yellow (total)	1	100			1
graphic	1	100			1
Brown (total)	1	100			1
pigment smear	1	100			1
Cream (total)	7	100			7
pigment blobs	2	100			2
stencil	5	100			5
Crimson (total)			1	100	1
graphic			1	100	1
Gestural subtractive (total)	6	100			6
pitting	2	100			2
rubbing	4	100			4
Orange (total)			5	100	5
Graphic			5	100	5
Red (total)	8	4.9	156	95.1	164
graphic	4	6.9	54	93.1	58
indeterminate	4	6.7	56	93.3	60
pigment blobs			2	100	2
pigment smear			2	100	2
print			8	100	8
stencil			34	100	34
Red and black (total)	3	60	2	40	5
graphic	3	60	2	40	5
Scratch (total)	14	100			14
graphic	4	100			4
indeterminate	2	100			2
scratching	8	100			8
White (total)	35	89.7	4	10.3	39
graphic	3	100			3
indeterminate	3	100			3
pigment blobs	1	100			1
pigment smear	1	100			1
stencil	27	87.1	4	12.9	31
Yellow (total)	1	100			1
graphic	1	100			1

Source: Table reproduced from Dibden (2011).

The sequential position of three or more motifs in superimpositions (17 instances) confirms previously identified trends and clarifies some other relationships (Table 7.6). Red and orange dominate the lowest positions and are the first in the sequence in 88 per cent of superimpositions as either graphic, indeterminate or stencil mark types. A white stencil occurs as the top layer in the one sequence containing four marks. However, in sequences of three marks, white motifs are relatively equally distributed between second (n = 5; 38.5%) or third layers (n = 7; 53.8%). All cream motifs are in the top of the sequence in the three instances they occur in these superimpositions. Likewise, black motifs are similarly relatively equally distributed between second (n = 10; 62.5%) and third (n = 6; 37.5%) layers. These data suggest that black and white can co-occur in the recent phase of the overall relative rock art sequence.

Table 7.6 Sequential position of the motifs in superimpositions of three or more
(1 = first in sequence, 2 = second, and so on) (R/DB).

Colour	1	2	3	4	Total
Black (total)		10 (62.5%)	6 (37.5%)		16
graphic		8	5		13
indeterminate		2	1		3
Black and white (total)		2 (66.7%)	1 (33.3%)		3
graphic		2	1		3
Black and yellow (total)			1 (100%)		1
graphic			1		1
Cream (total)			3 (100%)		3
pigment blobs			2		2
stencil			1		1
gestural		1 (50%)	1 (50%)		2
rubbing		1	1		2
Orange (total)	2 (100%)				2
graphic	2				2
Red (total)	15 (88.2%)	1 (5.9%)	1 (5.9%)		17
graphic	5	1			6
indeterminate	7		1		8
stencil	3				3
Red and black (total)		1 (100%)			1
graphic		1			1
Scratch (total)			1 (100%)		1
graphic			1		1
White (total)		5 (38.5%)	7 (53.8%)	1 (7.7%)	13
graphic		1			1
indeterminate			3		3
pigment blobs		1			1
stencil		3	4	1	8

Source: Table reproduced from Dibden (2011).

The superimpositions in the Research Database, as set out in accordance with the IPG recordings (and including those as recorded by the IPG in Table 7.4), are listed in Table 7.7. This demonstrates that the superimposition relationships in the Research Database are in general agreement with the IPG recordings. The following points are made:

- While recorded infrequently in superimpositions, white stencils are always over red stencils.

- Unlike the IPG Database, there are no instances of charcoal graphics being under red stencils and, instead, 23 instances of the reverse in the Research Database. The dominant trend is that charcoal graphics overlie red stencils in superimposed relationships.

- Red stencils do not occur in superimpositions with red wet graphics.

- White and scratched graphics occur infrequently in superimpositions with red stencils and, where they do, white and scratched are over red.

- Two instances of red drawn graphics overlying red stencils have been recorded. This result suggests that, generally, red drawn graphics were not produced in locales in which red stencils occur, and the two superimpositions tentatively indicate that red stencils may be older than red drawn graphics.

- The instances of 43 black graphics overlying red wet graphics (and red wet indeterminate marks) in the Research Database far outweigh the recordings of this relationship in the IPG Database. A dominant trend is inferred and, notably, this is comparable with that obtained between black graphics and red stencils. In the Research Database, there is one instance of a red wet graphic overlying a black graphic. It will be argued below that a small number of red graphics do occur in the most recent temporal phase in the study area.

- The 56 black graphics overlying red drawn graphics in the Research Database are greater than the number encountered in the IPG Database. Again, a dominant trend is inferred, however, as only four red drawn graphics over black graphics are recorded in the Research Database (these are all a component of the most recent rock art).

- Generally, white or cream stencils occur over black graphics. One instance of the reverse is recorded in the Research Database.

- Two instances of a superimposed relationship between white stencils and red drawn graphics occur, with the former being over the latter in the Research Database. This result suggests that, typically, white stencils were produced in locales where red drawn graphics do not occur, and that white stencils may be younger than red drawn graphics.

- White stencils and white graphics do not co-occur in superimpositions. This may indicate that different locales were used for each type of mark.

- White graphics occur infrequently with black graphics in superimpositions and, where they do, white is over black.

- Eleven instances of scratched graphics or non-graphic marks overlying black graphics are recorded in the Research Database, while one instance only of this superimposition is in the IPG Database. There are no instances of black graphics overlying scratched marks.

- Scratched marks and white graphics do not co-occur in superimpositions, and this may indicate that different locales were used for each type of mark.

- Scratched marks and white stencils do not co-occur in superimpositions, and this may indicate that different locales were used for each type of mark.

- Scratched marks and red wet or dry graphics occur infrequently in superimpositions, and, where they do, scratches overlie red graphics.

Table 7.7 Comparison of recorded superimposition relationships between the Research Database and the IPG Database.

Motif types	Superimposition	Number of instances	Superimposition	Number of instances
Red and white stencils	White (including cream) over red stencils	3 (IPG: 4)	Red over white stencils	Nil (IPG: Nil)
Charcoal graphics and red stencils	Charcoal graphics over red stencil and print	23 (IPG: 5)	Red stencil over charcoal graphics	Nil (IPG: 1)
White graphics and red stencils	White graphics over red stencil	Nil (IPG: 1)	Red stencils of white graphics	Nil (IPG: Nil)
Scratched graphics and red stencils	Scratched graphics over red stencils	Nil (IPG: 2)	Red stencils over scratched graphics	Nil (IPG: Nil)
Red wet graphics and red stencils	Red wet graphics over red stencils	Nil (IPG: Nil)	Red stencils over wet red graphics	Nil (IPG: Nil)
Red drawn graphics and red stencils	Red drawn graphics over red stencils	1 (IPG: 1)	Red stencils over red drawn graphics	Nil (IPG: Nil)
Charcoal graphics and red wet graphics (including red wet indeterminate)	Charcoal graphics over red wet graphic	43 (IPG: 2)	Red wet graphic over charcoal graphics	1 (IPG: Nil)
Charcoal and red (and orange and crimson) and red-and-black drawn graphics	Charcoal graphics over red or red-and-black drawing	56 (IPG: 6)	Red or red-and-black drawing over charcoal graphics	4 (IPG: Nil)
Charcoal graphics and white (and cream) stencils	White stencils over charcoal graphics	13 (IPG: 5)	Charcoal graphics over white stencil	1 (IPG: Nil)
Red drawn graphics and white stencils	White stencils over red drawn graphics	2 (IPG: 2)	Red drawn graphics over white stencils	Nil (IPG: Nil)
White graphics and white stencils	White stencils over white graphics	Nil (IPG: Nil)	White graphics over white stencil	Nil (IPG: Nil)
Charcoal and white graphics	White graphics over charcoal graphics	3 (IPG:2)	Charcoal graphics over white graphics	Nil (IPG: Nil)
Scratched (including non-graphic) and charcoal graphics	Scratched graphics over charcoal graphics	11 (IPG: 1)	Charcoal graphics over scratched graphics	Nil (IPG: Nil)
Scratched and white graphics	Scratched graphics over white graphics	Nil (IPG: Nil)	White graphics under scratched graphics	Nil (IPG: Nil)
Scratched and wet red graphics (and wet red indeterminate)	Scratched graphics over wet red graphics	2 (IPG: Nil)	Wet red graphics over scratched graphics	Nil (IPG: Nil)
Scratched and red dry graphics	Scratched graphics over red drawn graphics	1 (IPG: Nil)	Drawn red graphics over scratched graphics	Nil (IPG: Nil)
Scratched graphics and white stencils	Scratched graphics over white stencils	Nil (IPG: Nil)	White stencils over scratched graphics	Nil (IPG: Nil)

Source: Table reproduced from Dibden (2011).

In conclusion, red stencils and red wet graphics (and red wet indeterminate marks) occur frequently in superimpositions with black graphics. The dominant trend is that the former occurs under the latter. Based on a consideration of the assumed relative fragility of charcoal compared with red pigment, this trend is likely to have a temporal significance.

Red stencils and red wet graphics do not co-occur in superimpositions. Given that both mark types are comprised of red wet ochre and, therefore, both have the potential to be of an age greater than the majority of other pigment rock art in the study area, it is possible that these were produced more or less contemporaneously. Given that they do not co-occur in superimpositions, this is suggestive that they were, by choice, produced in different locales. The schema of red wet graphics is often comparable with the small intaglio engravings of the Sydney Basin.

These graphics are also qualitatively similar to McDonald's (1994:176) Phase 2 graphics. In the Upper Nepean catchment, their position within the relative sequence has been established to represent the earliest red graphic rock art.

Red stencils and red drawn graphics occur in four superimpositions (including those in the three-part sequence in Gill1 described earlier), but this is clearly an infrequent relationship. This result indicates the possibility that red drawn graphics are younger than red stencils and, or perhaps, a general preference to avoid the production of red drawings over red stencils.

The high numbers of superimpositions involving red drawn and black drawn graphics reveal a dominant trend for black drawings to occur over red. Given the relative fragility of charcoal compared with red ochre, it is probable that black drawings are younger than red drawn graphics, and that this relationship has a diachronic significance (see also Sefton 2003a:40).

Both white stencils and white graphics occur infrequently in superimposed relationships with any other motif, but, where they do, they each predominantly overlie other motifs. Charcoal and white pigment are relatively fragile, and it is assumed that both white and black motifs are of a generally comparable and relatively young age. In the Upper Nepean catchment, charcoal and white pigment do co-occur as bichromes in motifs, and one motif in site BR29 contains black and white pigment in two reversed superimpositions. Also, for example, site SCR10 contains a number of formally similar graphics in black and white that occur in superimpositions, thus strengthening the argument for their contemporaneity. Scratched motifs and non-graphic marks have been identified to occur above black graphics in 11 instances, above red wet marks in two, and above a red drawn graphic in one. Given that these marks never occur below other techniques, they are, therefore, most likely to be a part of the final art production phase.

7.3 Proposed Relative Sequence of the Upper Nepean Rock Art

A proposed relative sequence of rock art, and other marks, based on pigment colour and technique is listed in Table 7.8. This sequence is based on a consideration of the superimposed trends, and also the likely antiquity of the various pigment types. Two shelters in the Upper Nepean catchment contain intaglio engravings and these are added to the sequence, with reference to McDonald (2008a).

Table 7.8 Temporal sequence of sheltered art based on colour and technique.

Phase	Age	Mark type	Rock art
Phase 1	>4,000 years BP	Graphic	Intaglio engraved motifs
Phase 2	Uncertain; possibly <4,000 – >500 years BP	Gestural	Red hand stencils and handprints Red pigment smears usually over large areas
		Graphic	Red painted motifs Red, yellow and orange drawn motifs
Phase 3	Recent; possibly <500 years BP or even considerably less	Gestural	White and cream stencils Non-graphic pigment applications, including pigment blobs, circles, rock surface marking strokes and random Non-graphic scratched, pitted and rubbed marks
		Graphic	Charcoal drawn motifs (and black and white bichrome) Redrawing (usually outline only) of earlier red drawn graphics White painted or drawn motifs Scratched motifs Very small numbers of red drawn or wet motifs

Source: Table reproduced from Dibden (2011).

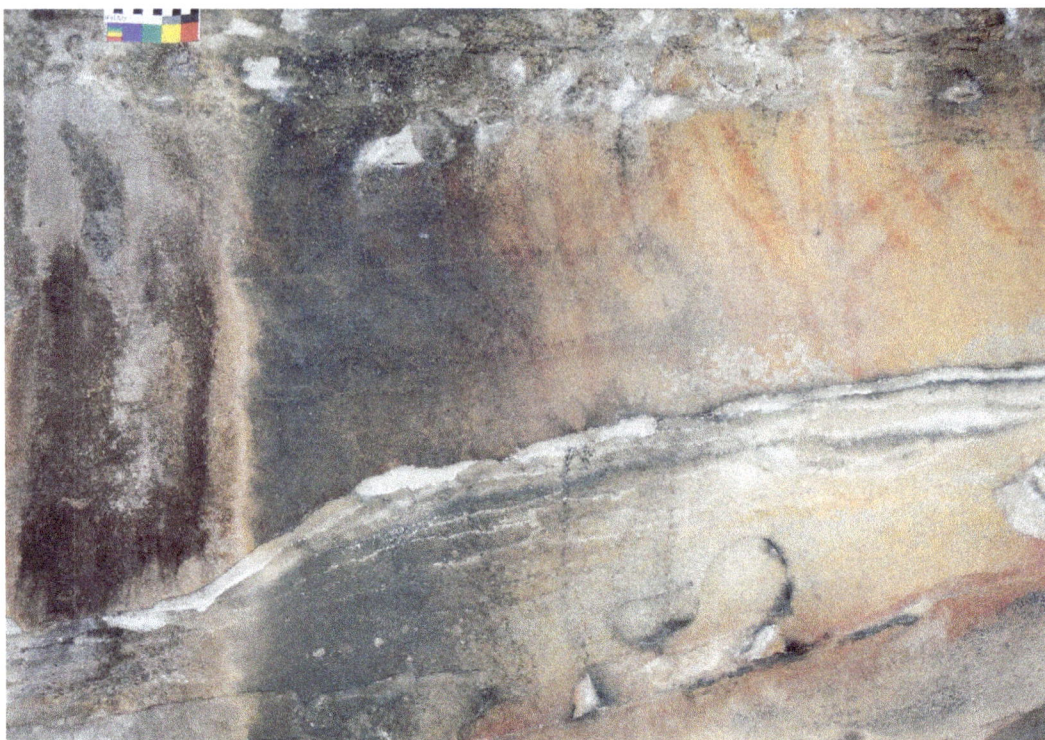

Plate 7.3 An example of a red wet 'trident' motif, which is assigned to Phase 2a (rock shelter EC5b).
Source: Photograph by Julie Dibden, 2011.

The analysis has identified a sequence of change that is comparable, in its broad structure, with that defined by McDonald (2008a:342–243), based on superimpositioning in the Upper Mangrove Creek catchment (see also Taçon et al. 2008:202). In the Upper Nepean, the two rock shelters with intaglio engravings do not contain pigment rock art. However, this type of rock art does occur in a shelter in the Southern Highlands (discussed further in Chapter 8), where it is superimposed under red hand stencils (pers. observ.), and so it is possible that the intaglio motifs are the earliest sheltered rock art in the study area. If such is the case, it is in agreement with McDonald's (2008a) Sydney Basin sequence.

The Upper Nepean Phase 2 rock art is not, however, entirely comparable with McDonald's Phase 2. There is no evidence that white stencils belong to this phase. The pigment rock art, which was identified as occurring frequently under other colours and techniques in the Upper Nepean catchment, includes red stencils and prints, gestural applications of red wet smeared pigment, and red painted motifs (simple forms, e.g. see Plate 7.3), and red drawn animal motifs (figurative forms). Based on four instances of red drawn motifs overlying red stencils, as discussed above, the Upper Nepean Phase 2 may contain a finer level of temporal ordering.

It is possible that the Phase 2 rock art, comprised of red drawn and yellow and orange painted animals and anthropomorphs, may be more recent than the stencils and, also, more recent than a small suite of red wet motifs that include simple forms (tridents and so on), which are formally comparable with the intaglio motifs (Plate 7.3). The superimpositioning analysis of the Upper Nepean rock art has defined the early relative position of the red wet simple form motifs, which McDonald (1994:176) placed within Phase 2 of her sequence. This will be discussed further in later chapters, but, for now, it is asserted that these motifs in the Upper Nepean catchment are also likely to be the earliest pigment rock art, and may be representative of an earlier sub-phase of Phase 2 (Phase 2a). It is also believed that some anthropomorphic motifs may also belong to Phase 2a.

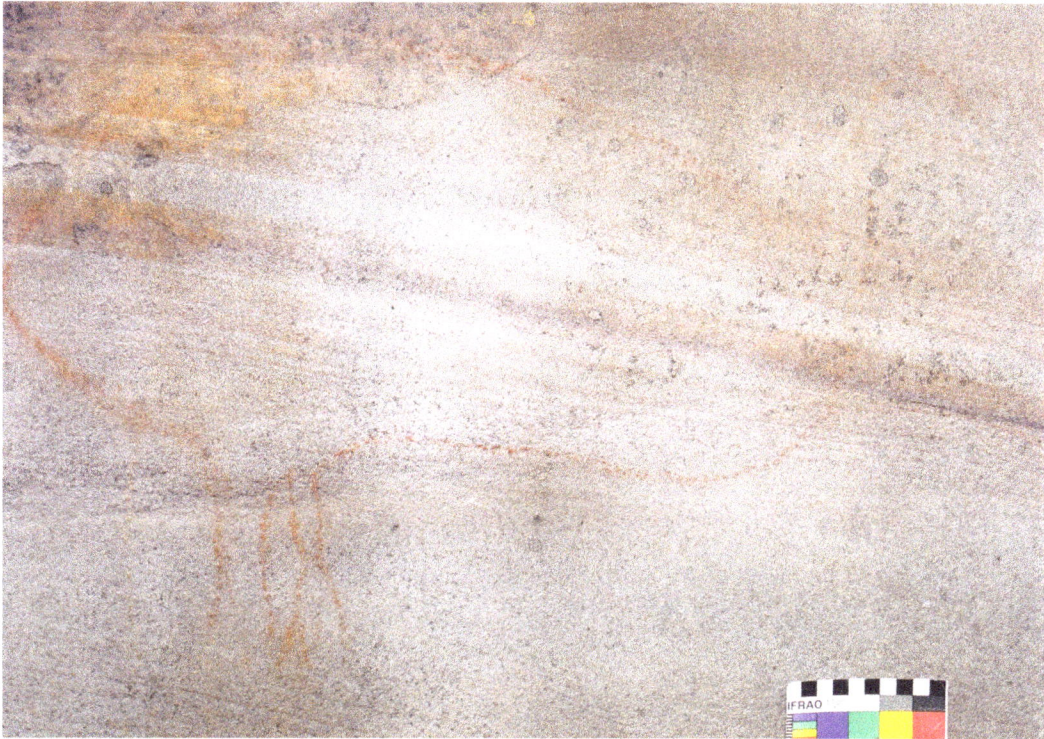

Plate 7.4 Example of red drawn animal motif, which is assigned to a possible later sub-phase of Phase 2 (rock shelter EC36).

Source: Photograph by Julie Dibden, 2011.

The red drawn animal motifs may be later in the Phase 2 sequence (Phase 2b). The analysis of the Upper Nepean superimpositioning has identified a dominant trend for red drawn graphics, most of which are large animal motifs (e.g. see Plate 7.4), to underlie charcoal and white motifs. This relationship was not identified by McDonald (1994:176), who placed them all within Phase 1. It is proposed that in the Upper Nepean catchment, these red drawn motifs, which are assigned to Phase 2, may represent an intermediate position between earlier red wet simple graphics, and the later charcoal and white motifs would, hence, be a later sub-phase of Phase 2.

The Upper Nepean Phase 3 rock art is, similar to the sequence identified in the Upper Mangrove Creek catchment (McDonald 1994:176), represented by a greater diversity of rock-marking behaviours, techniques and colours. Stencils in this phase are of white or cream pigment (also black), and a wide range of new gestural marks occur, produced by the addition of pigment or subtraction of the rock matrix. Graphics in this phase are predominantly charcoal drawings. In addition, black-and-white bichrome, white drawn and painted, scratched, and a small number of red (wet and dry) motifs occur (these latter motifs are the anomalous recordings in the superimposition analysis). Notably, in comparison with the Upper Mangrove Creek catchment sequence, Phase 3 rock art in the Upper Nepean catchment does not contain red pigment figurative (animal) motifs in either dry or wet applications. However, in Phase 3, the re-marking, and even 'repair', of older red animal imagery with charcoal is frequent (discussed further in Chapters 8 and 9).

While there are no direct dates yet available for the Upper Nepean rock art assemblages, the analysis of superimposition, in conjunction with a consideration of the likely longevity, or otherwise, of pigment indicates that rock art has been produced in this area for a considerable period of time, and is likely to have extended from at least the mid-Holocene through to the contact period (cf. McDonald 2008a:249). As discussed, McDonald employed a range of absolute and relative dating evidence to assign a broad temporal framework to her sequence. This included excavated evidence from a number of shelters, including buried panels of small intaglio engravings identified to represent Phase 1, and dated by their association with archaeological deposit (> 4,000 years BP or c. 6,000 years BP), buried ochre of the same colour as paintings in Dingo and Horned Anthropomorph shelter located above a dated horizon of 581 BP (Phase 3), and the identification of contact imagery that falls within Phase 3. McDonald (2008a:248) notes the absence of associated evidence for Phase 2, and indicates that defining the timing between Phases 2 and 3 is problematic.

Therefore, McDonald (2008a:247–248) defines the earlier and terminal rock art phases, but notes that assigning dates to the intervening period is more problematic. This same situation applies for the Upper Nepean catchment, although here the question of when rock art production ceased is even less secure as no obvious colonial imagery has been identified (this will, however, be discussed further in subsequent chapters). The small intaglio engraved rock art that occurs in two shelters, and several others in the immediate region, in accordance with McDonald's chronology, are likely to represent the earliest rock art in the Upper Nepean.

In the Upper Nepean catchment, red hand stencils (Plate 7.5), and a small suite of red painted graphic imagery (e.g. as shown in Plate 7.4), represent the earliest pigment art. McDonald (2008a:343) argues that the production of Phase 2 rock art in the Upper Mangrove Creek catchment commenced at some time prior to 4,000 years BP. It is possible that the earliest Phase 2 rock art in the Upper Nepean has a comparable antiquity; however, this cannot be confirmed at this time. The antiquity of the later Phase 2 rock art, comprised of large animal imagery, will be discussed further in Chapters 9 and 10. It is almost certainly not as old as the red stencils and red painted rock art.

Plate 7.5 Note the high degree of weathering of red stencil pigment (rock shelter SCR25).
Source: Photograph by Julie Dibden, 2011.

Phase 3 rock art in the Upper Nepean catchment is considered to be relatively recent. This conclusion is based on an assumption of the likely antiquity and durability of charcoal and white pigments (Plate 7.6 and 7.7); a consideration of Huntley's (Ford 2006) argument relating to the age of white stencils and pigment blobs in the Upper Nepean; and McDonald's (2000; 2008a) direct dates for charcoal motifs in the Upper Mangrove Creek catchment. However, Huntley's work was a trial project and the results, at this time, should perhaps most properly be considered as suggestive, rather than conclusive. Likewise, the AMS dating program of charcoal drawings in the north Sydney Basin produced results that are clearly not conclusive regarding the age of this rock art (McDonald 2000). It is proposed that Phase 3 rock art in the Upper Nepean may not be any older than 500 years BP. This is in general accordance with the AMS dates for charcoal drawings of the Sydney Basin, except for those obtained from Native Animals shelter. However, it is recognised that the organic environment of rock art pigments is so complex that any AMS dates should be viewed with caution (cf. Ridges 1995).

Plate 7.6 Phase 3 imagery (rock shelter A16). Black graphics.
Source: Photograph by Julie Dibden, 2011.

Plate 7.7 Phase 3 imagery (rock shelter SCR10).
Source: Photograph by Julie Dibden, 2011.

It is concluded that the Upper Nepean relative sequence is coarse grained, and is likely to be more nuanced than defined in the analyses. In addition, it is emphasised that the sequence is without firm chronological anchors. The rock art in each of the three phases in the Upper Nepean temporal sequence will be explored further in Chapters 8 and 9.

8

Rock Art and Temporal Variability

In this chapter, the rock art of the Upper Nepean catchment is examined within a temporal framework in accordance with the relative sequence defined in Chapter 7. The intent is to explore and define the nature of both synchronic and diachronic rock art variability according to the following criteria:

- abundance of sites and motifs
- shelter morphology variables
- the micro-topographic location of rock art within shelters
- the diversity of rock art, and its nature, in respect of behavioural expression, motif form and figurative referent.

8.1 Phase 1 Rock Art

Small intaglio engravings of Phase 1 rock art occur in two shelters in the Upper Nepean catchment: Cad5 and Bet37 (Figure 8.1). The low numbers of sites with this type of rock art is in keeping with the general pattern of their low density distribution in the broader Sydney Basin. Sefton (2003a) has previously described these shelters, and her discussion refers to others with this rock art, located to the south of the Woronora Plateau, including Bundanoon, Jubilee Rocks and Foxground. Sefton (2009b) has more recently described the engravings in FRC226 and FRC225, which are both located immediately to the north of the Upper Nepean study area in the Woronora River catchment (Figure 8.1).

This type of engraving in the Sydney Basin is often called Panaramitee, the name ascribed to a corpus of engravings in Australia, defined by Maynard (1979:92) as follows:

> [T]hey are composed of bands of solid forms; most figures measure up to 10 centimetres in height, and there is a very narrow range of motifs, dominated by macropod and bird tracks and circles, with a smaller number of crescents, groups of dots, human footprints, radiating lines, 'tectiforms' or line mazes, and a tiny fraction of other nonfigurative designs. Although rare, these 'other designs' are sometimes very distinctive and highly variable.

Maynard's definition is based on the criteria of technique, age and an assessment that the art is essentially non-figurative. She asserted that classic Panaramitee sites are widely distributed in the arid zone (Maynard 1979:95). Maynard (1979:95, 97), however, cast her net more broadly and included two Sydney Basin sites in her grouping and distribution of Panaramitee rock art. These additional areas, which she described as being peripheral, were seen to conform generally to the Panaramitee style, except in terms of the relative proportions of different motifs (Maynard 1979:95).

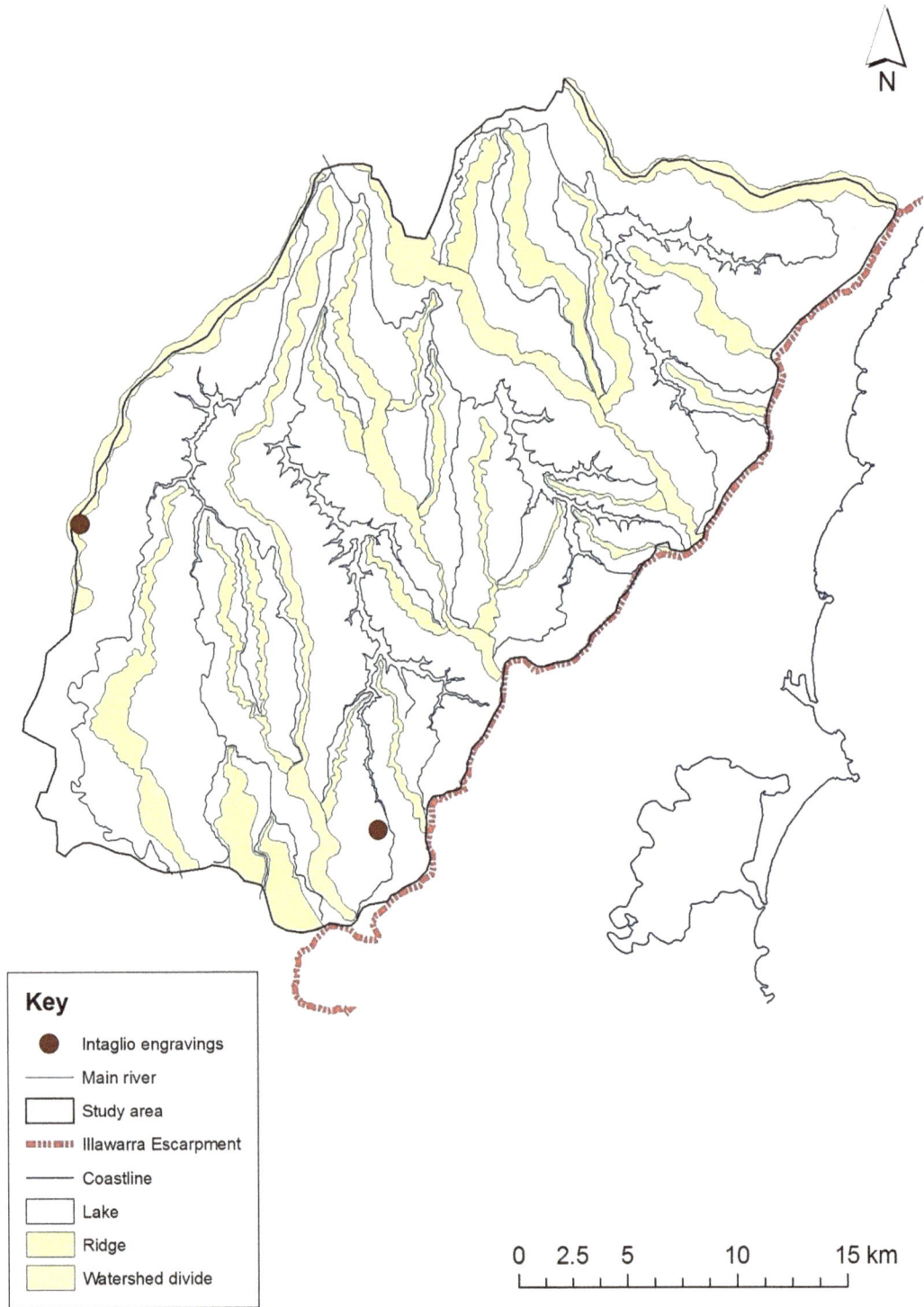

Figure 8.1 Location of shelters with Phase 1 rock art in the Nepean and Avon catchments.
Source: Map reproduced from Dibden (2011).

For some time, Panaramitee rock art was considered to be representative of the oldest rock art in Australia, and consistent in form over virtually the entire continent (e.g. see Figure 1 in Clegg 1987:238). The apparent pan-continental distribution was seen to contrast with the more regionally varied recent rock art. Maynard (1979:92) proposes a developmental sequence for Australian rock art based on three broad stylistic categories: Panaramitee, Simple Figurative and Complex Figurative. The assumed antiquity of Panaramitee, and its stylistic uniformity, was invoked as reflecting a high degree of cultural homogeneity during the Pleistocene, which subsequently gave way to cultural diversity, represented by the more regionalised, later rock art styles (Maynard 1979:108).

Panaramitee has since been identified to exhibit considerable motif and intra- and inter-site distributional diversity, which earlier researchers had failed to address (Rosenfeld 1991:137). There are also indications that many motifs are represented in pigment rock art in some regions. The significance of this is that not only has the antiquity and the duration of the Panaramitee tradition required revision, but also the epistemological foundation regarding the operational basis of artistic systems in the archaeological record has required rethinking. In her review, Rosenfeld (1991:140) concludes that Panaramitee engravings have a temporal dimension that extends from the late Pleistocene well into the Holocene and, in some cases, into the very recent past. Recognising this vastly inflated timescale for the phenomenon of Panaramitee, Rosenfeld (1991:141) proposes that it is not just 'assemblages of motifs, but also their stylistic regularities and the rules which govern their meaningful deployment' that characterise an artistic system, and that these may operate in a diversity of contextual modes of expression.

In considering the underlying assumptions of cultural uniformity, which prevailed at that time, and with reference to ethnographic understandings of how a comparable artistic system comprised of simple forms operates, Rosenfeld (1991:141) argues that social context and structure convey meaning as much as the graphic form itself. Accordingly, such a visual system of communication is highly flexible, and has the capacity to express a multiplicity of meanings, so that superficial similarities of form and motif frequencies that define Panaramitee do not necessarily imply the expression of cultural uniformity, either synchronically or diachronically. In regard to cultural change, such a graphic system can accommodate transformation, via the employment of existing forms, by the use of different structural change (Rosenfeld 1991:142). Hence, Rosenfeld (1991:143) argues that the 'apparent stability of the basic motif elements of these artistic traditions over more than 10,000 years need not reflect cultural stagnation'.

All current indications relating to the antiquity of the small intaglio engravings found in the Sydney Basin suggests that they are the earliest extant expression of rock art. However, this rock art has not yet been subject to a specific analysis and, hence, a deep understanding of its graphic form, and whether it possesses synchronic or diachronic diversity is not known. To date, there has been no suggestion that it was produced synchronically with any sheltered pigment art, but this possibility should not be discounted. As noted in Chapter 7, McDonald (1994, 2008a) has assigned a minimum age of 4,000 years BP for these engravings, and she considers them to be 'residual Panaramitee'. Sefton (2003a:14, 2009a:37, 2009b:9) also considers these motifs located on the Woronora Plateau, and others to the south, to conform to the Panaramitee style and, specifically, she argues for their expression during the earliest occupation of the region, and that they reflect sparse occupation. Given the location of shelters with this rock art at the 'margins' of the Woronora Plateau, and/or on major ridgeline travel routes, Sefton (2009a:13) argues that this distribution reflects early occupation patterns, indicating 'partial use of the landscape and avoidance of the rugged sandstone of the Woronora Plateau'. This notion will be discussed further in Chapter 10.

Plate 8.1 Small intaglio engravings at the Bundanoon rock shelter.

Source: Photograph by Julie Dibden, 2011.

The intaglio engraving shelters, Cad5 and Bet37, and others in the wider local area, are listed in Table 8.1. The seven shelters described in Table 8.1 represent the only sites south of the Georges River known to contain this rock art. As only two sites are in the study area, the following discussion takes into consideration the attributes relating to all seven sites in order to consider those in the Upper Nepean catchment more meaningfully.

Table 8.1 Description of shelters with small intaglio engravings in the Upper Nepean and adjacent environs (IPG/DB).

Name	Location	Description
Caddie 5 (Cad5)	Avon River	Shelter measuring 12 m long x 5 m wide x 4 m high; living area 8 square metres; located on a ridge top. Engraving on rear wall above a shelf: Sefton (1997:35) describes the engravings as Panaramitee-style tracks including two bird tracks and a double bird track. No pigment art in shelter.
Bethany 37 (Bet37)	Nepean River	Shelter measuring 6 m long x 2.8 m wide x 1.6 m high; living area 3 square metres; located on an upper valley slope of the major divide between the Nepean and Bargo rivers. Engravings on rear wall in two sections: one 0.8 metres above the floor and the other at floor level. The upper section has two bird tracks and three pairs of kangaroo tracks. The lower section contains a further series of weathered engravings, including three bird tracks, one pair of kangaroo tracks, one circle and two indeterminate. No pigment art in shelter.
FRC225	Woronora River Nth Woronora Plateau	Shelter measuring 14 m long x 4.6 m wide x 3 m high; living area 10 square metres; located on an upper valley slope. One pair of engraved kangaroo tracks on the rear face of a floating rock. Also on the rear wall of shelter two charcoal indeterminate drawings.

Name	Location	Description
FRC226	Woronora River Nth Woronora Plateau	Shelter measuring 24 m long x 4.5 m wide x 2.1 m high; living area 40 square metres; located on a ridge top. A panel on the rear wall of the shelter measuring 5.7 m long x 1.4 m high contains a total of 85 engravings, including 47 three-toed bird tracks (emu), 9 four-toed bird tracks, 7 right tick, 5 left ticks (this includes 3 pairs kangaroo tracks), 11 bars and 6 frontal human figures. The engravings are all pecked and extend to almost floor level. Also on a side wall one red indeterminate drawing superimposed by two charcoal indeterminate drawings. Three hatchet grinding grooves, two large ground (?food) depressions and four 1 cm diameter (1 cm deep) pits on a large boulder at front of shelter.
Bundanoon (Plate 8.1)	Southern Highlands	This small shelter (7 m long x 1 m wide x 1.5 m high) is located in a low boulder and does not contain any optimal living space. The site is divided into two sections by a protruding wall. The southern alcove measuring 2 m long contains an upper wall with large areas of what appears to be red wet pigment. No stencils are identifiable. The northern alcove measuring c. 2.5 m long contains a bottom panel that slopes to the ground on which is one pair of large macropod tracks and two adjacent small bird tracks; below this another pair of large macropod tracks with a smaller bird track between the two. The upper wall panel contains areas of wet red pigment and three identifiable red hand stencils.
Jubilee Rocks	Southern Highlands	Shelter measuring 18 m long x 8 m wide x 3 m high with a living area measuring 100 square metres on ridge. This large commodious shelter has a wall panel of red hand stencils and another containing red hand stencils and engravings. The engravings in this site are very weathered and are exfoliating from the wall suggesting some antiquity. The site contains a deep deposit and two grinding grooves. A grinding groove site is also located above the shelter on an open platform. Significantly, red stencils are superimposed over many of the engravings at this site.
Foxground	Kangaroo Valley	This shelter, similar to Bundanoon, is divided in two small parts, which are separated by a rock wall, and neither of which contain living space. The site contains an extensive (c. 60 m) suite of small engraved motifs, most of which are bird and macropod tracks. The site also contains an extensive suite of red hand stencils.

Source: Table reproduced from Dibden (2011).

8.1.1 Abundance of Sites and Rock Art

The engraved rock art in the seven shelters is comprised of small, pecked and abraded motifs, primarily trident-shaped bird and macropod tracks, the latter often being paired (Dibden 2011:Appendix 10). Rarer motifs include circles, bars and, notably, six frontal human figures (the latter all being in FRC226). The motifs are predominantly figurative, given that most represent animal footprints or tracks. However, their arrangement on rock surfaces is not in alignment and, accordingly, does not obviously denote movement (cf. Rosenfeld 2002:74). Rather than suggesting that they functioned as narrative, their formal qualities evoke more iconic, symbolic values.

The two Upper Nepean shelters, Cad5 and Bet37, are not associated with any other rock art type. However, the engravings in Jubilee Rocks are superimposed by red stencil pigment, and Bundanoon and Foxground also contain red stencils.

8.1.2 Shelter Morphology

Intaglio engravings in the study area occur in a small and a medium-sized shelter with small living areas, although Cad5 is slightly more commodious than Bet37. Neither shelter can be considered likely to have functioned as base camp habitation sites. However, variability in the size of shelters occurs across the local region. Jubilee Rocks and FRC226 shelters are both large and commodious, with abundant space; yet, Bundanoon and Foxground are small and contain no living area. This diversity in shelter size, and that some contain living space of significant dimensions and others not, suggests that either intaglio engravings were produced synchronically (i.e. if they are contemporaneous) within different sociofunctional contexts, on an ad hoc basis, or that the shelter space itself was incidental to their production. It is notable that when red hand stencils are present in these sites, shelters may be either commodious or small and, as will be discussed in the section dealing with Phase 2 rock art, this is a geographically widespread pattern.

The number of intaglio engraving sites is too low to make any interpretation regarding the sociocultural context in which this rock art was produced, based on a consideration of shelter morphology alone. Nevertheless, the diversity represented by the seven sites suggests that the nature of the shelter itself was not a significant determining factor relating to the choice of location for rock art production.

8.1.3 Micro-topography

The intaglio engravings in the shelters in the study area occur on vertical wall panels, as do the engravings in Jubilee Rocks, Foxground and FRC226. However, the engravings in Bundanoon shelter are located on a low, sloping wall/floor panel, and those in FRC225 are located on the rear face of a 'floating' rock. At Bundanoon, for example, there is no physical reason for this choice to engrave on a low, sloping panel, as vertical surfaces with stencils are present, and would presumably have been as suitable for the production of engravings as any of the other vertical surfaces used in the other sites. At Jubilee Rocks, a boulder is present in the shelter (containing grinding grooves), which could have been used similar to that in FRC225. From a perspective of embodiment, the practice of making these intaglio motifs was clearly as varied as the choice of the site in the first place.

8.2 Phase 2 Rock Art

Phase 2 rock art includes gestural and graphic rock art, and the use of red pigment is predominant. The red graphics in Phase 2, where their form is intact and recognisable, are most frequently comprised of large animal motifs that appear to have been drawn, and a small suite of more abstracted forms believed to have been painted. Some of these latter motifs are formally comparable with those in Phase 1 rock art, and this is consistent with McDonald's (2008a:238) findings in the Upper Mangrove Creek sequence. The majority of the rock art in Phase 2 is highly weathered, and in the majority of cases red pigment is present as a stain without any residue remaining on the rock surface. Accordingly, in respect of graphics in Phase 2 rock art, determining the method of application, by non-aided visual inspection alone, is problematic.

Huntley (Ford 2006; Huntley et al. 2011) has conducted pigment characterisation analyses of red (and a yellow) drawn motifs in the Upper Nepean, and argues that they were produced as a wet application of prepared paint. The implication of this argument is that many of the graphics in Phase 2 have been classified as drawn in both the IPG Database (IPG/DB) and

Research Database (R/DB), which is therefore incorrect. More importantly, Huntley's finding introduces a new dimension relating to the behavioural significance of all Phase 2 rock art, for it implies not only that people began to mark the land with a suite of new and diversified range of imagery, but that they also engaged with a new range of social and technological processes relating to the acquisition of pigment and preparation of paint.

8.2.1 Abundance of Sites and Motifs

A total of 1,169 Phase 2 rock markings are present in 173 (34%) shelters in the Upper Nepean catchment. Table 8.2 lists the distribution of these mark types by database. It is noted that 42 per cent of those marks are in the R/DB, with the remainder in the IPG/DB. The Phase 2 count of 1,169 motifs represents 23 per cent of rock art in the study area. Certain discrepancies between the two databases are evident. A total of 119 marks in the R/DB have been classified as indeterminate, and this refers to marks that are not distinguishable, based on a visual assessment alone as either graphic or gestural, although it is probable that most are weathered stencils. It is also notable that the R/DB contains a higher number of graphics and fewer stencils compared with the IPG/DB. On one hand, this bias reflects the emphasis in this research to record sites with high graphic counts and, on the other, avoidance of stencil sites for which it was considered that the IPG recordings were adequate for the purposes of this analysis.

The majority of Phase 2 rock art is represented by gestural marks, predominantly red stencils (n = 601; 51%). This frequency would be higher if the 119 (10%) indeterminate marks in the R/DB are indeed weathered stencils as suggested. Graphic marks account for approximately one-third (n = 415; 36%), and while not insignificant they are, nevertheless, a relatively minor component of Phase 2 rock art. The geographic distribution of shelters with Phase 2 rock art is shown in Figure 8.2, and it can be seen that marking the land became relatively widespread with the advent of the use of pigment and the production of gestural and figurative graphic imagery.

Table 8.2 Numbers of Phase 2 rock art types (R/DB and IPG/DB).

Motif type	Research Database	IPG Database	Total motif
Red indeterminate	119	–	119 (10%)
Red stencils	136	465	601 (51%)
Red handprints	16	5	21 (2%)
Red gestural other	6	7	13 (1%)
Red graphics	234	181	415 (36%)
Total	511 (44%)	658 (56%)	1,169 (100%)

Source: Table reproduced from Dibden (2011).

Phase 2 rock art is present in the 173 rock shelters in three main groups of associations: stencils only, graphics only, and stencils and graphics. Red stencils are present in 111 shelters, while graphics occur in 92. Given the fewer numbers of shelters with graphics, and a consideration of rock mark counts where stencils are more frequent than graphics, it is proposed that gestural expression within Phase 2 was the more common manner in which people marked the land. It is recognised that this assertion is based on an assumption of the relative contemporaneity of both rock art forms.

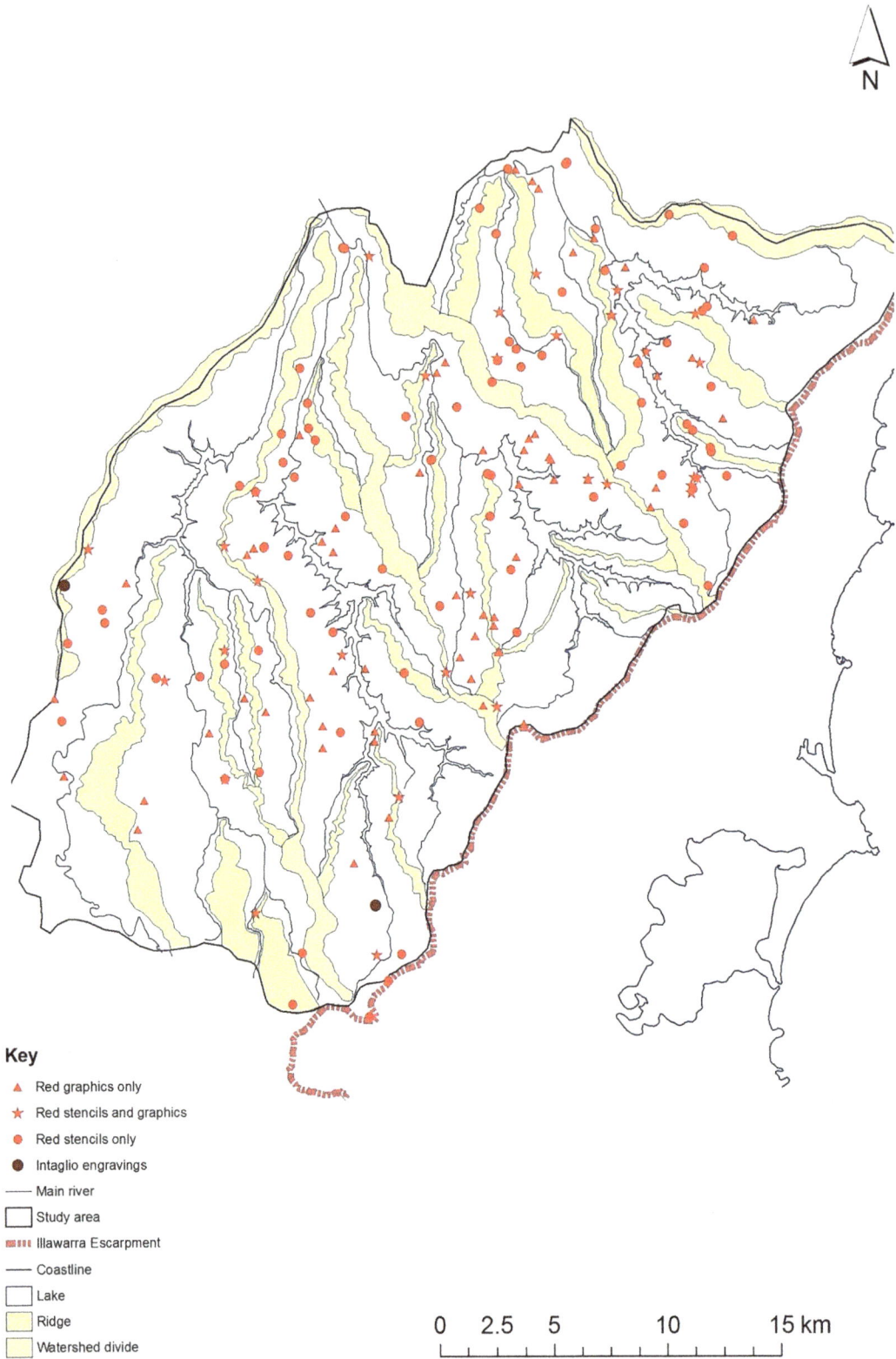

Key

▲   Red graphics only
★   Red stencils and graphics
●   Red stencils only
●   Intaglio engravings
―   Main river
☐   Study area
▰▰▰   Illawarra Escarpment
―   Coastline
☐   Lake
▨   Ridge
▨   Watershed divide

0   2.5   5   10   15 km

Figure 8.2 Location of Phase 2 rock art shelters.

Source: Map reproduced from Dibden (2011).

Gestural Marks

Gestural marks in Phase 2 include red stencils, handprints, and large smears of red wet pigment. The stencil shelter density in the entire study area is 0.1 sites per square kilometre, and the average stencil motif density is 0.8 stencils per square kilometre. A comparison of densities between catchments indicates that Phase 2 stencil site and motif densities decrease from north to south. The Cataract has a comparable site density to the Cordeaux and Avon, but a higher stencil density. The Nepean contains the lowest overall site and motif density. The Cataract, Cordeaux and Avon have comparable densities for all sheltered rock art sites (as discussed in Chapter 6), and this contrasts with individual rock art motifs that occur in the Cordeaux and Avon in higher densities (Table 8.3). A different pattern, however, occurs in respect of Phase 2 stencils, which, while present in comparable shelter densities between the three catchments, are more numerous in the Cataract. This suggests that within Phase 2 rock art, gestural marking of the land varies in intensity between the catchments, and it is noted that there is a strong correspondence between these calculations and the open context grinding groove site frequencies and densities, as outlined in Chapter 6. This stencil density distribution is suggestive of a greater intensity of land use in the Cataract within Phase 2.

Table 8.3 Comparison of Phase 2 stencil density with all shelter sites and motif densities (IPG/DB and R/DB).

Catchment	All sheltered rock art site density	All sheltered motif density	Phase 2 stencil site density	Phase 2 stencil motif density
Cataract	0.8	6.8	0.2	1.3
Cordeaux	0.7	9.1	0.1	0.5
Avon	0.8	9	0.2	0.8
Nepean	0.4	3	0.07	0.4
Average	0.6	6.4	0.1	0.8

Source: Table reproduced from Dibden (2011).

The highest frequency of shelters (41.4%) and stencil counts (45.8%) is in the Cataract catchment, which also has the highest average count per site (n = 6). The Nepean and Cordeaux have comparably low frequencies of sites and motif counts. The range of stencil counts per shelter is 1 to 46. The mode and median are both low, indicating that low stencil counts in individual shelters are frequent. Again, the structure of these data is similar to the pattern of grinding groove distribution per site, and indicates that stencil production was generally a low-level activity, with a few key sites being the focus of comparatively higher levels of this type of marking (Figure 8.3).

In all catchments, the majority of stencils are in shelters that do not contain any other Phase 2 rock art. Furthermore, the shelters that contain the highest stencil counts, except for the Cordeaux catchment, are also those that do not contain Phase 2 graphic rock art. These patterns suggest a general tendency for gestural marking to be undertaken in locations separate from those for which it was appropriate to produce graphic motifs. It is notable that when both stencils and graphics co-occur, each motif type is generally spatially separate (see Dibden 2011:Appendix 1). Generally, stencils are located at one end of a shelter and graphics at the other. This trend for spatial separation between the two motif types, either at the inter- or intra-site level, suggests that each is of a different order of sociofunctional significance, as Rosenfeld (1999) argues. It may also explain why the two motif types are rarely found in superimposed relationships.

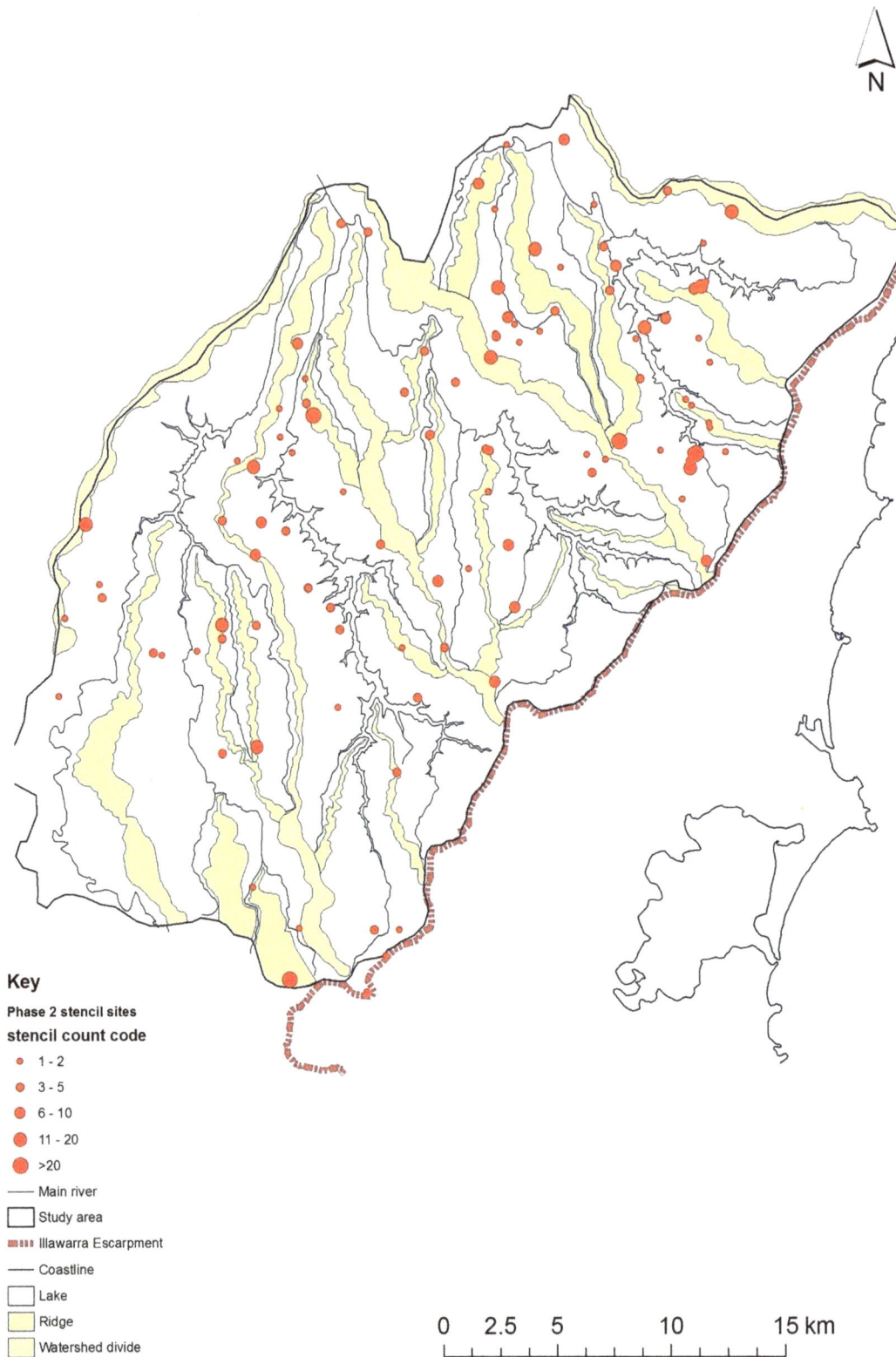

Key

Phase 2 stencil sites
stencil count code

- ○ 1 - 2
- ● 3 - 5
- ● 6 - 10
- ● 11 - 20
- ● >20
- —— Main river
- ☐ Study area
- ▬▬▬ Illawarra Escarpment
- —— Coastline
- ☐ Lake
- ☐ Ridge
- ☐ Watershed divide

0   2.5   5   10   15 km

Figure 8.3 Phase 2 shelters with stencils showing count variability in the Upper Nepean catchment.
Source: Map reproduced from Dibden (2011).

The other gestural marks in Phase 2 rock art are smears of red pigment. These are frequently, but not always, associated with red stencils. They occur in 11 shelters, most of which are in the Cataract catchment (e.g. LizCk17, AF3, Wall19, Wall26, Wall40, Gill10, Gill1, BMS5). These applications of pigment to the surface of shelter walls generally cover large areas of rock art panels (>1 metre) and are therefore considered to be more than incidental marks. While the productive context of these smears can only be speculated, at the very least as deliberate applications of prepared pigment, they are likely to have been meaningful actions relating, by means of the gesture, people to place.

Graphics

The Phase 2 graphic site density in the study area is 0.12 sites per square kilometre; average motif density is 0.31 graphics per square kilometre. Phase 2 graphic sites and motif densities are highest in the Cataract, Cordeaux and Avon catchments. The Nepean contains the lowest overall site and graphic density (Figure 8.4).

The Cataract, Cordeaux and Avon catchments have comparable site densities for all sheltered rock art sites, and this contrasts with all rock art motif counts that occur in the Cordeaux and Avon in higher densities. Therefore, the higher density of Phase 2 graphics in the Cordeaux and Avon catchments is comparable with the density patterns in respect of all sheltered rock art sites and motifs. The different pattern in respect of Phase 2 graphics, while occurring in comparable site densities between the three catchments, but in higher motif densities in the Cataract, is notable. This distribution suggests that the Cordeaux and Avon were the focus of marking the land with corporately defined rock art, although this is only a matter of degree in respect of a comparison with the Cataract (see Figure 8.4).

The catchment with the highest frequency of shelters with Phase 2 graphics is the Cordeaux (33.7%), while the Avon contains the highest frequency of motif counts (34.7%). The range of graphics per shelter is between 1 and 49. The mode and median are both low, indicating that low graphic counts in individual shelters are frequent. The structure of these data is similar to stencil distribution and indicates, likewise, that graphic production was generally a low-level activity, with a few key sites subject to relatively higher levels of marking (Figure 8.4). Shelters A12, UA1, UA47 (in the Avon), EC5b (in the Cordeaux) and Gill50, in the Cataract, are key Phase 2 shelters with high graphic counts. Notably, these sites, except for Gill50, contain graphics exclusively.

In the Avon and Cordeaux catchments, the majority of graphics occur in shelters that do not contain any other type of Phase 2 rock art. It is also in these catchments where the highest graphic counts occur in shelters that do not contain stencils. This contrasts with the Cataract and Nepean, where both the highest graphic counts and highest count per site occur in shelters that also have Phase 2 stencils. This distribution suggests that the Avon and Cordeaux may have been the foci for the production of graphic rock art and not gestural marking.

These patterns for Phase 2 graphic rock art contrast with stencil data, where typically shelters with stencils only are distributed across all catchments. However, the pattern that shelters with the highest stencil counts (except for the Cordeaux) contain Phase 2 graphic rock art is mirrored with the graphic data from the Cordeaux and Avon. With the exception of the Cataract and Nepean, there is a trend that marking of the land with corporate symbols was undertaken in locations that are separate from those for which it was appropriate to produce individualised gestural marks.

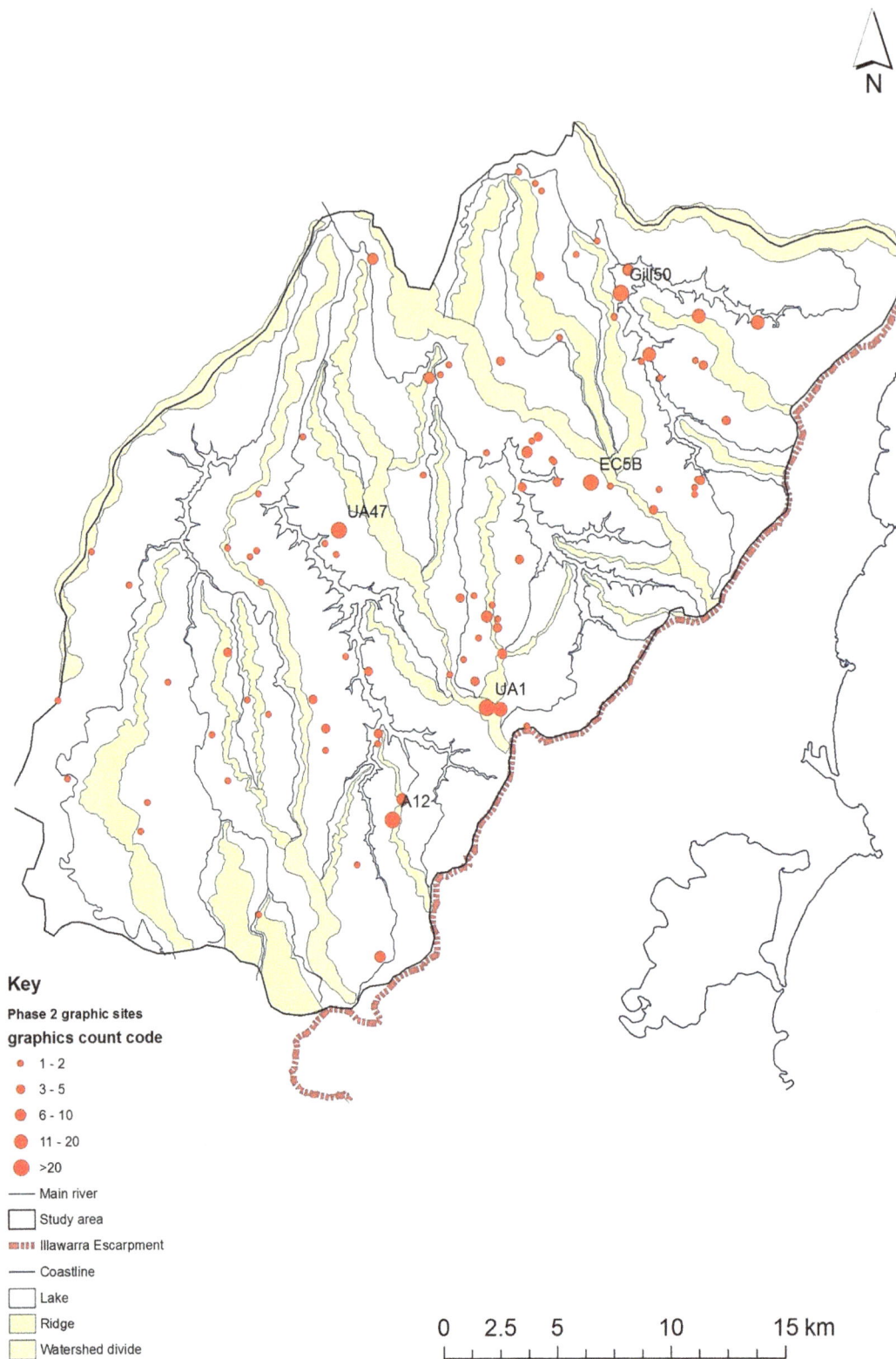

Figure 8.4 Phase 2 shelters with graphics showing count variability in the Upper Nepean catchment (sites with >20 graphics named).

Source: Map reproduced from Dibden (2011).

8.2.2 Shelter Morphology

Phase 2 rock art occurs in a wide variety of shelter morphological types. These range from shallow, scalloped niches in vertical rock faces to large, commodious shelters with abundant space.

Shelters with Phase 2 rock art that contain stencils only frequently have no, or very small, areas of living space. Some 71 per cent of these sites, including all shelters that have large stencil counts (>10), have a living space of 10 square metres or less. Sites with small stencil counts, particularly those with five or less, occur in the full range of living space sizes and, notably, in shelters with large living areas. By comparison, stencils that co-occur with Phase 2 graphics tend, frequently, to be in shelters that have larger living areas. This trend is particularly evident for larger stencil counts.

Shelters with Phase 2 graphics only have a wide range of living space sizes and, notably, slightly more than half contain either no living space or an area that measures 10 square metres or less. There is a trend for shelters with large graphics counts (>20) to possess large living areas, as do three of the four shelters with more than 20 graphics. Notably, two with graphic counts of 11 or more clearly have insignificant living area space.

The three shelters with 20 or more graphics with large living spaces are:

- EC5b: This shelter is a major rock art site in the Cordeaux catchment. It is large, contains high counts of graphics, and all indicators suggest it has been used for rock art pigment activity since the practice began in the Upper Nepean. It is notable for possessing a suite of red painted graphics, including four tridents and other trident configurations. These motif types are formally comparable with the bird track motifs of the Phase 1 small intaglio engravings.

- A12: This shelter, a major rock art site in the Avon catchment, is large, with high graphic counts, and is likely to have been used for rock art since the practice began in the area. It possesses a suite of red painted graphics, including tridents and trident configurations (Plate 8.2), and animal imagery of paired gliders (Plate 1.1), marsupials, eels and others.

- UA47: This shelter in the Avon is notable for containing an unusually wide range of animal imagery, including six echidnas, one marsupial glider, two animated marsupials, a lizard, a snake, an eel and a group of three wombats (the latter associated with a cluster of oval motifs [c. 17]). These wombats are the only examples that occur in Phase 2 rock art.

The two shelters with 11 or more graphics and negligible living spaces are:

- BC45: This shelter, at the eastern end of the Cataract catchment, contains a limited suite of graphic forms, and is dominated by a large trident motif associated with a cluster of six or seven circle motifs.

- UA1: This shelter in the Avon catchment is in many ways a counterpart of UA47 described above, as it too is dominated by groups of echidnas (2) and gliders (3), marsupials and macropods, but these are accompanied with small anthropomorphic figures that have their counterparts in the Phase 1 intaglio engraving site FRC226.

In summary, shelters that have large counts of Phase 2 graphics (without stencils) are variable in terms of shelter morphology and occupational living space, suggesting either that their sociocultural context was not uniform, or that the nature of the shelter morphology was unimportant. However, it is notable that these larger sites generally contain imagery that has formal counterparts in Phase 1 rock art. It is also noted that the tridents in EC5B, A12 and BC45 may represent an earlier sub-phase of Phase 2, as discussed in Chapter 7.

A different picture emerges in respect of shelters that contain Phase 2 stencils in addition to graphics. These tend to possess larger living areas, with correspondingly higher graphic numbers, and the four that have graphic counts of 11 or more all contain floor living areas measuring greater than 20 square metres. These sites are:

- BC6: This shelter, in the Cataract catchment, contains painted red pigment graphics including tridents, trident variations and other simple forms.
- BC41: The rock art in this shelter is highly weathered but is, nevertheless, one of the major sites in the Cataract. It contains relatively high numbers of red drawn animal motifs.
- Gill50: This shelter is the largest in the Cataract, and is notable for possessing a suite of red painted graphics, including four tridents and 10 elongated oval forms.
- SCR10: This shelter is the most commodious in the Upper Nepean catchment. The Phase 2 graphics are highly weathered, but the shelter contains much remnant red wet pigment over the majority of its wall surfaces, some of which are trident forms, including possible schematic anthropomorphic motifs.

The painted graphics in three of these sites are possibly representative of the earliest pigment rock art in the Upper Nepean. The trident and oval forms in BC6, Gill50 and SCR10, are rare in the study area, and may represent an earlier sub-phase of Phase 2 (also those in EC5B, A12 and BC45). The implication of this, with respect to shelter size, large living space and the inclusion of red stencils, will be discussed in a later section of this chapter. However, here it is noted that the specific location, chosen for the production of the very earliest pigment rock art, may have been influenced by shelter size and the ability to house relatively large numbers of people. All Phase 2 rock art is in ground-level shelters. None are perched in elevated contexts in cliff faces, or the like.

8.2.3 Micro-topography

In Chapter 6, the location of rock art within the micro-topographic context of shelters was examined in respect of the data from the Research Database (Table 8.4). It was found that the majority of rock marks had been produced on walls; however, marks were also on ceilings (10%), and in concavities (10%). It was also found that the most marks were located in contexts of open visibility, but that 16 per cent occurred in hidden or only moderate visibility contexts. The analysis of the micro-topographic location of Phase 2 rock art can only be conducted on the Research Database and, accordingly, the results should be considered to be indicative of typical patterns only.

Table 8.4 Frequency distribution of the micro-topographic location of Phase 2 stencil rock art (R/DB).

Location	Frequency		Visibility	Frequency	
Wall	98	72%	Open	118	86.8%
Ceiling	10	7.4%	Moderate	18	13.2%
Concavity	28	20.6%	Hidden	0	–
Total	136	100%	Total	136	100%

Source: Table reproduced from Dibden (2011).

Phase 2 rock art occurs most frequently on wall locations and in contexts of open visibility. Stencils occur normally on wall panels (72%). They do not occur in relationships of isomorphic congruence, although this is hardly surprising given their mechanically imposed form. However, they do occur in concavities in 20.6 per cent of recorded instances. In all cases, this position is apparently a very deliberate choice, because other wall surfaces are available in each of the shelters in which this occurs. SCR10 contains over 10 Phase 2 stencils (all children's) in a concavity. However, this is an unusual example, and more frequently a single stencil is present in a concavity (e.g. TL31, Ana3).

It is also notable that, while the majority of stencils occur in contexts of open visibility, 13.2 per cent occur in locations of only moderate visibility. Furthermore, while stencils occur at an average height above the floor of 1.21 metres (median = 1.15), they occur in a wide range of heights that vary between 0.6–2.9 metres. The location of stencils in very high places in shelters is unusual and certainly unexpected.

The majority of graphic rock art occurs on wall panels (89%); however, 6 per cent is on ceilings and 5 per cent within concavities. Most graphics are located in open visibility contexts (95%), while 5 per cent occur in locations where their visibility is moderate only, generally on ceiling locations (Table 8.5).

Table 8.5 Frequency distribution of the micro-topographic location of Phase 2 graphic rock art (R/DB).

Location	Frequency		Visibility	Frequency		Isomorphic congruence	Frequency	
Wall	209	89%	Open	222	95%	Yes	4	1.7%
Ceiling	13	6%	Moderate	12	5%	No	230	98.3%
Concavity	12	5%	Hidden	0	–			
Total	234	100%	Total	234	100%	Total	234	100%

Source: Table reproduced from Dibden (2011).

It is noted that the most commonly recognisable Phase 2 graphic—eel motifs—are the only identifiable form that occur in contexts of moderate visibility on ceilings (Codes 2.3 and 2.4)[1]. An additional rare graphic of 'unknown' figurative referent (Code 6.6) is also present in a moderate location. The remainder are weathered and, hence, formally indeterminate (Table 8.6). Notably, no Phase 2 graphic rock art occurs in 'hidden' contexts.

Phase 2 graphic rock art occurs in isomorphic, congruent relationships with natural rock features on art panels in four instances only. This is clearly rare and unusual. These motifs include one eel (Code 2.3), one 'unknown'—that is, a simple elongated oval form (Code 2.25) and two gliders (Code 8.2; see Plate 1.1).

Table 8.6 Locational data for Phase 2 graphics as per figurative referent (R/DB).

Graphic referent	Moderate	Open	Total
Bird		4	4
Echidna		8	8
Eel	3	13	16
Female human		3	3
Glider		8	8
Human		2	2
Human imaginary		10	10
Indeterminate	8	99	107
Lizard		2	2
Macropod		8	8
Male human		2	2
Marsupial		4	4
Snake		1	1
Wombat		3	3
Unknown	1	54	55
Total	12	221	233

Source: Table reproduced from Dibden (2011).

---

1   All imagery is coded—see Appendix 3 in Dibden (2011).

8.2.4 Rock Art Diversity

It has been beyond the scope of this research to analyse stencil diversity. Nevertheless, Phase 2 stencils can be summarised in general terms. Red stencils are human hands. The range in hand size indicates that men and children participated in stencilling activity. Medium-sized stencils, which do occur, are rather more ambiguous to interpret, as they may represent either women or adolescents.

The following analysis of Phase 2 graphic rock art is undertaken on two levels. First, an overview is presented that is based on motif data from both the Research and IPG Databases (Table 8.7). Thereafter, a detailed analysis of the graphics from the Research Database will be undertaken. More than half (53%) of Phase 2 graphics are indeterminate in form. A total of 89 (21.8%) graphics are classified as 'unknown'. These are generally formal graphics comprising circles, ovals, elliptical shapes, tridents and other comparably simple motifs (these will be discussed further below). Anthropomorphic figures account for 6.8 per cent (n = 28) of Phase 2 graphics. The remainder are animal forms, the most common of which are eels (n = 21). There are 19 macropod and other marsupial forms, and small numbers each of echidnas (n = 11), gliders (n = 8), lizards (n = 5), snakes (n = 5), birds (n = 4) and wombats (n = 3).

The animal motifs do not all occur in all catchments, except for eels and the 'unknown' category. Bird motifs occur in the Cordeaux only, and gliders and wombats in the Avon only. Macropod and anthropomorphic motifs occur in all catchments except the Nepean; lizard, snake and marsupial forms are present in the Avon and Cataract only. The spatial distribution of these motifs will be examined further in Chapter 9.

Table 8.7 Counts of Phase 2 motif categories based on model/referent per catchment (R/DB and IPG/DB).

Model	Avon		Cordeaux		Cataract		Nepean		Total
	IPG/DB	R/DB	IPG/DB	R/DB	IPG/DB	R/DB	IPG/DB	R/DB	
Indeterminate	23	42	28	52	54	10	13		222
Echidna	1	8			1		1		11
Bird				4					4
Eel	1	8		8	1		3		21
Glider		8							8
Lizard		1			3	1			5
Wombat		3							3
Snake		1			4				5
Marsupial		4			2				6
Macropod	1	4	1	3	3	1			13
Human	1	9	6	7	4	1			28
Unknown	2	29	1	18	30	8	1		89
Total	29	117	36	92	102	21	18	0	415

Source: Table reproduced from Dibden (2011).

Table 8.8 examines the formal diversity represented in the anthropomorphic, animal and 'unknown' categories of Phase 2 graphic rock art. This analysis is conducted on the Research Database only. Given this, and taking into consideration the high numbers of Phase 2 indeterminate motifs, the analysis is considered to be indicative of diversity only. Of the 126 motifs (other than indeterminate) in Phase 2 graphic rock art, 54 different motif forms occur. This ratio of 2.3:1 indicates considerable diversity in this small sample. However, as noted in Table 8.8 below, while motifs such as gliders, echidnas and eels be slightly schematically different, they are, nevertheless, relatively similar in graphic construction.

Table 8.8 Phase 2 graphic diversity (R/DB).

Motif type	Code	Count	Total	Discussion
Bird	0.3 (incomplete)	1	4	Four bird motifs occur in three shelters. Two bird motifs occur in the one form: Code 11.17 (both in a single shelter: SCR12).
	11.14	1		
	11.17	2		
Echidna	8.4	6	8	Eight echidna motifs occur in two shelters in the Avon; their form is very similar, however, they occur in three slightly different forms
	8.16	1		
	8.18	1		
Eel	2.2	1	16	16 eel motifs occur in seven shelters in four slightly different forms, the most common of which is Code 2.3
	2.3	10		
	2.4	4		
	2.21	1		
Glider	8.2	5	8	Eight glider motifs occur in three shelters in three slightly different forms, the most common of which is Code 8.2
	8.5	1		
	8.6	2		
Lizard	13.2	2	2	Two lizards in two shelters; same form
Wombat	5.18	2	3	Three wombat motifs occur in a composition in a single shelter, in two slightly different forms, one of which appears animated (running)
	5.42	1		
Snake	4.7	1	1	Large, broad and curved
Marsupial	5.7	1	4	Four marsupial motifs occur in three shelters, they are formally diverse and animated
	5.9	1		
	5.14	1		
	5.16	1		
Macropod	0.3 (incomplete)	2	8	Eight macropod motifs occur in six shelters; they are formally diverse
	5.2	1		
	5.11	2		
	5.13	1		
	5.15	1		
	5.28	1		
Anthropomorph Female	7.49	1	3	Three female anthropomorphs occur in three shelters; they are each partnered with a male. Two are formally the same
	7.12	2		
Anthropomorph Male	7.48	1	3	Three male anthropomorphs occur in three shelters; they are each partnered as above. Two are formally the same
	7.13	2		
Anthropomorph	7.6	2	2	Two anthropomorphs (human-like) in two shelters; they are formally comparable

Motif type	Code	Count	Total	Discussion
Anthropomorph Imaginary	incomplete	1	9	These nine anthropomorphic motifs (unhuman like) are formally diverse
	7.11	1		
	7.18	2		
	7.19	2		
	7.22	1		
	7.42	1		
	7.58	1		
Unknown	1.5	1	1	Simple form
	1.7	6	6	Trident form
	1.16	1	1	Triangular line arrangement
	1.17	2	2	Double-ended trident
	1.19	3	3	Double-ended trident (variation)
	2.1	4	4	Long oval with elliptical ends
	2.5	6	6	Sinuous long oval
	2.7	1	1	Long oval with rounded ends
	2.9	1	1	Long oval with elliptical ends with barred middle
	2.11	1	1	Short oval with pointy end
	2.17	8	8	Circle
	2.18	14	14	Short oval with pointy ends
	2.25	1	1	Curved long oval with one pointy end
	4.8	1	1	Long angular zig-zag form
	6.6	6	6	'Tadpole' shape
	8.14	1	1	Organic form (perhaps an animal)
	9.11	1	1	Trident form
	11.18	1	1	Organic form (perhaps an animal)

Source: Table reproduced from Dibden (2011).

The majority of motifs in Phase 2 rock art are, of course, new additions to the graphic repertoire. Yet several are not, and these are formally comparable with the small intaglio engravings of Phase 1. Notably, these motifs all appear to have been produced with paint, rather than drawn. These are listed as follows:

- Two anthropomorphic motifs in UA1 (Code 7.19) are schematically similar in form to the engraved human motifs in FRC226. One graphic in BC45 has been tentatively called an anthropomorphic figure due to its large size (and shape); however, it is essentially formally a trident and therefore comparable with Phase 1 bird track motifs.

- The 'unknown' category includes a number of simple-shaped motifs, including circle (Code 2.17) and elongated ovals or linear forms (Code 2.1) that are similar to 'line' engravings (see FRC226). In addition, the various trident forms and trident variations (Codes 1.7, 1.17, 1.19 and 9.11) are all formally similar to bird track motifs (see Plate 8.2).

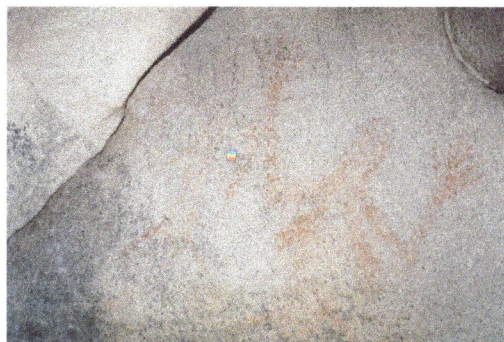

Plate 8.3 A pair of Phase 2 anthropomorphs that have subsequently been redrawn in charcoal (rock shelter EC17).

Source: Photograph by Julie Dibden, 2011.

Plate 8.2 Large trident-shaped Phase 2 motif (rock shelter A12).

Source: Photograph by Julie Dibden, 2011.

Plate 8.4 A composition of three large (c. 80 cm high) marsupial gliders (Phase 2) superimposed by Phase 3 charcoal anthropomorphic drawings (rock shelter UA1).

Source: Photograph by Julie Dibden, 2011.

The Phase 2 drawn graphics that are new additions to the Upper Nepean rock art include anthropomorphic motifs, which are sometimes male and female pairs (Plate 8.3), and animals, which are also commonly drawn in pairs or triplets (Plate 8.4).

Phase 2 graphic rock art is summarised as follows:

- Approximately half of graphic motifs are formally indeterminate, due to weathering.
- Approximately one-quarter of Phase 2 graphics are images of animals.
- Animal motifs occur in a limited number of sites, and the same animal is often in groups of two or more. Exceptions include a snake, which occurs once only, and lizards, which occur singly in two sites.
- Animal motifs occur in a limited number of forms (as per motif code) and, hence, are relatively homogeneous.
- Animal motifs are either formal (static) or animated. Those that are animated have a narrative quality and invoke an imagined space.
- Animal motifs are generally large.
- Animal motifs are always located on walls in highly visible locations, except for eels, which can occur on ceilings.

- Animal motifs can occur, albeit rarely, in isomorphic congruence with natural rock features. Those that do, similar to animated motifs, invoke an imagined space.
- Anthropomorphs occur infrequently (n = 15) in Phase 2.
- The three pairs of male and female anthropomorphs are each in association (side by side).
- Two pairs of anthropomorphs are not in association with animal imagery of Phase 2, although one (in BR29) is strongly associated with eels; these are the only animal form in Phase 2 rock art in this site.
- All anthropomorphic figures are in highly visible locations.
- All anthropomorphic figures are relatively small (<1 metre in height).
- No anthropomorphic figures are in isomorphic association with natural rock features.
- Phase 2 graphics do not usually possess elaborate infill patterns, and are executed simply, in either solid or outline pigment applications. The exceptions include a wombat and echidnas in UA47.
- Phase 2 graphics, either animal or anthropomorphic, do not 'occupy' the viewers' imagined space. No Phase 2 graphics have 'eyes'.
- Approximately one-quarter (n = 55) of Phase 2 graphics are 'unknown' in terms of model or referent. The majority of images in the 'unknown' category are simple forms, particularly tridents, circles, ovals and elliptical forms. Some occur in relatively high numbers in composition with other motifs: elliptical forms (n = 14) with wombats in UA47, and circles (n = 7) with a very schematic trident/anthropomorphic figure in BC45.

8.3 Phase 3 Rock Art

Phase 3 rock art is comprised of graphics, most of which are charcoal drawings and a wide range of gestural marks including stencils. Phase 3 pigment marks, both graphic and gestural, are generally highly weathered and, in respect of graphics, their form is commonly indeterminate. Charcoal is frequently used to redraw, usually in outline, older red graphics.

Red pigment was used very infrequently for the production of this rock art. It was used for a few small motifs, most of which are schematically similar to Phase 1 and 2 tridents, and other simple forms. Their place within Phase 3 is recognised by their superimposed position in stratified layers, and their generally 'fresh' appearance. Red pigment also occurs occasionally on rock surfaces as random lines, which do not appear to be remnant motifs. There is no indication that red pigment was used for stencilling in Phase 3. The use of white pigment apparently occurs for the first time in Phase 3 rock art. Its use for graphic production is uncommon, and generally confined to small, simple motifs, which are also schematically comparable with Phase 1 and 2 trident and simple forms; however, several animal motifs are also produced with white pigment. In addition, white pigment is used in Phase 3 rock art for the embellishment of a few charcoal motifs, and occasionally to re-mark older red motifs. White- or cream-coloured pigment is predominantly used for stencilling, and one site contains three black stencils that are regionally rare. While relatively infrequent, light scratching is also used to create motifs and sometimes simply to mark (gesturally) the rock surface.

8.3.1 Abundance of Sites and Motifs

A total of 3,938 Phase 3 rock markings are present in 449 (88%) rock shelters in the Upper Nepean catchment. They occur in shelters used previously for Phase 2 rock art, and in a range of 'new' shelters. A list of the distribution of these marks is presented in Table 8.9. These markings are distributed relatively evenly between the Research and IPG Databases. The Phase 3 rock art (and other marks) count of 3,938 represents 77 per cent of all rock art in the study area.

Table 8.9 Numbers of Phase 3 rock art types (R/DB and IPG/DB).

Rock marking type	R/DB	IPG/DB	Total
Graphic	1,744	1,797	3,541 (89.9%)
Indeterminate	75	0	75 (1.9%)
Pigment blobs	14	0	14 (0.4%)
Pigment circles	9	0	9 (0.2%)
Pigment marking	14	0	14 (0.4%)
Pigment random	9	0	9 (0.2%)
Pigment smear	10	0	10 (0.3%)
Pigment strokes	11	0	11 (0.3%)
Pitting	4	0	4 (0.1%)
Ridge bashing	1	0	1 (0.02%)
Rubbing	14	0	14 (0.4%)
Scratching	15	25	40 (1%)
Stencil	113	83	196 (5%)
Total	2,033 (51.6%)	1,905 (48.4%)	3,938 (100%)

Source: Table reproduced from Dibden (2011).

The majority of Phase 3 rock art is graphic. Unlike Phase 2, stencils are a minor component (n = 196; 5%). The Research Database includes marks that are indeterminate, in regard to whether they are graphic or gestural (n = 75; 1.9%). A new suite of gestural marks occur in Phase 3. The location of Phase 3 rock art shelters is shown in Figure 8.5, in which it can be seen that marking the land during this phase is much more geographically widespread and abundant than when compared with Phase 2.

Gestural Marks

The distribution of shelters with Phase 3 white/cream stencils (e.g. Plate 8.5) is listed in Table 8.10. Their geographic distribution is shown on Figure 8.6. The Cataract catchment possesses more than half the shelters with white/cream stencils (n = 20), and the Cordeaux has the next highest frequency (n = 11). The Avon has five shelters with stencils, and the Nepean one only. Three black stencils are located in one shelter in the Cataract. It is assumed that these occur only within the period represented by Phase 3.

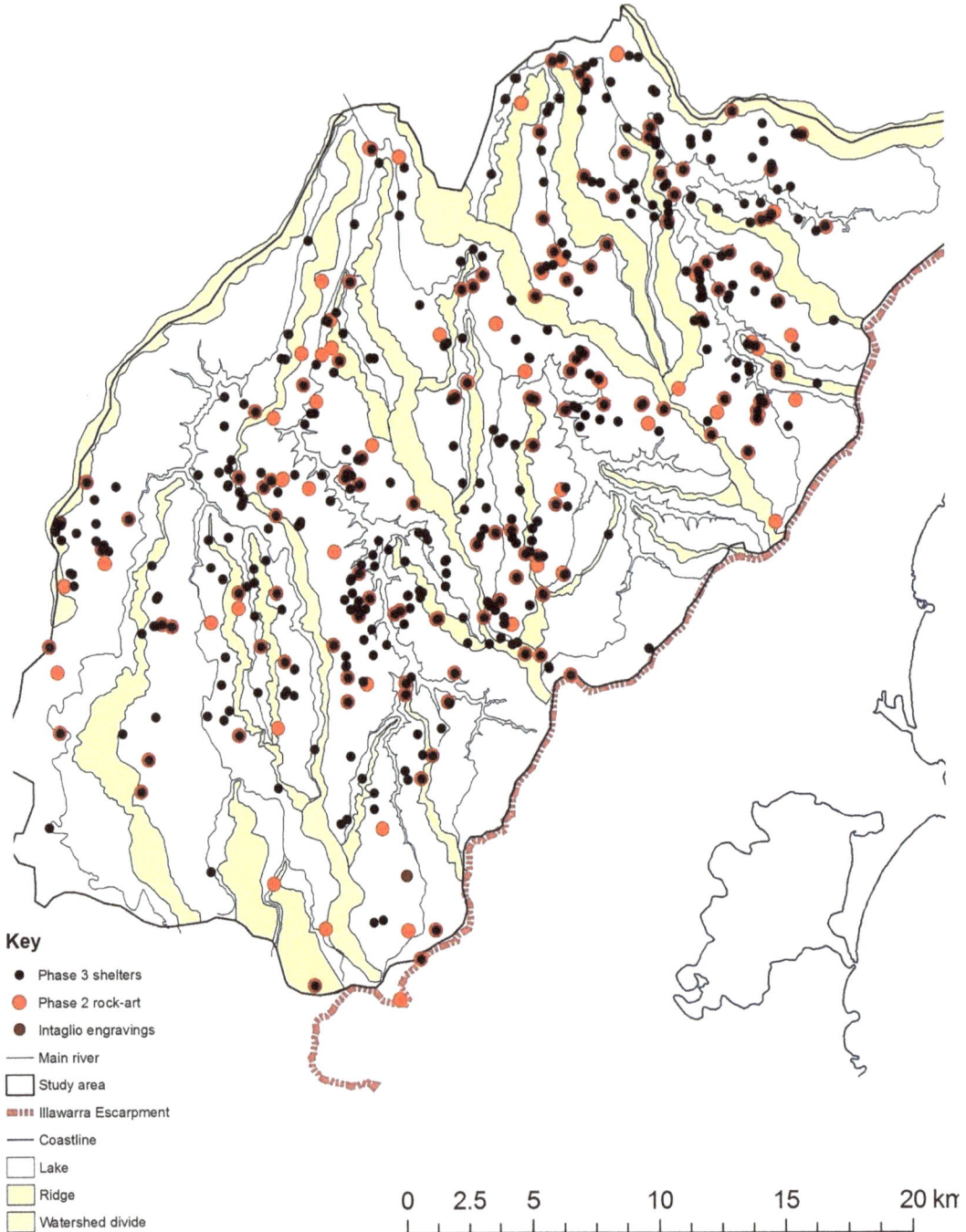

Figure 8.5 The distribution of all rock art shelters in the Upper Nepean catchment.
Source: Map reproduced from Dibden (2011).

Plate 8.5 Phase 3 gestural marks (rock shelter Cad39). Cream-coloured hand and feet stencils.

Source: Photograph by Julie Dibden, 2011.

Table 8.10 Distribution of shelters and stencil counts of Phase 3 white/cream stencils per catchment (R/DB and IPG/DB).

Count/site	Avon	Cataract	Cordeaux	Nepean	Total
1		4	3	1	8
2	1	6	3		10
3		3	1		4
5			1		1
6		1			1
7		3			3
8	2	1	1		4
9			2		2
12		1			1
15		1			1
21	1				1
23	1				1
Total	5	20	11	1	37

Source: Table reproduced from Dibden (2011).

The distribution of stencils between the catchments similarly compares with the distribution of Phase 2 stencils. The pattern of white/cream stencils, which decreases as one moves north to south, is comparable with Phase 2, as is their frequency in each catchment. The notable difference is the Nepean, which contains one white stencil only. Almost half the shelters possess one or two stencils only, and this pattern is similar to the distribution of Phase 2 stencils. However, two shelters, located in proximity to each other in the Avon catchment, each contain relatively large stencil counts of 21 (C44) and 23 (C39). In Figure 8.6, it can be seen that Phase 3 stencilling activity generally occurs within the interior of the catchment. This contrasts with the geographic distribution of the earlier Phase 2 stencilling, and this phenomenon will be discussed further in Chapter 9.

Key

Phase 3 stencils

stencil count code

- ⊙ 1 - 2
- ⊙ 3 - 5
- ⊙ 6 - 10
- ⊙ 11 - 20
- ⊙ >20
- —— Main river
- ▢ Study area
- ▰▰▮▮ Illawarra Escarpment
- —— Coastline
- ▢ Lake
- ▢ Ridge
- ▢ Watershed divide

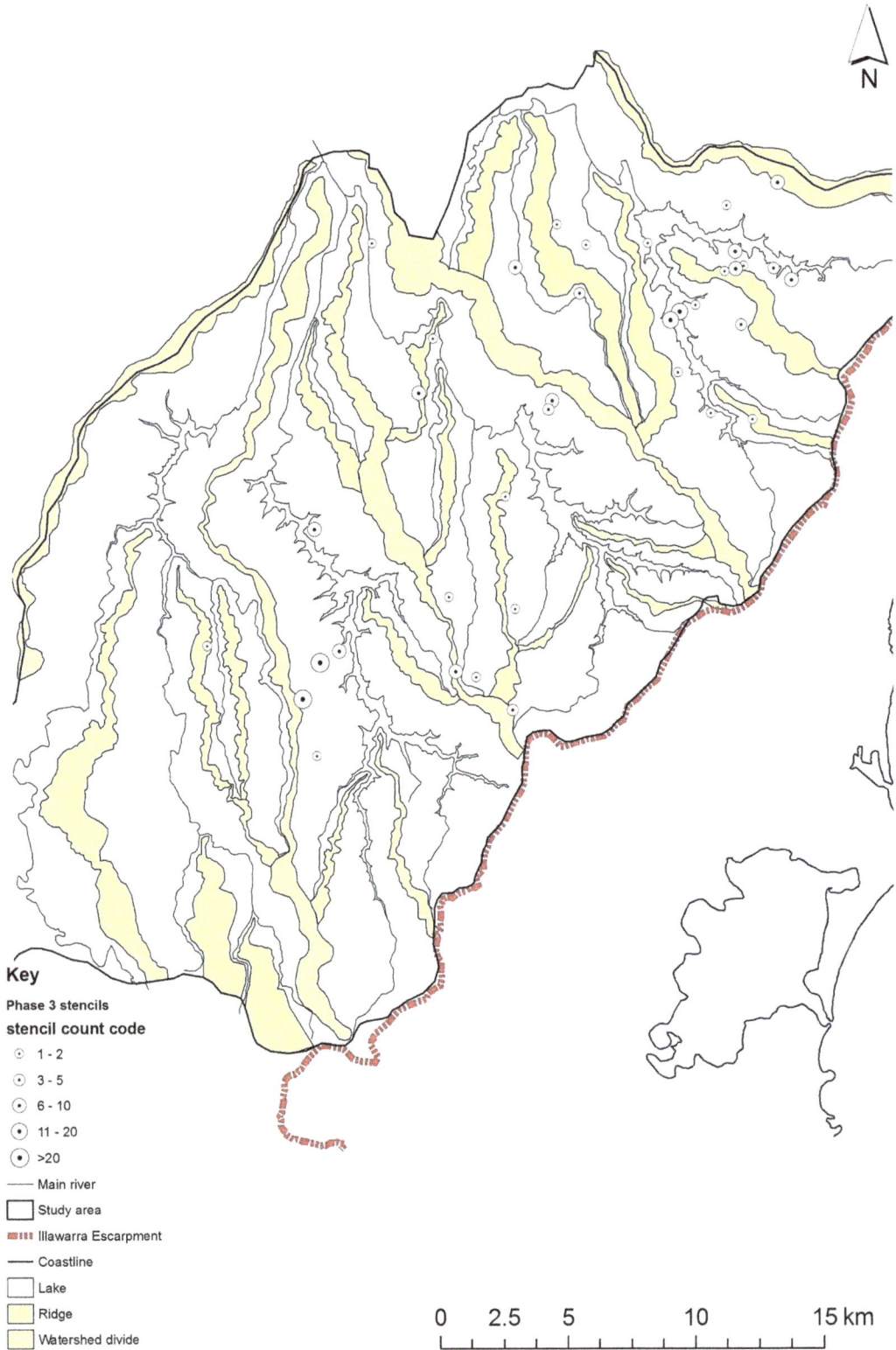

Figure 8.6 The geographic distribution of Phase 3 stencils.

Note the location of the two shelters with large counts situated in close proximity to each other in the Avon catchment.

Source: Map reproduced from Dibden (2011).

Gesturally subtractive marks, including scratched, pitted,, and rubbed rock panel surfaces, occur within Phase 3. These marks are usually in association with charcoal graphics. Two instances of ridge bashing have been recorded, one of which is certainly caused by humans. The origin of the other is ambiguous. In addition, a range of new gestural marks, which entail the application pigment, appear in Phase 3.

Graphics

Phase 3 graphics occur in 439 of the 449 shelters with Phase 3 rock art. Phase 3 graphic site density in the entire study area is 0.6 sites per square kilometre. Average motif density is 4.5 graphics per square kilometre. Phase 3 graphic shelter densities are comparable between the three northern catchments, and typically higher than in the Nepean. This shelter density distribution contrasts with Phase 2 rock art, in which graphic shelters are distributed at higher densities in the Cordeaux and Avon.

Phase 3 graphic motif density is considerably higher in the Cordeaux and Avon than when compared with the Cataract, and this distribution mirrors Phase 2 graphic motif densities. The distribution of Phase 3 shelters is shown on Figure 8.7.

The catchment with the highest percentage frequency of shelters with Phase 3 graphics is the Cataract (31.2%). However, it contains a relatively low percentage frequency of motifs, and a relatively low average count per shelter. Similar to Phase 2 graphics, the Avon has the highest percentage frequency of motifs (31.4%), although this is comparable with the Cordeaux. The range of graphics per shelter is 1 to 129. The mode and median are low, which indicates that low graphic counts in individual shelters are frequent. The structure of this data indicates that Phase 3 graphic production was a low-level activity, and that a few key sites were the focus of comparatively higher levels of marking (Figure 8.7).

8.3.2 Shelter Morphology

The types of shelters in which Phase 3 stencils and graphics occur are explored in this section. The first series of analyses is conducted on the Research and IPG Databases, and the last is conducted on the Research data only. The range of measurements for all variables is high. Shelters vary in size from very small to large. The average shelter measurements are 12 metres in length, 3 metres in width and 2.7 metres in height. The minimum width of 0.5 metres and minimum height of 0.8 metre is notable. The variability in living area sizes is significant, as is the mode of zero.

Phase 3 stencils are preferentially located in shelters with living areas that measure more than 6 square metres. The three shelters with relatively high stencil counts all possess relatively large living area measurements. This contrasts with Phase 2 stencils, which were commonly produced in shelters with very small or no living area. Also, shelters with high Phase 2 stencil counts generally contain no, or minimal, living areas.

In Phase 3, stencilling as a practice apparently declines significantly. However, it is feasible that the production of white stencils was undertaken over a relatively short period, when compared with Phase 2 and, hence, the decline in abundance may simply be a factor of time, rather than a shift in motivation. It is also important to recognise that white stencil pigment may not endure long. Accordingly, interpreting the behavioural significance of this decline is problematic. The contrast in shelter morphology between the two phases of stencilling suggests that the sociocultural context did change in the most recent past.

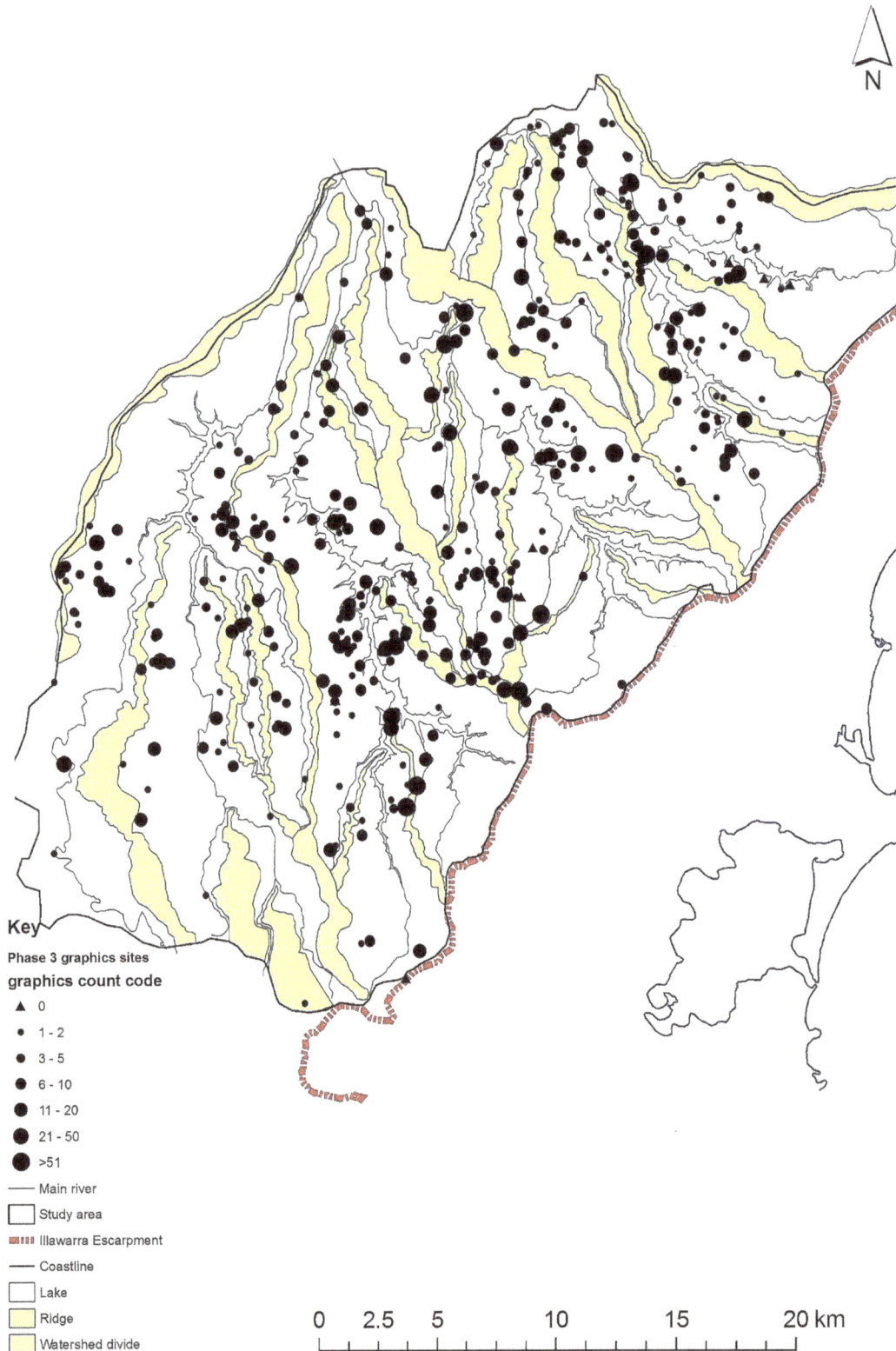

Key

Phase 3 graphics sites
graphics count code

▲ 0
• 1 - 2
● 3 - 5
● 6 - 10
● 11 - 20
● 21 - 50
● >51
—— Main river
☐ Study area
▦▦▦ Illawarra Escarpment
—— Coastline
☐ Lake
☐ Ridge
☐ Watershed divide

0   2.5   5   10   15   20 km

Figure 8.7 Shelters with Phase 3 graphics showing count variability in the Upper Nepean catchment (0 = no graphics; white stencils only).

Source: Map reproduced from Dibden (2011).

Of the 439 shelters that contain Phase 3 graphics, 43 per cent possess either no or otherwise negligible (1–5 square metres) living area, and this includes two shelters that contain more than 50 graphic counts. The shelters with graphic counts of 50 or less have the full range of living areas in a more or less equal distribution. However, shelters with more than 50 graphics commonly possess large living areas. These patterns are comparable with those observed for Phase 2 graphics and indicate that graphic rock art production was not generally an activity that depended on a shelter's potential to be used for habitation.

Potential Art Surface Areas (PASA) in shelters range in size from 0.96 to 103 square metres. Their average measurement is 18.5, with a median of 12.6. The percentage calculation of the Surviving Art Surface Area (SASA) is also variable, and ranges from 2.4 to 100 per cent. The average SASA calculation is 34, with a median of 31 per cent. The SASA calculations indicate that rock art panels generally are not filled with rock art. With a consideration of weathering processes, these figures should be read with caution.

The relationship between Phase 3 graphic abundance and the amount of rock art panel surface area available for rock art production has been analysed for the purpose of determining whether or not the PASA in shelters determines the abundance or otherwise of graphic production. The trend suggests that rock art panel size in shelters does normally influence the abundance of rock art. For example, most frequently, shelters with counts of 50 or more motifs do have PASA that measure more than 21 square metres. Similarly, shelters with motif counts of 11 or more trend towards possessing larger PASA areas. However, notably, some shelters, albeit in low frequencies, that have small motif counts have very large PASA. This analysis suggests that, while generally a shelter's potential to host rock art influences the abundance of rock art present, this is not always the case.

Most shelters contain Phase 3 graphic rock art that occupies a quarter or less of the PASA, and the trend is for these shelters to have low rock art counts. However frequently, shelters with relatively high graphic counts do have rock art occupying less than half of available rock art panels. Nevertheless, it is only shelters with high graphic counts that contain rock art panels that are nearly full (>75%).

In contrast to Phase 2 rock art, during Phase 3, rock art was produced in eight rock shelters that are perched in elevated positions within vertical faces of cliffs or boulders. These shelters possess a range of spatial measurements, although, notably, they generally do not contain any living space due to their rock floors. The rock art in these shelters share some similarities and they each typically contain remarkable assemblages. UA36, a huge shelter, contains a range of very large, commanding anthropomorphic motifs (e.g. see Plate 1.2), each of which are unique and possess 'eyes', and a huge macropod and emu, the latter being relatively frequent motif combinations in both Phases 2 and 3. SCR15 contains a suite of highly weathered imagery, including anthropomorphic motifs and several eels (discussed in more detail later in this chapter), and also several instances of gestural rock rubbing and pitting. RL18 contains mostly anthropomorphic motifs, including a male and female pair in association and, unusually, one additional female. Other motifs include snake and eel forms. Both SCR14 and Gill49 contain small assemblages dominated by large snakes. SCR14 is situated within 100 metres of SCR15, and so they are likely to have been associated. Other than the macropod and emu in UA36, these shelthers notably do not contain marsupial motifs. However BR13, which has a very low roof, contains a small suite of marsupial motifs located in 'hidden' contexts.

A sociocultural context can tentatively be inferred for these shelters based on a consideration of their location within elevated, vertical rock faces. It is suggested that given the potential danger they pose to small children, they may have been used exclusively by men. It is notable that these sites are each also located away from major thoroughfares. That they have been used for the production of Phase 3 rock art, apparently for the first time, suggests that these otherwise 'marginal' locales became relevant at this time for the pursuit of certain social strategies.

8.3.3 Micro-topography

Similar to Phase 2 rock art, the analysis of Phase 3 marks is conducted on the Research Database, and hence the results are indicative only (Table 8.11). Comparably with Phase 2, Phase 3 stencils occur predominantly on wall panels in contexts of open visibility. However, fewer Phase 3 stencils occur in concavities. Similar to Phase 2, a small percentage of Phase 3 stencils occurs on ceilings, and notably one is located in a 'hidden' location.

Phase 3 stencils occur at an average height above the floor of 1.25 metres (median = 1.2) and their heights range from 0.5 and 2.5 metres. These height locations are comparable with the position of Phase 2 stencils. Similar to the earlier red stencils, Phase 3 stencils occasionally occur in unusual places, some of which are very high within shelters. For example, the IPG reports a white stencil in BC6 located high in the shelter wall, to which access is only possible via a series of ledges. In summary, there is no notable difference between the micro-topographic contexts in which Phase 2 and 3 stencilling occurred.

Table 8.11 Frequency distribution of the micro-topographic location of Phase 2 and 3 stencils (R/DB).

Location	Phase 2 stencils frequency		Phase 3 stencils frequency		Visibility	Phase 2 stencils frequency		Phase 3 stencils frequency	
Wall	98	72	101	89	Open	118	86.8	101	89
Ceiling	10	7.4	11	10	Moderate	18	13.2	11	10
Concavity	28	20.6	1	1	Hidden			1	1
Total	136	100%	113	100%	Total	136	100%	113	100%

Source: Table reproduced from Dibden (2011).

Table 8.12 lists the locational attributes of Phase 3 non-graphic gestural marks. The majority of these marks were produced on wall panels. A relatively high frequency occur in concavities, the majority of which are charcoal pigment applications.

Table 8.12 Cross-tabulation of Phase 3 non-graphic gestural marks and location (R/DB).

Type	Ceiling	Concavity	Wall	Total
Pigment blobs			14	14
Pigment circles		8	1	9
Pigment marking	1	11	2	14
Pigment random	1	2	6	9
Pigment smear			10	10
Pigment strokes		5	6	11
Pitting			4	4
Ridge bashing		1		1
Rubbing			14	14
Scratching	1	2	12	15
Total	3 (3%)	29 (28.7%)	69 (68.3%)	101 (100%)

Source: Table reproduced from Dibden (2011).

The frequency distribution of Phase 2 and 3 graphics is presented in Table 8.13. While wall locations for Phase 3 graphics are typical, greater numbers occur on ceilings and in concavities than with Phase 2 graphics. Likewise, Phase 3 graphics occur mostly in visible locations but in greater numbers in moderate visibility contexts compared with Phase 2 and, notably, for the first time in hidden places. These results indicate a change and diversification in the micro-topographic locations chosen for the production of Phase 3 graphics.

Table 8.13 Frequency distribution of the micro-topographic location of Phase 2 and 3 graphics (R/DB).

Location	Phase 2 graphics frequency		Phase 3 graphics frequency		Visibility	Phase 2 graphics frequency		Phase 3 graphics frequency	
Wall	209	89	1,357	78	Open	222	95	1,396	80
Ceiling	13	6	203	12	Moderate	12	5	200	11
Concavity	12	5	184	11	Hidden	0		148	8
Total	234	100%	1,744	100%	Total	234	100%	1,744	100%

Source: Table reproduced from Dibden (2011).

The height above the floor of Phase 3 graphics ranges between 0.05 centimetres and 300 centimetres as measured from the base of the image. The average height is 103 centimetres and the mode and median height is 100 centimetres.

The choice to produce graphics and other marks in hidden locations raises questions in regard to new motivations and sociocultural context in Phase 3. As quantified previously, the reason for this practice cannot be attributed to a lack of available space and, hence, a necessary retreat to previously unused spaces. An explanation for this practice must reside solely in choice and a new purpose. Their hidden location implies that, fundamentally, the motivation to produce these marks was not predicated upon their being viewed by a human audience. The majority of hidden marks occur on very low ceilings above bedrock, although, occasionally, motifs are tucked behind a protruding piece of rock. In all instances, both the contexts of production and perception are necessarily restricted to either one person or very few people because these spaces are physically limiting. Generally, motifs in hidden locations require a person to crawl. These aspects regarding the production of hidden imagery suggest an intimacy between people, and people and place, and the practice of rock marking. Given that an audience, beyond that of the makers, is not implied by this practice, it also suggests that the motivation resided primarily in the act of marking, itself.

A total of 51 Phase 3 graphics occur in this relationship with natural features of rock surfaces in shelters. Additionally, seven indeterminate marks and 21 non-graphic gestural pigment marks (all Phase 3) occur in isomorphic congruent situations.

An example of isochrestic congruence is the drawn black wombat shown in Plate 8.6 (rock shelter Gill22). Another notable example is an eel in SCR15. The image is on a low section of a large panel immediately below a charcoal macropod. Its form is drawn diagonally on the rock panel, and its tail end follows the slightly raised ridges on the rock surface. The image is highly weathered and only its front end, including its head and fins, and tail remain intact. However, remnant pigment is present along the ridges, which extend from both the head and tail ends, confirming their unity as a single image. The relationship between the tail end of the motif and the natural rock is unambiguous. In addition, it is notable that the eel motif (tail end), raised ridges and areas below the image are also extensively pitted from being bashed. The practice of marking the rock in this manner, which incorporates the natural 'lines' on the rock into the graphic, is highly suggestive of a union between the eel and the rock on, *or within*, which it is situated. The animal and the rock have in effect been rendered physically, and thus conceptually, as one.

Plate 8.6 Charcoal wombat motif in relationship of isomorphic congruence in a small concavity (rock shelter Gill22; mark ID 1722).

Source: Photograph by Julie Dibden, 2011.

8.3.4 Rock Art Diversity

Whereas all Phase 2 stencils in the Research Database are hands (or indeterminate), a greater range of objects is present in the suite of Phase 3 stencils. Hands are most common, and include men's, children's and possibly women's. In addition, one fist and six feet are present. One object, which is unidentified (see Dibden 2011:Appendix 1: Gill33), and six animal paws occur in Phase 3 stencil rock art. While infrequent, the IPG has recorded a small number of stencilled hatchets (including one believed to be European; Sefton, pers. comm., April 2001). All stencilled tools on the Woronora Plateau were made with white pigment (Sefton, pers. comm., April 2001).

It was suggested earlier that the difference between Phase 2 and 3 stencil locations, in respect of the morphology of shelters and living area size, may relate to some shift in the sociocultural context of stencil production. It was also noted that the geographic distribution of Phase 3 stencil shelters was patterned differently to Phase 2 stencils. The addition of a new suite of objects to the stencilling repertoire of Phase 3 rock art further suggests a change in motivation and purpose. The Phase 3 six foot stencils are located in the two Avon catchment shelters, which each contain the highest numbers of Phase 3 stencils (C39 and C44). This relationship is notable. These shelters also contain gestural applications of white/cream pigment blobs and smears in relatively high numbers. C39 contains five pigment blobs and three pigment smears, and C44 has four pigment blobs and two pigment smears. All the recorded pigment blobs in the Research Database occur in these two shelters.

The one fist stencil (women or adolescent size) occurs in a shelter that has a relatively large number of hand stencils (UA49), and an unusual suite of Phase 3 graphic imagery, much of which has been produced by scratching. The graphics in the site include a large, two-legged animal, which has the facial characteristics of a cow or horse, and 'eyes'. These rock marks are all representative of the most recent phase of marking in the study area, which may well have been in the contact period. The rock art panel in UA49 also contains an area of gestural rubbing and two areas of gestural scratching. This repertoire of marks is suggestive of rock marking activity undertaken with a motivation to connect intimately, and with a very powerful reason, with the rock. However, whether this provides illumination as to the purpose behind the inclusion of a stencilled fist is equivocal.

The addition of animal feet to the Phase 3 suite of stencils, while rare, is nevertheless a significant change. It is noted that no other animal feet stencils, other than those in the Research Database, are known in the Upper Nepean catchment. One animal paw is present in C39. This stencil is weathered and, accordingly, its identification is uncertain. However, it is large and likely to be either a wombat or kangaroo paw. This shelter contains several Phase 3 graphics, most of which are indeterminate in form; however, notably, it has a large (83 centimetres long x 52 centimetres high) charcoal-and-white pigment wombat motif located in a central position on the rock art panel. This motif has been gesturally marked by the application of pigment blobs. The stencilling and graphic rock art in C39 strongly evokes an emphasised relationship between humans, animals and place.

The stencilled animal paws in EC25 include kangaroo paws and emu feet, and these are associated with four hand stencils, two of which are children's. This shelter does not contain graphic rock art. Given the assumed relative contemporaneity of the human hand and animal feet stencilling events, again the gesture, implied by the concurrence of these, suggests that a relationship between humans and animals was emphasised in this shelter.

While non-graphic gestural marks are infrequent during Phase 3, when present they normally occur in association with other gestural mark types. Pigment blobs occur in only two shelters, and these have been discussed above. The most common pigment application gestural mark is 'pigment strokes' (Plate 8.7). This type occurs in five instances in TL18, a shelter notable for containing eight gestural pigment marks out of a total of 18 marks (see Dibden 2011:Appendix 1). All graphic rock art in this site is schematically unusual and rare, and two motifs have tentatively been identified as horse heads. An example of the 'pigment marking' category in the TL18 shelter is shown in Plate 8.8.

Plate 8.7 Example of non-graphic pigment gestural mark 'pigment strokes' on left in photo (rock shelter TL18; mark ID 859).

Source: Photograph by Julie Dibden, 2011.

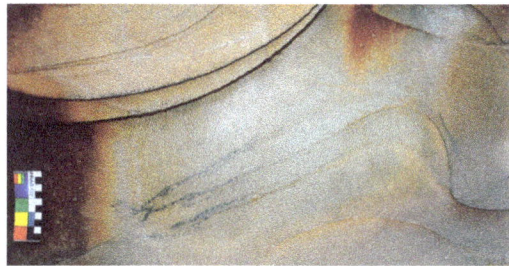

Plate 8.8 Examples of non-graphic charcoal 'pigment marking' highlighted with arrows, showing pigment application to the edges of natural rock features (rock shelter TL18; mark ID 847).

Source: Photograph by Julie Dibden, 2011.

Rock shelter EC5b contains at least 13 non-graphic gestural pigment marks, most of which are charcoal embellishments of small concavities. While not commonly reported in the literature, these types of markings are known to occur in Central Australia (see Smith and Rosenfeld 1992). This category of rock mark is possibly underrepresented in the Research Database because, generally, all charcoal rock marks are weathered and it is not always possible to discriminate between graphic and non-graphic forms with certainty. Unlike Phase 2, in which gestural applications of pigment entailed wiping large areas of rock art panels with wet red pigment, Phase 3 non-graphic pigment marks are discrete, and typically embellish natural features of rock art panels, particularly concavities. Despite their relatively uncommon occurrence, they feature in approximately a quarter of the Research

Database shelters. The motivation behind this form of rock marking can only be speculated. However, if it is as deliberate as it appears to be, it may be interpreted to indicate a concern simply to connect people physically, and/or conceptually via the gesture, with the locale.

Similar to Phase 2, the analysis of the Phase 3 graphic rock art is undertaken on two levels and includes, first, an analysis of figurative category data from both databases, followed by an analysis of the Research Database. The distribution of each Phase 3 figurative graphics as per catchment location is listed in Table 8.14. A total of 2,365 Phase 3 graphics are formally indeterminate (67%) due to weathering.

Table 8.14 List of Phase 3 figurative graphics per catchment (R/DB and IPG/DB); new figurative categories italicised.

Model	Cataract		Cordeaux		Avon		Nepean		Total
	R/DB	IPG/DB	R/DB	IPG/DB	R/DB	IPG/DB	R/DB	IPG/DB	
Indeterminate	129	474	516	188	350	348	27	333	2,365
Echidna	1	5			3	1		6	16
Bird	1	3	3	3	7	17		2	36
Eel	1	7	21		5	1	1	6	42
Glider	3	2	19	4	3				31
Lizard	1	2	3		2	3		4	15
Wombat	2				3		1		6
Snake	5	2	14	2	10	5	2	2	42
Marsupial	6	4	24	2	13	1	1		51
Macropod	9	86	14	16	9	7	2	15	158
Human	8	39	64	22	58	55		80	326
Unknown/other	41	4	122		185	7	3	8	370
Fish	6	7	2		4	1		1	21
Animal with joey			1						1
Koala							2		2
Macropod with joey	1	2				1			4
Tortoise	1		3		3	1	1		9
Animal: other (possibly European)	2		1		2				5
Dog							1		1
Profile anthropomorph		5	22	4		10			41
Total	217	642	829	241	657	458	41	457	3,542

Source: Table reproduced from Dibden (2011).

In Phase 3 rock art, animal motifs occur that have their referential counterparts in Phase 2. While this will be discussed in further detail below, it is noted here that the schema of many motifs also remain unchanged in Phase 3. A summary of motifs occurring in Phase 2 and Phase 3, and described as per the figurative referent variable, is listed below.

Bird motifs were drawn infrequently in Phase 2 and all are in the Cordeaux (n = 4). In Phase 3, birds occur in all catchments but occur most frequently in the Avon (n = 36).

Echidna motifs occur in all catchments other than the Cordeaux, in both Phase 2 (n = 11) and Phase 3 (n = 16). In Phase 2, echidnas were most frequent in the Avon catchment (and most [8] are in two sites). In Phase 3, they are distributed relatively evenly between the catchments in which they occur, and older Phase 2 echidnas are typically redrawn in charcoal.

Plate 8.9 Phase 3 eel motif (front end) drawn with charcoal and white pigment and 'v'-shaped infill (rock shelter A12).

Source: Photograph by Julie Dibden, 2011.

Eel motifs occur in all catchments in both Phase 2 (n = 21) and Phase 3 (n = 42). In Phase 3, higher counts occur more frequently in the Cordeaux. It is noted that shelter BR29 in the Cordeaux has large counts of eels, most of which were drawn in Phase 3 (Phase 3: n = 7). In Phase 3, eel motifs are sometimes highly inscripted with the use of different coloured pigment and elaborate infill (Plate 8.9), and older Phase 2 motifs are frequently redrawn, sometimes in multiple colours (e.g. see Plate 1.7).

Glider motifs were drawn infrequently in Phase 2 (n = 8). All are in the Avon catchment in three shelters, including the same two sites that have the eight echidnas. In Phase 3, gliders occur in all catchments (n = 31), except the Nepean. In Phase 3, older Phase 2 gliders are typically redrawn in charcoal. Similar to Phase 2, glider motifs in Phase 3 are relatively uniform in schematic construction. However, the majority of Phase 3 gliders are very small (c. 30 centimetres with tail); this contrasts with Phase 2, where they were all drawn as relatively large (c. 80 centimetres with tail) motifs. A single and notable exception is a Phase 3 glider in UA8, which is equivalent in size as those produced during Phase 2. Similar to Phase 2, in Phase 3, glider motifs are usually in small groups of two or three, yet one cluster of at least 10 are in a small alcove in EC17 (see Dibden 2011:Appendix 1). Another two in this shelter have been drawn immediately adjacent to the pair of Phase 2 anthropomorphic motifs that are shown in Plate 8.3. Given the very small size of this shelter, and the highly restricted range of motif forms it contains, these associations tentatively suggest that, in Phase 3, a relationship between these motifs was emphasised in this locale.

Lizard motifs were drawn infrequently in Phase 2: three are in the Cataract catchment, and one is in the Avon. In Phase 3, lizards occur in an even distribution between all catchments (n = 15).

Three wombat motifs occur in one shelter in Phase 2 (UA47). They were drawn infrequently in Phase 3 also (n = 6), but occur in all catchments except the Cordeaux. The three Phase 2 wombats in UA47 were drawn in association with a cluster of elliptical motifs (Plate 8.10).

A similar association occurs between a large Phase 3 wombat and a clutch of circle motifs, in AF4, in the Cataract (Plate 8.11) (see Dibden 2011:Appendix 1). Another small wombat motif occurs in the Cataract. It is in a reasonably strong isomorphic congruent relationship with a small concavity (Gill22). Previously in this chapter, the association between Phase 3 human hand and feet stencils and a wombat motif has been discussed. Given that only nine wombat motifs occur in the Upper Nepean, and that frequently they are embellished, either by association with other motifs or by other means, this is suggestive that they had some unique significance.

Plate 8.10 Phase 3 wombat with some of its associated circular motifs (rock shelter AF4).
Source: Photograph by Julie Dibden, 2011.

Plate 8.11 Phase 2 wombat with some of its associated elliptical motifs (rock shelter UA47).
Source: Photograph by Julie Dibden, 2011.

Snake motifs were drawn infrequently in Phase 2: one is in the Avon catchment, and four are in the Cataract. This distribution is comparable with that of lizard imagery, although in reverse. In Phase 3, snakes were drawn relatively frequently (n = 42), and are present in all catchments (Plate 8.12). Mirroring Phase 2 distribution, they occur in greater abundance in the Avon and Cataract. Similar to wombats and eels, snakes also occur occasionally in compositions with clutches of large numbers of small circle, or elliptical-shaped motifs. Like eels, they are often in associations with anthropomorphic motifs.

Plate 8.12 Phase 3 snake graphic (rock shelter Wade5).
Source: Photograph by Julie Dibden, 2011.

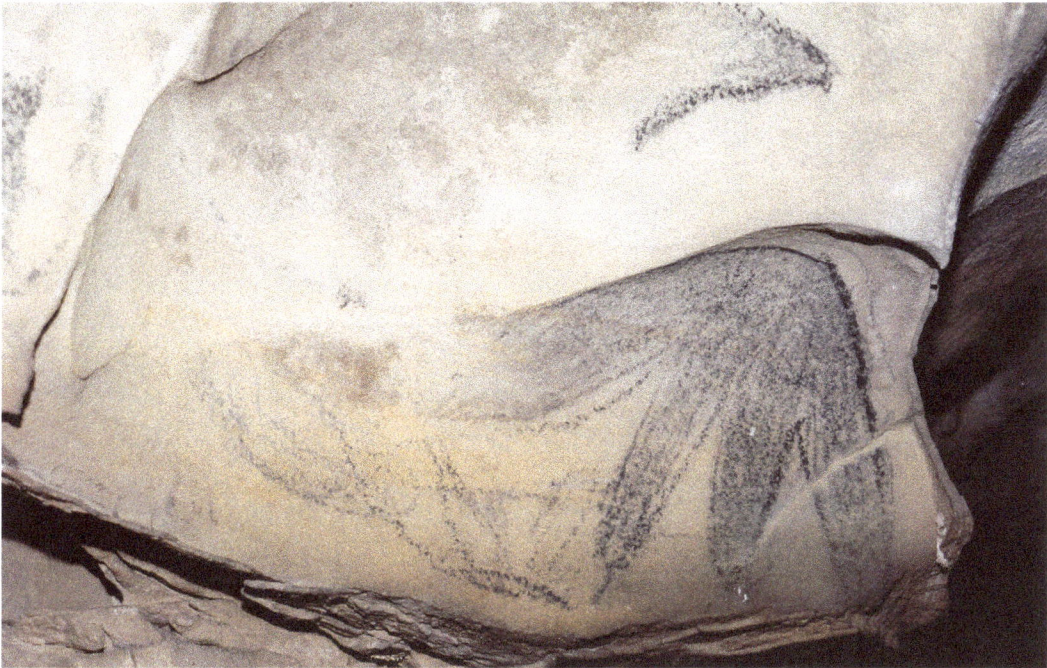

Plate 8.13 Phase 3 'unknown/other' graphic (rock shelter SCR15).
Source: Photograph by Julie Dibden, 2011.

Marsupial motifs were drawn infrequently in Phase 2: two in the Cataract catchment and four in the Avon. This distribution is comparable with that of lizard and snake imagery. In Phase 3, marsupial motifs were drawn relatively frequently (n = 51) and are in all catchments, although only one is recorded in the Nepean. They are most common in the Cordeaux and Avon. These motifs include animals that look like bandicoots and quolls. In both phases, marsupials are sometimes animated and drawn as though they are leaping downwards or standing. In Phase 3, small bandicoot motifs in identical schema (Code 5.8) are introduced. They are typically drawn in groups of three, at the base of rock art panels (see Dibden 2011:Appendix 1:EC1, UA1, UA47, DCC4).

Macropod motifs were drawn in all catchments except the Nepean in Phase 2 (n = 13). They became particularly abundant in Phase 3 (n = 158). In both phases, they were occasionally drawn with their heads turned backwards, evoking an imagined place.

Anthropomorphic motifs occur in all catchments except for the Nepean in Phase 2 rock art (n = 28). In Phase 3, 326 anthropomorphic motifs have been recorded, and they are schematically highly diverse.

The 'unknown/other' category will be described more fully below; however, it is noted here that there is a strong formal continuity between Phases 1, 2 and 3 in many of the motifs within the grouping. In addition, this category includes a large number of motifs that are new to the Upper Nepean rock art repertoire in Phase 3 (Plate 8.13).

While the above discussion has referred to the introduction in Phase 3 of new motifs that are schematically different from Phase 2, within the broad figurative categories, a range of new animal referents appear in Phase 3. These are discussed below in summary form.

- Fish motifs occur in 21 instances in Phase 3, and are certainly not common. They occur in all catchments, although they are infrequent in the Cordeaux and Nepean catchments.

- Macropod with joey motifs occur in four instances and, as well, one weathered animal (indeterminate as to species) with a 'joey'. Three are in the Cataract and one each in the Avon and Cordeaux.

- Koala motifs occur as a pair in a single shelter in the Nepean.

- Tortoise motifs occur in nine instances in Phase 3. They occur in all catchments, although they are infrequent in the Cataract and Nepean.

- A dog motif has been identified once, in the Nepean.

- Profile anthropomorphs occur in 41 instances in all catchments except the Nepean, and most frequently in the Cordeaux. One shelter (T4) in the Cordeaux contains 18 small profile anthropomorphic motifs in a composition (see Dibden 2011:Appendix 1). It is also notable that the two in BR29, associated with large numbers of eels and other anthropomorphic motifs, are highly inscripted, having been drawn in black and white pigment and with cross-hatch infill (Plate 8.14).

Plate 8.14 Phase 3 charcoal-and-white pigment (white is very faint) profile anthropomorph with complex infill (rock shelter BR29).

Source: Photograph by Julie Dibden, 2011.

The discussion below describes the formal diversity present in the anthropomorphic, animal and 'unknown' graphic categories of Phase 3 rock art in the Research Database. A total of 722 motifs (other than indeterminate) have been identified in Phase 3 graphic rock art. These occur in 234 different schematic forms and indicate considerable formal diversity. The graphic diversity of each animal motif category listed above is summarised and discussed below:

Bird: The 11 bird motifs are drawn in five different forms (see codes in Dibden 2011:Appendix 3). Two resemble emus and the remainder are highly schematic. Ten are drawn in charcoal and one is scratched. Formally, bird motifs can be similar to profile anthropomorphs and, occasionally, discriminating between the two can be arbitrary. The most common bird form is Code 11.1, four of which occur in one site (UA12). These are notable for being small (<20 centimetres), and three in a cluster on a ceiling appear to have been drawn in such a way that their heads coincide with natural red marks on the panel (see Dibden 2011:Appendix 1). Code 11.9 occurs once only and is weathered; its entire form is uncertain, although its rear end is strongly evocative of a bird. Like the birds in *UA12*, it is also small and occurs in a less-than-visible locale in a concavity.

The remaining birds are all large and in highly visible locations. Code 11.7 is a tall bird form, with its head turned backwards, and this motif also occurs in the Phase 2 assemblage. It occurs twice in Phase 3. One is in UA49, discussed previously in relation to the stencilled fist. In UA49, the motif is scratched, is in association with a large scratched macropod and also has its head turned backwards.

Code 11.6 are tall bird forms, with certain emu characteristics (in the rear end). These motifs also occur with macropods in very obvious association. One is present in UA36 with an extremely large macropod. The other is in Wall13 with two large macropods, and in association with one that has a joey (see Dibden 2011:Appendix 1). The Code 11.17 bird is very emu-like in form. It occurs in one shelter only (SCR10), but, significantly, is schematically comparable with the only emu motif in an open engraved context in the study area (BC4).

Echidna: The four echidna motifs are drawn in two different forms (see codes in Dibden 2011:Appendix 3), both of which first appeared in Phase 2. Code 8.16 occurs once in UA47, as an addition to the six drawn previously during Phase 2. It is elaborately drawn with a complex 'v'-shaped infill. The addition of this motif in UA47 suggests that the motif form continued to be relevant and meaningful in that site in the most recent sociocultural context. The three Code 8.4 echidnas occur in two sites, UA43 and Wall27. The shelter UA43 is a Phase 3 counterpart of two similar Phase 2 shelters, UA1 and UA47. It contains a very similar range of animal motifs, some of which are animated or paired, as in UA47 in particular. The echidnas in UA43 are drawn together and contain linear infill. The other Code 8.4 echidna is in a large shelter (Wall27) and unusually occurs singly rather than in a pair. However, the echidna is accompanied, as was always the case in Phase 2, by gliders (three), which are located immediately above it in Wall27 (see Dibden 2011:Appendix 1).

Eel: A total of 28 eel motifs are drawn in six different forms and occur in 15 shelters, the most common of which is Code 2.3. The majority are drawn in charcoal; however, eel motifs, more than any other animal, are most likely to be inscripted with the use of other coloured pigment. Several shelters are dominated by eel imagery. A16 has one Phase 3 eel, and this is an addition to the four Phase 2 red eels. The other motif dominant in A16 is Code 2.5: small, simple-form elliptical shapes (not unlike eels), which occur on the south end of the panel in a large group. It is notable that A16 has gestural marks in the form of rubbed and pitted surfaces. The other notable shelter with Phase 2 eels is BR29, with seven large, highly inscripted (colourful and with complex infill) Phase 3 eels, which are also additions to the earlier Phase 2 eel motifs in that site. The other dominant motif in BR29 is anthropomorphs, which are all highly inscripted with colour and complex infill. Notably, BR29 also includes a snake drawn parallel and in association with an eel. In these two shelters, Phase 3 eels, as additions to earlier eel-dominated sites, indicate continuity of the formal relevance of this motif between the two phases. While occurring with other Phase 2 animal imagery, including gliders and macropods, A12 likewise suggests continuity with the addition of a highly inscripted Phase 3 eel (Plate 8.9) to the earlier eel repertoire. SCR10 is notable for containing not only a huge 3-metre-long yellow-and-black eel, but also large numbers of the small, elliptical Code 2.5 motifs that occur in abundance in A16 with eels.

While typically large and dominant, eel motifs may also be small and subtle, such as in BR12, a small, low shelter containing mostly hidden imagery on a low ceiling. BR12 has three small eels, two drawn in charcoal, and one that is scratched (Plate 1.6). The other imagery in the shelter is abstracted 'unknown' motifs. This shelter suggests the production of imagery with a more individualised, participatory motivation, rather than being informed by corporately structured and motivated goals.

The remainder of shelters with Phase 3 eels appear to be more diverse and inclusive in regard to the suite of imagery they contain. BR24 is notable for containing a large panel of many Phase 3 anthropomorphs, side by side, in a row. At one end of the panel a small, upright eel is drawn beside a small glider, the pair clearly associated. In Wade5, a shelter containing only Phase 2 imagery, a charcoal eel with complex infill is associated with a diverse range of imagery, including a snake and, notably, two large 'downward-leaping' marsupial/macropods.

Eel motifs are gesturally marked by scratching or pitting in three instances, and sometimes rubbed surfaces are in close association (A16, SCR15). In 8 out of 28 Phase 3 cases, eels also are drawn in isomorphic congruence with natural rock features.

Glider: In 23 of 24 cases, glider motifs are drawn in one form (Code 8.2). This motif first appeared in three shelters (A12, UA1 and UA47) in Phase 2. Phase 3 gliders (Code 8.2) occur in seven shelters. They are small, except for one in UA8 (discussed further below in the Lizard category). Phase 3 gliders are all drawn in charcoal and frequently in compositions of two, three or more. The exceptions include the one in UA8, and one in BR24, discussed above in the eel category. Two occur in A12, which is one of the three shelters where they first appeared in Phase 2. Their addition in Phase 3 suggests a continuity of their formal relevance in this shelter. They occur in small clusters in BR32, DCC4 and Wall27, all of which contain Phase 2 red hand stencils and/or handprints, and EC17, which contains a pair of small Phase 2 anthropomorphs. There is a strong tendency for Code 8.2 gliders to occur in shelters with Phase 2 rock art, whether graphic or gestural. A very different form of glider (Code 5.27) is in AF3, a Phase 3 shelter, which is dominated by a large panel of 'fighting' macropods.

Lizard: The six lizard motifs are drawn in four different schema, one of which occurs in Phase 2. They are always drawn with charcoal in Phase 3, and occur singly in sites. The Code 9.1 forms are highly schematised. This motif occurs twice (A12 and EC21), and both are very small. Code 13.1 also occurs twice (UA8 and UA13) in shelters containing Phase 2 rock art only. UA8 contains six motifs, all of which are large, and three are unique. One is a large anthropomorph with 'Daramulan' characteristics (Code 7.15), and two are 'unknown' (Codes 8 and 8.1). One is a large glider, the size of which is comparable with Phase 2 gliders, but unique in Phase 3, during which they are normally small. UA13 contains a limited suite of motifs, including eel, snake and profile anthropomorphic forms, in addition to the large lizard. The Code 13.2 lizard first appears in Phase 2. It is formally similar to Code 13.1, in that it is also sinuous in form, suggesting movement. In Phase 3, it occurs in one shelter (Gill27), which also has a limited suite of only Phase 3 imagery. Again, it is associated with a snake and an anthropomorphic motif. In summary, there is a tendency for large, sinuous lizards to be associated with snakes and anthropomorphic motifs. The two code 13.3 lizards occur in separate shelters located in close proximity.

Wombat: Six wombats occur in Phase 3 and, similar to Phase 2, they are a minor, albeit arguably significant, component of Phase 3 rock art. Other than the black-and-white wombat in Cad39 (discussed previously in regard to Phase 3 stencils), all Phase 3 wombats are drawn in charcoal. They always occur singly in shelters; this contrasts with Phase 2, where three wombat motifs occur together in one shelter (UA47). Notably, a Phase 3 wombat has been added to UA47. Except for the small wombat in a concavity in Gill22, they are normally large, and there is a tendency for Phase 3 wombats to be the dominant motif in a shelter—for example, AF4, with its clutch of circles, and C39, with its associated animal paw and human stencils, the two of which have been discussed previously. Not unexpectedly, a large 'running' wombat occurs in UA43, a Phase 3 counterpart (with a similar suite of imagery, some of which is paired) of the predominantly Phase 2 shelter UA47. The other Phase 3 wombat occurs in Wade5 (with Phase 3 rock art only), a shelter with a range of motifs, including a spectacular pair of large, downward-leaping marsupial/macropods.

Snake: A total of 31 snake motifs occur in 12 different forms (see codes in Dibden 2011:Appendix 3) and in 22 shelters. Snakes are abundant and, similar to eels, are likely to be embellished by complex infill, by different colours, and be associated with other motifs (i.e. circles or elliptical forms). Two shelters contain large groups of small elliptical motifs (Code 2.5): A16, where they are strongly associated with eel imagery; and in SCR10, where they occur around a large snake. This motif (Code 2.5) also occurs as infill (c. n = 40) in a huge (2.7 metres long) 'death adder' snake in the shelter Ana50 (see Plate 8.12). The relationship between the small elliptical motifs and eels and snakes is very strong, and suggests a conceptual union, although this is emphasised in only a few locales. Snake motifs may also occur in association with groups of large numbers (c. 20 or so) of small circles: UA11, a shelter dominated by snake, eel, lizard and profile anthropomorphic imagery, and SCR3 and A29 with circles as infill. Snakes often occur in shelters with a limited number and range of other motifs and, in these cases, frequently occur with anthropomorphic motifs (Gill49, Gill27, SCR14, BR29).

Marsupial: A total of 49 marsupial motifs occur in 11 different forms (see codes in Dibden 2011:Appendix 3), and are distributed between 19 shelters. The most common (n = 17) marsupial motif is Code 5.8, with the physical characteristics of a bandicoot. This is a new Phase 3 addition to the Upper Nepean, and occurs in eight shelters. The typical manner of depiction occurs in alignments of three or four and, most commonly, at the base of a rock art panel (EC1, DCC4, UA1, UA47). They mostly occur in shelters used previously in Phase 2 for either gestural or graphic marks and, notably, occur in UA1 and UA47 Phase 2 shelters with groups of animals. All except two Phase 3 marsupials are drawn in charcoal; however, one Code 5.8 motif occurs in a shelter (Gill44) as a single motif and, unusually, is drawn in white pigment. The highly structured organisation of the Code 5.8 motifs, their relative abundance and the nature of the shelters in which they occur suggests that this image was a significant addition to the animal repertoire in Phase 3 rock art. A number of marsupial motifs are drawn in a manner suggestive of movement (Codes 5.14, 5.16 and 5.17), the first two of which also occur in Phase 2 rock art.

Macropod: A total of 29 macropod motifs occur in 11 different forms (see codes in Dibden 2011:Appendix 3) and are distributed between 19 shelters. The most common macropod motif is Code 5.11, which also occurs in Phase 2. Generally, macropod motifs occur singly in shelters. They are drawn in a variety of poses including very formal stances; however, frequently, they are in a state of animation. The AF3 shelter is notable for containing seven in a row, upright and in a 'fighting pose'.

Anthropomorphic Categories

In Phase 2, anthropomorphic imagery was relatively uncommon (n = 17) and occurred in 11 different forms. Anthropomorphic motifs have been categorised in five overall categories: female, male, anthropomorph, anthropomorph imaginary, and profile anthropomorph. The female category is identified on the basis of having breasts. The male group is distinguished usually by the presence of a penis, although sometimes solely by association with what appears to be obviously a female. The male category was reasonably coherent in regard to Phase 2, where paired anthropomorphs were more common, and is less so for Phase 3. The anthropomorph category includes images that appear human in a 'life-like' manner. The imaginary category is somewhat arbitrary, but captures motifs that are only slightly modelled on a human form. The profile anthropomorphic category is a new category that does not occur in Phase 2.

Phase 3 anthropomorphic imagery is described below:

Female anthropomorphs: A total of 15 charcoal female anthropomorphic motifs occur in seven forms in seven shelters (two occur in Phase 2). In Phase 2, the few anthropomorphic motifs were frequently drawn in male and female pairs—for example, in EC17. This small shelter has four anthropomorphs added in Phase 3, one of which is female, in addition to the large numbers of small gliders, as discussed previously. It has already been noted that two gliders were added to the panel in which the earlier pair of anthropomorphs reside and, in addition to those on a panel in a group of 10, one has also been drawn with the four new Phase 3 anthropomorphs. The association between anthropomorphs and gliders in Phase 2 is dominant in this site. The shelter UA36 has been referred to before in that it is a Phase 3 counterpart to UA47, with paired animal imagery. It contains a similar suite of animal pairs and, in addition, a pair of anthropomorphs, one of which is female (with 'eyes'). While anthropomorphic motifs have not been added to UA47 in Phase 3, the shelter UA1, which is comparable with UA47 but has anthropomorphs in the Phase 2 suite of rock art, has had numerous Phase 3 anthropomorphs added to it, one of which is female.

The Phase 3 shelter (RL18) contains a pair of female and male anthropomorphs, the female being larger than the male. A large female anthropomorph with complex infill is beside the pair. This shelter, located in a cliff, contains a limited number and a small range of motifs, and the anthropomorphs appear to be significant in this site. A small pair occurs in SCR11. These motifs have their formal counterparts in SCR10. A12 has one small female motif, which, unusually, is in a hidden location, and is an addition to an animal motif dominated Phase 2 site. Two females occur in a row of around eight large anthropomorphic motifs that dominate the rock art panel in BR24. A similar configuration of Phase 3 anthropomorphs occurs in one other shelter only, Cad44. Notably, the anthropomorphs in BR24 are accompanied by a pair of motifs, a small eel and a small glider, these being the only other recognisable motifs in the shelter. The eel and anthropomorphic-dominated shelter BR29 has one female anthropomorph (also two others that are weathered, which may be female). SCR15 is largely an eel and anthropomorphic-dominated site, and has one female. DCC12 contains a large number of graphics, including eel, snake, macropod, marsupial and three rare or unique anthropomorphic motifs, one of which is female. DCC30 is dominated by marsupial motifs and has one female anthropomorphic motif.

Male anthropomorphs: A total of 15 male anthropomorphs occur in five different forms (one of which occurs in Phase 2) in six shelters, the majority of which have been discussed above.

Anthropomorph imaginary: This category of anthropomorph is a significant addition to the graphic imagery in Phase 3. A total of 83 motifs occur in 37 different forms (many of which are similar). This category is distributed between 28 shelters in the Research Database. Two major forms occur: one that is large, elaborate and often highly inscripted, with colour and/or complex infill (and other accoutrements such as long appendages, which extend from the head, 'rays', 'hair' and 'eyes') and another that is small and highly schematic. While occurring in single instances in 13 shelters, frequently they occur in groups of two, three or more. The large category will be described first.

This category of anthropomorph was intended to be seen and is visually dramatic. This is evident on the basis of numerous criteria. They are typically in locations, both geographically (but not always) and micro-topographically (always), where they are visually dominant. They are large (c. 80 centimetres or more high) and sometimes very large (see Plate 1.2). As indicated above, they are highly inscripted and frequently contain complex infill. They occur commonly in rows, usually of three or more, and are sometimes the only motif type or the visually dominant motif in a shelter (TL6, C38, BR24). Typically they have long 'tails' or 'penises', 'hair' or 'rays', and sometimes long appendages extending from their heads, mouths or bodies. Frequently this motif has 'eyes', a trait shared only with other anthropomorphs and two unique animal motifs (Codes 11.8 and 2.41). While visually dominating on all levels, the presence of 'eyes' in these motifs creates an imagined space where the image is read as entering the viewer's actual lived space.

The other type of anthropomorph in this category is less visually dramatic, but while being a highly schematic and simplified form, it is frequently inscripted with the use of colour. This motif occurs in two main and significant shelters, BR29 and SCR10 (see Plate 7.7).

Profile anthropomorph: This category of anthropomorph is also a new, and arguably a significant addition to the suite of rock art in the Upper Nepean. A total of 32 motifs, in seven different forms, occur in 11 shelters. This motif is also sometimes large and dramatic (see motif in DCC12 located 3 metres above the ground, on the outside face of the shelter: Plate 6.3), but can also occur as very small motifs. It commonly has 'eyes'. A group of small profile anthropomorphic figures in a single small panel in T4 is a composition. This is a unique occurrence. Profile anthropomorphs occur frequently in shelters that have rows or groups of other anthropomorphic types (BR24, BR29, C44, UA1). They also occur singly, or with very few other motifs in shelters, such as BR17, which is simply a small, scalloped surface in a cliff, rather than a shelter (see Dibden 2011:Appendix 1). With their typically large size, 'eyes' and prominent micro-topographic locations, profile anthropomorphs frequently create an imagined space that occupies that of the viewer.

A small range of new animal imagery occurs in Phase 3. One macropod with a joey is associated with an emu in Wall13. Another unidentified animal with a joey, in EC5b, has a highly schematic form and drawn in black and white. Both shelters also possess Phase 2 imagery, and EC5b is a significant early site. Fish can occur in groups (schools) of three or more, where their schematic construction is identical (e.g. UA1 and BMS18: see Dibden 2011:Appendix 1). In BMS18, a school of six fish occurs in a small concavity. All fish motifs are relatively small, however; one very large fish (c. 2 metres) dominates a rock art panel in SCR10. This motif is formally comparable with an engraved whale/fish motif, which occurs as a single motif in the open context site EC12. It is also notable that a unique emu form in SCR10 is also represented in one instance in the open engraved rock art of the Upper Nepean catchment (as discussed above). Tortoise motifs are uncommon (n = 8), and occur in three different forms in five shelters. Significantly, three occur in UA43, the Phase 3 counterpart of UA47 that contains the paired animals. The three tortoise motifs in UA43 are the only ones inscripted with complex infill.

The 'possible European animal' category has been defined for the purposes of capturing, in the analysis, motifs that possess characteristics of European animals. There is no certainty in the identification of these motifs, but it is considered worthwhile to contemplate their form and the resulting implications, if they are indeed representative of introduced species. Two appear to be horse heads, including Codes 5.19 and 5.21, and both occur in the one shelter, TL18. The motifs have long 'heads' and tall 'ears'. This shelter is rare because it contains relatively few charcoal rock marks (n = 18), but many of them are gestural pigment marks (n = 8). The other motifs, while relatively well preserved, are figuratively unidentifiable.

The Phase 3 shelter UA49, remarked upon previously for its rare collection of scratched graphics, a stencilled fist and scratched gestural marks, contains a large motif (Code 11.8), which appears to be a cow or horse/emu-morphed animal. The animal is typically drawn in profile, but, unusually, with the head turned to the viewer. It has a long cow/horse type head, with a large, upright 'ear' and, notably, two large 'eyes'. Its rear end is emu shaped and it has two legs, although its feet are neither hoof-like nor emu feet. The shelter EC5b was noted above for the large charcoal-and-white animal with joey it contains. On the same panel, another highly weathered but large charcoal-and-white animal is present (Code 11.15); only the bottom of the image remains. It is possibly a cow or horse with four legs. Three other smaller animal motifs have been identified as possibly European (Codes 5, 5.25 and 5.36).

The Phase 3 'unknown' categories are described minimally below:

- A number of motifs include simple trident form motifs, some of which also occur in Phases 1 and 2. Their inclusion in Phase 3 is normally as small charcoal drawings; however, they also occur in white and in red in two instances.

- Several motifs include simple circle, or slightly elongated circle, shapes. Numerous oval shapes occur, some of which are slightly eel-like. Many motifs are only subtly different and frequently occur once only. Several unknown motifs in this grouping have forms evocative of animals (e.g. Codes 2.27 and 2.28), but are nevertheless figuratively unidentifiable. They may be entirely imagined in form, or simply not recognisable to the uninformed eye. The most frequently occurring of these is Code 2.5, which appears in 103 instances in a highly restricted distribution and, primarily, in A16 with eels and SCR10 with a large snake. Four occur in A12, one of the Phase 2 sites in which this motif is present; notably, six occur in SCR15, a significant eel shelter with gestural marking (pitting).

- Codes 2.31, 2.32, 2.33, 2.34 and 2.35 occur in a single panel in EC5b. Their figurative model, given their shape and short, stubby tails, can only be conjectured, but it is grub-like. One has 'eyes' and 'hair', and two have complex infill. They occur with a large, slightly anthropomorphic type motif (but categorised as 'unknown'), which has complex infill and a long appendage. Similar motifs, Codes 11.13 and 2.36, occur in DCC4 and Gill34 shelters respectively, and these also have complex infill. These motifs are all unique and, given their large size and inscription, are significant motifs.

- Many motifs in the 'unknown' category are relatively large and animal-like, such as those in the code sequence 8. The motifs in the code sequence 9 are all small, highly schematic motifs.

8.4 Summary: Rock Art in the Upper Nepean Catchment

In this chapter, the analyses have sought to describe and quantify the formal and material nature of the rock art of the Upper Nepean catchment within a temporal framework. The approach has identified that the imagery possesses considerable variability, both formally and materially, and that many images are either unique or rare. However, it has also demonstrated that the repetition of specific motifs, both on an inter- and intra-site basis, is a strong characteristic of this rock art. Furthermore, the analysis has established that, while there is considerable change and innovation in a diachronic context, there is also some continuity of motif production. The analyses have also confirmed that there is significant intra- and inter-site structure in the rock art, particularly in Phases 2 and 3. The patterns in inter-site variability will form the basis for exploring spatial and geographic distribution in Chapter 9. Table 8.15 summarises the nature of temporal variability in the rock art in the Upper Nepean.

Table 8.15 Summary of temporal change in the rock art of the Upper Nepean catchment.

Phase	Rock art	Object/model
Phase 1	Intaglio engravings	Bird and macropod tracks; other simple forms (and anthropomorphs elsewhere on Woronora Plateau)
Phase 2a	Gestural: red hand stencils and handprints; red pigment smears usually over large areas	Hands located in a range of shelter morphologies. Sites with large counts are small, non-habitation shelters
	Red wet graphics	Limited range of motifs: trident forms and simple motifs. Present in a restricted number of shelters and all motifs in highly visible locations

Phase	Rock art	Object/model
Phase 2b	Red drawn graphics	Animal and anthropomorphic imagery: macropods, marsupials, birds, eels, snakes, lizards, echidnas, gliders, 'unknown': simple forms. Frequently in habitation shelters, but also in non-habitation sites. All imagery in visible locations and some in isomorphic congruence.
Phase 3	Gestural: white and cream stencils; non-graphic pigment applications, including pigment blobs, circles, rock-surface marking, strokes and random; non-graphic scratch, pitted and rubbed marks	Stencilling activity of decreased abundance. Stencils predominantly hand, but including a fist, small numbers of human feet, animal paws, and objects. Sites with large counts are potential habitation shelters Significantly greater diversity in non-graphic pigment applications and the introduction of non-graphic, gestural rock marking
	Charcoal graphics; white wet or drawn graphics; scratched graphics; small numbers of red drawn or wet graphics (usually highly schematic)	Animal imagery, including most of the forms previously produced; however, with the addition of others, macropods with joeys, tortoise, fish and small marsupials, such as bandicoots, etc. A wide range of anthropomorphic motifs, and the addition of a range of unique or rare forms, many of which have an 'unknown' figurative referent Shelter morphologies highly variable, and include locations perched within cliffs. A diversification in the micro-topographic contexts of graphic locations and imagery produced in 'hidden' locales

Source: Table reproduced from Dibden (2011).

The temporal patterns in the Upper Nepean rock art sequence that have emerged in this chapter are summarised below:

Phase 1

Only two Phase 1 rock art shelters occur in the Upper Nepean catchment. These are clearly distributed in very low density in the broader local area (south of the Georges River). The Phase 1 engraved rock art is comprised of a restricted range of graphic forms that are predominantly trident-shaped bird feet and macropod feet/tracks. This rock art is mostly figurative and, given its formal and iconic properties, is interpreted as reflecting the encoding of symbolic values of the animals and beings they represent. Taking into consideration the seven shelters on the Woronora Plateau with this art (albeit a small sample), the engraved intaglio rock art occurs in a diverse suite of shelter types that vary considerably in terms of their morphology, size and whether they contain living space. This diversity suggests that the nature of the shelter itself was largely incidental to its choice for marking. The micro-topographic location of imagery within shelters is similarly diverse.

Phase 2

Phase 2 rock art occurs in 173 rock shelters in the Upper Nepean catchment, and is comprised of both graphic and gestural marks. The analyses have identified that, during the Phase 2 period, stencilling was the dominant mode of marking the land, but that graphic production was not insignificant. The overall distributional pattern of stencils and graphics is such that the majority of shelters contain low numbers of motifs, contrasting with a small number that contain relatively high counts. The frequency of stencilling is geographically varied and decreases from north to south. The Cataract contains the greatest abundance and density of Phase 2 stencils. Graphic rock art, however, has a different spatial distribution. While the general trend is one of decreasing graphic production, north to south, in contrast to Phase 2 stencils and open grinding groove densities, higher densities of graphics occur in the Cordeaux and Avon.

The strong separation between stencils and graphics, in respect of inter- and intra-site distribution, suggests that the two rock art categories were produced within different sociocultural contexts. Furthermore, while stencils occur in a range of shelter morphological types, those shelters with stencils only typically do not contain living areas, and all shelters that have high stencil counts have no or negligible living areas. These trends indicate that shelter morphology was largely incidental to stencilling activity and, generally, stencilling took place in locales that were separate from those that may have been used for habitation or other activities. A contrast with this pattern is evident in shelters that have a combination of stencils and graphics. These sites typically have large living areas, especially if high stencil counts are present. More than half the shelters that have graphics only do not contain significant potential living space. Typically, shelters with high graphic counts do. This is not to imply, necessarily, that the space was used for habitation. The relationship may relate simply to the size of either the rock art panels or the shelter itself, to accommodate on one hand an abundance of art and, on the other, larger numbers of people for rock art production and associated activities.

It has been argued that within the suite of Phase 2 graphic rock art, an earlier sub-phase is probable (Phase 2a). This rock art is formally comparable with the Phase 2 rock art identified by McDonald (2008a) in the Upper Mangrove Creek catchment. In the Upper Nepean, it is comprised of painted motifs, including tridents, trident configurations, other simple forms and possibly highly schematic anthropomorphs. This rock art is not abundant. It occurs in very few shelters, and this density distribution is comparable with Phase 1 rock art distribution; although, in contrast to Phase 1, it occurs almost exclusively in large shelters that have large floor spaces. Accordingly, the location of Phase 2a rock art is strongly tethered to shelter morphology and, arguably, an ability to accommodate large numbers of people. The nature of the data, and level of analysis used in this research, does not provide the capacity to unravel the implication of the presence of these motifs in the suite of earliest pigment rock art. Given that it is formally comparable with Phase 1 engraved motifs, doing so may be of considerable interest. It is possible that the pigment motifs were produced synchronically with the intaglio motifs and, accordingly, they may each be contextually different. On the other hand, if they are temporally discrete and separate, the formally comparable Phase 1 motifs in Phase 2a may represent some continuity of tradition. However, it is also noted that this analysis has not actually identified, with any certainty, the temporal order of these two types of rock art in the Upper Nepean, other than that they are both early in the relative sequence.

It has been argued in this chapter that stencils, and also pigment smears, via their gestural and participatory manner of production (embodied connection with the land), may have emphasised people and land relationships. Graphic rock art, on the other hand, given its potential to encode conceptual meanings, may have been used to mark localities within a supra-individualised context, thus serving to establish and maintain, via inscription, a corporately mediated social geography.

The figurative element of Phase 2 graphic rock art is believed to be a later component of this phase (Phase 2b). It includes animal and anthropomorphic motifs in low counts, and a generally restricted range of formal diversity. Anthropomorphic motifs are uncommon. They are frequently paired, including a male and female form. Animal motifs can be either formally static or animated. They often occur in pairs, in triplicate or more, in individual shelters. As noted above, the Avon and Cordeaux contain the highest Phase 2 graphic density. The analyses have also shown that these catchments contain more shelters with graphics only, compared with either the Cataract or

Nepean. Furthermore, the shelters in these catchments with high graphic counts do not contain stencils. These patterns suggest that the Cordeaux and Avon were contextually significant areas for the production of this earliest figurative rock art. The analyses have demonstrated the highly restricted distribution of animal motifs. Several animal species are present only in the Avon and in either one or very few shelters.

The similarity of schematic organisation (as grouped in individual codes), the relatively few motifs that occur in the various figurative and code categories, their typical patterns of co-occurrence, and the highly restricted range of shelter and geographic locales in which Phase 2 rock art occurs indicate that its production is likely to have been generated within a highly organised corporate structure.

Phase 3

Phase 3 rock art occurs in 449 rock shelters in the Upper Nepean catchment, and this contrasts with the 173 Phase 2 shelter frequency. Phase 3 rock art accounts for three-quarters of all rock markings, and is mostly graphic imagery. There is no indication that stencilling with red pigment occurs during the Phase 3 period. All stencils were produced with white or cream pigment, except for three black stencils. Stencilling is significantly less frequent compared with Phase 2, and is a minor practice within this phase. Stencils are distributed in a pattern comparable with that encountered in Phase 2, decreasing in abundance from north to south. Notably, one Phase 3 stencil only occurs in the Nepean. This result is in accordance with the overall pattern of Phase 3 stencilling, which is largely confined to the interior of the study area. The two shelters located near each other in the Avon each contain the highest stencil counts.

It has been argued that the motivation and meaning of stencilling changed in Phase 3. A shift in the sociocultural context of stencilling is indicated by its preferential location in shelters with relatively large living space, the diversity and nature of objects stencilled, including animal paws and feet, and their association with graphic imagery. Where animal paws and feet occur, human stencils accompany them, and this suggests the emphasis of a relationship not only between people and land, but also in association with animals. In Cad39, the prominence of a highly inscripted black-and-white pigment wombat on the rock art panel, in association with the human and animal paw stencils, may well be amplifying this conceptual relationship.

Phase 3 graphic production happened in a wide range of shelter types and sizes. A greater diversification of micro-topographic contexts used within shelters occurs, with 'hidden' locales employed for the first time. In addition, shelters located high within the vertical faces of cliffs were utilised. These shifts suggest that the sociocultural context of graphic production became diversified, and this may represent both a sociocultural structural difference and change in purpose and motivation when compared with Phase 2 graphic rock art. In respect of hidden imagery, an audience beyond that of the makers is not implied by this practice, and this suggests that the purpose resided primarily in the act of marking itself. The use of new shelter types in Phase 3, such as those located in cliffs, suggests a new restriction in sociocultural context, in which the production and perception of rock marking was enjoyed by a select group within society, in these locales.

The majority of Phase 3 graphic motifs are drawn with dry pigment; however, white pigment and scratching are also used. Phase 2 graphics are frequently redrawn, usually with charcoal. During Phase 3, pigment is used in a greater diversity of ways to gesturally mark the land. Non-graphic, gestural pigment marking occurs in one-quarter of the Phase 3 shelter assemblages in the Research Database. Accordingly, this practice is not infrequent and, hence, can be considered to be purposeful marking of the land. Given that the form of these marks is not regulated by corporately defined conventions, as graphics are, they may reflect, similar to stencils, individualised expressions of people and land relationships. These types of marks, typically, have been applied to natural features within rock art panels and, therefore, the shelter morphology appears to strongly influence their nature and location. The expressive behaviour implied by these marks may well have been motivated by the simple need of uniting people and land. It is possible that this type of marking may well have functioned similar to stencils in this regard, and may have occurred as a substitute in a context, for example, where the acquisition of suitable stencil pigment was hindered.

Similar to Phase 2, the graphic rock art in Phase 3 is comprised of animal, anthropomorphic and 'unknown' motifs. There is the continued production of schematically similar motifs and indications that, furthermore, many of these continued to be conceptually meaningful and relevant. This is suggested by the additions to specific shelters of motifs of the same figurative referent and schema as those that already existed, the production of older comparable imagery in those sites, the re-marking of older imagery and the inscription of imagery with colour and complex infill. Many Phase 2 shelters do have new and different images added to them; however, these motifs are frequently restricted in number, and are made in intra-site locales where they do not interfere visually with older graphics. This pattern is particularly evident in the few shelters that contain very formal displays of animal imagery. For example, in UA47, with its suite of gliders, echidnas and other Phase 2 imagery, a row of 'new' animal motifs (bandicoots) are drawn close to the floor at the base of the panel. However, there does not seem to be an aversion to creating Phase 3 rock art, gestural or graphic, on panels that contain Phase 2 stencils. These results indicate that the corporate graphic imagery of Phase 2, unlike the individualised marks (stencils), given that they were frequently curated and reproduced by subsequent generations, continued to be relevant to the needs and concerns of people in the period encompassed by Phase 3 rock art.

The motif categories echidna and glider continue always to co-occur in Phase 3 shelters as they did in Phase 2. However, notably, gliders become considerably smaller. All Phase 3 gliders, except for one, are small. The association between large bird (emu) and macropod motifs also continues in Phase 3. While many Phase 2 motifs exhibit a highly restricted geographic distribution, the same motifs occupy a greater spatial distribution in Phase 3. Snakes, for example, are infrequent in Phase 2, and restricted to two catchments. In Phase 3, not only do they become more abundant, they are drawn in all catchments. Anthropomorphic imagery becomes significantly diverse and abundant in Phase 3, and profile anthropomorphic forms are added to this category. It is particularly within the anthropomorphic category that motifs, for the first time, are drawn with 'eyes'. This feature, and their often large and commanding presence, act to occupy the viewer's actual lived space. It is notable that an emu motif, a macropod motif and a whale motif, which occur in three open engraved sites, have their formally comparable counterpart in Phase 3 images in a single shelter (SCR10). In summary, Phase 2 imagery continues to be produced in Phase 3 in a structured manner that is comparable with the earlier patterns.

However, there are also significant changes. Many new motifs, both animal and figuratively 'unknown', occur in Phase 3. Tortoises appear for the first time in a very similar structural pattern as existed during Phase 2, when animals are first introduced to the rock art repertoire of the Upper Nepean catchment. That is, they are rare, occurring in eight instances only, and are distributed between a small number of shelters. Three, which are highly inscribed with complex infill, occur in one site. Furthermore, this shelter, UA43, is used in Phase 3 for the first time; it does not contain Phase 2 art. The shelter UA43, in terms of its contents and structural organisation, is comparable with UA1 and UA47, two of the three significant Phase 2 animal motif shelters.

In addition, a suite of new and usually unique motifs, which are frequently large and drawn with complex infill, and which have no obvious figurative referent, suggests that while older motifs continued to be relevant, newer forms were required to satisfy corporate goals. This may imply that the sociocultural context had undergone change, and that a new ideational system came into being in order to mediate that change.

In this chapter, the nature of the rock art of the Upper Nepean catchment has been explored in accordance with the structure of the relative temporal sequence. The nature and diversity of the expressive behaviours relating to rock art, as practised within each phase, have been described, and they have formed the basis for conceiving the nature of the relationships between people and their world, and how these changed over time. The environmental and spatial signature of each temporal phase will be examined in Chapter 9, in order to expand the interpretive potential of the patterns identified in this chapter.

9

Rock Art and Spatial Variability

> When practices continue at the same locations over many generations these places and their surrounding landscapes become increasingly symbolically charged, patterned, and contextualised— traditions of landscape experience and enrichment are perpetuated and expressed as 'Ancestral Law'.
> (Taçon 1999:41)

In previous chapters, the analyses revealed trends in the structure of the distribution of rock markings in the Upper Nepean catchment. All site types and the abundance of their contents decline in numbers as one moves from north to south. This pattern is a southerly extension of a broader trend on the Woronora Plateau (cf. Sefton 1988). Significantly, two rock-marking practices—the engraving of images and groove channels on open sandstone platforms—did not occur south of the central Upper Nepean.

In Chapter 6, differences in the distribution of the abundance of grinding grooves in open context and rock art in shelters were identified. The incidence of high groove counts in certain open grinding groove sites has been interpreted to reflect spatially focused nodes of grinding activity. Likewise, the analysis of the distribution of rock art motif counts indicates that a small number of rock shelters were crucial locales in which extensive rock marking occurred. Higher density grinding groove and stencilling activity in the Cataract catchment contrasts with higher densities of graphic rock art in the Avon and Cordeaux.

The distribution of open context grinding grooves, engraved groove channels and engraved rock art, in respect of spatial organisation and environmental variables, has been addressed in Chapter 6. Apart from broad-scale geographic patterns in the location of these sites, it was established that all grinding groove sites with large groove counts, engraved rock art and engraved groove channels have an environmental signature. These sites are preferentially situated on upper valley slopes or crests and on, or very near to, ridge and watershed divide landforms. These rock markings frequently co-occur in discrete locales or within proximity of each other. Except in the Cataract catchment, the majority of rock shelters that contain large motif counts are preferentially situated on the same landforms.

Over time, it can be expected that the motivations and referential contexts for the production of rock art change. In Chapter 7, a relative temporal sequence for the rock art of the Upper Nepean catchment has been defined. In Chapter 8, abundance and density, shelter-specific locational signatures, and the nature and variability of the rock art, in each of the defined phases, has been examined. In this chapter, the analyses will look at the environmental and geographic distribution of rock art, in each of the defined phases. The analyses seeks to explore changes in the way people engaged with the land, via the practice of inscription on stone, throughout the late Holocene. The focus is to explore change via a consideration of the geographic and environmental signature of each temporal phase. The analysis is premised upon the proposition that the rock markings are elements that represent patterns of social life (cf. Thomas 2008). The distribution of specific shelters and their contents will be explored in order to discriminate different cultural contexts in which rock art was produced (cf. Layton 2000a). By examining the locational patterning of shelters and rock art, and how this changes over time, the analysis explores the dynamics of the social geography made materially manifest by the people of the Upper Nepean.

The discussion will address the topic according to the following criteria:

- abundance and the nature of rock art locales
- distribution and environmental location
- clusters and site associations
- motif distribution
- trends in Phase 3 additions, or otherwise, compared with Phase 2 shelters.

The analysis is based on tabulations presented in Appendix 11 of Dibden (2011). In these tables, the location of each rock art shelter and its contents is described in respect of its location on or adjacent to major watershed and ridge landforms. The focal patterns relating to site type, contents, site clusters and associations are summarised. The location of the major landforms are numbered and shown on the key map in Dibden (2011:Appendix 11) and are referred to here. The geographic distribution of various site types shown in maps in Chapters 6 and 8 illustrate many of the trends that are discussed.

The textually based analysis seeks to describe general trends in the spatial and environmental signature of each of the temporal phases. In particular, the discussion aims to identify the specific preferences relating to rock-marking distribution that may be inferred from the location of site and rock mark type. This analysis forms the primary basis for conceptualising the nature and transformation of the social geography in the Upper Nepean.

9.1 Phase 1 Rock Art

In Chapter 8, it was argued that the nature of shelter morphology was largely incidental to the choice of location for the production of Phase 1 rock art on the Woronora Plateau. By contrast, geographic and environmental variables appear to have strongly influenced the choice of places marked. In the Upper Nepean, the shelters Cad5 and Bet37 are located on the periphery of the plateau, at its southern and western margins, respectively. They are situated on, or immediately adjacent to, broad crest landforms and in upper valley slope contexts. The shelter Cad5 is on an east–west thoroughfare between the coast and the Southern Highlands, which is coincident with the southern margin of the Woronora Plateau. Bet37 is on a major north–south thoroughfare between the Cumberland Plain and the Southern Highlands, and flanks the western margin of the plateau. Further north, the two shelters in the Woronora River catchment are on a major divide/watershed between the Georges/Woronora and Cataract river catchments and, hence, on an east–west thoroughfare between the coast and the interior. They are also situated in upper valley slope contexts. To the south, the Phase 1 shelters in the Southern Highlands are all similarly located on broad, relatively flat and accessible landforms.

The spatial and environmental signature of these sites is characterised as geographically widespread in a low-density distribution, and preferentially on landforms that are readily accessible. Other than the two shelters located in the Woronora catchment, the areas located within the interior of the plateau were not chosen for marking the land with Phase 1 rock art.

9.2 Phase 2 Rock Art

In the following sections the geographic and environmental signatures of Phase 2 rock art are discussed on a catchment basis.

9.2.1 The Cataract Catchment

The Cataract catchment is bounded to the north and south by two major watershed divides (Watersheds 1 and 2), and these are major thoroughfare landforms between the coast and its hinterland. Two minor divide landforms (Minor Divides 1 and 2) extend from the escarpment westward into the heart of the Cataract. Three minor divides (3, 4 and 5) extend north to the Cataract gorge from the Cordeaux/Cataract divide. Unlike the southern catchments, the main river valleys of the Loddon and Cataract rivers are also likely to have been utilised as thoroughfares in this catchment.

In the Upper Nepean, almost half the grinding groove sites and 54 per cent of grooves are in the Cataract catchment. Two major clusters of grinding groove sites, engraved groove channels, and engraved rock art occur in the north-east sector of the catchment. The eastern end of the Watershed 1 landform is notable for its absence of rock shelter sites. However, this is likely to be determined by a general absence of shelter exposures. A large number of grinding groove locales occur in this area, some of which have significant groove counts. An open engraving site (Lod47) in this cluster has a single motif that is unique in the Upper Nepean: a human figure with a hatchet. In Chapter 6, it was noted that ground-edge hatchets were significant items of material culture in the south-east. It was proposed that grinding groove sites may over time become meaningful locales and mnemonic of individual and group history. The strong spatial association between grinding groove locales and the engraving in this area may reflect a mutually constituted dialectic, in which the significance of hatchets was expressed.

The eastern end of Minor Divide 2 also contains large numbers of grinding groove sites. Several have high counts, including BMS1, which also has engraved rock art. Open engraving sites BC3 and BC4 are located within 500 metres of each other at the western end of this divide near the Cataract River, and are associated with four grinding groove sites. BC3 and BC4 each contain a single engraved image: a macropod and an emu. These are the only animal motifs in the engraved rock art of the Upper Nepean catchment. Macropod and emu motifs occur in obvious association in individual shelters in Phase 2 and Phase 3 rock art, and their inscription in this pair of open sites supports an interpretation that they are conceptually related.

In Chapter 8, the analysis of Phase 2 stencil shelters and their motif abundance revealed that, similar to grinding groove sites, they occur in relatively higher density in the Cataract catchment. Across the Upper Nepean, they are frequently associated with open sites that have large grinding groove counts. The following associations occur in the Cataract:

- Lod8 with Lod5 (45 grinding grooves)
- AF11 and AF12 with AF8 (28 grinding grooves)
- BC49, BC51 and BC6 with BC7 (67 grinding grooves)
- Wall37 with Wall39 (32 grinding grooves)
- Wall13 with Wall15 (52 grinding grooves)
- Gill38 with Gill29 (19 grinding grooves)
- Gill45, Gill50 and Gill56 with Gill51 (54 grinding grooves)
- LizCk17 with LizCk19 (45 grinding grooves).

These clustered associations suggest a relationship between the two types of rock-marking locales. The grinding groove sites may have accumulated in size over considerable time, and long after the practice of Phase 2 stencilling ceased. Whether or not the motivation to continue to grind hatchet heads in these locales over time was inspired by their proximity to stencil sites, or that the relationships resulted from some other behaviour or purpose, is unknown.

Of the 160 rock art shelters in the Cataract, Phase 2 rock art occurs in 58 shelters. A total of 46 contain stencils, and this represents almost half of the Phase 2 stencil locales in the Upper Nepean. Phase 2 graphic rock art occurs in 26 shelters. In the Cataract, Phase 2 rock art was geographically widespread, and produced in shelters located on the ridge crests and valley slopes and bottoms, and this contrasts with patterns in the southern catchments. However, some geographic patterns exist in respect of where each of these different rock markings were produced, and the intensity of their production. Other than the engraved image in Lod47, the watershed divide (Watershed 1) between the Cataract and Georges/Woronora rivers does not contain graphic rock art. Yet, hand stencils were made in five shelters. One in the central area contains relatively large stencil counts (Lod8), and AF13 in a cluster of three at the west end of the divide does also.

In the Upper Nepean generally, Phase 2 stencils were normally produced at the extremities of thoroughfare landforms, as well as throughout each catchment, and this pattern of geographic distribution is evident in the Cataract. In the Cataract, Phase 2 stencilling also has a strong environmental signature. It was undertaken most frequently on crests or upper valley slopes, and in highly accessible locations. This contrasts with the graphic rock art, particularly all significant Phase 2 sites, which are located in interior locations in the main valleys and lower slope contexts.

Stencil counts vary between sites and several nodes of stencilling activity are represented by site clusters across the catchment. Other than the cluster referred to above, several others are notable. Minor Divide 2 contains a cluster of three, BC49, BC51 and BC6, and the latter contains relatively rare early Phase 2a graphics (various trident forms). The relatively short Minor Divide 1 landform contains only stencils in its suite of Phase 2 rock art. A short spur that extends north into the Cataract from near the east end of the watershed between the Cataract and Cordeaux (Watershed 2) contains a cluster of five stencil sites. Of the 46 shelters with stencils, 33 do not contain Phase 2 graphics, and 13 do. This structural pattern in the distribution of the two rock art types in shelters is repeated across the Upper Nepean.

In chapter 8, the analyses revealed that shelters with only stencils, and, in particular, those with high counts, are normally small and possess no living area. By comparison, those that also have relatively high numbers (>10) of Phase 2 graphics are typically large and have large living floors. Several of these sites are in the Cataract catchment, including BC6, BC41 and Gill50. What is notable about BC6 and Gill50 is that they contain formally simple motifs, likely to be representative of the earliest graphic rock art (Phase 2a). These sites are each located close to the valleys of the Loddon and Cataract, respectively. The choice to mark these sites with stencils and graphics may have been based on an interplay between their ability to accommodate relatively large numbers of people, the large size of their rock art panels and their geographic and environmental location. This relationship is also evident in comparable sites in the southern catchments.

Other shelters in the Cataract catchment contain Phase 2 stencils and graphics in low motif counts. They differ from those described above in that they do not exhibit patterned trends in respect of shelter size or location. However, the majority of these sites with Phase 2 graphics (irrespective of graphic numbers) and stencils do appear to have influenced the nature of their subsequent Phase 3 rock marking (discussed below).

9.2.2 The Cordeaux and Avon Catchments

The Cordeaux and Avon are discussed together in this section primarily because the watershed (Watershed 3) between the two catchments is a significant and focal area of Phase 2 graphic rock art.

Of the 114 rock art shelters in the Cordeaux, Phase 2 rock art occurs in 42. Eighteen sites contain stencils and 31 shelters have graphics. The Avon contains 140 rock art shelters, 45 of which have Phase 2 rock art: 29 have stencils and 22 have graphics. Compared with the Cataract, in these catchments the production of Phase 2 graphic rock art was undertaken in relatively higher frequency than the making of hand stencils.

Also in contrast to the Cataract, in the Cordeaux and Avon, valley bottoms generally do not contain Phase 2 rock art shelters. The exception is in the Avon, where two occur in lower slope contexts in its upper reaches near Gallahers Creek, where the valleys are broad and accessible. Like the Cataract, both catchments exhibit strong geographic patterns in respect of where Phase 2 rock markings were produced, and the intensity of their production.

Unlike the divide between the Cataract and Georges/Woronora rivers, the Watershed 2 between the Cataract and Cordeaux catchments was the focus of relatively intensive and significant Phase 2 rock art production. As noted in the discussion regarding the Cataract, a cluster of Phase 2 stencil sites is located immediately to the north of the Cataract/Cordeaux divide (at c. 3.5 kilometres west from the escarpment). A large cluster, likewise, is located on and adjacent (south-west side) to this landform, at a distance of c. 7.2 kilometres north-west from the escarpment. The large stencil site G23 is also located close to this cluster on the Cataract side of the divide. Notably, this cluster includes EC2 and EC12, the southernmost open engraving sites in the Sydney Basin. EC12 contains a single whale motif and EC2 has what the IPG describe as a female sex symbol, and large numbers of grinding grooves. The cluster includes three shelters with Phase 2 stencils, two of which (EC1 and EC5a) contain graphic motifs. EC5a is located adjacent to EC5b, a major Phase 2 shelter that has trident-form graphics (Phase 2a), comparable with those in Gill50 and BC6 in the Cataract. EC5b is also morphologically similar to Gill50 and BC6 (commodious with a large living floor area). This cluster represents a significant Phase 2 node of rock-marking activity, including both graphic production and gestural marking. A small Phase 2 graphic site with a pair of anthropomorphs (EC17) is located approximately 1.5 kilometres further west. What is notable about this cluster of sites is the absence of animal imagery in the Phase 2 suite of graphics.

In the central area of Watershed 2 and near to the Cordeaux River, a small cluster of minor Phase 2 graphic sites occur. These do contain animal motifs including, notably, EC36 with macropod and emu imagery. While not immediately associated with a Phase 2 rock art shelter, the largest open grinding groove site in the Upper Nepean catchment, EC34, is located in the central area of this major thoroughfare landform.

The watershed (Watershed 3) situated between the Cordeaux and Avon rivers contains a significant suite of Phase 2 graphic sites, including several mentioned in Chapter 8. The south-eastern end of this landform was a focal area for grinding hatchets. This clustering at the eastern end of watershed landforms is a locational pattern, noted above in respect of landforms in the Cataract catchment, and the watershed divide between the Cataract and Cordeaux. One of the most significant rock art shelters in the upper Nepean, SCR10, is located at the south-eastern end of Watershed 3. Similar to Gill50, BC6 and EC5b (in its association with EC5a), SCR10 contains early Phase 2a graphics and stencils, and is commodious with a huge living area floor. UA1 is located approximately 600 metres to the west in the cluster of large numbers of grinding groove sites, including UA3 with its high groove count of 41. UA1 is one of two significant Phase 2 animal motif shelters on this major thoroughfare. The other, UA47, is located approximately 12 kilometres north-west of UA1, on a minor divide landform (Minor Divide 12). These two shelters may have been the focus for the visual expression of a totemic geography in the Upper Nepean. Minor stencil and graphic sites are distributed along the remainder of Watershed 3.

A minor divide (Minor Divide 8) that extends northwards between Wongawilli and Sandy Creek contains a cluster of Phase 2 graphic shelters in its central area. The most notable of these is BR29, with its anthropomorphic and eel motifs. Shelters with stencils are distributed along the length of this thoroughfare landform. The remainder of the minor divides between the Cordeaux and Avon rivers contain a sparse, continuous but unfocused distribution of shelters with stencils and graphics in low numbers, all of which are on, or immediately adjacent to, crests and, hence, are accessible. However, a large stencil site, RL11, located in close proximity to a relatively large grinding groove site in the central area of Watershed 3 is loosely associated with two other stencil sites. Similar to the Cataract, Phase 2 stencil sites in the area between the Cordeaux and Cataract rivers are geographically widespread and present at their terminal ends.

In the Avon catchment proper, a minor divide landform (Minor Divide 14) extends northward from the escarpment into its upper reaches. Two Phase 2 shelters are located on the crest in the central area of this ridge. A12 is a significant Phase 2 graphic site, and contains both early Phase 2a motifs and Phase 2b animal imagery. It does not contain stencils, but its counterpart, A16, located 1 kilometre further to the north, does. Similar to the other shelters with Phase 2a motifs (Gill50, BC6, EC5b and SCR10), this shelter is commodious and has a large living area floor. A12 is the southernmost shelter in the Upper Nepean of this type. A16 contains stencils at one end, and Phase 2 eel motifs at the other. At the terminal end of this ridge and adjacent to the Avon River, two shelters, A29 and A26, are in a cluster, and each contains a small suite of Phase 2 graphics, including animal imagery.

The watershed between the Avon and Nepean rivers (Watershed 4), and a short minor divide, which extends to the north-east from near its southern end, does not contain any major Phase 2 graphic or stencil shelters. Shelters with generally very low stencil counts occur along the length of the landform in a relatively continuous distribution. Three small clusters of Phase 2 stencil sites occur, and one is in close association with a large grinding groove site.

Major Phase 2 graphic rock art sites in the Avon and Cordeaux catchments are clearly tethered to major thoroughfares and crest landforms, and are highly accessible.

9.2.3 The Nepean Catchment

The Nepean catchment contains 95 rock art shelters, 13 with stencils only, 8 with graphics only and 5 with both stencils and graphics. The Nepean is characterised by a relative dearth of Phase 2 graphics shelters and motifs.

The Nepean side of the long watershed landform (Watershed 4), between the Nepean and Avon rivers, has only two Phase 2 shelters, both of which contain a single red stencil. A minor divide landform (Minor Divide 16) extends north between Burke and Explorers creeks from the Nepean and Avon watershed. From Minor Divide 16, a shorter ridge (Minor Divide 17) extends north between Explorers Creek and Little Burke River. Shelters with Phase 2 stencils occur at either end of both landforms, and several are loosely clustered. One shelter on each minor divide contains relatively high stencil counts: Ana28 has 14 stencils, and three rare handprints, and Ana15 has 17 stencils. Both minor divides each have a single Phase 2 graphic site containing only eel imagery: Ana28 has one eel motif, and its association with hand stencils and prints is notable; Ana20 has two. All Phase 2 shelters on these minor divides are on crests or elevated slope contexts. Infrequent and minor grinding activity occurred. On Minor Divide 16, those locales with higher groove counts are located in the central area of the ridge.

Two short minor divides (18 and 19), separated by a minor tributary, extend north from the southern boundary of the study area. Minor Divide 18 has two rock art shelters only, both of which contain Phase 2 stencils. *Ana1*, located at the southern end, is a major stencil site. The other site has two stencils and a single Phase 2 graphic of uncertain figurative model. Minor Divide 19 contains two grinding groove sites, both of which have relatively high groove counts. These peripheral landforms, at the edge of the catchment, display a similar spatial association between Phase 2 stencil and grinding groove sites with that of the eastern end of major watersheds, in the Cataract, Cordeaux and Avon catchments.

Minor Divide 20 is a significant, long landform extending north from the southern boundary of the study area, between the Nepean and Burke rivers. It contains a relatively high number of grinding groove sites, but very little Phase 2 rock art. Grinding groove locales occur at the southern end of the ridge, and a cluster in the central area has two large sites, including one with 53 grooves (Sab24). Two shelters contain counts of two and three indeterminate graphics, and two clustered shelters contain minor counts of stencils, one of which has one indeterminate graphic.

The major watershed (Watershed 5) that forms the western boundary of the study area has very little Phase 2 rock art, and low numbers of grinding groove sites. The rock art sites cluster in the central area. Five contain stencils, mostly in low counts, and four shelters have graphics in very low counts.

The Nepean catchment contrasts significantly with its northern neighbours, in terms of the abundance of Phase 2 graphic-marking activity; there is a paucity of Phase 2 graphic production in the Nepean. However, it is broadly comparable in its geographic and environmental structure of site distribution. Grinding groove and stencilling locales are widely distributed. Several open sites contain high groove counts, and some site clustering occurs. Their environmental signature is also comparable with the other catchments; all Phase 2 sites are located on obvious thoroughfares and in accessible locales. The absence of significant grinding groove and Phase 2 rock art sites along the western margin of the Upper Nepean Catchment is notable, and suggests that interior locations were preferred areas of rock-marking activity.

9.3 Phase 3 Rock Art

The geographic and environmental signatures of Phase 3 rock art are described in the following sections. The majority of rock shelters used for the production of Phase 2 graphic rock art were reused for Phase 3 marking. As noted in Chapter 8, additions made to rock art panels during Phase 3, typically, did not obscure earlier graphic rock art, but Phase 2 stencils were not preferentially avoided. In Phase 3, Phase 2 animal and anthropomorphic graphics were frequently redrawn (re-marked) with charcoal. These trends strongly indicate that the relevance of the referential properties of early graphic rock art remained in place during the most recent period of rock marking. Because of this, it is inferred that the separation in time between the production of Phase 2b graphic rock art and Phase 3 may not have been significant.

In Chapter 8, it was noted that Phase 3 stencils were geographically circumscribed compared with Phase 2 stencils, and restricted generally to the interior of the Upper Nepean. The location of shelters with Phase 3 stencils, in respect of major landforms, reflects this pattern. While the majority of Phase 3 stencils do occur on the main travel route landforms, 35 per cent are on spurs off minor divides that are interior locales in the catchment. This contrasts with the locational patterns relating to Phase 2 stencils, and indicates a retreat away from major thoroughfares into more secluded locales within the catchment for the production of Phase 3 stencils. It is in the

Cataract that this pattern contrasts most obviously with Phase 2. Of the 20 shelters with Phase 3 stencils, 11 occur on spurs off minor divides and are in shelters that are close to the river. This differs significantly from Phase 2 stencil-only sites in that catchment, where only seven of 33 occurred in this context.

The inter- and intra-site spatial separation evident between Phase 2 stencils and graphics does not occur in Phase 3 rock art. In contrast, Phase 3 stencils and graphics frequently co-occur on an inter- and intra-site basis, and the patterns suggest a strong mutual association. It is in this sense that they may have functioned within the same social context, and '[t]hey may therefore, ultimately be linked in reinforcement or in dialectic' (Rosenfeld 1999).

In Phase 3, the production of graphic rock art was predominant and stencilling was a minor practice. This suggests a greater emphasis on the use of rock art in the pursuit of corporate or supra-individualised social strategies. However, the character, nature and environmental and micro-topographic location of some Phase 3 graphics and other marks is suggestive of individualised activity. It was suggested in Chapter 8 that the non-graphic pigment marking in rock shelters (charcoal embellishment of natural features and so on) may have functioned to unite people and place in a manner comparable with stencilling.

During Phase 3, rock art was produced in 449 shelters; this abundance contrasts significantly with shelter numbers used for Phase 2 rock art production. Typically, shelters used previously were reused in Phase 3, although this is not always the case. Phase 2 shelters with relatively large graphic counts were normally reused for Phase 3 rock art, and sometimes this was extensive. While the majority of Phase 3 rock art was produced in very low counts in 'new' shelters, some of these sites contain high numbers, and this indicates that corporate pursuits required the use of sites that were additional to those previously used.

9.3.1 The Cataract Catchment

Of the 160 rock art shelters in the Cataract catchment, Phase 3 graphic rock art occurs in 137 of those shelters. Stencils were produced in 20 shelters and, except for Lod8 located on Watershed 1, stencilling occurred predominantly in the interior of the catchment in close association with the main river valleys. Two shelters located close together at the western end of this watershed contain remarkable and rare suites of Phase 3 graphics. The rock art panel in AF3 is dominated by a line of macropod motifs that face in one direction and are drawn in an animated and fighting stance. This composition suggests the expression, via narrative, of new concerns that may relate to stress. The panel in AF4 is dominated by a large wombat, with a clutch of circle motifs. While the pose of the macropods in AF3 is novel, the wombat and its association with circles in AF4 exemplifies a referential continuity between Phase 2 and 3 graphic rock art. The location of these sites on a prominent thoroughfare and near Appin at the north-west corner of the Cataract catchment is notable. Appin is a site of early contact, conflict and violence between European settlers and Aboriginal people.

Phase 3 graphic shelters mostly contain very low graphic counts, and are geographically widespread across the remainder of the Cataract, with no obvious environmental patterns in distribution. Because of the generally amorphous nature of the terrain in the Cataract, this is not unexpected. The intensive Phase 3 rock marking appears to have occurred in larger shelters that contain Phase 2 rock art. In these shelters, Phase 2 graphic forms were reproduced, and novel forms were introduced. As well as the production of Phase 3 graphics, new forms of gestural marking were undertaken, including gestural non-graphic pigment marking and rubbing, pecking and scratching of rock art panels. Shelters that exemplify this trend in the Cataract include LizCk17 and Wall13. This pattern, which occurs in the southern catchment also, suggests that shelters with older graphics may have been influential in regard to their reuse and the nature of subsequent rock marking. In particular, there is a tendency for gestural marking in these sites, which suggests that during the production of Phase 3 rock art they were symbolically charged locales.

9.3.2 The Cordeaux and Avon Catchments

In the Cordeaux and Avon catchments, 217 of the 254 rock art shelters contain Phase 3 graphic and stencil marks. Significant Phase 2 shelters were reused, and the patterns identified in the Cataract exist also in the Cordeaux and Avon. The prominent Phase 2 shelters, SCR10, UA1 and UA47, located on Watershed 3, were each used differently during Phase 3, suggesting the expression of a greater complexity of concerns on this major thoroughfare. In SCR10, early Phase 2a graphics were superimposed by large and imposing animal motifs—an emu, macropod and whale. These are formally comparable with the three rare animal motifs in the Upper Nepean's open context engraved sites. While other Phase 3 graphics occur in this major site, the addition of these motifs indicates not only their continued relevance, but a shift away from open to 'closed' contexts. UA1 is located in a prominent position on the crest and at the eastern end of the Watershed 3 thoroughfare landform. The Phase 3 imagery in this site is comprised primarily of large imposing anthropomorphic motifs, and these are superimposed over the early Phase 2b animal imagery. This contrasts with its counterpart UA47, which is located adjacent to a ridge crest but away from the thoroughfare itself. Here, the Phase 2 animal imagery was redrawn in charcoal and carefully curated during Phase 3. SCR10 and UA47, located slightly away from the main thoroughfare area of Watershed 3, appear to have been used to reaffirm traditional themes. In contrast, UA1, located in a very obvious thoroughfare locale, exhibits a dominant new referential system, which appears to have been used to express more contemporary concerns.

In the Cordeaux and Avon catchments, rock marking at this time was not tethered to major thoroughfares and accessible landforms. In the rugged terrain located away from ridge landforms, Phase 3 shelters are distributed in a geographic and environmental pattern that is widespread and diverse. This pattern corresponds with a greater diversity in shelter types used for the production of Phase 3 graphics. While many graphics produced in these more marginal landforms and shelters include motifs, which are formally structured and referential in a manner comparable with those in accessible places, typically graphics and gestural rock marking exhibit a greater diversity in their form and nature. This suggests a retreat from the restrictions of corporate strategies to a more individualised expression and relationship to land.

9.3.3 The Nepean Catchment

In the Nepean catchment, the environmental patterns of Phase 3 rock art do not differ significantly from those in Phase 2. This similarity is likely to be to be environmentally determined, and a reflection of the nature of the terrain (the significant gorge and cliff lines that dissect the plateau in this catchment). Phase 3 stencilling is largely absent in the catchment and occurs as a single motif. Of the 95 rock art shelters, 85 contain Phase 3 graphics, most of which were produced in low counts. Similar to Phase 2, rock art production was not a high-level activity, despite the existence of suitable shelters (Sefton, pers. comm., 2003).

9.4 Discussion

The archaeological implications of the geographic pattern of diminishing site densities, as one moves from north to south along the Woronora Plateau, is not easily understood or explained. The higher densities of grinding groove sites and groove counts, and Phase 2 stencilling in the Cataract, may indicate a greater intensity of occupation in that catchment. However, this inference is by no means axiomatic. Cultural choice made in response to the increasingly rugged environment encountered south of the Cataract, or purely social factors relating to social and technological organisation, may have resulted in this pattern. It is possibly a product of a nexus between both. However, other indicators suggest that a social parameter may have existed. These include the cessation, south of the central Upper Nepean, of the production of the Sydney–Hawkesbury open context engraved imagery and engraved groove channels, and the paucity of Phases 2 and 3 graphic rock art, south and west of the Cordeaux and Avon divide. While these locational patterns demand an explanation, they are outside the empirical basis and thrust of this monograph.

The geographically widespread practice of Phase 2 stencilling contrasts with the spatially focused signature of Phase 2 graphic rock art sites and motifs. The engagement with this pattern from a perspective of rock art as praxis indicates that Phase 2 graphic rock art was produced in a highly organised social milieu. Very few graphic motifs were produced, and their careful inscription and ordered arrangement on rock art panels within shelters reflects a highly structured productive and social context. Phase 2 rock art shelters are in environmental contexts that are accessible. They occur on landforms that are likely to have been those normally, if not habitually, used for movement through country and base camp habitations. The earliest Phase 2 graphics occur exclusively in shelters that have the capacity to accommodate relatively large numbers of people. These situational contexts, in which Phase 2 graphic rock art was produced, suggest that fundamentally the inscription of corporate signatures on the land at this time may not have been governed by any meaningful significance of the specific locale. The location of Phase 2 rock art may instead relate to the opportunities and amenity presented by the morphological attributes of shelters and their location on landforms that people habitually occupied.

This scenario is significantly different in respect of the locational and environmental signature of the later Phase 3 rock art. However, a tendency for rock art production and new expressions of gestural marking, to have taken place in Phase 2 shelters indicates that these locales may have possessed highly charged symbolic properties and resonances. The spatially widespread, diverse and abundant rock marking that took place in the recent past suggests that rock art as practice was of increased importance.

10

Transformations in Social Geography

For archaeology, only the world of experience is left. (Layton 2000b:51)

The Sydney Basin has been occupied since the late Pleistocene, yet it was not until the mid-Holocene that rock art was produced in shelters. It is instructive to question and explore philosophically the implications of an earlier lack of engagement with this form of cultural practice. To do so may pave a way toward an understanding of its first appearance and subsequent change in the archaeological record.

While referring to an earlier absence of image-making in Europe and Africa, Soffer and Conkey's (1997:6) discussion is of relevance in attempting to understand change and transformation in the production of rock art, and the practice of marking the land. They remark:

> What was absent, then, was what we have termed *performance*, the habitual use of the capacity [for image-making] in patterned behaviour. What was absent were the social and cultural contexts within which such material practice would have been efficacious and would have had appropriate meanings. Such a perspective requires us to begin examining the circumstances under which image making becomes habitual, an approach that can help us understand the temporal and regional discontinuities in the global record.

Soffer and Conkey (1997:5) are concerned with the evolutionary context for the emergence of image-marking at c. 40,000 years BP, associated with anatomically modern humans and thought to signal the 'advent of [a] fully modern way of life – one embedded in and shaped by culture, dependent upon the making of meaning'. In Australia, it can be assumed that a *modern way of life* has been in place for as long as people have been present. Consequently, the concern is not related to the origins of symbolic and modern behaviour, but the apparent absence, then making and eventual efflorescence of rock art as praxis. While not framed in evolutionary terms, the aim here has been to explore the historical dimension of change and transformation in regard to image-making. This topic has been approached from the perspective of embodiment and experience, i.e. the *performance* of rock art as practice. The question as to why people commenced to produce imagery in rock shelters is important because this practice represents a significant shift in people's engagement with their social and physical world.

The discussion in this chapter is concerned with the manner in which the object world was constituted, the situated experience of this, and how, in turn, this material world may have shaped being and social life. Materiality is situated in the context of people and social relations: 'bodies of artifacts [*sic*] … implicate particular cosmologies where the role of materiality may have been central to people's relationships to each other and to the deities' (Meskell 2005b:52). One of the material features of rock art is its potential for permanence, and that it may continue to mark the land long after its production. A consideration of this requires acknowledgement of the notion that rock art, irrespective of its original significance, is 'continually socially reconstituted in the process of its observation and, possibly, its repainting or augmentation' (Rosenfeld 1997:296).

That is, imagery itself, and other marks on rocks, are constantly coming into being (cf. Boast 1997:181). But more than this is the question of whether rock art can have a productive power of its own (cf. Bennett 2010:2).

Two major pigment phases of rock art have been recognised in the Sydney Basin (McCarthy 1988b; McDonald 2008a). In its broad structure, this sequence has been identified to be applicable to the Upper Nepean catchment, although some differences have been defined. The two major temporal phases of pigment rock art have been identified to have their own specific and nuanced formal signatures. In addition, this research has revealed that temporal variability also has a complex locational, environmental and spatial signature, which has not been previously identified in the Sydney region.

At some time, and probably in the early to mid-Holocene, a fundamental change occurred in Aboriginal society in the Upper Nepean catchment and surrounds, when people began to mark stone in rock shelters. The archaeological record in the Sydney Basin demonstrates change in a number of behavioural and technological indices, particularly in the late Holocene. This is a general trend observed across much of the continent (cf. David 2002:150). However, the temporal framework of change in rock art in the Sydney Basin, and correlations with the dynamics evident in other archaeological material, is not well understood. McDonald (2008a) formulated her chronological ordering of the Sydney Basin rock art based on an assumption of the contemporaneity of her defined Phase 3 pigment imagery, and the period of greatest intensity of occupation, inferred from archaeological deposits in rock shelters. However, the empirical basis for this correlation is not accepted by all Sydney Basin specialists (cf. Attenbrow 2004:225).

At this time, the chronological dimensions (the timing and duration) of the Upper Nepean relative sequence are not possible to define. The sequence that is proposed is coarsely conceived, given the limitations of the data. It is likely that there are chronological nuances within the sequence that have not yet been revealed.

In western Arnhem Land, where the sequence of change has been well delineated, Taçon (1993:113) argues that rock art was not produced at a 'steady, constant rate over time'. Instead, the pattern is one of 'many outbursts … over time rather than a continuous, non-varying output' (Taçon 1993:113). He identifies intervals when very little rock art was produced, which punctuate periods in which there was a relatively high rate of production. A similar pattern appears to exist in the Upper Nepean catchment, although here, quantifying the timing of the rock art phases and the intervals is not possible. Nevertheless, the analyses have revealed that each phase is different in its structural character. What is notable about graphic rock art production in Phase 2 of the Upper Nepean sequence is how little of it appears to have been produced. This, and the distributional nature of Phase 2 rock art, indicates that it was generated within a highly organised corporate structure. In contrast, the character of Phase 3 graphic rock art has a much more diversified organisation. The relative abundance and variability in structural patterns, suggests that, in Phase 3, rock art was produced in a greater range of contexts, and that corporate and individual goals and motivations were more diverse.

In Chapter 1, it was proposed that one possible motivation for the marking of rock shelters with imagery is that, within these environments, there exists the potential for durability and permanence (cf. Forge 1991; Rosenfeld 2002). If this notion is invoked to explain the motivation to commence producing imagery in rock shelters, there is the implication that the impetus for the practice of rock art may have been to satisfy a requirement relating to intransience. Rock shelters may have been marked because there was a perceived potential that they may facilitate a process of objectifying an ideology in a material and durable manner. Referring again to the quote from Soffer and Conkey (1997) set out earlier, the question is posed as to why the performance of producing imagery specifically in rock shelters in the Upper Nepean began, and whether or not this may be answered by considering that marking the land was undertaken as a social strategy, not only to materialise people's concerns and beliefs, but also to do so in an enduring and permanent way.

The corollary of this is that previously this need was absent. This does not imply an absence of beliefs, but instead that the performance of inscripting the land in respect of an ideology was not a practice that was a part of experience and occupation of the world. Fundamentally, it suggests that the need to conceptualise the immaterial, via its materialisation in a permanent and durable form, was absent. This may be read to imply that a land-based ideology and social geography may not have been in place at this time, or was expressed in some other way.

The putative widespread distribution and homogeneity of Panaramitee-style rock art has been interpreted to reflect extensive and open communication networks, the function of which is to support the economic and biological viability of small, dispersed populations (cf. Rosenfeld 1997:290). While Phase 1 rock shelters south of the Georges River are distributed in low density, their geographic range (within a c. 50-kilometre radius) is not extensive, and not greater than would be expected of people to traverse during their seasonal rounds. Sefton (2009b:13) argues that these sites relate to the earliest occupation of the region, that their distribution indicates a partial use of the landscape and, specifically, 'the rugged sandstone of the Woronora Plateau' was avoided.

However, the watershed divides and ridges in the Upper Nepean catchment are gently undulating, and do not pose impediment to movement or occupation. Boot's (2002) investigations of the forested and rugged south coast hinterland reveals occupation of these types of landscapes in the Pleistocene and early Holocene, some of which was of high intensity. In the absence of detailed and adequate archaeological investigation of the Woronora Plateau and Southern Highlands, it may be premature to interpret the occupational significance of the low density distribution of Phase 1 rock art. The absence of rock art need not imply the absence of people, and a low density distribution of rock art need not necessarily reflect low population levels (*contra* Sefton 2009b:13). Rock art, as a technology to convey meaning, may not have been a practice that required marking the land in a spatially dense manner.

Given the nature of the mechanics for the production of engravings, a suitable material is required to penetrate sandstone, and this could only be stone. Such stone must be of a kind that can withstand the stress of impact, and is likely to be a type with similar qualities to hatchet head stone (i.e. toughness) (Dickson 1978:66–67; McBryde & Harrison 1981:183). Stone with these qualities is not found in the sandstone country of the Sydney Basin, and so it can be inferred that the production of engravings was predicated upon the acquisition of suitable stone from elsewhere. This consideration implies a relational context between people and other places. However, the spatial distribution of Phase 1 rock art does not provide any firm clues as to the arena of social geography in which it was relevant.

The current view in regard to the antiquity of Phase 1 engravings in the Sydney Basin is that they were produced in the mid-Holocene, which is more or less coincident with the stabilisation of the post-glacial sea level rise. The lack of ability to precisely define the contemporaneity, or otherwise, of engraving activity and environmental change precludes any attempt to correlate the two and make behavioural inferences. If there was a correspondence, consideration could be given to whether or not engraving the land with imagery developed as a social strategy motivated by the need to mediate social change in light of reduced land mass and shifts in resource type and abundance.

Phase 1 rock art in the Upper Nepean catchment is comprised of small engraved bird and macropod foot/paw motifs. It is essentially figurative and is an ostensive referential system (cf. Layton 2000b:51). Although sometimes paired, the motifs are not arranged in track alignments and, therefore, do not evoke a narrative depiction. In Chapter 8, it was suggested that, based on a consideration of their formal, iconic qualities, this rock art may be interpreted to have been produced to refer to symbolic values (cf. Rosenfeld 2002:75). In respect of these types of motifs in Central Australia, Rosenfeld (2002:74) distinguishes between those in alignment, and others that are formal depictions, to infer different contextual significances of the locales in which they were situated. Rosenfeld argues that alignments of tracks are common in occupation sites (secular), and while not discounting that these illustrative compositions may evoke mythological values, she proposes that their narrative may have been understood at a lesser esoteric level 'and hence be the more appropriate visual form in secular contexts' (Rosenfeld 2002:75). When these motifs occur in single or non-narrative compositions, their iconic form is suggestive that they served to encode symbolic values pertaining to the representational being that was depicted (Rosenfeld 2002:74–75).

It is premature to characterise Phase 1 engravings in the Sydney Basin as being homogeneous in form because a broad-scale, regional analysis of the topic has not been undertaken. In any case, if they were, this need not imply social or cultural unity. Similarity in material culture does not necessarily reflect uniformity at the structural level (cf. Rosenfeld 1999; Thomas 2004:100). While some motif diversity is apparent on the Woronora Plateau (e.g. the inclusion of anthropomorphic images in FRC226 in the Woronora River catchment), all Phase 1 shelters in the local area do contain bird and macropod foot images. The widespread distribution of this limited suite of iconic imagery suggests a pan-regional ideational system that articulated a mythology predominantly associated with the symbolic values evoked by the production of these motifs. The addition of anthropomorphic motifs to this basic repertoire, in the single shelter FRC226 in the middle of the Woronora Plateau, is notable. The inclusion of the anthropomorphs in the heart of the plateau suggests that this area may have been a focal node, with a unique significance. However, the widespread distribution of formally comparable imagery suggests the presence of an ideational mythology that was inclusive and relevant over a broad geographic area. This rock art and its relative uniformity does not conform to a pattern that suggests the existence of a totemic geography (cf. Layton 2000a).

However, the production of engravings in the Phase 1 rock art of the Upper Nepean catchment and its local region signals the initiation of a people/land relationship that was mediated, at least in part, by the practice of inscripting imagery on stone. Their production can be interpreted to reflect the assumed beginning, in the Upper Nepean and its surrounds, of the use of a material technology of marking meaning onto the land. In the practice of taking advantage of the environments that rock shelters afford, rock art as praxis became an enduring feature of being and experience in the Upper Nepean.

The graphic form of the Phase 1 engravings in the seven local shelters in the Woronora Plateau (including the two in the Upper Nepean catchment) is found in subsequent phases of rock art. Macropod paw and emu feet motifs are represented in Phase 2 and 3 rock art, in graphic and/or stencilled form. Likewise, circles, bars and formally comparable human motifs occur as graphics in later phases. Macropod and emu bodied motifs become a significant component of the pigment rock art. While a concern to mark the land, with reference to these animal forms, commenced with the production of the engraved bird and macropod foot/paw motifs, their materiality exerted considerable influence on the trajectory of the symbolic worldview in the Upper Nepean.

The rock art in Phase 2 indicates that the materialisation of the ideological system diversified. It is probable that there are two sub-phases of Phase 2 rock art: an earlier phase of motifs that have their formal counterparts in Phase 1; and a later phase, in which animal depictions were produced and rendered in their full bodily form. As well, Phase 2 includes a gestural category or rock art: human hand stencils and prints, and non-graphic pigment smears. While recognising problems relating to the implications of the contemporaneity or otherwise of different categories of materials (cf. Attenbrow 2004; Pinney 2005), it is possible that Phase 2 rock art was produced more or less contemporaneously with the use of ground-edge stone hatchets and, by association, the grinding grooves distributed across the plateau.

The use of pigment to mark the land provided people with the means for a new and different engagement with their physical and social world. It is not known where red ochre was obtained for the production of Phase 2 red motifs in the Upper Nepean catchment. Pigment may have been sourced from outside, although there are no known significant ochre quarries in the region. Red pigment is available on the plateau in the form of iron-rich seams in sandstone, laterite on ridges, ooze in shelters that is re-precipitated material, and decomposed sandstone, which breaks down behind case-hardened crusts in shelters (Sefton, pers. comm., 2003). Huntley (Ford 2006:87–88; Huntley et al. 2011) found that all paints examined in the Upper Nepean were clay based. She argues that the clay was most likely derived from the Wianamatta group and Camden sub-group shales of the Illawarra Coal Measures. This result implies that clay, used in the preparation of paints for the production of Phase 2 rock art, was sourced from outside the Woronora Plateau, although the likelihood of this is questionable. However, given that this research is in its infancy and requires further work (cf. Ford 2006:96), it is premature to speculate about spheres of sociality and relationships across the region that may be inferred. But more importantly, this issue introduces a new dimension relating to the practice of Phase 2 rock art. It implies not only that people began to mark the land with a suite of novel and diversified range of imagery, but also that they engaged with a new range of social and technological processes, relating to the acquisition of materials and preparation of paint.

In the Upper Nepean catchment, Phase 2 rock art is comprised predominantly of stencils. Forge (1991:40) and Rosenfeld (1999) consider stencils as marks that are individual in their referential content and, hence, that they refer to an individual's relation to place. This view is in keeping with ethnographic understandings of the motivation for stencilling (see Peterson 1972:16; Layton 1992:75). While marking the land at this time may be interpreted to have been most frequently an individualised and participatory expression, it is likely to be both more complex and interesting than this.

In Chapter 8, the analyses revealed that Phase 2 stencilling activity was normally undertaken in shelters used exclusively for that purpose. In addition, stencilling commonly occurs in shelters that are small and possess no living area. This contrasts with the types of shelter typically used for the production of graphic rock art. Where stencilling and graphics co-occur, they were produced in separate intra-site locales. This trend in the Upper Nepean is not unique. Cole et al. (1995:63) report that in the Laura area of north-eastern Australia, red stencils are concentrated in shelters that have few or no other motifs. Rosenfeld (1999) argues that such trends suggest that they reflect different sociocultural contexts. Accordingly, in Phase 2 of the Upper Nepean sequence, a contextual diversification in rock art production is evident.

The Phase 2 stencilled rock art is comprised of human hands. Stencilling as practice, inscribing images of body parts that are inalienable (cf. Thomas 2002:41), may have been motivated by a concern to emphasise a connection between people and place. If stencilling acts to locate people, who are mobile within the landscape, to place, its expression in Phase 2 rock art may have been motivated by a need to negotiate people and land relationships. Rosenfeld (1999) has referred to stencils in Tasmania produced during the terminal Pleistocene when significant adjustments in subsistence strategies were required. She argues that gesturally marking the land at this time is an expression of person–land relationships being emphasised during a period of severe stress. In the Sydney Basin, the dating of red stencils is not secure enough to correlate their appearance with either climatic, environmental or archaeological change, and the duration of red pigment hand stencilling as a practice is not known. If the motivation for stencilling was constituted in a manner comparable with the scenario Rosenfeld suggests, it may have occurred at any number of times during the Holocene, including, for example, environmental or climatic shifts associated with sea level rise, or the onset of the ENSO pattern. Stencilling as practice is worthy of considerably more attention than given in this current research.

The earliest Phase 2 graphic rock art (Phase 2a) is comprised of motifs, which are formally similar to Phase 1 intaglio engravings, and they typically co-occur with Phase 2 stencils. These motifs were produced in a small number of large, commodious shelters, on major thoroughfare landforms. Thus, their environmental signature is comparable with Phase 1 rock art. However, their restricted location in large shelters is a significant change, and implies a productive and social context that related to abundant space. It was noted in Chapter 8 that the temporal relationship between engravings and Phase 2a pigment graphics is actually not understood in the Upper Nepean catchment. They may be either temporally discrete, in accordance with McDonald's (2008a) chronology, or contemporaneous. While this poses an interpretative constraint, the production of Phase 2a pigment graphics with stencils, and only in commodious shelters, nevertheless represents the emergence of a shift in the productive context in the practice of rock art.

However, these formally similar Phase 2a motifs are distributed across space in low density, and in a pattern that is comparable with Phase 1 rock art. This suggests that the corporate signature of Phase 2a graphic rock art does not exhibit evidence of significant structural change in social geography. The nature of Phase 2a graphic rock art, and its locational patterning, suggests the continued emphasis of an inclusive ideology, which was relevant over a broad geographic area. The introduction to rock art practice (the production of human hand stencils) is a significant development. This phenomenon, in which individual and land connections began to be emphasised, may be informative in regard to the impetus and motivation that led to subsequent shifts expressed in Phase 2b graphic rock art.

A number of notable formal and locational changes are evident in Phase 2b rock art. The production of rock art occurred more intensively, and in a relatively denser distributional pattern, than in Phase 1 or Phase 2a, although the environmental signature of Phase 2b is similar to earlier locational patterns. The shelters used for the production of Phase 2b imagery are normally located on or near to major thoroughfares in accessible environmental locales. With the exception of some eel motifs, Phase 2b rock art is located on highly visible rock art panels in shelters.

Phase 2b rock art suggests a reconfiguration of social geography, which was accompanied by the formulation of a new ideology. This rock art is dominated by fully formed animal imagery, and these motifs are frequently large. While different animal species occur within this suite of imagery, there also exists variability in qualitative traits and, from this, it is inferred that not all Phase 2b animal imagery was equivalent in its purpose and meaning. This variability is evident in three primary categories: manner of depiction, associations between imagery and spatial distribution.

Certain motifs have a narrative quality, which is evoked by their depiction in movement or action, and by their formal arrangement in respect of natural features in rock-shelters. These motifs conjure an imagined space that is three dimensional, animated and fluid (cf. Taçon & Ouzman 2004; Dobrez 2009). Motifs, such as eels, which may possess these qualities are also those that are abundant and distributed widely across geographic space. The eel motif animates the earth, and the nature of its inscription and distribution suggests a deep connection and relatedness between people across the Upper Nepean catchment (cf. Tamisari & Wallace 2006:216, 218). Eel motifs, and others, suggest their function in the depiction of stories and narration relating to the land and water ways.

Motifs that contrast with this pattern tend to be more formal in their schema, limited in number, occur in groups of pairs or more (e.g. gliders and echidnas), and are present in spatially discrete locales within the landscape. It is the production of the latter group of imagery in focal points in the landscape that suggests the existence of a totemic geography (cf. Layton 1992:77). The Phase 2b rock art has a structural pattern that is generally consistent with a model of social organisation based on clan totemism. According to Layton (2000a:181), totemic rock art is spatially patterned. Animal species are preferentially depicted at sites within the territory of the group for whom it is a totemic emblem. Large numbers of species are represented in totemic rock art, but each occurs with more or less the same frequency (Layton 2000a:181). In the Upper Nepean, Phase 2b animal imagery is patterned in accordance with these criteria.

In his review of Aboriginal rock art, Layton (1992:242) argues that the archaeological patterns in the Georges River rock art, identified by Officer (1984), closely correspond to a totemic model of social geography. The patterns remarked upon by Layton (1992:242) include the highly varied range of motifs, with only a few repeated consistently; the emphasis on certain motifs in individual sites; motifs that were repeated several times in sites; and the functional separation between large and small sites. Given the proximity of the Georges River, it is not surprising that a similar pattern exists in the rock art of the Upper Nepean catchment.

The emergence of clan totemism, which may be inferred from the patterning of Phase 2b rock art, indicates that social group and place relationships were expressed by this practice of rock art production. This may be seen to be a development that materialised from the practice of mediating individual and place connections, as expressed via Phase 2 stencilling. During Phase 2b, the infrequent use of rock art, its formal constraint, and restricted geographic and environmental location are suggestive of rock art functioning to mediate a relatively stable social geography. Given uncertainty in regard to the age of Phase 2b rock art and the absence of an archaeological context (excavated data), it is not appropriate to speculate in regard to what might have motivated this change. It is, however, highly unlikely to have been a single cause, and there is the possibility that transformation was an endogenous, gradual and distributed process (cf. Hodder 2011:18) of being and experience.

In contrast to Phase 2, the patterning of rock art and contextual variables indicate that, in Phase 3, the marking of rock with imagery was produced within a greater number and range of social contexts to that which had previously existed. Graphics continued to be produced in commodious shelters situated on thoroughfares, but the range of that imagery increased dramatically. Some older graphic forms, specifically animals, continued to be produced, and older motifs were redrawn (re-marked) in charcoal. However, a new suite of models and graphic schema were added to the repertoire and the graphic art is considerably more heterogeneous. While some forms were repeated across the land, rare and unique forms were produced. Most graphics and other marks were drawn with charcoal (scratching was also used), but others were highly inscripted with colour and complex infill patterns. Stencils were made with white clay rather than red ochre.

The source of the white pigment is not currently known, and could have been obtained either within or outside the Woronora Plateau. The use of charcoal for the production of the majority of graphic imagery within the Phase 3 rock art is notable. Because it is a readily accessible material and likely to have been available almost anywhere in the landscape as a result of bush fires, land management practices or domestic activities, its use was not predicated upon complex procurement and processing strategies. It is for this reason that the use of charcoal for rock art production is usually considered to be convenient and expedient (cf. Frederick 2000:320). Charcoal is often the material used for the production of rock art in contexts of cross-cultural exchange between Aboriginal people and Europeans (Smith & Rosenfeld 1992:11; Frederick 2000:320). Explanations, which are posited to account for its use, include considerations relating to difficulties and limitations in obtaining ochres, or because of its convenient availability, while people were on the move during contact contexts (Rosenfeld, pers. comm., 2003). Given that the production of charcoal drawings in Phase 3 rock art was undertaken on an unprecedented and prolific scale, the use of charcoal at this time may simply have met a requirement for an abundant, readily available material.

In the Upper Nepean catchment, scratching was a recent method for the production of imagery and making of non-graphic marks. The use of this technique may be interpreted as reflecting expeditious marking of the land, and this hints also at a social context of adjustment and flux, which may have been the colonial encounter. At this time, the nature of the implement/s used for scratching is not known, but it is possible that, given the fineness of the etched marks, these were metal (e.g. nails), and had been obtained from the European colonisers.

The most recent rock art shows a greater diversity in graphic form, and this is accompanied by a significant shift in the locations that were chosen to mark rock. Instead of graphic rock art practice being limited to typically large shelters on major thoroughfares, and in readily accessible locales, the land everywhere became marked with graphic imagery and other gestural marks. In addition, a greater diversity of shelter types is chosen for the production of rock art. Many of these do not contain floors or living spaces, are small and otherwise difficult to move around in, and are located within cliffs and places that are difficult or awkward to access. Rock art and other marks are commonly produced in 'hidden' locales within rock shelters.

Many of these physical contexts suggest the presence of one, or only a few, individuals at any one time. Furthermore, they indicate that people were occupying and using remote and out-of-the-way places. Both these contexts contrast with the embodied experience of Phase 1 and 2 rock art production. The production of white stencils away from major thoroughfares, and the significant contrast of this pattern with the earlier Phase 2 stencil sites, further emphasises the changed spatial signature of rock marking in the recent past. The functional and social contexts, in which Phase 3 rock art was produced, appears to have diversified, and both corporate and individualised motivations appear to have been expressed via rock marking. The social geography, as meditated by rock art in relation to country, thus shifted. The significant use of previously unused rock shelters for the production of Phase 3 rock art is suggestive that art practice functioned at this time to achieve a much greater level of mediation between people and land.

A model of the use of rock art during colonial encounters has been constructed by Frederick (1997), based on her work at Watarrka National Park in Central Australia. Her thesis is underpinned by the proposition that Aboriginal people encountered and responded to white society not as passive victims, but as active social agents. The use of a graphic system on rock, within the context of contact, can act as an intervening force during a period of stress and insecurity. The structural patterns in Phase 3 rock art in the Upper Nepean catchment are consistent with Frederick's (1997) model of rock art produced within a contact context. It is particularly the change in the use of landscape, the diversity displayed in both gestural and graphic rock art, and the nature of the material used (charcoal) that conform most closely to this model.

In the Upper Nepean catchment, and more generally the Woronora Plateau, imagery that overtly represents contact items or themes is rare and otherwise ambiguous. However, a number of other variables directly related to some Phase 3 rock art are relevant to an assumption of its recent age and production within the contact period. The main pigments used during the recent period are charcoal and white clay, both of which are relatively unstable and do not bind strongly to rock surfaces. Imagery produced with these materials is unlikely to be old. Additionally, the graphic imagery is produced with dry rather than prepared pigment, and by scratching rock surfaces. This is suggestive of a more expedient mode of rock art production, which can be expected during a period of conflict and alienation. Other more qualitative attributes of Phase 3 rock art indicate a significant shift in people's concerns. The emphasis placed on the drawing of a new suite of large and imposing anthropomorphic imagery (with 'eyes') exemplifies a different and more outward-looking manner of depiction. These motifs were produced in highly visible locales, and are read as entering actual lived space. This quality evokes a purpose that seeks to transcend or go beyond the earth itself, and this contrasts with the manner with which Phase 2 anthropomorphs and animal imagery were inscripted.

However, the production of new graphic forms, and the diversity represented in Phase 3 imagery, tends to mask a fundamental continuity between older and newer rock art. During the production of Phase 3 rock art, many of the choices, made in regard to motif and location, appear to have been significantly influenced by earlier rock art. While continuity in the drawing of some imagery and re-marking of older imagery indicates the referential relevance of these motifs, the significance of certain locales in which earlier imagery was present appears to have been symbolically charged. It is in many of these shelters that recent gestural marking was undertaken, particularly rubbing and pecking, and this suggests a ritual context.

The historical records that attend to the intellectual and cultural response of Aboriginal people in south-east Australia during the early colonial and post-colonial period, while scant, nevertheless reveal the dynamic nature of people's concerns and ritual practice. While the impacts of European occupation were devastating at all conceivable levels (e.g. population and land loss, and personal and social stress and dislocation), it is highly probable that, as elsewhere across the continent, in the Upper Nepean catchment, people also responded ritually to the European encounter, and sought to mediate their position vis-à-vis the new colonial geography. The topography of this spatial milieu, being one of general diminishment and impoverishment, of loss of life and land, was one in which the maintenance of a totemic geography became to some extent untenable and, furthermore, not now fully relevant to being and experience. It is inconceivable that occupation within the colonial milieu in the Upper Nepean was not accompanied by a reformulation of ideology. In the suite of Phase 3 imagery, a host of new anthropomorphic motifs indicates the ascendance of novel referential beings that are likely to have 'served to order social space and meaning in the world' (cf. David 2002:204). Swain (1993:121–122) argues that a twofold cosmological orientation existed in south-east Australia during the early colonial period, and the diversity in the recent rock marks in the Upper Nepean is consistent with this.

Given its geographic situation away from the hub of colonial settlement, the Woronora Plateau potentially provided the opportunity for Aboriginal people to maintain connections with country. In the negotiation of social relations during this time, the marking of place with individual gestures and religious iconography indicates that, despite devastation and loss, Aboriginal people actively sought to maintain social and moral order. In the words of Swain (1993), 'Aboriginal people trusted, as they still trust, in the powers of regeneration'.

The land of the Upper Nepean catchment, with its abundance of sandstone, provided Aboriginal people with an opportunity to formulate and enact a visual language for the objectification of their social geography. Now, as in the past, this marked landscape resonates with its visual marks and motifs. The diachronic sequence evident in this body of rock art has revealed a rich and complex history of a dialogue between people and the land, which, brokered by inscription in rock shelters, was mutually influencing and transformative. The continuity over time of many motifs suggests that the placement of certain images within shelters by earlier generations successfully served to fulfil a role of transmitting information generationally. It is likely that in the most recent past, when people were mediating cross-cultural exchange within the colonial period, they drew heavily on the existing technology to convey meaning, and earlier imagery to reaffirm their relationship with their land.

The rock art of the Upper Nepean possesses a diversity of themes and behavioural signatures that have both synchronic and temporal significance. It is likely that previous studies, which have assumed functional equivalence in Sydney Basin sheltered rock art, have failed to sufficiently explore the variability, and the contextual and historical narratives, this may inscribe.

In this engagement, the approach has been to explore rock art as embodied practice. This has focused attention and consideration on notions of experience in space, the manner of producing or crafting marks, and where and how they reside in the land. These are the extant elements of the patterns of how humans experienced and lived in the Upper Nepean, and the material discourse they produced and were created by.

References

Andrews, A. 1998 *Earliest Monaro and Burragorang 1790 to 1840 with Wilson Bass Barrallier Caley Lhotsky Jauncey Lambie Ryrie*. Tabletop Press, Palmerston.

Attenbrow, V. 1976 Aboriginal Subsistence Economy on the Far South Coast of New South Wales, Australia. Unpublished BA Honours thesis, University of Sydney, Sydney.

Attenbrow, V. 1987 The Upper Mangrove Creek Catchment. A Study of Quantitative Changes in the Archaeological Record. Unpublished PhD thesis, University of Sydney, Sydney.

Attenbrow, V. 2002 *Sydney's Aboriginal Past: Investigating the Archaeological and Historical Records*. University of New South Wales Press, Sydney.

Attenbrow, V. 2004 *What's Changing: Population Size or Land Use Patterns? The Archaeology of Upper Mangrove Creek, Sydney Basin*. Terra Australis 21. ANU E Press, Canberra.

Bell, J. H. 1959 Official policies towards Aborigines of New South Wales. *Mankind*. Vol. 5, No. 8, pp. 345–355. doi.org/10.1111/j.1835-9310.1959.tb00319.x

Bennett, J. 2010 *Vibrant Matter a Political Ecology of Things*. Duke University Press, Durham and London.

Berndt, R. 1969 *The Sacred Site: The Western Arnhem Land Example*. Australian Aboriginal Studies No. 29. Australian Institute of Aboriginal Studies, Canberra.

Biosis 2007 Dendrobium Area 3 Archaeological and Cultural Heritage Assessment. Unpublished report for BHP Billiton, Chippendale.

Binford, L. R. 1980 Willow smoke and dog's tails: Hunter-gatherer settlement systems and archaeological site formation. *American Antiquity*. Vol. 45, pp. 4–20. doi.org/10.2307/279653

Binns, R. & I. McBryde 1972 *A Petrological Analysis of Ground-Edge Artefacts from Northern New South Wales*. Australian Institute of Aboriginal Studies, Canberra.

Black, M. P., S. D. Mooney & V. Attenbrow 2008 Implications of a 14 200 year continuous fire record for understanding human climate relationships at Goochs Swamp, New South Wales, Australia. *The Holocene*. Vol. 18, No. 3, pp. 437–447. doi.org/10.1177/0959683607087933

Boast, R. 1997 A Small Company of Actors: A Critique of Style. *Journal of Material Culture*. Vol. 2, No. 2, pp. 173–198.

Boot, P. 1994 Recent research into the prehistory of the hinterland of the South Coast of New South Wales. In M. Sullivan, S. Brockwell & A. Webb (eds) *Archaeology in the North: Proceedings of the 1993 Australian Archaeological Association Conference*, pp. 319–340. North Australian Research Unit, The Australian National University, Darwin.

Boot, P. 1996 Aspects of prehistoric change in the south coast hinterland of New South Wales. In S. Ulm, I. Lilley and A. Ross (eds) *Australian Archaeology '95: Proceedings of the 1995 AAA Annual Conference*, pp. 63–79. Tempus Vol. 6. University of Queensland, St Lucia.

Boot, P. 2002 Didthul, Gulaga and Wadbilliga: An Archaeological Study of the Aboriginals of the New South Wales South Coast Hinterland. Unpublished PhD thesis, The Australian National University, Canberra.

Bowdler, S. 1970 Bass Point: The Excavation of a South-East Australian Shell Midden Showing Cultural and Economic Change. Unpublished BA Honours thesis, University of Sydney, Sydney.

Bradley, R. 1991 Rock art and the perception of landscape. *Cambridge Archaeological Journal*. Vol. 1, No. 1, pp. 77–101. doi.org/10.1017/S0959774300000263

Branagan, D., C. Herbert & T. Langford-Smith 1979 *An Outline of the Geology and Geomorphology of the Sydney Basin*. Science Press, Sydney.

Brück, J. 2005 Experiencing the past? The development of a phenomenological archaeology in British prehistory. *Archaeological Dialogues*. Vol. 12, No. 1, pp. 45–72. doi.org/10.1017/S1380203805001583

Butlin, N. G. 1983 *Our original aggression: Aboriginal populations of south-eastern Australia 1788–1850*. George, Allen & Unwin, Sydney.

Capell, A. 1970 Aboriginal languages in the south Central Coast, New South Wales: Fresh discoveries. *Oceania*. Vol. 41, pp. 20–27. doi.org/10.1002/j.1834-4461.1970.tb01112.x

Carey, H. M. & D. Roberts 2002 Smallpox and the Baiame Waganna of Wellington Valley, New South Wales, 1829–1840: The earliest nativist movement in Aboriginal Australia. *Ethnohistory*. Vol. 49, No. 4, pp. 821–869. doi.org/10.1215/00141801-49-4-821

Chippindale, C. & G. Nash 2004 Pictures in place: Approaches to the figured landscapes of rock-art. In C. Chippindale & G. Nash (eds) *Pictures in Place: The Figured Landscapes of Rock-Art*, pp. 1–36. Cambridge University Press, Cambridge.

Clarkson, C., M. Smith, B. Marwick, R. Fullagar, L. A. Wallis, P. Faulkner, T. Manne, E. Hayes, E., R. G. Roberts, Z. Jacobs, X. Carah, K. M. Lowe, J. Matthews & S. Anna Florin 2015 The archaeology, chronology and stratigraphy of Madjedbebe (Malakunanja II): A site in northern Australia with early occupation. *Journal of Human Evolution*. Vol. 83, pp. 46–64.

Clegg, J. K. 1971 A ?'metaphysical' approach to the study of Aboriginal rock painting. *Mankind*. Vol. 8, pp. 37–41.

Clegg, J. 1977 A method of resolving problems which arise from style in art. In P. Ucko (ed.) *Form in Indigenous Art: Schematisation in the Art of Aboriginal Australia and Prehistoric Europe*, pp. 260–276. Gerald Duckworth & Company Ltd, London.

Clegg, J. 1983 From the study of Aboriginal art to the archaeology of prehistoric pictures. *Australian Archaeology*. No. 16, pp. 87–91.

Clegg, J. 1985 Prehistoric pictures as evidence of religion. Unpublished paper presented to the 80th Congress of the International Association for the History of Religions, Sydney.

Clegg, J. 1986 The archaeological approach to prehistoric pictures in Australia. In G. Bailey & P. Callow (eds) *Stone Age Prehistory Studies in Memory of Charles McBurney*, pp. 55–65. Cambridge University Press, Cambridge.

Clegg, J. 1987 Style and tradition at Sturt's Meadow. *World Archaeology*. Vol. 19, pp. 236–255. doi.org/10.1080/00438243.1987.9980037

Cole, N., A. Watchman & M. Morwood 1995 Chronology of Laura rock art. In M. Morwood & D. Hobbs (eds) *Quinkan Prehistory: The Archaeology of Aboriginal Art in South East Cape York Peninsula, Australia*, pp. 147–160. Tempus Vol. 3. Anthropology Museum, University of Queensland, St Lucia.

Collins, D. 1798 *An Account of the English Colony in New South Wales*. A. H. & A. W. Reed, London.

Comaroff, J. & J. Comaroff 1989 The colonization of consciousness in South Africa. *Economy and Society*. Vol. 18, No. 3, pp. 267–296.

Comaroff, J. & J. Comaroff 1991 *Of Revelation and Revolution: Colonialism and Consciousness in South Africa*. University of Chicago Press, Chicago. doi.org/10.7208/chicago/9780226114477.001.0001

Conaghan, P. J. & J. G. Jones 1975 The Hawkesbury Sandstone and the Brahmaputra: A depositional model for continental sheet sandstones. *Journal of the Geological Society of Australia*. Vol. 22, pp. 275–283. doi.org/10.1080/00167617508728897

Conkey, M. 1978 Style and information in cultural evolution: Toward a predictive model for the Paleolithic. In C. Redman, M. Berman, E. Curtin, J. Langhorn, N. Versaggi & J. Wanser (eds) *Social Archaeology: Beyond Subsistence and Dating*, pp. 61–85. Academic Press, New York.

Conkey, M. 1990 Experimenting with style in archaeology: Some historical and theoretical issues. In M. Conkey and C. Hastorf (eds) *The Uses of Style in Archaeology*, pp. 5–17. Cambridge University Press, Cambridge.

Conkey, M. 1997 New approaches in the search for meaning? A review of research in 'Paleolithic art'. *Journal of Field Archaeology*. Vol. 14, pp. 413–430.

Conkey, M. 2001 Hunting for images, gathering up meanings: Art for life in hunting-gathering societies. In C. Panter-Brick, R. H. Layton & P. Rowley-Conway (eds) *Hunter-Gatherers: An Interdisciplinary Perspective*, pp. 267–291. Cambridge University Press, Cambridge.

Cox, J., L. Maynard & J. V. S. Megaw 1968 The excavation of a rock-shelter at Audley, Royal National Park, N.S.W. *Archaeology & Physical Anthropology in Oceania*. Vol. 3, No. 2, pp. 94–104.

Curson, P. H. 1985 *Times of Crisis: Epidemics in Sydney 1788–1900*. University of Sydney Press, Sydney.

David, B. 1991 Fern Cave, rock art and social transformations: Rock art regionalism and demographic models in southeastern Cape York Peninsula. *Archaeology in Oceania*. Vol. 26, No. 2, pp. 41–57. doi.org/10.1002/j.1834-4453.1991.tb00263.x

David, B. 1999 Whither landscapes. *Cambridge Archaeological Journal*. Vol. 9, No. 2, pp. 294–295. doi.org/10.1017/S0959774300015468

David, B. 2002 *Landscapes, Rock-Art and the Dreaming: An Archaeology of Preunderstanding*. Leicester University Press, London.

David, B. & N. Cole 1990 Rock art and inter-regional interaction in northeastern Australian prehistory. *Antiquity*. Vol. 64, pp. 788–806. doi.org/10.1017/S0003598X00078881

David, B. & M. David 1988 Rock pictures of the Chillagoe-Mungana Limestone Belt, North Queensland. *Rock Art Research*. Vol. 5, No. 2, pp. 147–156.

David, B. & J. Thomas 2008 Landscape archaeology: Introduction. In B. David & J. Thomas (eds) *Handbook of Landscape Archaeology*, pp. 27–43. Left Coast Press, Walnut Creek, CA.

David, B., M. Lecole, H. Lourandos, A. Baglioni Jr. & J. Flood 1999 Investigating relationships between motif forms, techniques and rock surfaces in north Australian rock art. *Australian Archaeology*. Vol. 48, pp. 16–22. doi-org/10.1080/03122417.1999.11681620

Davidson, I. 1995 Paintings, power, and the past: Can there ever be an ethnoarchaeology of art? *Current Anthropology*. Vol. 36, No. 5, pp. 889–892. doi.org/10.1086/204455

Davidson, I. 1997 Review of rock Art and Regionalism in North Queensland Prehistory. By B. David and D. Chant. *Archaeology in Oceania*. Vol. 32, No. 3, pp. 217–218. doi.org/10.1002/j.1834-4453.1997.tb00392.x

Denham, T. & S. Mooney 2008 Human-environment interactions in Australia and New Guinea during the Holocene. *The Holocene*. Vol. 18, No. 3, pp. 365–371. doi.org/10.1177/0959683607087926

Dickson, F. 1978 Australian Ground Stone Hatchets. Unpublished PhD thesis, Macquarie University, Sydney.

Dibden, J. 1996 Hatchet Hatchment: A Study of Style in a Collection of Ground-Edge Hatchet Heads from South Eastern NSW. Unpublished BA Honours thesis, The Australian National University, Canberra.

Dibden, J. 2011 Drawing in the Land: Rock-Art of the Upper Nepean Sydney Basin, New South Wales. Unpublished PhD thesis, The Australian National University, Canberra.

Dobrez, L. 2009 New and old paradigms: The question of space. In G. Dimitriadis (ed.) *Landscape in Mind: Dialogue on Space between Anthropology and Archaeology*, pp. 5–7. BAR International Series 2003, British Archaeological Reports, Oxford.

Dodson, J. & S. Mooney 2002 An assessment of historic human impact on south-eastern Australian environmental systems, using late Holocene rates of environmental change. *Australian Journal of Botany*. Vol. 50, pp. 455–464. doi.org/10.1071/BT01031

Dodson, J. & B. Thom 1991 A late Pleistocene to Holocene vegetation history from the Hawkesbury Valley, New South Wales. *Proceedings of the Linnean Society of New South Wales*. Vol. 113, pp. 121–134.

Domingo Sanz, I., D. Fiore & S. K. May 2008 Archaeologies of art: Time, place and identity in rock art, portable art, and body art. In I. Domingo Sanz, D. Fiore & S. K. May (eds) *Archaeologies of Art. Time, Place and Identity*, pp. 15–28. Left Coast Press, Walnut Creek, CA.

Eades, D. K. 1976 *The Dharawal and Dhurga Languages of the New South Wales South Coast*. Australian Aboriginal Studies Research and Regional Studies No. 8. Australian Institute of Aboriginal Studies, Canberra.

Edwards, R. 1971 Art and Aboriginal prehistory. In J. Mulvaney & J. Golsen (eds) *Aboriginal Man and Environment in Australia*, pp. 356–367. Australian National University Press, Canberra.

Flood, J. 1980 *The Moth Hunters: Aboriginal Prehistory of the Australian Alps*. Australian Institute of Aboriginal Studies, Canberra.

Flood, J. 1982 Katungal, Paiendra and Bemeringal. In S. Bowdler (ed.) *Coastal Archaeology in Eastern Australia. Proceedings of the 1980 Valla Conference on Australian Prehistory*, pp. 29–31. Department of Prehistory, Research School of Pacific Studies, The Australian National University, Canberra.

Ford, J. 2006 Painting Contact: Characterising the Paints of the South Woronora Plateau Rock Art Assemblage, Wollongong, New South Wales. Unpublished BA Honours thesis, The Australian National University, Canberra.

Forge, J. A. 1991 Handstencils: Rock art or not. In P. Bahn & A. Rosenfeld (eds) *Rock Art and Prehistory: Papers Presented to Symposium G of the AURA (Australian Rock Art Research Association) Congress, Darwin 1988*, pp. 39–44. Oxbow Monograph 10. Oxbow Books, Oxford.

Frederick, U. K. 1997 Drawing in Differences: Changing Social Contexts of Rock Art Production in Watarrka (Kings Canyon) National Park, Central Australia. Unpublished MA thesis, The Australian National University, Canberra.

Frederick, U. K. 1999 At the centre of it all: Constructing contact through the rock art of Watarrka National Park, central Australia. *Archaeology in Oceania*. Vol 34, pp. 132–144. doi.org/10.1002/j.1834-4453.1999.tb00443.x

Frederick, U. K. 2000 Keeping the land alive: Changing social contexts of landscape and rock art production. In R. Torrence & A. Clarke (eds) *The Archaeology of Difference: Negotiating Cross Cultural Engagements in Oceania*, pp. 132–144. Routledge, London.

Gamble, C. 1982 Interaction and alliance in Palaeolithic society. *Man* (NS). Vol. 17, pp. 92–107. doi.org/10.2307/2802103

Giopoulis, G. 1986 Edge Ground Axes of South Eastern Australia. Unpublished BA Honours thesis, University of Sydney, Sydney.

Gott, B. 1999 Cumbungi, *Typha* species, a staple Aboriginal food in southern Australian. *Australian Aboriginal Studies*. Vol.1, pp. 33–50.

Gunn, R. G. 2005 Motif structure and Australian rock art analysis: An example from Gariwerd, Victoria. *Rock Art Research*. Vol. 22, No. 1, pp. 34–47.

Gunson, N. (ed.) 1974 *Australian Reminiscences and Papers of L. E. Threlkeld, Missionary to the Aborigines, 1824–1859*. Vol. 1. Australian Institute of Aboriginal Studies, Canberra.

Haskovec, I. 1992 Mt. Gilruth revisited. *Archaeology in Oceania*. Vol. 27, No. 2, pp. 61–74. doi.org/10.1002/j.1834-4453.1992.tb00285.x

Hazelton P. & P. Tille 1990 *Soil Landscapes of the Wollongong-Port Hacking 1:100 000 Sheet*. Soil Conservation Service of NSW, Sydney.

Head, L. 2008 Is the concept of human impacts past its use-by date? *The Holocene*. Vol. 18, No. 3, pp. 373–377. doi.org/10.1177/0959683607087927

Herbert, C. 1980 Wianamatta Group and Mittagong Formation. In C. Herbert & R. Helby (eds) *A Guide to the Sydney Basin*. Geological Survey of NSW, Bulletin 26, pp. 10–53. Department of Mineral Resources, Sydney.

Hiscock, P. 1981 Comments of the use of chipped stone artefacts as a measure of 'intensity of site usage'. *Australian Archaeology*. No. 13, pp. 30–34.

Hiscock, P. 1982 A technological analysis of quartz assemblages from the South Coast. In S. Bowdler (ed.) C*oastal Archaeology in Eastern Australia. Proceedings of the 1980 Valla Conference on Australian Prehistory*, pp. 32–35. Department of Prehistory, Research School of Pacific Studies, The Australian National University, Canberra.

Hiscock, P. 1986 Technological change in the Hunter River valley and the interpretation of late Holocene change in Australia. *Archaeology in Oceania*. Vol. 21, No. 1, pp. 40–50. doi.org/10.1002/j.1834-4453.1986.tb00123.x

Hiscock, P. 2008 *Archaeology of Ancient Australia*. Routledge, London. doi.org/10.4324/9780203448359

Hiscock, P. & V. Attenbrow 1998 Early Holocene backed artefacts from Australia. *Archaeology in Oceania*. Vol. 33, No. 2, pp. 49–62. doi.org/10.1002/j.1834-4453.1998.tb00404.x

Hiscock, P. S. O'Connor, J. Balme & T. Maloney 2016 World's earliest ground-edge axe production coincides with human colonisation of Australia, *Australian Archaeology*. Vol. 82, No. 1, pp. 2–11. doi.org/10.1080/03122417.2016.1164379

Hodder, I. 1982 *Symbol in Action*. Cambridge University Press, Cambridge.

Hodder, I. 2011 *Catalhoyuk The Leopards Tale. Revealing the Mysteries of Turkey's Ancient 'Town'*. Thames and Hudson, London (1st paperback ed.).

Howitt, A. 1904 The Native Tribes of South East Australia. London: Macmillan & Co. Limited.

Hughes, P. 1976 Inferred Rates of Weathering in Sandstone Shelters in Southern N.S.W.: Some Implications for the Preservation of Rock Art. In C. Pearson & G. L. Pretty (eds) *Proceedings of the National Seminar on the Conservation of Cultural Material, Perth 1973*. pp. 51–54. ICCM (Institute for Conservation of Cultural Material), Canberra.

Hughes, P. 1977 A Geomorphological Interpretation of Selected Sites in Southern Coastal New South Wales. Unpublished PhD thesis, University of New South Wales, Sydney.

Hughes, P. & R. Lampert 1982 Prehistoric population changes in southern coastal New South Wales. In S. Bowdler (ed.) *Coastal Archaeology in Eastern Australian: Proceedings of the 1980 Valla Conference on Australian Prehistory*, pp. 16–28. Occasional Papers in Prehistory 11. Department of Prehistory Research School of Pacific Studies, The Australian National University, Canberra.

Huntley, J., A. Watchman & J. Dibden 2011 Characteristics of a pigment art sequence: Woronora Plateau, New South Wales. *Rock Art Research*. Vol. 28, No. 1, pp. 85–97.

Hurcombe, L. 2007 A sense of materials and sensory perception in concepts of materiality. *World Archaeology*. Vol 39, No. 4, pp. 532–545. doi.org/10.1080/00438240701679346

Ingold, T. 1993 The temporality of the landscape. *World Archaeology*. Vol. 25, No. 2, pp. 152–174. doi.org/10.1080/00438243.1993.9980235

Johnson, A. 2000 Fine resolution palaeoecology confirms anthropogenic impact during the late Holocene in the lower Hawkesbury Valley, NSW. *Australian Geographer*. Vol. 31, No. 2, pp. 209–235. doi.org/10.1080/713612247

JMcD CHM (Jo McDonald Cultural Heritage Management Pty Ltd) 2005 Archaeological Salvage Excavation of Site RTA G1 109–113 George St Parramatta, NSW. Unpublished report to Landcom, Sydney.

Jones, R. 1990 Hunters of the Dreaming: Some ideational, economic and ecological parameters of the Australian Aboriginal production system. In D. E. Yen & J. M. J. Mummery (eds) *Pacific Production Systems: Approaches to Economic Prehistory. Papers from a Symposium at the XV Pacific Science Congress, Dunedin, New Zealand 1983*, pp. 25–53. Department of Prehistory, Research School of Pacific Studies, The Australian National University, Canberra.

Jones, R. L. 1990 Late Holocene vegetation changes on the Illawarra coastal plain, New South Wales, Australia. *Review of Palaeobotany and Palynology*. Vol. 65, pp. 37–46. doi.org/10.1016/0034-6667(90)90054-M

Kamminga, J. 1982 *Over the Edge. Functional Analysis of Australian Stone Tools.* Occasional Papers in Anthropology. No. 12. University of Queensland, St Lucia.

Keen, I. 1986 Stanner on Aboriginal religion. *Canberra Anthropology*. Vol. 9, No. 2, pp. 26–50. doi.org/10.1080/03149098609508534

Keen, I. 2004 *Aboriginal Economy and Society: Australia at the Threshold of Colonisation.* Oxford University Press, South Melbourne.

Kershaw, A. P., D. D'Costa, J. McEwen Mason & B. Wagstaff 1991 Palynological evidence for Quaternary vegetation and environments of mainland southeastern Australia. *Quaternary Science Reviews*. Vol. 10, pp. 391–404. doi.org/10.1016/0277-3791(91)90003-D

Knight, T. 2001 Stepping Stones to the Sky: Archaeological Perspectives on the Cultural Significance of the Weddin Mountains in Prehistory. Unpublished Masters thesis, The Australian National University, Canberra.

Lampert, R. 1971 *Burrill Lake and Currarong: Coastal Sites in Southern New South Wales.* Terra Australia 1. Department of Prehistory, Research School of Pacific Studies, The Australian National University, Canberra.

Lattas, A. 1993 Gifts, commodities and the problem of alienation. *Social Analysis*. No. 34, pp. 102–117.

Layton, R. 1989 The political use of Australian Aboriginal body painting and its archaeological implications. In I. Hodder (ed.) *The Meaning of Things: Material Culture and Symbolic Expression*, pp. 1–11. Unwin Hyman, London.

Layton, R. 1992 *Australian Rock Art: A New Synthesis*. Cambridge University Press, Cambridge.

Layton, R. 2000a Shamanism, totemism and rock art: *Les chamanes de la préhistoire* in the context of rock art research. *Cambridge Archaeological Journal*. Vol. 10, No. 1, pp. 169–186. doi.org/10.1017/S0959774300000068

Layton, R. 2000b Intersubjectivity and understanding rock art. *Australian Archaeology*. No. 51, pp. 48–53. doi.org/10.1080/03122417.2000.11681680

Lee, G. 2002 Wahi Pana legendary place on Hawai'i Island. In B. David & M. Wilson (eds) *Inscribed Landscapes: Marking and Making Place*, pp. 79–92. University of Hawai'i Press, Honolulu.

Lewis, D. 1988 *The Rock Art Paintings of Arnhem Land, Australia: Social, Ecological and Material Culture Change in the Post-Glacial Period*. BAR International Series 415. British Archaeological Reports, Oxford.

Lewis, D. & D. Rose 1988 *The Shape of the Dreaming: The Cultural Significance of Victoria River Rock Art*. Australian Institute of Aboriginal Studies, Canberra.

Lewis-Williams, D. & T. Dowson 1990 Through the veil: San rock paintings and the rock face. *The South African Archaeological Bulletin*. Vol. 45, No. 151, pp. 5–16. doi.org/10.2307/3887913

McBryde, I. 1984 Exchange in South Eastern Australia: An ethnohistorical perspective. *Aboriginal History*. Vol. 8, No. 2, pp. 132–153.

McBryde, I. 1986 Artefacts, language and social interaction: A case study from southeastern Australia. In G. Bailey & P. Callow (eds) *Stone Age Prehistory: Studies in Memory of Charles McBurney*, pp. 77–93. Cambridge University Press, Cambridge.

McBryde, I. & G. Harrison 1981 Valued good or valuable stone? Consideration of some aspects of the distribution of greenstone artefacts in South-eastern Australian. In F. Leach & J. Davidson (eds) *Archaeological Studies of Pacific Stone Resources*, pp. 183–208. BAR International Series 104. British Archaeological Reports, Oxford.

McCarthy, F. D. 1959 Cave art of the Conjola district, NSW. *Records of the Australian Museum*. Vol. 24, No. 13, pp. 191–202. doi.org/10.3853/j.0067-1975.24.1959.651

McCarthy, F. D. 1961 A remarkable gallery of cave paintings in eastern New South Wales. *Records of the Australian Museum*. Vol. 25, No. 7, pp. 115–120. doi.org/10.3853/j.0067-1975.25.1961.659

McCarthy, F. D. 1964 The archaeology of the Capertee Valley, New South Wales. *Records of the Australian Museum*. Vol. 26, No. 6, pp. 197–246. doi.org/10.3853/j.0067-1975.26.1964.674

McCarthy, F. D. 1979 *Australian Aboriginal Rock Art*. The Australian Museum, Sydney.

McCarthy, F. D. 1988a Rock art sequences: A matter of clarification. *Rock Art Research*. Vol. 5, No. 1, pp. 16–19.

McCarthy, F. D. 1988b Reply. *Rock Art Research*. Vol. 5, No. 1, pp. 38–41.

McDonald, J. 1988 Comment on FD McCarthy's rock art sequences: A matter of clarification. *Rock Art Research*. Vol. 5, No. 1, pp. 28–30.

McDonald. J. 1994 Dreamtime Superhighway: An Analysis of Sydney Basin Rock Art and Prehistoric Information Exchange. Unpublished PhD thesis, The Australian National University, Canberra.

McDonald. J. 1999 Bedrock notions and isochrestic choice: Evidence for localised patterning in the engravings of the Sydney region. *Archaeology in Oceania*. Vol. 34, pp. 145–160. doi.org/10.1002/j.1834-4453.1999.tb00444.x

McDonald, J. 2000 AMS dating charcoal drawings from the Sydney region: Results and issues. In G. K. Ward & C. Tuniz (eds) *Advances in Dating Australian Rock Markings: Papers from the First Australian Rock Picture Dating Workshop*. AURA Occasional Publication No. 10, pp. 90–94. Australian Rock Art Research Association, Melbourne.

McDonald. J. 2008a *Dreamtime Superhighway: Sydney Basin Rock Art and Prehistoric Information Exchange*. Terra Australis 27. ANU E Press, Canberra. doi.org/10.26530/OAPEN_459083

McDonald, J. 2008b Rock art and cross-cultural interaction in Sydney. How did each side perceive the other? In P. Veth, P. Sutton & M. Neale (eds) *Strangers on the Shore: Early Coastal Contacts in Australia*, pp. 94–112. National Museum of Australia, Canberra.

McDonald, J., K. Officer, T. Jull, D. Donahue, J. Head & B. Ford. 1990 Investigating C14 AMS: Dating prehistoric rock art in the Sydney Sandstone Basin, Australia. *Rock Art Research*. Vol. 7, No. 2, pp. 83–92.

McDonald, R., R. Isbell, J. Speight, J. Walker, & M. Hopkins 1998 *Australian Soil and Land Survey Field Handbook*. CSIRO (Commonwealth Scientific and Industrial Research Organisation) Australia.

McDonald, W. 1966 *Earliest Illawarra by its Explorers and Pioneers*. Illawarra Historical Society, Wollongong.

Macdonald, W. K. 1990 Investigating style: An exploratory analysis of some Plains burials. In M. Conkey & C. Hastorf (eds) *The Uses of Style in Archaeology*, pp. 52–60. Cambridge University Press, Cambridge.

Macintosh, N. W. G. 1977 Beswick Creek cave two decades later: A reappraisal. In P. Ucko, P. (ed.) *Form in Indigenous Art: Schematisation in the Art of Aboriginal Australia and Prehistoric Europe*, pp. 191–197. Gerald Duckworth and Company Ltd, London.

McMah, L. 1965 A Quantitative Analysis of the Aboriginal Rock Carvings of the District of Sydney and the Hawkesbury River. Unpublished BA Honours thesis, University of Sydney, Sydney.

McNiven, I. & L. Russell 2002 Ritual response place marking and the colonial frontier in Australia. In B. David& M. Wilson (eds) *Inscribed Landscapes. Marking and Making Place*, pp. 27–41. University of Hawai'i Press, Honolulu.

Mathews, R. H. 1895 Australian rock pictures. *The American Anthropologist*. Vol. VIII, No. 3, pp. 268–278. doi.org/10.1525/aa.1895.8.3.02a00050

Mathews, R. H. 1898 Initiation ceremonies of Australian Tribes. *Proceedings of the American Philosophical Society*. Vol. 37, No. 157, pp. 54–73.

Mathews, R. H. & M. M. Everitt 1900 The organisation, language and initiation ceremonies of the Aborigines of the south-east coast of N. S. Wales. *Journal and Proceedings of the Royal Society of NSW*. Vol. XXXIV, pp. 262–281.

Maynard, L. 1977 Classification and terminology in Australian rock art. In P. J. Ucko, (ed.) *Form in Indigenous Art: Schematisation in the Art of Aboriginal Australia and Prehistoric Europe*, pp. 387–402. Australian Institute of Aboriginal Studies, Canberra.

Maynard, L. 1979 The archaeology of Australian Aboriginal art. In S. M. Mead (ed.) *Exploring the Visual Art of Oceania*, pp. 83–111. University of Hawai'i Press, Honolulu.

Megaw, J. V. S. 1974 The recent archaeology of the south Sydney district—a summary. In J. V. S. Megaw (ed.) *The Recent Archaeology of the Sydney District. Excavations 1964–1967*, pp. 35–38. Australian Institute of Aboriginal Studies, Canberra.

Merlan, F. 1989 The interpretive framework of Wardaman rock art: A preliminary report. *Australian Aboriginal Studies*. No. 2, pp. 14–24.

Meskell, L. 2005a Introduction: Object orientations. In L. Meskell (ed.) *Archaeologies of Materiality*, pp. 1–17. Blackwell, Malden. doi.org/10.1002/9780470774052.ch1

Meskell, L. 2005b Objects in the mirror appear closer than they are. In D. Miller (ed.) *Materiality*, pp. 51–71. Duke University Press, Durham and London. doi.org/10.1215/9780822386711-002

Miller, D. 2005a Afterword. In L. Meskell (ed.) *Archaeologies of Materiality*, pp. 212–219. Blackwell, Malden. doi.org/10.1002/9780470774052.ch9

Miller, D. 2005b Materiality: An introduction. In D. Miller (ed.) *Materiality*, pp. 1–50. Duke University Press, Durham and London. doi.org/10.1215/9780822386711-001

Mills, K., R. Muston, C. Sefton & A. Young 1985 (eds) Environmental Values of the Metropolitan Catchment Areas – A Submission to a Metropolitan Water, Sewerage & Drainage Board (MWSDB) Study. Unpublished report by the Geography Department, Wollongong University, Wollongong.

Morphy, H. 1999 Encoding the Dreaming – A theoretical framework for the analysis of representational processes in Australian Aboriginal art. *Australian Archaeology*. No. 49, pp. 13–22. doi.org/10.1080/03122417.1999.11681648

Morwood, M. J. 1980 Art and Stone: Towards a Prehistory of Central Western Queensland. Unpublished PhD thesis, The Australian National University, Canberra.

Morwood, M. J. 1981 Archaeology of the central Queensland highlands: The stone component. *Archaeology in Oceania*. Vol. 16, pp. 1–52. doi.org/10.1002/j.1834-4453.1981.tb00001.x

Morwood, M. J. 1984 The archaeology of social complexity in south-east Queensland. *Proceedings of the Prehistoric Society*. Vol. 53, pp. 337–350. doi.org/10.1017/S0079497X00006265

Morwood, M. J. & C. E. Smith 1994 Rock art research in Australia 1974–94. *Australian Archaeology*. No. 39, pp. 19–38. doi.org/10.1080/03122417.1994.11681525

Morwood, M. & P. Trezise 1989 Edge-ground axes in Pleistocene greater Australia: Evidence from S. E. Cape York Peninsula. *Queensland Archaeological Research*. Vol. 6, pp. 77–90. doi.org/10.25120/qar.6.1989.138

Mountford, C. P. 1976 *Nomads of the Australian Desert*. Rigby Limited Adelaide.

Mulvaney, K. 2006 What to do on a rainy day. Reminiscences of Mirriuwung and Gadjerong artists. *Rock Art Research*. Vol. 13, No. 1, pp. 3–20.

Myers, F. 1986 *Pintupi country, Pintupi Self: Settlement, Place, and Politics among the Western Desert Aborigines*. Smithsonian Institution Press, Aboriginal Studies Press, Washington and Canberra.

Officer, K. L. C. 1984 From Tuggerah to Dharawal: Variation and Function within a Regional Art Style. Unpublished BA Honours thesis, The Australian National University, Canberra.

Officer, K. L. C. 1991 What's in an anthropomorph? In P. Bahn & A. Rosenfeld (eds) *Rock Art and Prehistory: Papers Presented to Symposium G of the AURA (Australian Rock Art Research Association) Congress, Darwin 1988*, pp. 112–119. Oxbow Monograph 10. Oxbow Books, Oxford.

Officer, K. L. C. 1994 Style and Graphic: An Archaeological Model for the Analysis of Rock Art. Draft PhD thesis, The Australian National University, Canberra.

Ouzman, S. 2001 Seeing is deceiving: Rock art and the non-visual. *World Archaeology*. Vol. 33, No. 2, pp. 237–256. doi.org/10.1080/00438240120079271

Packham, G. H. (ed.) 1969 The geology of New South Wales. *Journal of the Geological Society of Australia*. Vol. 16, No. 1, pp. 1–654. doi.org/10.1080/14400956908527964

Paton, R. 1994 Speaking through stones: A study from northern Australia. *World Archaeology*. Vol. 26, No. 2, pp. 172–184. doi.org/10.1080/00438243.1994.9980271

Penman, T., D. Binns, T. Brassil, R. Shiels & R. Allen 2009 Long-term changes in understorey vegetation in the absence of wildfire in south-east dry sclerophyll forests. *Australian Journal of Botany*. Vol. 57, pp. 533–540. doi.org/10.1071/BT09079

Peterson, N. 1972 Totemism yesterday: Sentiment and local organisation among the Australian Aborigines. *Man*. Vol. 7, No, 1, pp. 12–32. doi.org/10.2307/2799853

Pinney, C. 2005 Things happen: Or, from which moment does that object come? In L. Meskell (ed.) *Archaeologies of Materiality*, pp. 256–272. Blackwell, Malden. doi.org/10.1215/9780822386711-011

Plomley, N. 1990–1991 Aborigines and governors. *Bulletin of Centre for Tasmanian Historical Studies* Vol. 3, No 1, pp. 1–18.

Poiner, G. 1976 The process of the year among Aborigines of the central and south coast of New South Wales. *Archaeology and Physical Anthropology in Oceania* Vol. 11, pp. 186–206.

Rainbird, P. 2002 Making sense of petroglyphs: The sound of rock-art. In B. David & M. Wilson (eds) *Inscribed Landscapes: Marking and Making Place*, pp. 93–103. University of Hawai'i Press, Honolulu.

Ridges, M. 1995 An Investigation into the Aboriginal Rock Paints of the Selwyn Ranges Region in North West Queensland. Unpublished BA Honours thesis, University of New England, Armidale. doi.org/10.1017/S0003598X00098446

Robertson, G., V. Attenbrow & P. Hiscock 2009 Multiple uses for Australian backed artefacts. *Antiquity*. Vol. 83, pp. 296–308.

Rose, D. 1990 Gulaga. A Report on the Cultural Significance of Mt Dromedary to Aboriginal People. Unpublished report presented to the Forestry Commission of New South Wales and the New South Wales National Parks and Wildlife Service, Hurstville.

Rose, D., D. James & C. Watson 2003 *Indigenous Kinship with the Natural World in New South Wales*. NSW National Parks and Wildlife Service, Hurstville.

Rosenfeld, A. 1975 The Early Man sites: Laura, 1974. *Australian Institute of Aboriginal Studies News Series*. No. 3, pp. 37–40.

Rosenfeld, A. 1982 Style and meaning in Laura art: A case study in the formal analysis of style in prehistoric art. *Mankind*. Vol. 13, No. 3, pp. 199–217. doi.org/10.1111/j.1835-9310.1982.tb01231.x

Rosenfeld, A. 1991 Panaramitee: Dead or alive? In P. Bahn & A. Rosenfeld (eds) *Rock Art and Prehistory: Papers Presented to Symposium G of the AURA (Australian Rock Art Research Association) Congress, Darwin 1988*, pp. 136–144. Oxbow Monograph 10. Oxbow Books, Oxford.

Rosenfeld, A. 1992 Recent Developments in Australian Rock Art Studies. Unpublished paper presented to the Fourth World Congress of Aegean Archaeologists, Hobart, Tasmania.

Rosenfeld, A. 1997 Archaeological signatures of the social context of rock art production. In M. Conkey, O. Soffer, D. Stratmann & N. G. Jablonski (eds) *Beyond Art: Pleistocene Image and Symbol*, pp. 289–300. California Academy of Sciences, San Francisco.

Rosenfeld, A. 1999 Rock art and rock markings. *Australian Archaeology.* No. 49, pp. 28–33. doi.org/10.1080/03122417.1999.11681653

Rosenfeld, A. 2000 Minor Variations in a Stable Tradition: Rock Art in the Central Ranges, Australia. Unpublished paper presented at the AURA (Australian Rock Art Research Association) Congress, Alice Springs.

Rosenfeld, A. 2002 Rock-art as an indicator of changing social geographies in central Australia. In B. David & M. Wilson (eds) *Inscribed Landscapes: Marking and Making Place*, pp. 61–78. University of Hawai'i Press, Honolulu.

Rosenfeld, A. & P. Bahn 1991 Introduction. In P. Bahn & A. Rosenfeld (eds) *Rock Art and Prehistory: Papers Presented to Symposium G of the AURA (Australian Rock Art Research Association) Congress, Darwin 1988*, pp. v–vii. Oxbow Monograph 10. Oxbow Books, Oxford.

Ross, J. 1997 Painted Relationships: An Archaeological Analysis of a Distinctive Anthropomorphic Rock Art Motif in Northwest Queensland. Unpublished BA Honours thesis, University of New England, Armidale.

Ross, J. & I. Davidson 2006 Rock art and ritual: An archaeological analysis of rock art in arid Central Australia. *Journal of Archaeological Method and Theory.* Vol. 12, No. 4, pp. 305–341. doi.org/10.1007/s10816-006-9021-1

Rumsey, A. 1989 Language groups in Australian Aboriginal land claims. *Anthropological Forum.* Vol. VI, No. 1, pp. 69–79. doi.org/10.1080/00664677.1989.9967396

Sackett, J. R. 1986 Isochrestism and style: A clarification. *Journal of Anthropological Archaeology.* Vol. 5, pp. 266–277. doi.org/10.1016/0278-4165(86)90008-5

Sefton, C. 1988 Site and Artefact Patterns on the Woronora Plateau. Unpublished MA thesis, University of Sydney, Sydney.

Sefton, C. 1989 Archaeological Survey of the Cordeaux River and Woronora River by the Illawarra Prehistory Group. Unpublished report for the Australian Institute of Aboriginal Studies, Canberra.

Sefton, C. 1990 1989–1990 Archaeological Survey of the Cordeaux River and Woronora River by the Illawarra Prehistory Group. Unpublished report for the Australian Institute of Aboriginal and Torres Strait Islander Studies, Canberra.

Sefton, C. 1991 1990–1991 Archaeological Survey of the Cordeaux River by the Illawarra Prehistory Group. Unpublished report for the Australian Institute of Aboriginal and Torres Strait Islander Studies, Canberra.

Sefton, C. 1992 Red Ochre and Charcoal Drawing Distributions on the Woronora Plateau with Special Reference to Motif Variation. Unpublished paper presented to the AURA (Australian Rock Art Research Association) Congress, Cairns.

Sefton, C. 1994 1993–1994 Archaeological Survey of the Avon River by the Illawarra Prehistory Group. Unpublished report for the Australian Institute of Aboriginal and Torres Strait Islander Studies, Canberra.

Sefton, C. 1995 1994–1995 Archaeological Survey of Kangaroo Creek Royal National Park by the Illawarra Prehistory Group. Unpublished report for the Australian Institute of Aboriginal and Torres Strait Islander Studies, Canberra.

Sefton, C. 1996 1995–1996 Archaeological Survey of North and Western Side of the Hacking River including Royal National Park and Carrawarra State Recreation Area by the Illawarra Prehistory Group. Unpublished report for the Australian Institute of Aboriginal and Torres Strait Islander Studies, Canberra.

Sefton, C. 1997 1996–1997 Archaeological Survey of the Avon River by the Illawarra Prehistory Group. Unpublished report for the Australian Institute of Aboriginal and Torres Strait Islander Studies, Canberra.

Sefton, C. 2000 Archaeological Survey of the Nepean River by the Illawarra Prehistory Group. Unpublished report for the NSW Heritage Office, Sydney.

Sefton, C. 2003a Archaeological Survey of the Nepean and Western Catchment of Burke River to the Confluence by the Illawarra Prehistory Group. Unpublished report for the NSW Heritage Office, Sydney.

Sefton, C. 2003b Near and Far Rock Engravings of the Woronora Plateau. Unpublished paper presented at the AURA (Australian Rock Art Research Association) Congress, Hamilton.

Sefton, C. 2009a Archaeological Survey of the Head of Waratah Rivulet by the Illawarra Prehistory Group. Section One. Unpublished report, Wollongong.

Sefton, C. 2009b Recording of Flat Rock Creek 326 Woronora Catchment Area by the Illawarra Prehistory Group. Section Two. Unpublished report, Wollongong.

Sharp, L. 1952 Steel axes for Stone Age Australians. Reprinted in Y. Cohen (ed.) *Man in Adaptation: The Cultural Present*, pp. 69–91. Aldine, Chicago.

Shaw, A. G. L. 1992 British policy towards the Australian Aborigines, 1830–1850. *Australian Historical Studies*. Vol. 25, No. 99, pp. 265–286. doi.org/10.1080/10314619208595910

Sherwin, L. & G. G. Holmes (eds) 1986 *Geology of the Wollongong Port Hacking 1:100 000 Sheets 9029, 9129*. Geological Survey of New South Wales. Department of Mineral Resources, Sydney.

Shulmeister, J. 1999 Australasian evidence for mid-Holocene climate change implies precessional control of Walker Circulation in the Pacific. *Quaternary International*. Vol. 57/58, pp. 81–91. doi.org/10.1016/S1040-6182(98)00052-4

Smith, C. 1994 Situating Style: An Ethnoarchaeological Study of Social and Material Context in an Australian Aboriginal Artistic System. Unpublished PhD thesis, University of New England, Armidale.

Smith, L. J. 1983 What's in the Size of a Macropod? A Study of Variance in Prehistoric Pictures from the Mangrove Creek Area. Unpublished BA Honours thesis, University of Sydney, Sydney.

Smith, M. A. & A. Rosenfeld 1992 Archaeological Sites in Watarrka National Park: The Northern Sector of the Plateau. A report to the Conservation Commission of the Northern Territory on Fieldwork in 1991. Unpublished, Darwin.

Soffer, O. & M. Conkey 1997 Studying ancient visual cultures. In M. Conkey, O. Soffer, D. Stratmann & N. G. Jablonski (eds) *Beyond Art: Pleistocene Image and Symbol*, pp. 1–16. California Academy of Sciences, San Francisco.

Standard, J. C. 1964 Stratigraphy, Structure and Petrology of the Hawkesbury Sandstone. Unpublished PhD thesis. University of Sydney, Sydney.

Stanner, W. E. H. 1969 After the Dreaming: Black and White Australians. The Boyer Lectures, ABC Press, Sydney.

Stanner, W. E. H. 1977 The history of indifference thus begins. *Aboriginal History*. Vol. 1, No. 1, pp. 3–26.

Stockton, E. D. & W. Holland 1974 Cultural sites and their environment in the Blue Mountains. *Archaeology and Physical Anthropology in Oceania*. Vol. 9, pp. 36–65.

Sutton, P & B. Rigsby 1979 Linguistic communities and social networks on Cape York Peninsula. In S. Wurm (ed.) *Australian Linguistic Studies*, pp. 713–732. Research School of Pacific Studies, The Australian National University, Canberra.

Swain, T. 1993 *A Place for Strangers: Towards a History of Australian Aboriginal Being*. Cambridge University Press, Cambridge. doi.org/10.1017/CBO9780511552175

Taçon, P. S. C. 1989 From Rainbow Serpents to 'X-ray' Fish: The Nature of the Recent Rock Painting Tradition of Western Arnhem Land, Australia. Unpublished PhD thesis, The Australian National University, Canberra.

Taçon, P. S. C. 1991 The power of the stone: Symbolic aspects of stone use and tool development in Western Arnhem Land, Australia. *Antiquity*. Vol. 65, pp. 192–207. doi.org/10.1017/S0003598X00079655

Taçon, P. S. C. 1993 Regionalism in recent rock art of Western Arnhem Land, Northern Territory. *Archaeology in Oceania*. Vol. 28, No. 3, pp. 112–120. doi.org/10.1002/j.1834-4453.1993.tb00302.x

Taçon, P. S. C. 1994 Socialising landscapes: The long-term implications of signs, symbols and marks on the land. *Archaeology in Oceania*. Vol. 29, No. 3, pp. 117–129. doi.org/10.1002/arco.1994.29.3.117

Taçon, P. S. C. 1999 Identifying ancient sacred landscapes in Australia: From physical to social. In W. Ashmore & A. B. Knapp (eds) *Archaeologies of Landscape Contemporary Perspectives*, pp. 33–57. Blackwell, Oxford.

Taçon, P. S. C. 2002 Rock-art and landscapes. In B. David & M. Wilson (eds) *Inscribed Landscapes. Marking and Making Place*, pp. 122–136. University of Hawai'i Press, Honolulu.

Taçon, P. S. C. 2008a Rainbow colour and power among the Waanyi of northwest Queensland. *Cambridge Archaeological Journal*. Vol. 18. No. 2. pp. 163–176. doi.org/10.1017/S0959774308000231

Taçon, P. S. C. 2008b Marks of possession: The archaeology of territory and cross-cultural encounter in Australia and South Africa. In B. David & J. Thomas (eds) *Handbook of Landscape Archaeology*, pp. 218–227. Left Coast Press, Walnut Creek, CA.

Taçon, P. S. C. & S. Ouzman 2004 Worlds within stone: The inner and outer rock-art landscapes of northern Australia and southern Africa. In C. Chippindale & G. Nash 2004 (eds) *Pictures in Place: The Figured Landscapes of Rock-Art*, pp. 39–68. Cambridge University Press, Cambridge.

Taçon, P. S. C., M. Wilson & C. Chippindale 1996 Birth of the Rainbow Serpent in Arnhem Land rock art and oral history. *Archaeology in Oceania*. Vol. 31. No. 3. pp. 103–124. doi.org/10.1002/j.1834-4453.1996.tb00355.x

Taçon, P. S. C., M. Kelleher, W. Brennan, S. Hooper & D. Pross 2006 Wollemi petroglyphs, N.S.W., Australia: An unusual assemblage with rare motifs. *Rock Art Research*. Vol. 23. No. 2. pp. 227–238.

Taçon, P. S. C., M. Kelleher, G. King & W. Brennan 2008 Eagle's Reach: A focal point for past and present social identify within the Blue Mountains World Heritage Area, New South Wales, Australia. In I. Domingo Sanz, D. Fiore & S. K. May (eds) *Archaeologies of Art: Time, Place and Identity*, pp. 195–214. Left Coast Press, Walnut Creek, CA.

Tamisari, F & J. Wallace 2006 Towards an experiential archaeology of place: From location to situation through the body. In B. David, B. Barker & I. McNiven (eds) *The Social Archaeology of Australian Indigenous Societies*, pp. 204–223. Aboriginal Studies Press, Canberra.

Thomas, J. 1996 *Time, Culture and Identity. An Interpretive Archaeology*. Routledge, London.

Thomas, J. 2002 Archaeology's humanism and the materiality of the body. In Y. Hamilakis, M. Pluciennik & S. Tarlow (eds) *Thinking through the Body Archaeologies of Corporality*, pp. 29–45. Kluwer Academic/Plenum Publishers, New York. doi.org/10.1007/978-1-4615-0693-5_2

Thomas, J. 2004 *Archaeology and Modernity*. Routledge, London.

Thomas, J. 2008 Archaeology, landscape and dwelling. In B. David & J. Thomas (eds) *Handbook of Landscape Archaeology*, pp. 300–306. Left Coast Press, Walnut Creek, CA.

Tilley, C. 1994 *A Phenomenology of Landscape*. Berg, Oxford.

Tindale, N. B. 1974 *Aboriginal Tribes of Australia*. The Australian National University, Canberra.

Tomásková, S. 1997 Places of art: Art and archaeology in context. In M. Conkey, M., O. Soffer, D. Stratmann & N. G. Jablonski (eds) *Beyond Art: Pleistocene Image and Symbol*, pp. 265–287. California Academy of Sciences, San Francisco.

Troy, J. 1990 *Australian Aboriginal Contact with the English Language in New South Wales: 1788 to 1845*. Pacific Linguistics Series B-103. Department of Linguistics, Research School of Pacific Studies, The Australian National University, Canberra.

Tyerman, D. & G. Bennett 1840 *Voyages and Travels Round the World*. John Snow, London.

Ucko, P. J. & A. Rosenfeld 1967 *Palaeolithic Cave Art*. World University Library. Weidenfeld and Nicolson, London.

Vallance, D. 1983 Fishing, Weather and Site Location: An Esoteric Essay. Unpublished B. Litt. thesis, The Australian National University, Canberra.

van Dommelen, P. 1999 Exploring everyday places and cosmologies. In W. Ashmore and A. B. Knapp (eds) *Archaeologies of Landscape Contemporary Perspectives*, pp. 277–285. Blackwell, Massachusetts.

Vinnicombe, P. 1980 Predilection and Prediction: A Study of Aboriginal Sites in the Gosford-Wyong Region. Unpublished report to the New South Wales National Parks and Wildlife Service, Sydney.

Whittaker, B. 2005 *Appin: The Story of a Macquarie Town*. Kingsclear Books, Alexandria.

Wiessner, P. 1983 Style and social Information in Kalahari San projectile points. *American Antiquity*. Vol. 48, No. 2, pp. 253–276. doi.org/10.2307/280450

Williams, N. 1986 The *Yolngu and their Land: A System of Land Tenure and the Fight for its Recognition*. Australian Institute of Aboriginal Studies, Canberra.

Wilson, M. 1999 Bringing the art inside: A preliminary analysis of black linear rock-art from limestone caves in Erromango, Vanuatu. *Oceania*. Vol. 70, pp. 87–97. doi.org/10.1002/j.1834-4461.1999.tb02991.x

Wilson, M. & B. David 2002 Introduction. In B. David & M. Wilson (eds) *Inscribed Landscapes: Marking and Making Place*, pp. 1–9. University of Hawai'i Press, Honolulu.

Wobst, M. 1977 Stylistic behaviour and information exchange. In C. E. Cleland (ed.) *Papers for the Director: Research Essays in Honor of James B. Griffin*, pp. 317–342. Anthropology Papers No. 61. Museum of Anthropology, University of Michigan, Michigan.

Young, A. 1982 Upland Swamps (Dells) of the Woronora Plateau, NSW. Unpublished PhD thesis, University of Wollongong, Wollongong.

Young, A. 1985 Submission on the Preservation of Geomorphic Resources within the M.W.S.D.B. Southern Catchment Area. In Mills, K., Muston, R., Sefton, C. & A. Young (eds) Environmental Values of the Metropolitan Catchment Areas—A Submission to a MWSDB Study. Unpublished report by the Geography Department, Wollongong University, Wollongong.

Young, R. 1980 *The Illawarra Escarpment, Wollongong*. Studies in Geography No. 2. Department of Geography, University of Wollongong, Wollongong.

Young, R. & A. Johnson 1977 The physical setting: Environmental hazards and urban planning. In R. Robinson (ed.) *Urban Illawarra*, pp. 38–57. Sorrett Publishing, Melbourne.

www.ingramcontent.com/pod-product-compliance
Lightning Source LLC
Chambersburg PA
CBHW061239270326
41926CB00060B/4781